Hub exchange operations in intermodal hub-and-spoke networks

Comparison of the performances of four types of rail-rail exchange facilities

Hub exchange operations in intermodal hub-and-spoke networks

Comparison of the performances of four types of rail-rail exchange facilities

Proefschrift

ter verkrijging van de graad van doctor
aan de Technische Universiteit Delft,
op gezag van de Rector Magnificus prof. dr. ir. J.T. Fokkema,
voorzitter van het College voor Promoties,
in het openbaar te verdedigen op maandag 6 februari 2006 om 15.30 uur
door Yvonne Margaretha BONTEKONING
Landbouwkundig ingenieur
geboren te Berkhout.

Dit proefschrift is goedgekeurd door de promotoren:
Prof. dr. ir. H. Priemus
Prof. dr. ir. R. Dekker

Samenstelling promotiecommissie:

Rector Magnificus, voorzitter
Prof. dr. ir. H. Priemus   Technische Universiteit Delft, promoter
Prof. dr. ir. R. Dekker   Erasmus Universiteit Rotterdam, promotor
Prof. M.B.M. de Koster   Erasmus Universiteit Rotterdam
Prof. dr. C. Macharis   Vrije Universiteit Brussel, België
Prof. dr.-Ing. I.A. Hansen   Technische Universiteit Delft
Prof. dr. G.P. van Wee   Technische Universiteit Delft
Prof. ir. J.C. Rijsenbrij   Technische Universiteit Delft

Het proefschrift is tot standgekomen in het kader van het TU Delft onderzoeksprogramma (1997–2002): 'Freight Transport Automation and Multimodality (FTAM); Towards a breakthrough in the technological and organizational conditions for competitive and sustainable multimodal freight transport'.

TRAIL Thesis Series nr. T2006/1, The Netherlands TRAIL Research School

The Netherlands TRAIL Research School
Delft University of Technology
Erasmus University Rotterdam
Radboud University Nijmegen
University of Groningen
University of Twente

TRAIL-office
P.O. Box 5017
2600 GA Delft
The Netherlands
Telephone: +31 (0) 15 27 86046
Telefax: + 31 (0) 15 27 84333
E-mail: info@rsTRAIL.nl

ISBN 90-5584-072-6

Keywords: freight, intermodal, rail, terminals, shunting, hub-and-spoke

© Copyright 2006 by Y.M. Bontekoning.
All rights reserved. No part of the material protected by this copyright notice may be reproduced or utilized in any form or by any means, electronic or mechanical, including photocopying, recording or by any information storage and retrieval system, without written permission from the author.

Table of contents

Preface and Acknowledgements — xi

1. Comparison of the performances of hub exchange facilities — 1
1.1 Introduction — 1
1.2 Problem definition — 1
1.2.1 The intermodal hub-and-spoke concept — 2
1.2.2 Hub-and-spoke concepts in other freight transport industries — 4
1.2.3 Conclusion — 9
1.3 Research objectives — 10
1.4 Research design and outline of the thesis — 11
1.4.1 Three phases of research activities — 11
1.4.2 Phase I: a comprehensive exploration — 11
1.4.3 Phase II: modeling — 12
1.4.4 Phase III: numerical analysis — 14
1.5 Scope of the research — 15
1.6 Scientific and societal relevance — 16
1.7 Summary and conclusions — 16

2. Is a new applied transportation research field emerging? – A review of intermodal rail-truck freight transport literature — 19
2.1 Introduction to the chapter — 19
2.2 Introduction to the article — 19
2.3 Methodology — 21
2.4 Results — 22
2.4.1 General statistics about the review — 22
2.4.2 Research categories — 22
2.4.3 Common definition and conceptual model of intermodal transport — 26
2.4.4 Coherence of the transportation research field — 26
2.5 Current knowledge base — 28
2.5.1 Drayage — 28
2.5.2 Rail haul — 29
2.5.3 Transhipment: road-rail terminals and rail-rail terminals — 31
2.5.4 Standardisation — 32
2.5.5 Multi-actor chain management and control — 32
2.5.6 Mode choice and pricing strategies — 33
2.5.7 Transportation policy and planning — 34
2.5.8 Miscellaneous — 36
2.5.9 Applied methods and technique — 36
2.6 Towards an intermodal research agenda — 37
2.7 Conclusions — 38

3. Hub exchange operations: a system description — 39
3.1 Introduction — 39
3.2 Approach — 40
3.2.1 System analysis — 40

3.2.2	Analytical framework	41
3.2.3	Data collection	42
3.3	Description of the system component Demand	42
3.4	Description of the component Resources	46
3.4.1	New hub terminal infrastructure and resources	47
3.4.2	Hump shunting yard infrastructure and resources	48
3.4.3	Flat shunting yard infrastructure and resources	49
3.4.4	Road-rail terminal infrastructure and resources	49
3.4.5	Side yard infrastructure	50
3.5	Description of system component Process	50
3.5.1	Strategic process control principles	51
3.5.2	Hub exchange operations at new hub terminals	51
3.5.3	Hub exchange operations at hump shunting yards	53
3.5.4	Hub exchange operations at flat shunting yards	54
3.5.5	Hub exchange operations at road-rail terminals	55
3.6	Relationship between elements and environment	55
3.7	Relationship elements and performance criteria	56
3.8	Summary and conclusions	57
4.	**Conceptual modeling of hub exchange operations**	**61**
4.1	Introduction	61
4.2	Approach	62
4.3	Modelling Demand	64
4.4	Modelling train access control to the exchange facility	65
4.5	Modelling Resources and Process for new hub terminals	67
4.5.1	Modelling infrastructure, equipment and labour	67
4.5.2	Modelling exchange operations–synchronized	68
4.5.3	Modelling exchange operations–non-synchronised	70
4.6	Modelling Resources and Process for hump shunting and flat shunting yards	71
4.6.1	Modelling infrastructure, equipment and labour	71
4.6.2	Modelling exchange operations–synchronized	73
4.6.3	Modelling exchange operations–non-synchronised	73
4.7	Modelling Resources and Process for road-rail terminals	73
4.7.1	Modelling infrastructure, equipment and labour	73
4.7.2	Modelling exchange operations at road-rail terminals–synchronized	75
4.7.3	Modelling exchange operations at road-rail terminals–non-synchronized	75
4.8	Summary and conclusions	76
5.	**Computerised modeling**	**79**
5.1	Introduction	79
5.2	Approach	80
5.3	Specification of the computer models	81
5.3.1	Module: Train arrivals	81
5.3.2	Module: Operations access control	82
5.3.3	Module: Generation of load units and assignment of job classes/rail wagons	83
5.3.4	Module: Exchange operations	83
5.3.5	Module: Operations control	85
5.3.6	Module: Train departures	86

5.4	Estimation of service time probability distributions	87
5.4.1	Estimation of service time distributions for servers in terminal models	87
5.4.1.1	A tool for simulating crane cycles	87
5.4.1.2	Application of the simulation tool to generate crane service times	91
5.4.1.3	Estimation of crane service time probability distributions	93
5.4.1.4	Estimation of transport service time distributions in terminal models	95
5.4.2	Estimation of service time distributions for servers in hump shunting models	97
5.4.3	Estimation of service time distributions for servers in flat shunting models	99
5.4.4	Estimation of service time distribution function for shunting from side yard to exchange facility	99
5.5	A cost model	100
5.6	Summary and conclusions	103

6. Experiments and results — 105

6.1	Introduction	105
6.2	Approach	106
6.2.1	Initial set of experiments	106
6.2.2	Experiments to test sensitivity of initial results for variables: load order, load factor and costs	109
6.2.3	Experiments to test the sensitivity of initial results for variables arrival time, delay and strategic control principle	112
6.2.4	Simulation output, replications and confidence intervals	114
6.3	Evaluation of performances: time and cost benchmark criteria	115
6.4	Impact of the variable demand on handling time and costs	119
6.4.1	Identification of favourable options	119
6.4.2	Analysis of train service times and sojourn times	122
6.4.3	Required minimum network volume	125
6.4.4	Cost structures	128
6.4.5	Conclusions	130
6.5	Sensitivity of favourable options for load order, load factor, annual costs and arrival times	132
6.5.1	Impact of a planned load order on the set of favourable options	133
6.5.2	Impact of a smaller and larger load factor on the favourable options	136
6.5.3	Impact of an increase in costs on the favourable options	139
6.5.4	Impact of cheaper but slower cranes on the favourable options	143
6.5.5	Conclusions	146
6.6	Impacts of variable arrival schedules, delays and non-cynchronised operations on handling time	147
6.6.1	Impact of different arrival schedules	148
6.6.2	Delays	151
6.6.3	Non-synchronised operations	163
6.6.4	Conclusions	168
6.7	Conclusions	169

7. Conclusions and recommendations — 175

7.1	Introduction	175
7.2	Main research findings and conclusions	176

7.2.1	Model development	176
7.2.2	Favourable operational conditions for new hub terminals	177
7.2.3	Large gap between practice and favourable conditions	179
7.2.4	Alternatives for new hub terminals	180
7.3	Main findings and conclusions with respect to secondary objectives	181
7.4	Recommendations for further research	183

Summary 187

Samenvatting 199

References 211

Appendix A Specification of parameters and variables of the crane service time simulation tool 221

Appendix B Justification of the number of crane service times to be generated by the crane service time simulation tool 225

Appendix C Validation of the crane service time simulation tool 227

Appendix D Overview of collected time data on hump shunting activities 229

Appendix E Simulating sorting locomotive behaviour and service times at a flat shunting yard 231

Appendix F Specification of variables in the cost model 233

Appendix G Specification of additional costs per load unit due to changes in rail haul costs 237

Appendix H Specification of half-width confidence intervals average train sojourn times 239

Appendix I Specification of number of load units and rail wagons to be exchanged per train 241

Appendix J Specification of results of cases in quadrants II, III and IV 243

Appendix K Specification of infrastructure dimensions, number of equipment and labour in cost model 247

Appendix L Selected cases for sensitivity analyses 253

Appendix M Specification of results flat shunting alternatives 255

Appendix N Specification of results for different load orders 257

Appendix O Specification of results for different load factors 259

Appendix P	Specification of results of costs per load unit for different increases in costs	263
Appendix Q	Specification of results for initial versus ideal train interarrival times	265
Curriculum Vitae		267

Preface and Acknowledgements

This thesis is a continuation of the work carried out by the author for the EU project "Terminet". The project ran from 1997 to 2000 as part of the Fourth EU Framework Programme. The central objective of the Terminet project was to identify promising developments for innovative freight bundling networks and new-generation terminals for intermodal transport within Europe[1].
This thesis was co-funded by the TU Delft research programme 'Freight Transport Automation and Multimodality: towards a breakthrough in the technological and organisational conditions for competitive and sustainable multimodal freight transport'. The growing awareness of the need for breakthrough innovations in intermodal freight transport prompted a multiyear (1997–2002) research programme. This programme set out to provide knowledge and tools for developing an intermodal freight transport system capable of offering high-quality and sustainable overland transport services at different geographical network levels. This thesis was carried out in the context of a sub-programme entitled: 'Intermodal Networks and a New Generation of Terminals and Multimodal Transfer Points'. Parallel to this thesis two other PhD research projects were carried out:
- 'New-generation terminal concepts and innovative bundling concepts for combined transport: identification of promising and missing developments' by my colleague Ekki Kreutzberger (forthcoming).
- 'Network design for intermodal barge transport' by my colleague Rob Konings (forthcoming).

I received support from a number of people whilst carrying out my PhD research. Firstly, I would like to thank my family and friends. I am immensely grateful to my partner Carin for her indefatigable encouragement and moral support. Throughout my PhD adventure we have shared all my ups and downs, my doubts and my triumphs. She is just as relieved as I am that the job is finally over. I would like to thank my former roommate Erik for being my informal "life coach" with whom I could share any doubts about my PhD work and who could always motivate me to persevere. Fortunately, we spent a lot of time discussing personal and societal issues extraneous to my research over the past few years. I would like to thank my parents for their encouragement and sympathy whenever I complained about my thesis. I would also like to thank my good friend Sandrina. Through our regular cultural, walking and dining sessions I was able to escape from the stress of my PhD and recharge my batteries.

Secondly, I would like to thank those people who have supported me at a professional level. I thank my promoters Professor Rommert Dekker and Professor Hugo Priemus and colleagues Dr Milan Janic and Ir. Ekki Kreutzberger for their valuable comments and sometimes lengthy but interesting discussions. I would like to thank Danielle Stekelenburg who programmed my computer models and her supervisor Corné Versteegt. I wish to thank Dr Klaus-Peter Franke and Dr Peter Meyer for their support with the validation of the crane cycle tool. I am grateful to Truus Waai-

---

[1] At that time consisting of 15 countries.

jer, Martine Lansbergen, Ineke Groeneveld, Monique Hazewinkel, Caroline van Eijk, Dirk Dubbeling, Herman Toneman and Hans Ruigrok who undertook a number of supportive roles in the realisation of this thesis. Finally, I would like to thank the OTB management for giving me the opportunity to study for this PhD, and towards the end for providing OTB time to finish it.

At last, my PhD study is complete. Now that I've done it, I know how I should have done it.

Yvonne Bontekoning
Gouda, June 2005

1 Comparison of the performances of hub exchange facilities

1.1 Introduction

Intermodal freight transport can be defined as the movement of goods in one and the same load unit using several successive modes of transport without handling of the goods themselves in changing modes (European Conference of Ministers of Transport, 1993). The trend is for intermodal operators and railway companies to focus on the reliable and time- and cost-effective point-to-point bundling concept. Point-to-point bundling implies that all load units loaded onto a train at an origin terminal have the same destination terminal. This concept requires a constantly high transport volume on specific routes. Intermodal transport competes on cost on these routes with road transport and has a rather strong position. Traditional markets for intermodal transport on these routes are large flows over long distances, seaport hinterland flows, flows between production plants and to depots, and bulk commodities and hazardous goods (Cardebring, 2002). Despite this strong position, intermodal transport accounts for little more than 5% of the total surface traffic (tonne-km) of the EU15[1] (Savy & Aubriot, 2005). This reflects the small size of these traditional markets compared to the total transport market. Since intermodal transport already has a strong position in the traditional markets, a growth of the market share in these market segments is not obvious. The growth potential lies in the markets for flows over medium distances (between 200km and 500km), for perishable and high-value commodities, for small consignments, for small flows and for flows demanding speed, reliability and flexibility. These markets are large, while the market share of intermodal transport is so close to zero as to be almost negligible (Cardebring, 2002; European Commission, 1998).

1.2 Problem definition

The implementation of hub-and-spoke networks in intermodal transport is suggested as one of the potential solutions for helping to increase the intermodal market share (Beisler, 1995; European Commission, 1997; Kreutzberger, 1999a; 1999b; Cardebring et al., 2002). The proposed hub-and-spoke networks with exchange operations (also called transfer operations) at hubs differ from the traditional rail production system. In the traditional rail production system each rail wagon has a unique "trip plan" which shows the planned sequence of trains and shunting yards through the railway network. While the proposed hub-and-spoke networks imply that train services are organised as batches[2] (groups) of trains with synchronised arrivals and departures for compact exchange operations at a hub. The intermodal hub-and-spoke concept is further elaborated in section 1.2.1.

The interest of scientists in hub-and-spoke networks and hubs in freight transport is rather recent, while they have extensively been studied in the passenger airline industry. In addition to transfer operations in the intermodal rail industry, transfer

---

[1] 15 countries of the EU prior to expansion.
[2] See Section 3.3 for a further definition and explanation of the batch concept.

operations were studied for freight consolidation terminals[3] in the parcel delivery industry (see Hall, 2001; McWilliams et al. 2005), less-than-truck-load industry (see Taha & Taylor, 1994; Gue, 1999), retail business (see Gue, 1999) and for marine (see Zijderveld, 1995; Vis & de Koster, 2002) and road-rail terminals in intermodal transport (see Boese, 1989; Brunner, 1994; Rizzoli et al, 2002). At first sight analogous transfer operations are expected. If analogous operations exist, an existing model applied to another freight industry may be used to analyse rail-rail hub exchange operations. In this way a generic approach may be used. If transfer operations are not analogous a new model to analyse rail-rail hub operations needs to be developed. In this section typical features of transfer operations in other freight industries are described and compared with rail-rail exchange operations. In subsection 1.2.2 transfer operations for these other freight transport industries are briefly reviewed and compared with rail-rail transfer operations.

1.2.1 The intermodal hub-and-spoke concept

In this thesis a hub-and-spoke network[4] (see Figure 1–1) is defined as follows: trains with load units for various destination terminals run from various origin terminals to a hub with an exchange facility. At this hub exchange facility either rail wagons (at a shunting yard) or load units (at a terminal) are exchanged between trains such that load units for one destination terminal are regrouped on one train. Next, trains head for their destination terminal. The exchange of load units or rail wagons, defined as hub exchange operations, takes place between a group of related trains called a batch. Arrivals and departures of the trains belonging to a batch are synchronised within a certain time window. This definition is based on the concepts of complex bundling networks described by Kreutzberger (1999a) and the terminology applied in documentation that describes the proposed new hub terminals (summarised in Bontekoning & Kreutzberger, 1999).

I define an exchange facility as a set of equipment, layout and operations used to unload and load transport units such as trains. To distinguish exchange facilities applied as a hub from other exchange facilities (e.g. for road-rail transhipment). I shall call the former "hub exchange facilities". Logically, exchange operations at a hub exchange facility are called hub exchange operations.
Functioning of hub-and-spoke networks and hub exchange facilities in intermodal transport is further elaborated in Chapter 3.

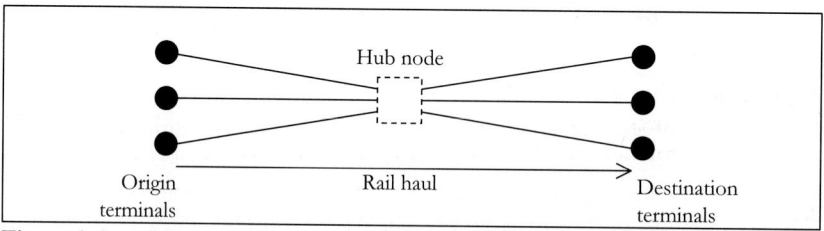

Figure 1–1: **A hub-and-spoke network connecting three origin terminals and three destination terminals.**

---

[3] Freight consolidation terminals are also called hub terminals or crossdocks.

[4] Sometimes known as a star network, but as Figure 1-1 indicates, depending on trade relations a hub-and-spoke network may also have a west-east/east-west or north-south/south-north shape.

The advantages that hub-and-spoke networks may offer compared to point-to-point networks are a higher frequency of transport services per transport relation, an increase in the number of transport relations (serving small flows) and economies of scale. This is illustrated in Figure 1–2. In a point-to-point network commonly one train service per day is maintained between one origin terminal and one destination terminal. The upper part of Figure 1–2 gives an example of a point-to-point network with one transport relation for each origin terminal. If the point-to-point network is replaced by a hub-and-spoke network each origin terminal can offer more destinations, three instead of one, with an equal number of trains. Due to bundling of flows for various destination terminals at an origin terminal the threshold value per transport relation is lower in a hub-and-spoke network. In addition, as a result of the integration of flows of transport relations that cannot justify a point-to-point connection the three trains will transport more load units, resulting in economies of scale and therefore lower costs per load unit.

With respect to the point-to-point network depicted in example 2 of Figure 1–2 the frequency of service may be increased with the introduction of a hub-and-spoke network. Due to the exchange at the hub node, each train leaving the origin terminal can be loaded with load units for all destination terminals. Consequently, instead of running one train per transport relation directly, all destination terminals can be served three times a day from each origin terminal. Instead of an increase in frequency, larger trains may be used, resulting in economies of scale.

However, additional time and costs incurred by hub exchange operations counteract these advantages.

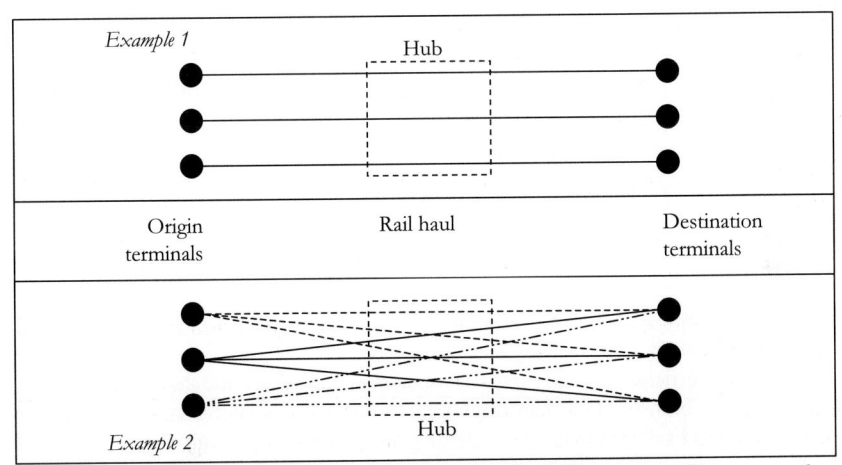

Figure 1–2: **Two examples of point-to-point bundling networks connecting three origin terminals and three destination terminals being transformed to a hub-and-spoke network**

Besides several national hub-and-spoke networks in for instance France and Germany, three international hub-and-spoke networks became operational in Europe in the 1990s. Two of them were abandoned at the end of this thesis work, in December 2004. ICF operated *Qualitynet* with a hub in Metz (France) and *X.net* with a hub in Herne (Germany). Interferry Boats operates the *North European Network* (NEN) with a hub at Muizen (Belgium). Traditionally, trains are shunted at these hubs. These networks reveal some advantages, such as serving small flows, but still within the traditional markets due to time-consuming shunting. In Europe, shunting operations may account for a significant part of the total transit time of trains. Vogtman and Franke (2000) calculated for the shunting hub Metz rail wagon sojourn times of several hours to 2 days. Therefore, shunting cannot meet the quality requirements for commodities sensitive to time and reliability.

Since the early 1990s a new type of intermodal terminal, specifically designed for nodes in hub-and-spoke networks, has been introduced in Europe. These hub terminals could replace time-consuming shunting. At these terminals standardised load units (such as containers, swap bodies and sometimes semi-trailers) are transhipped from one train to another, instead of shunting rail wagons. Studies on the new hub terminals suggest that they may perform more efficiently than shunting yards (European Commission, 1997; Jourquin, 1999; Bontekoning & Kreutzberger, 2001; Bontekoning & Trip, 2004). However, a systematic comparison to reveal the operational and costs differences between shunting and these new hub-terminals for a broad range of situations still lacks.

Studies into the new hub terminals themselves deal with terminal design optimisation (Alicke, 1999, 2002; Meyer, 1998; Bostel, 1996; Bostel & Dejax, 1998). Simulation and analytical models were developed to determine capacity dimensions and terminal equipment work routines for just one specific batch[5] size (number of trains and number of load units to be exchanged) and one specific train arrival schedule. How the new hub terminals perform for different batch sizes or different arrival schedules has not been studied.

Shunting operations, especially at yards with a shunting hill, have been studied much longer than new hub-terminal operations (see Petersen, 1977; Daganzo, 1983; Ferguson, 1993; Timian, 1994; Kraft, 2000 and 2002). However, the shunting operations studied are the common railway operations (explained above), while for intermodal hub-and-spoke networks batch-organised and synchronised exchange operations are proposed. The implication of such organisation for the shunting operations has not been studied. So, it is interesting to study the proposed hub-and-spoke network concept with shunting operations at the hub and to compare them with hub-and-spoke operations with operations at these proposed new hub terminals. In addition, in order to complete the comparison, also hub-and-spoke operations with a flat shunting yard and a road-rail terminal as hub should be studied.

1.2.2 Hub-and-spoke concepts in other freight transport industries

Hub-and-spoke networks with transfer operations at a hub are also applied in the parcel delivery industry, less-than-truck-load industry and retail business. In addition, marine and road-rail terminals are sometimes also considered as hub. In this section I look into various transfer operations as documented in the literature in order to identify whether we can speak of analogous operations.

The comparison is carried out for typical features of hub-and-spoke networks and transfer operations, being: organisation of the hub-and-spoke network, the type of unit to be processed, level of synchronisation of arrivals at the hub, material handling equipment and type of process.

Less-than-truck-load and retail industry
A schematic representation of the organisation of the hub-and-spoke network in the less-than-truck-load and retail industry is depicted in Figure 1–3. Hub terminal opera-

---

[5] See Section 3.3 for a further definition and explanation of the batch concept.

tions, also called crossdocking, in the less-than-truck-load (LTL) trucking industry can be described as follows. After pick-up and delivery trucks return in the evening from their routes to the crossdock. Freight is sorted, consolidated with other products, and loaded onto outbound trucks, which is for other crossdocks in other service areas. In the early morning, trucks arrive from other crossdocks. Freight from these trucks is sorted and loaded onto pick up and delivery trucks. Some crossdocks serve as midway consolidation points for freight that neither originates from, nor is destined for, the local area crossdock.

The idea is to transfer incoming shipments directly to outgoing trailers without storing them in between. Workers unload the products from the inbound trailer, often on pallets, and transport them by means of forklift trucks or pallet trucks to an outbound trailer bound for the appropriate destination. Crossdocking operations are labour-intensive and most of the variable cost of labour is devoted to travel between doors (Gue, 1999; McWilliams et al., 2005).

There are two main differences with the proposed hub-operations in intermodal freight transport:

1. The function of the transfer operation. In intermodal transport, the purpose of the hub exchange is to make inbound trains with multiple destinations outbound trains for just one destination. In the LTL industry, inbound trucks do not exchange load units with each other. The function of pick-up & delivery trucks is to collect freight for other service areas and to deliver freight from other service areas. Other (often larger) trucks are assigned to the task of the (long) truck haul.

2. The unit processed. The units processed are, different from rather standardised load units and rail wagons in intermodal transport, very heterogeneous in size and shape. In addition, smaller units (parcels) may be consolidated to a pallet and pallets may be deconsolidated in smaller units. These features make the handling process much more complicated with respect to resource allocation and processing steps.

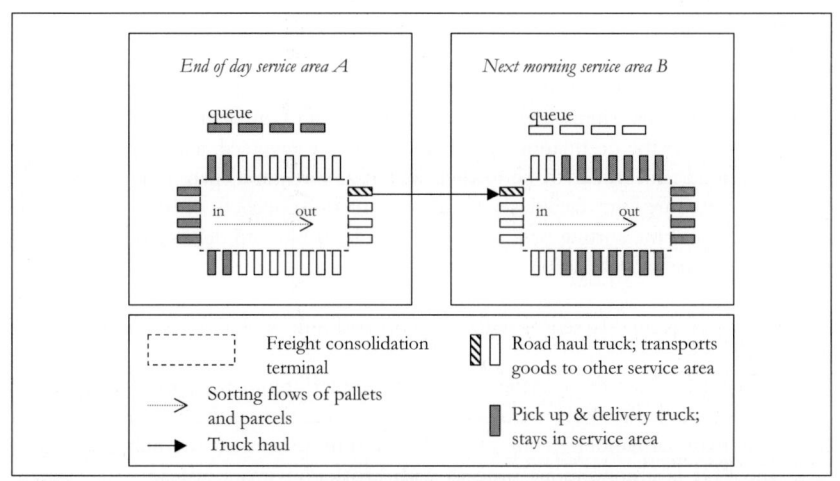

Figure 1–3: Schematic representation of the organisation of a hub-and-spoke network for the less-than-truck-load, retail and parcel delivery industry.

Parcel delivery industry
A similar organisation as for the LTL and retail industry applies to the parcel delivery industry (PDI). Hence, also Figure 1–3 applies to the parcel delivery industry. However, two characteristics differentiate at the hub terminal in the LTL industry from a hub terminal in the parcel delivery industry (PDI). First, the material equipment used in LTL terminals are forklifts and pallet trucks; however, in the PDI, the primary material handling equipment used is a network of fixed cross conveyors. The reason for this is that freight in the LTL industry is often oddly shaped, so automation is difficult. Second, the docks in LTL terminal can be used for loading and unloading due to the flexible material handling equipment. While in the PDI, docks are dedicated as loading or unloading because of the stationary conveyors. However, also in the LTL industry a fixed number of doors is permanently assigned for inbound trucks. (McWilliams et al, 2005; Gue, 1999).

There are two main differences with the proposed hub-operations in intermodal rail transport:
1. The function of the transfer operation. The same arguments apply as above for the LTL industry.
2. The material handling equipment. The sorting process at the hub terminal in the PDI is a continuous process with cross conveyors instead of a discrete process with cranes or locomotives.

Truck-air parcel industry
The organisation of the hub-and-spoke network in the truck-air parcel industry (see for a schematic overview Figure 1–4) is to some extent similar to that of the truck-truck parcel delivery industry. However, there are also some typical differences. Similar is that shipments arrive at the transfer terminal by pick-up and delivery trucks and that parcels are sorted by a conveyor sorting line. Different is that trucks are scheduled to arrive within a certain time span, with the goal of keeping the conveyor line productive, minimizing the queue of shipments awaiting processing and to meet departure due time of the aircrafts. This coordination between truck arrivals and aircraft(s) departure is called a 'sort' and shows similarities with the batch organisation of trains in intermodal hub-and-spoke networks. A 'sort' ends when all the packages have been processed for an individual aircraft, or for a group of aircrafts. Different from PDI is also that shipments are consolidated in air containers, which are loaded onto aircrafts. At the destination airport the steps are reversed, allowing the aircraft to be unloaded, and trucks to be loaded, within a 'sort' time span. Due to the sort-organised structure, the facilities and labour are only needed within concentrated time periods and the sorting process is susceptible to random delays in the arrival of trucks and aircrafts (Hall, 2001).

There are three main differences with the proposed hub-operations in intermodal rail transport:
1. The function of the transfer operation. Similar arguments apply as above for the LTL industry. Yet, aircrafts carry out the function of the long haul trucks.
2. The material handling equipment. The sorting process at the hub terminal in the PDI is a continuous process with cross conveyors instead of a discrete process with cranes or locomotives.
3. The unit processed. Two types of units are processed, parcels and air containers. Consolidation and deconsolidation are compared to rail-rail exchange operations addition steps in the exchange process. Parcels are consolidated to air

containers and air containers are deconsolidated in smaller units. These features make the handling process much more complicated with respect to resource allocation and processing steps.

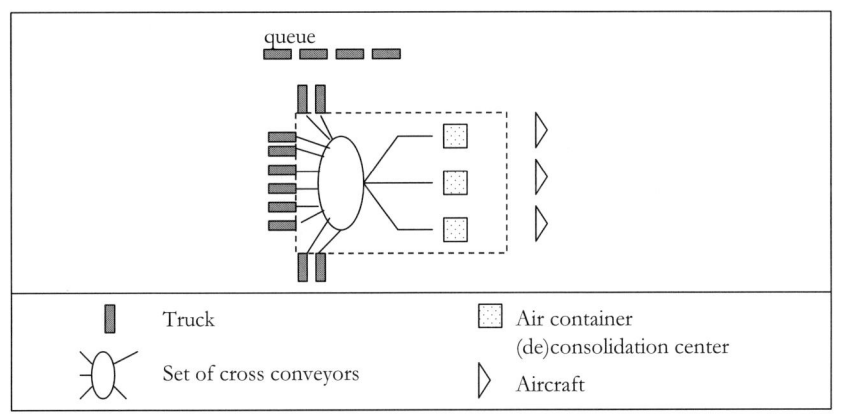

Figure 1–4: Schematic representation of the organisation of a hub-and-spoke network for the truck-air parcel industry

Container marine terminal operations
A marine container terminal serves as interface between different modes: sea on the one side and the hinterland modes road and rail, and for some marine terminals also inland waterway, on the other side. Figure 1–5 illustrates the typical transfer operations between these modes. The arrival and departure pattern of containerships generates the flows of containers to and from the marine terminal. A vessel delivers containers from various origins that need to be transported by the hinterland modes to many different hinterland destinations. And, the other way around, trucks, trains and inland vessels, deliver containers from many origins that need to be transported by container vessels to various destinations. As a consequence, sorting of containers is required for destination and for mode. In addition, sorting is required per carrier. Typical for the exchange between modes is that containers are always stacked before they move on to the succeeding modality. Dwell times in the stack vary from 1 to 6 days. Direct connections, and as a consequence synchronised availability of transport units in a certain time span, are very rare, because it is very difficult to organise.

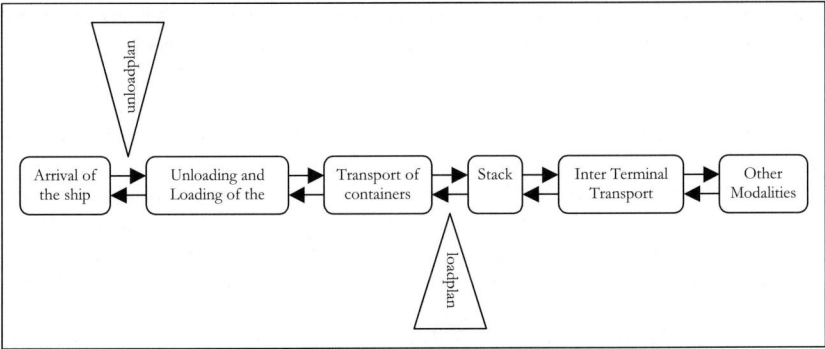

Figure 1–5: Transfer operations at a container marine terminal
Source: Vis, 2005 http://www.ikj.nl/container/

The stack functions as decoupling point of the different networks, such that the exchange of flows between modes can be managed. Each modality has it own terminal. As a consequence, inter terminal transport is required to connect the different modalities.

Handling equipment at marine terminals are the following. Quay cranes unload and load the vessels. Vehicles such as straddle carriers, single chassis truck, multiple chassis trucks or automated guided vehicles transport containers between quay cranes and storage area, but also between storage area and the terminals of the other modes. The stack consists of a number of lanes. Equipments, like cranes or straddle carriers, serve these lanes (Zijderveld, 1995; Vis, 2005).

There are two main differences with the proposed hub-operations in intermodal rail transport:
1. The function of the transfer operation. In intermodal transport, the purpose of the hub exchange is to make inbound trains with multiple destinations outbound trains for just one destination. At the marine terminal, inbound modalities do not exchange load units with each other. The function of the hinterland modes is to feed the sea transport system and vice versa to distribute flows from it.
2. The level of synchronisation of arrivals at the hub. At the marine terminal transport units of the different modes are not synchronised in a short time span as for rail-rail exchange operations, because it is too complex to organise. On the contrary, intermediate stacking of the containers interrupts the exchange of flows.

Road-rail terminal operations
A road-rail terminal has a collection and distribution function for intermodal load units in a certain service area. Load units are consolidated to a train, which travels to a road-rail terminal in another service area. At this road-rail terminal load units are distributed again. This process is depicted in Figure 1–6 for a point-to-point network. At a road-rail terminal standardised load units are transferred by gantry cranes or reach stackers between trucks and trains. Trucks arrive at the terminal to:
- deliver one or two load units,
- pick-up one or two load units, or
- both deliver one or two load units and pick-up one or two load units.

Trains arrive at the terminal to deliver or pick-up a train load of load units. Truck and train arrivals are not synchronised. Trucks delivering load units usually arrive before the train leaves, while trucks picking-up load units usually arrive after the train arrival, so that they can minimise the length of stay in the terminal. Combined delivery and pick-up of load units by one truck are very rarely related to just one train.

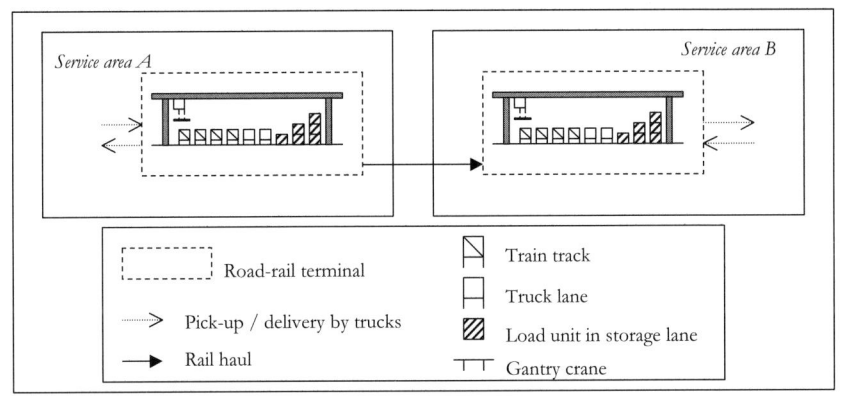

Figure 1–6: Schematic presentation of a point-to-point network with road-rail transfer terminals.

Most exchange between train and trucks is via the storage area. Load units dwell time at the terminal is usually much shorter than at marine container terminals, approximately 24 hours. However, load units could directly be transferred between train and truck (Boese, 1989; Brunner, 1994; Rizzoli et al., 2002).

There are two main differences with the proposed hub-operations in intermodal rail transport:
1. The function of the transfer operation. In intermodal transport, the purpose of the hub exchange is to make inbound trains with multiple destinations outbound trains for just one destination. At the road-rail terminal, there is a task division between trucks and trains. Trucks take care of the pick-up & delivery in a service area; trains take care of the long haul between service areas.
2. The level of synchronisation of arrivals at the hub. At the road-rail terminal truck and train arrivals are not synchronised in a short time span as for rail-rail exchange operations. As a result unloading and loading of trains and trucks is via the storage area.

1.2.3 Conclusion

I conclude, firstly, that for the further development of the use of hub-and-spoke networks in intermodal transport, it is important to find out whether implementation of new hub terminals implies improved performance levels compared to shunting. Shunting is rather time-consuming, while new hub-terminals claim fast exchange.

Secondly, the proposed hub exchange operations differ from current shunting practise, from transfer operations in other freight transport industries and from operations at marine and road-rail terminals. Differences apply to:
- The function of the exchange
- Handling of standardised units versus additional (de)consolidation of load units
- Discrete versus continuous transfer operations
- Synchronised versus non-synchronised arrival, implying exchange via the storage area.

Thirdly, due to these differences, existing models for transfer operations may be of limited use. As a consequence, a new model should be developed in order to determine the conditions under which new hub terminals perform better than shunting.

1.3 Research objectives

Departing from the problem definition in section 1.2 I was able to formulate the following main research objective of this thesis: *develop a model that can be used to identify favourable operational conditions for new hub terminals to be implemented, and quantify their operational performances in relation to alternative hub exchange facilities.*

This objective can be specified as follows.
Develop a model implies to develop one or various models in which different parameter and variable settings can represent different hub-and-spoke systems and make the model as transparent and as aggregated as possible without losing specific features. The purpose of the modelling was to evaluate performances of hub exchange operations at various exchange facilities under various operational conditions in general and specifically to identify favourable operational conditions for new hub terminals. The purpose of a transparent and aggregated model is to be able to keep track of effects of the interaction of certain parameter settings. The objective is not to imitate the entire hub-and-spoke system in detail, but to have a tool that helps to understand the dynamics of the system. Essential differences of the various systems must become clear.

Operational conditions are defined by demand on the one hand and *facility capacity* on the other hand. Within *demand* I make a distinction between volume characteristics, such as the number of trains per batch, number of batches, number of load units/rail wagons (load factor) per train, load position and type of load units, and arrival schedule characteristics such as train interarrival times, extent of synchronisation of arrivals and delays. The number and type of equipment, service times and the operations strategy determine *facility capacity*.

Operational performance is expressed as speed, flexibility and costs of operations. Speed of handling operations is defined as train and batch service and sojourn times respectively. Flexibility is defined as the capability of an exchange facility to adapt to changing demand volume and arrival patterns, expressed as relative increases/decrease in time and costs. Costs for exchange operations are expressed as costs per load unit based on the annual hub-and-spoke network volume.

In this thesis I consider hump shunting yards, flat shunting yards and road-rail terminals used for (rail-rail) hub exchange as *alternative hub exchange* facilities for new hub terminals.

As preliminary and transitional steps towards and as a spin-off of the main research objective, four secondary research objectives were formulated. As a prologue to the main research objective the first secondary objective was formulated as "*Provide a general assessment of the state of the art of road-rail intermodal transport research*".
The purpose of this objective was to provide a comprehensive overview of the field, to define an intermodal research agenda and to select a thesis topic. Despite the fact that:
- in transport practice, intermodal transport is considered a competitive transport mode and can be used as an alternative to unimodal transport;
- a specific intermodal industry for equipment and services exists;
- in the 1980s and 1990s intermodalism in general became an important policy issue, and

- since 1990 a substantial number of analytical publications specifically addressing intermodal transport issues have appeared;
- a comprehensive literature review and a research agenda on road-rail intermodal transport was still lacking at the time when work on this thesis started.

To achieve the main research objective two transitional steps were required and could be formulated as secondary research objectives. First, provide a thorough assessment of the functioning of existing and proposed hub-and-spoke systems.

The purpose of this analysis is to understand the functioning of existing and proposed hub-and-spoke systems and to obtain new empirical data. A hub-and-spoke system is defined as the combination of hub-and-spoke networks, hub exchange facilities and hub exchange operations.

Second, as a spin-off of the main objective: provide new and additional performance data for various hub exchange facilities for different operational conditions.

The purpose of this research objective is to provide other studies with values for time and costs parameters for hub exchange operations, which until now have been assumed and seem to be poorly underpinned by empirical data. Once the main objective is achieved new data will be available for presentation.

1.4 Research design and outline of the thesis

1.4.1 Three phases of research activities

The research consisted of three phases, which are presented in Figure 1–7. Phase I can be identified as a comprehensive exploration of the research topic and problem definition. The results of this phase are documented in Chapters 1 and 2. The research activities of this phase are elaborated in subsection 1.4.2. Phase II and Phase III cover the research activities relating to the simulation approach chosen to achieve the main objective. Phase II covers activities (see subsection 1.4.3.) that structure the research subject and help to identify the most relevant elements to be included in a simulation approach. Phase III covers the numerical analysis and interpretation of the results. These activities are elaborated in subsection 1.4.4.

1.4.2 Phase I: a comprehensive exploration

Phase I consisted of three related explorative research activities aimed at identifying a suitable research topic. Two parallel activities were a general literature study on intermodal transport and participation in the EU project Terminet. The general literature study aimed to provide an assessment of the state of the art of road-rail intermodal transport research and a research agenda from which a topic could be selected. The results of this activity are presented in Chapter 2 and have been published in *Transportation Research A* (Bontekoning et al., 2004). Research into complex bundling networks and the functioning of terminals were among other areas identified as knowledge gaps.

The Terminet project ran from 1997 to 2000 as part of the Fourth EU Framework Programme. The central objective of the Terminet project was to identify promising developments for innovative freight bundling networks and new-generation terminals for intermodal transport within Europe[6]. Participation in the Terminet project provided insight into promising developments for innovative freight bundling net-

---

[6] At that time consisting of 15 countries.

works and new-generation terminals for intermodal transport within Europe. The project consisted of an inventory study into networks other than the common point-to-point (see Vleugel et al., 2001) and into innovative transhipment techniques/terminals (see Bontekoning & Kreutzberger, 1999) and analysis of their functioning and performances (see Bontekoning & Kreutzberger, 2001). The findings of Terminet gave rise to the idea of further investigating hub-and-spoke networks and new hub exchange facilities.

Phase I: Comprehensive exploration

Inventory study within Terminet project → Specific literature review / Problem definition / Research design (Chapter 1) ← General literature review (Chapter 2)

Phase II: Modelling

Descriptive empirical model (Chapter 3)

Abstraction

Conceptual model (Chapter 4)

Programming and determination of parameters and variables

Computer simulation model and costs model (Chapter 5)

Phase III: Numerical analysis

Experimental design

Experiments and results (Chapter 6)

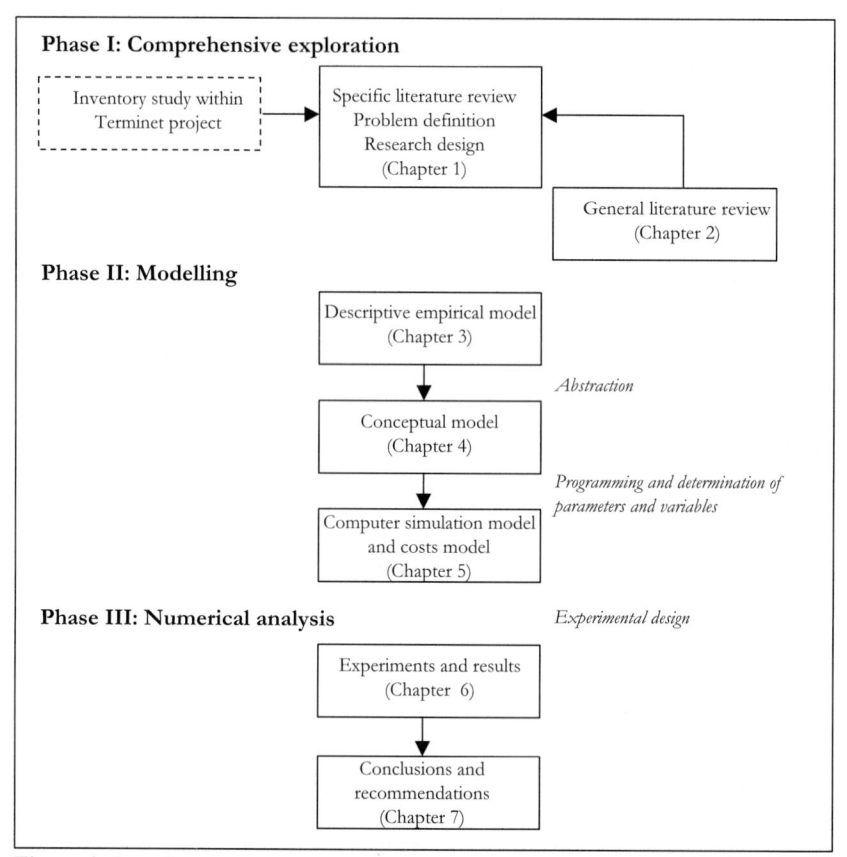

Conclusions and recommendations (Chapter 7)

Figure 1–7:   Outline of the research design and thesis

Finally, and once the research topic had been selected, an additional literature study focusing on the state of the art of hub-and-spoke networks, hub exchange facilities and hub exchange operations in road-rail intermodal transport was carried out. The objective of this literature study was to determine the problem definition and to identify the research objectives for this PhD research. The results of this literature study are included in sections 1.1 and 1.2 of this chapter.

1.4.3   Phase II: modelling

To achieve the main objective of this thesis, static simulation (see van Duin & van Ham, 1998, pp. 412-423; Winston, 1994, Chapter 23) was applied in combination with business economic costs spreadsheet calculations. Simulation may be defined as a technique that imitates the operation of the empirical (real-world) system. The em-

pirical system is captured in a model in a set of assumptions about the operation of the system, expressed as mathematical or logical relations between elements in that system (Winston, 1994, Chapter 23). A simulation model with an animation tool allows for assessment of the functioning and performance of various hub-and-spoke systems. Common steps in a simulation approach are (Banks, 1998) as follows:
1. Description of the empirical system.
2. Conceptualisation of the empirical system.
3. Specification of the conceptual model into a computer model.
4. Verification and validation of the computer model.
5. Carrying out experiments with the computer model.

Steps 1 to 4 were carried out in Phase II and are reported in three chapters. Step 5 belongs to Phase III: numerical analysis.

A first step towards the construction of a simulation model is to describe the empirical system, which is reported in Chapter 3. In this thesis the empirical system consists of one proposed (not existing) hub-and-spoke system with new hub terminals and three existing ones with hump shunting, flat shunting and road-rail terminals.

System analysis (see Clementson, 1988; Flood & Carson, 1990) was used to investigate and describe the empirical systems, resulting in a descriptive empirical model. An analytical framework was developed in order to carry out a uniform assessment of different hub-and-spoke systems and to identify the most relevant system elements that needed to be modelled. This first step was primarily used to gain a better understanding of the problem area.

Input for the system analysis was a mixture of empirical data and assumptions related to concepts and ideas for new hub terminals and hub-and-spoke networks. To obtain information and data the following approaches were used:
- Desk research on scientific journals, informal reports, professional magazines and commercial documentation.
- (Telephone) interviews with facility manufacturers, and facility and network operators.
- Site visits to shunting yards, rail-road terminals, pilot plants for new hub terminals.
- Observation of scale models and animations of new hub terminals.
- Case studies.

In the second step of the modelling, in Chapter 4, an abstraction was made of the essential parts of the descriptive empirical model. The result was a descriptive conceptual model. This model was used to represent the essential and generic elements of the problem area under investigation. The modelling objective was as follows:
- Develop a model in which different parameter and variable settings can represent different types of hub-and-spoke networks, hub exchange facilities and hub exchange operations.
- Keep the model as transparent and as aggregated as possible without losing typical features.
- Conceptualisation of the empirical hub-and-spoke system is inspired by logistics theory, regarding thinking in flows, stationary points and flow control (De Vaan, 1998 in: Goor, 1992; Goor et al., 2000), and queuing theory. In queuing theory systems are perceived as processes in which jobs are processed by servers in front of which queues may occur when the number of jobs exceeds server capacity (Hall, 1991). In addition, conceptualisation of the functioning

of hub-and-spoke systems is carried out from the viewpoint of the hub exchange facility (as opposed to the network, for instance).

It turned out that one conceptual model could not sufficiently represent all variations of exchange operations due to fundamental differences between types of resources and routing of flows along these resources and train access and departure control routines to and from exchange operations. As a result six conceptual models were constructed, which are all based on the same general framework and modelling principle.

In the third modelling step, in Chapter 5, the six conceptual models were programmed into computer models and values for parameters and variables were estimated. ARENA was chosen as the modelling software. The task of simulation software evaluation and selection, which involves multi-criteria decision-making, is usually time-consuming (Nikoukaran et al., 1999). Due to time and budget constraints along with the researchers' previous experiences with ARENA, an evaluation of ARENA was carried out. A set of criteria developed by Nikoukaran et al. (1999) was used as a guideline for the evaluation. The conclusion was that the features of the ARENA software package would suit the purpose of our modelling.

Chapter 5 also includes the fourth modelling step: verification and validation of the computer models.

Chapter 5 also includes a description of the modelling of costs. Since a simulation model does not include a cost evaluation module, a separate cost calculation model was constructed in a spreadsheet. The common business economic perspective on costs evaluation is used. Total annual costs and costs per load unit for greenfield situations are evaluated. Hence, costs calculations imply a total costs approach, implying that both capital (depreciation and interest) and operational costs are included. Input and output variables for the simulation model were used as input variables in the cost calculation module in addition to data collected from the literature and questionnaires (see Chapter 5). Cost categories in the spreadsheet were as follows:
- capital costs (depreciation and interest) for fixed assets such as infrastructure (rail tracks, storage area, surface, buildings), equipment and operational control software;
- operational costs such as labour costs, consumption costs (fuel), maintenance costs and administration and management costs.

1.4.4 Phase III: numerical analysis

In the fifth step of the modelling, experiments were carried out with the computer simulation models and costs models (Chapter 6). I hoped to answer the following questions in these experiments:
- What are favourable combinations of demand and capacity input for the new hub terminal in order to achieve an attractive time and costs performance for new intermodal markets?
- What are the effects of changes in demand with respect to the number of trains per batch, number of batches per day, number of load units/rail wagons (load factor) per train and load order on the time and costs performance of new hub terminals compared to other hub exchange facilities?
- What are the effects of changes in costs parameter values on the costs performances for various hub exchange facilities?

- What are typical levels of synchronisation of arrivals and operations for new hub exchange operations that will help to attract new markets?
- What is the effect of delays on the time performances of new hub terminals?
- What changes in the design and resources of new hub terminals could make the new hub terminal more favourable?

Various individual variables as well as various combinations of variables could be applied. To focus the search on the most favourable operational conditions for new hub terminals experiments were carried out in a controlled and structured manner. Controlled experiments imply that the effect of a single variable on certain performance indicators was studied. Structured experiments imply that the experiments in which single variables were studied were carried out in a specific order.

I started our experiments by studying three volume variables: number of load units/rail wagons per train, number of trains per batch and number of batches per day. Based on the outcomes of these so-called initial experiments only (nearly) favourable demand conditions and capacity levels were further explored. To determine favourable conditions, benchmark criteria for maximum train sojourn time and costs per load unit for time-sensitive flows were applied. Once favourable options for variable demand were determined, the sensitivity of the results for changes in the variables load order and load factor as well as for different costs levels was studied. In a third and final set of experiments variations in arrival times, delays and strategic operations control principle were studied.

1.5 Scope of the research

This thesis focuses on the identification of favourable operational conditions for new hub terminals and the quantification of their operational performances in relation to alternative hub exchange facilities in a European context. The research interest lies in the relation between demand variables such as number of trains in a batch and performance variables such as batch handling time at a hub exchange facility. Other elements of the intermodal system such as pre- and end-haulage and road-rail exchange operations at origin and destination terminals are not considered. The design of hub-and-spoke networks and operations (e.g. location of nodes, scheduling and routing of trains) is not considered either. There are no comparisons of transport systems or transport chains. Consequently, it is impossible to state whether or not a hub exchange concept could contribute to the improvement of the competitiveness of intermodal transport compared to road transport, based on the results of this study. However, the findings can be used to formulate statements on which concept would be most suitable for which type of hub-and-spoke network (exchange demand profile). The box with the thick black line in Figure 1–8 indicates the focus of this thesis.

The main performance parameters considered are time and costs. Land use is incorporated into the cost parameter. Other parameters such as noise, energy consumption, emissions, risk of damage to freight and safety are not included.

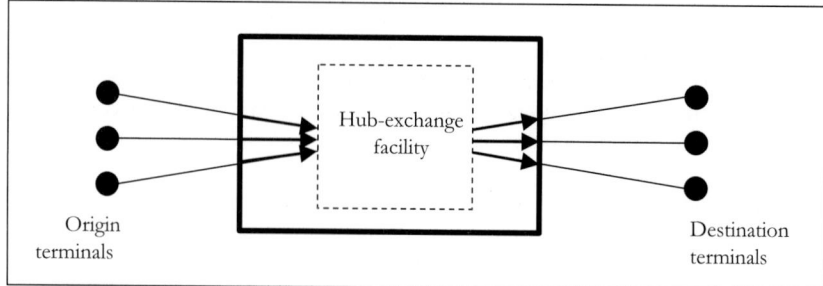

Figure 1–8 Scope of thesis: hub exchange operations from a hub exchange facility operator's point of view- outlined by the box with thick black line

1.6 Scientific and societal relevance

Scientifically, my aim is for this thesis to contribute to the advancement of intermodal transport research in general and theoretical approaches towards hub-and-spoke networks and hub exchange facilities in particular. The scientific contribution of this thesis concretely implies:
- Structuring the intermodal research field.
- A systematic analysis of hub exchange operations in intermodal transport which is successful in understanding its nature and the complex interactions between features of exchange demand and characteristics of hub exchange facilities.
- Theoretical approach and conceptualisation of hub exchange facilities and operations by applying logistics and queuing theory.
- Modelling of hub exchange operations and estimating time and cost performances.
- Complementing studies and models on hub-and-spoke networks in intermodal transport with time and cost data for hub exchange operations.

Besides its scientific contribution, this study also aims to have societal relevance. This study will offer actors and stakeholders in the intermodal industry new insight into hub-and-spoke networks in general and the functioning of hub exchange operations in particular. Fresh insight into the relationship between network (demand) features and hub exchange operations can be used to support decisions on hub-and-spoke network design and operations and hub-node selection. I hope that the results will inspire decision-makers to develop and improve hub-and-spoke networks to boost the market share of intermodal transport.

1.7 Summary and conclusions

Hub-and-spoke bundling networks in intermodal freight transport are suggested as a potential solution to help increase the intermodal market share. No more than three intermodal hub-and-spoke networks have become operational in the past decade in Europe[7]. However, trains are shunted at the hubs in these networks. Shunting is very time-consuming and counteracts the advantages of hub-and-spoke networks. A new

---

[7] Two of them were in the final stages of this thesis work, in December 2004, abandoned.

type of terminal, specifically designed for nodes in hub-and-spoke networks, has been introduced. At these terminals standardised load units (such as containers) are transhipped very efficiently from one train to another, instead of shunting rail wagons. Explorative evaluation studies suggest that under certain conditions these new terminals perform more efficiently than shunting yards. In order to further develop the use of hub-and-spoke networks in intermodal transport, it is important to ascertain whether implementation of new hub terminals would imply lower additional costs and time than shunting. If so, the counteracting of the advantages of hub-and-spoke networks may be reduced. Proposed hub-and-spoke networks and hub-exchange operations are different from transfer operations in other freight transport industries and operation at marine and road-rail terminals. Therefore existing models are of limited use and a model that can be used to identify favourable operational conditions for new hub terminals to be implemented, and quantify their operational performances in relation to alternative hub exchange facilities needs to be developed.

2 Is a new applied transportation research field emerging? – A review of intermodal rail-truck freight transport literature

2.1 Introduction to the chapter

This chapter reports on the general literature study that was carried out as one of the explorative research activities in Phase I. This general literature review tries to provide the state-of-the-art of road-rail intermodal transport research and a research agenda from which a thesis research topic could be selected. The review was carried out in 2001 in cooperation with C. Macharis and J.J. Trip. The results of the literature review have been published in Transportation Research A (Bontekoning et al., 2004). This article is reprinted in this chapter.

I thank Elsevier Ltd for the granted permission for this reprint.

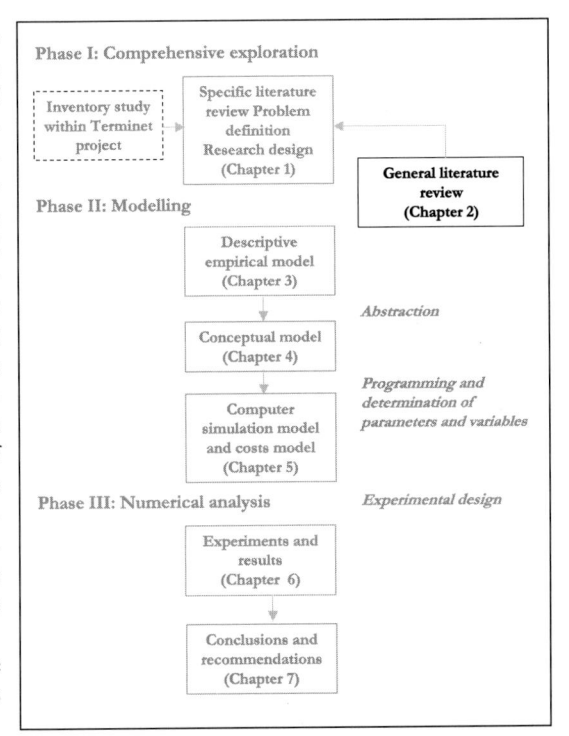

Phase I: Comprehensive exploration
- Inventory study within Terminet project
- Specific literature review Problem definition Research design (Chapter 1)
- General literature review (Chapter 2)

Phase II: Modelling
- Descriptive empirical model (Chapter 3)
  Abstraction
- Conceptual model (Chapter 4)
  Programming and determination of parameters and variables
- Computer simulation model and costs model (Chapter 5)

Phase III: Numerical analysis
  Experimental design
- Experiments and results (Chapter 6)
- Conclusions and recommendations (Chapter 7)

2.2 Introduction to the article

Intermodal freight transport is the movement of goods in one and the same loading unit or vehicle by successive modes of transport without handling of the goods themselves when changing modes (European Conference of Ministers of Transport, 1997). In examining intermodal freight transport, we can observe the following. First, in transport practice, intermodal transport is considered as a competing mode, alternative to unimodal transport. We also observe the existence of a specific intermodal industry for equipment and services. Second, in the 1980s and 1990s, intermodalism has become an important policy issue. It has been strongly advocated because of environmental concerns, reasons of overall efficiency and the benefits of co-ordination of modes to cope with growing transport flows (OECD, 1997). To illustrate this, the European Union has funded a good deal of research into intermodal transport in the past ten years. Third, handbooks and reference texts about transportation address intermodal transport separately from other modes such as road, rail, air, and waterborne transportation (Coyle et al., 2000; Button, 1994). Fourth, handbooks specifically addressing intermodal transport have now been published (Mahoney, 1985; Muller, 1995; Hayuth, 1987; McKenzie et al., 1989; DeBoer, 1992). Finally, since 1990 a substantial number of analytical publications specifically addressing intermodal transport have appeared. Various authors claim that intermodal research problems differ from other modes and mention the lack of analytical intermodal studies related to their field of study (Feo & González-Velarde, 1995; Yan et al., 1995; Morlok, 1994; Nozick & Morlok, 1997; Powell & Carvalho, 1998; Loureiro, 1994; Newman & Yano, 2000a, 2000b).

We thus contend that intermodal freight transportation research is emerging as a new transportation research field; while it is still in a pre-paradigmatic phase, it is now time to move on to a more mature state. Characteristics of a pre-paradigmatic phase, defined by the science philosopher Kuhn (Koningsveld, 1987) are:
- Several small research communities working on their own problems;
- Little references to other researchers (or only within the own research group);
- Lack of common problem definitions, hypothesis, definitions and concepts.

The situation will improve for the intermodal research field, intermodal practice and also for transport policy makers, when a distinct research community exists, directed by a consensus on definitions, concepts, problems to be investigated, and methodology. Kuhn calls this the period of "normal science" in which research is conducted within the framework of a hypothetical paradigm. Our contribution attempts to provide a comprehensive overview and classification of existing intermodal research, to identify possibilities for integration of intermodal research areas, and to extrapolate a fundamental integrated research agenda. With our contribution, we aim to bring the intermodal research field a step closer to "normal science".

In order to focus our review, we decided to concentrate on the rail-truck intermodal chain, primarily for geographical reasons. In most countries, shippers have access to rail, in fewer countries they have access to the sea, and in very few countries they have access to inland shipping. Intermodal rail-truck freight transport can be characterised by:
- task division between modes regarding the short-haul and long-haul parts of the chain. Road transport is assigned to the short haul, or collection and distribution of freight, rail to the long-haul leg of the transport chain. The rail haul involves large transport units that require bundling of flows in order to reduce transport costs, which is a common objective in transportation;
- synchronised and seamless schedules between different modes. This implies that freight is neither stored nor handled during its journey from origin to destination;
- the use of standardised load units, which increases the efficiency. Many commodities can be handled by standardised transport and transfer equipment, and can easily switch between any sequence of modes. By contrast, different types of bulk cargo each require dedicated equipment. For example, grain and oil require different of equipment;
- transhipment of load units is inherent to the division of tasks between modes;
- multi-actor chain management. The level of complexity is higher in intermodal transport chains with various organisations, each controlling a part of the transport chain. We could call this decentralised control, opposite to single-actor, centralised co-ordination.

With this review, we seek to answer the following questions:
- What are the characteristics of the rail-truck intermodal research community?
- To what extent does consensus exist about definitions and concepts?
- Which subjects and problems are studied?
- What is the current knowledge base?
- What are fundamental contents of a rail-truck intermodal research agenda?

The structure of this chapter is as follows. In section 2.3, we discuss our search strategy. The results of this review are presented in sections 2.4 and 2.5. Section 2.4 comprises the relevant descriptive statistics, research categories, definitions and conceptual models, and an assessment of the coherence of the research field. Section 2.5 briefly reviews the 92 publications which represent current leading-edge rail-truck intermodal knowledge. In section 2.6, we propose an intermodal research agenda. Section 2.7 contains our conclusions.

2.3 Methodology

Cooper (1989) argues that research reviews can be designed in a systematic, objective way, instead of the intuitive, subjective, narrative "traditional" style. The design of an integrative research review contains five stages:
- formulation of problem and hypothesis, guiding the review;
- determination of data collection strategy and selection of multiple channels in order to avoid a bias in coverage;
- evaluation and selection of retrieved data, including determining appropriate selection criteria;
- analysis and interpretation of the literature reviewed, including statistics about sources, number of retrievals and literature finally reviewed;
- presentation/reporting of the results.

These stages are followed in this chapter.

A computerised search was chosen, because it is fast and efficient. However, electronic sources such as databases have limited coverage. Their earliest date is 1988. Nevertheless, this relatively short period of coverage is not really a significant bias in our review, as we presume that most intermodal literature has been published in the last ten years. To locate studies, a number of channels, primarily including the Transport, Dissertation Abstracts and Social Sciences Citation Index databases, was used. In addition, studies were retrieved by tracking cited references. The review covers the period 1988-2001 as much as possible.

Based on search keys in the title, abstract, keywords, and type of media, a preselection of the literature was made. Studies concerning the short-haul, the long-haul, synchronisation of schedules, the use of standardised load units, transhipment and multi-actor co-ordination in intermodal rail-truck transport as well as studies covering intermodal rail-truck transport in general have been selected. Literature about intermodal passenger transport, as well as literature appeared in professional magazines or belonging to the category "best practice" has been included. As a result, the review is mainly based on English literature published in scientific transport journals and dissertations.

The characteristics of the intermodal scientific field can be expressed in terms of geographical scope, size, and coherence, and can be quantified. Indicators that can be retrieved from the literature reviewed and that give an indication of scope include: "countries of affiliation" (working location of scientists, not nationality) and "countries to which research applies". Indicators for size are "the number of scientists involved per country" and "the number of publications (per year)", for coherence the "citation relations". To determine to which extent consensus exist about definitions and concepts, all definitions and concepts applied in the literature reviewed have been noted. Next, the argumentation has been analysed, and definitions and concepts have been compared. We assessed the current knowledge by analysing the intermodal problems investigated and how they have been investigated. The analysis and description have been carried out with the aim of elaborating a fundamental intermodal research agenda, based on the integration of separate intermodal subjects.

2.4 Results

2.4.1 General statistics about the review

We reviewed 92 publications: 54 articles in scientific journals, 12 dissertations, 3 chapters in a book, 11 books/reports, and 12 papers in conference proceedings. Figure 2–1 shows that intermodal research is an emerging research field that really started to evolve in the last decade. In our opinion the data is not affected by a bias in database coverage, which only contains publications from 1988 till present. Such bias would be made visible in Figure 2–1 by a significant increase in the number of publications as from 1988. Instead, the number of publications increases rather gradually.

Table 2–1 shows that intermodal research is carried out mainly in North America (USA and Canada) and Europe. In North America, 88 researchers are involved in intermodal freight transport research, versus 47 in Europe. The number of publications is respectively 52 and 42. Other continents are barely, or not at all, covered by the literature reviewed. In Europe, the Netherlands and the United Kingdom are strongly represented. This may be explained by a language bias. German and French are world languages, while Dutch is not. The fact that four out of the five German publications are written in German supports this explanation. Further, there is a bias towards our own research, which accounts for 6 of the 16 publications by Dutch researchers.

2.4.2 Research categories

Eight research categories have been distinguished. Five are based on typical characteristics of intermodal transport described in section 2.2: 1) drayage; 2) rail haul; 3) transhipment; 4) standardisation; 5) multi-actor chain management and control. However, also studies related to the transport economical and policy context were identified. Two additional categories have been distinguished; 6) mode choice and pricing strategies; 7) transportation policy and planning. Finally, an eighth category "miscellaneous" has been defined. In section 2.5, we will discuss the literature reviewed per category.

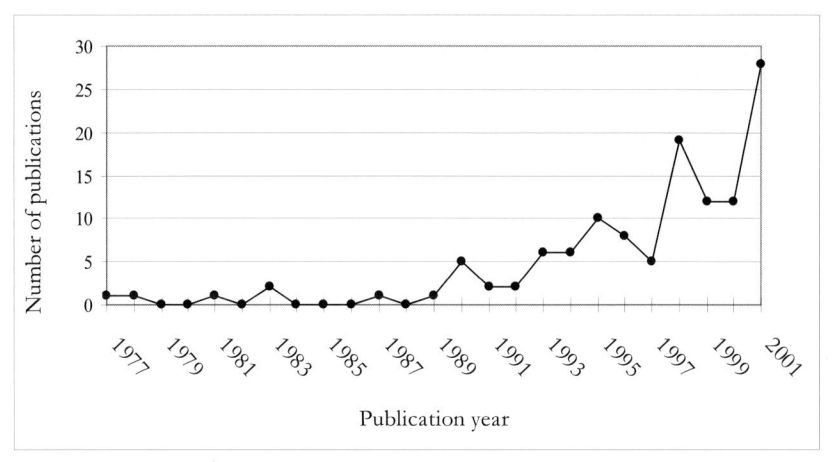

Figure 2–1: Number of publications per year: period 1977 to 2001
This figure includes 92 reviewed papers and 2 not obtained papers for the period up till 2000. A similar search and selection strategy for 2001 would lead to 28 publications. However, this number might be overestimated, because after the review process some publications still may be excluded.

The review shows that the involvement of North American and European scientists is not equally distributed over the research categories described above. Due to different geographical situations and development paths of intermodal freight transport in both regions, the research focus differs. North American researchers dominate the research concerning drayage, mode choice and pricing, and rail haul with respect to operational management topics. European research dominates the category of rail haul in terms of the strategic and tactical level, as well as the category transhipment. In other categories, there is not such a sharp distinction between North American and European scientists. For a description of intermodal transport development in North America see Thuong (1989) and Slack (1990, 1995), for Europe see Bukold (1996) and Charlier & Ridolfi (1994).

Table 2–1: Geographical distribution of publications, 1977-2000

Country	Number of researchers involved*	Number of publications	Country to which research applies
USA	79	44	47
Canada	9	8	5
Europe**	47	42	18
- The Netherlands	13	16	6
- United Kingdom	9	7	3
- Belgium	6	1	1
- Germany	5	5	6
- Greece	4	2	-
- Italy	3	3	1
- France	3	2	4
- Sweden	2	3	2
- Norway	1	1	1
- Switzerland	1	1	-
- Luxembourg	-	1	-
- Denmark	-	-	1
- Finland	-	-	1
Australia	4	4	3
Mexico	1	1	1
Taiwan	1	1	-
Brazil	-	-	2
No specific country	-	-	4
Total	141	100 ***	-

*   Based on affiliation, not on nationality of the researchers.

** In the first two columns the figure for Europe is the sum of the figures stated for the individual countries.

*** > 92 publications reviewed, because some articles are written by more than one author. Authors could be from different countries.

Table 2–2: Definitions of intermodal transport - ranging from rather general to more specific definitions

Authors	Definition
(Jones et al., 2000)	The shipment of cargo and the movement of people involving more than one mode of transportation during a single, seamless journey.
(Southworth & Peterson, 2000)	Movement in which two or more different transportation modes are linked end-to-end in order to move freight and/or people from point to origin to point of destination.
(Min, 1991)	The movement of products from origin to destination using a mixture of various transportation modes such as air, ocean lines, barge, rail, and truck.
(Schijndel, 2000)	The movement of cargo from shipper to consignee using two or more different modes under a single rate, with through billing and through liability (Hayuth, 1987).
(D'Este, 1995)	A technical, legal, commercial, and management framework for moving goods door-to-door using more than one mode of transport.
(TRB, 1998)	Transport of goods in containers that can be moved on land by rail or truck and on water by ship or barge. In addition, intermodal freight usually is understood to include bulk commodity shipments that involve transfer and air freight (truck-air).
(Ludvigsen, 1999)	The movement of goods in the same load-carrying unit, which successively use several transport modes without handling of goods under transit.
(Tsamboulas & Kapros, 2000)	The movement of goods in one and the same loading unit or vehicle, which uses successively several modes of transport without handling the goods themselves in changing modes (European Conference of Ministers of Transport, 1997)
(van Duin & van Ham, 1998)	The movement of goods in one and the same loading unit or vehicle, which uses successively several modes of transport without handling the goods themselves in changing modes (European Conference of Ministers of Transport, 1997)
(Murphy & Daley, 1998)	A container or other device which can be transferred from one vehicle or mode to another without the contents of said device being reloaded or disturbed (Jennings & Holcomb, 1996).
(Newman & Yano, 2000a, 2000b)	The combination of modes, usually ship, truck or rail to transport freight.
(Taylor & Jackson, 2000)	The co-ordinated transport of goods in containers or trailers by a combination of truck and rail, with or without an ocean-going link (Muller, 1995).
(Slack, 1996)	Unitised loads (containers, trailers) that are transferred from one mode to another.
(Spasovic & Morlok, 1993)	The movement of highway trailers or containers by rail in line-haul between rail terminals and by tractor-trailers from the terminal to receivers (termed consignees) and from shippers to the terminal in the service area.
(Niérat, 1997)	A service in which rail and truck services are combined to complete a door-to-door movement.
(Harper & Evers, 1993)	One or more motor carriers provide the short-haul pick up and delivery service (drayage) segment of the trip and one or more railroads provide the long haul or line haul segment.
(Evers, 1994)	The movement of truck trailers/containers by both railroads and motor carriers during a single shipment.
(Nozick & Morlok, 1997)	The movement of trucks and containers on railcars between terminals, with transport by truck at each end.

2.4.3 Common definition and conceptual model of intermodal transport

Typical for a research field in the pre-paradigmatic phase is the lack of a consensus on definitions and a common conceptual model, which is the case for the intermodal transportation research field. The purpose of a common definition and conceptual model is to provide integrated frameworks for analysis of the intermodal transport system in a methodical fashion.

Table 2–2 shows all definitions explicitly stated in the literature reviewed. It reveals that no commonly accepted definition exists. Although the European Conference of Ministers of Transport and United Nations et al. (1997) have proposed a common definition, only van Duin & van Ham (1998) and Tsamboulas & Kapros (2000) apply it. Why do authors not use this definition? Obviously, authors use a definition reflecting the scope of their research. Different scopes lead to different definitions. Something similar applies with respect to a standard conceptual model. Hayuth (1987), Jensen (1990), D'Este (1995), Woxenius (1994, 1998) and Bukold (1996) have developed conceptual models, but except for Woxenius, who built on Jensen's model, authors did not elaborate each other's model. Each researcher develops a model for the purpose of one's own research.

However, a comprehensive common definition and model may be useful when they reflect the distinguishing characteristics of intermodal transport and the general research problem. Only then they may serve as a common framework for a research field and can researchers use them to position their contribution to the general problem. It seems unlikely that the definition of European Conference of Ministers of Transport et al. (1997) can serve as common definition, because it only covers the physical characteristics of intermodal transport. Typical organisational aspects such as synchronised schedules, task division between modes, and multi-actor chain management are lacking, aspects emphasized in the definitions of Hayuth (1987) and D'Este (1995). The models by D'Este (1995) and Woxenius (1994, 1998) are the most comprehensive, and may be used for further elaboration.

2.4.4 Coherence of the transportation research field

One of the characteristics that can be used to determine the stage of development of a research field is its coherence. An indicator for coherence is the "citation relations". Citations provide insight into how an author positions his/her work in relation to others; they also give an indication of how a research topic is developing. We developed the following approach to measure the level of coherence of the intermodal transport research field. We traced all citation relations within the group of 92 publications reviewed. Between 46 of the 92 publications citation relations have been found. Hence 50% of the publications reviewed has not been cited. We grouped the citations into the eight research categories in order to provide information about the number of citations within a research category and between categories.

However, this absolute number of citations does not indicate anything in specific about the level of coherence. Therefore, we must relate the number of citations to the maximum number of possible citations within a research category and between two different categories. This results in a citation ratio, shown in Table 2–3. Assuming that the most recent publication theoretically could refer to all earlier publications, a maximum possible number of citations can be calculated. However, the time gap between when a paper is written and when it is published could be more than one year. Therefore, a time-gap of two years is taken into account.

Table 2–3: Coherence of the research field expressed in citation ratios within and between research categories

Cited FROM Cited TO	1	2	3	4	5	6	7	8
Drayage (5)	0.25							
Rail haul (22)	0.04	0.09	0.03			0.01	0.01	0.01
Transshipment (9)		0.02	0.21			0.09		
Standardisation (2)								
Multi-actor chain management and control (8)	0.03	0.02			0.12	0.04	0.02	0.02
Mode choice and pricing strategies (16)	0.07			0.25		0.14	0.02	0.04
Intermodal transportation policy and planning (19)	0.06	0.02	0.02				0.03	0.02
Miscellaneous (11)		0.02					0.03	0.03

The number of publications per category is indicated between brackets.
For a definition of citation ratio see subsection 2.4.4.

The citation ratio lies between 0 and 1. A ratio close to 1 means a high coherence of the research field; authors refer to each other and are aware of each other's work. When the ratio approaches 0, this could imply three things:
- researchers are not acquainted with each others' work, hence there is no coherent research field;
- the research field has become so large that it is no longer possible to refer to even a small part of all other relevant literature;
- the work of other researchers is not considered relevant or of less importance.

Table 2–3 shows many empty squares (no citations at all), while the ones that are filled show low ratios. Does this imply that there is no coherent intermodal research field? We reject the possibility that the research field has become too large, because then there would be references to review articles or a few authoritative publications. This is not the case. A few publications are being more cited than others, but still to a limited extent. The works most often cited are by Harper & Evers (1993), Fowkes et al. (1991) and Nierat (1987; 1997), with respectively 6, 5 and 3 citations. Taylor & Jackson (2000) and Bontekoning (2000a) incorporate the most citations to others. Each accounts for six citations.

The third point mentioned above certainly applies. Authors in general do not cite more than about 20 publications, implying that authors make a selection of most relevant and/or well-known citations. Considering that researchers could either take a methodical or a problem perspective, this perspective may direct the sort of citations. Verification of the citations indicates that most authors have a problem perspective. Implying that they could have refereed to other intermodal publications. Consequently, the low ratios could imply that authors are not aware of each other's work as is suggested in point 1. But it could also imply that researchers value the work of others as not close enough to their own research problem. Based on the citation ratio, which is a quantitative indicator, it is difficult to tell. However, overlooking the content of all publications reviewed (see Section 4) in combination with the citation relations, it appears that when the set-up and outcomes of studies had been set off more against results of other studies, the citation ratios would have been higher and the existing knowledge about various aspects of intermodal transport better integrated. Instead, we observe many isolated research (about 50% of the work reviewed is not cited) and small research communities focusing on a specific aspect of intermodal transport. As a result, we claim that the intermodal research field has a low coherence, which is typical for an emerging research field.

2.5 Current knowledge base

In section 2.2, we argued that intermodal transportation research is emerging as a new transportation research application field, that it still is in a pre-paradigmatic phase, and that it is time to move on to a more mature independent research field. The results of section 2.4 are in line with the characteristics of a pre-paradigmatic phase described in section 2.2. We think that the intermodal research field is ready to become a research field in its own right: there is a large variety of intermodal researchers, a large variety in research specialties, as well as a range of intermodal characteristics that justify a separate research field. The next step is to integrate existing knowledge and to identify an intermodal research agenda. In this section and in section 2.6 we will take this step.

The purpose of this section is to review the literature, analyse the problems being investigated and assess the knowledge needs. The emphasis lies on problems addressed in the literature, rather than methods and techniques applied. The structure of this section is based upon the eight research categories identified in subsection 2.4.2. In subsection 2.5.1 to 2.5.8 we address the problems addressed in the literature. In subsection 2.5.9 we discuss the theories, methods and techniques applied to investigate the problems mentioned. We will draw up an intermodal research agenda in section 2.6.

2.5.1 Drayage

Drayage operations take place by truck between a terminal and shippers or receivers. Drayage operations have some distinct features, different from simple pick up and delivery in rail and road transport. Despite the relatively short distance of the truck movement compared to the rail line haul, drayage accounts for a large fraction (25% to 40%) of total transport expenses. High drayage costs seriously affect the profitability of intermodal service, and limit the markets in which it can compete with road transport (Morlok et al., 1995; Morlok, 1994; Spasovic & Morlok, 1993; Höltgen, 1996; Fowkes et al., 1991; Niérat, 1997). Consequently, it affects the competitiveness of intermodal transport. Alternative operations need to be developed. Walker (1992) and Spasovic (1990), Morlok et al. (1995), Morlok (1994) and Spasovic & Morlok (1993) developed tools to study the behaviour of drayage operations. These studies show that substantial cost savings could be realised with a centrally planned operation in which trips can be combined in a more efficient manner, leading to fewer "empty hauls".

With respect to the influence drayage costs have on overall transport costs, we would have expected much more research in this category. Spasovic and Morlok contributed largely to new insights into the behaviour of drayage operations. However, more research is required in order to validate the model. Furthermore, the model can still be extended, for example by the inclusion of other parts of the intermodal chain, external costs, or by incorporating multiple objectives and more constraints.

2.5.2 Rail haul

The rail haul is the terminal-to-terminal segment of the intermodal trip. There is a vast literature about rail modelling (Assad, 1980; Crainic, 1999), but intermodal rail transport distinguishes itself from traditional rail in four points. First, fixed schedules are used, essentially without classification between origin and destination, while in traditional rail haul networks, trains run only when full and a lot of classification at intermediate nodes takes place. Second, fleet management issues in intermodal transport are more complex, because of the separation of the transport unit (rail flatcar) and the load unit (container/trailer). One aspect of the flatcar management problem is the tremendous variety of flatcars (including doublestack cars), along with the variety of trailers and containers. In contrast, in traditional rail transport, only boxcars are modelled. Third, because the transport unit can be separated from the load unit, rail-rail transhipment terminals can replace intermediate rail yards for classification. Fourth, location decisions for intermodal rail-road terminal are different from rail yards, as the former connect two types of infrastructure.

The main objective of intermodal rail haul research is to find an efficient, profitable and competitive way of organising the rail haul. We can distinguish three levels of planning and decision making with respect to this: strategic planning, tactical planning and operational planning.

At the strategic level, the configuration of the service network is determined. This includes decisions about which rail links to use, which regions to serve, which terminals to use and where to locate new terminals. It is not evident what would be more efficient: a few large terminals, or many small terminals. Arguments are put forward in both directions. Slack (1990) concludes that, to realise economies of scale, a large number of terminals have been closed and traffic has been concentrated on a few corridors and traffic hubs. Nine years later Slack (1999) himself proposes introducing satellite facilities to outplace some functions from congested terminals. Howard (1983) opposes to the rationalisation of the intermodal network, arguing that larger terminals do not lead to economies of scale. He suggests an expansion of the intermodal terminal coverage through a denser network of smaller terminals.

Another issue is the location of terminals. In this respect, the question is which objectives to optimise, for instance: minimising transportation costs on the links, maximising terminal profitability, maximising modal shift, minimising total transport costs or minimising drayage distance and costs. In addition, the problem can be split in the search for an optimal location in the whole network or the selection of an optimal location among a discrete number of possibilities. Five papers address the location of road-rail terminals. Four consider the issue from a network perspective, the fifth from a discrete choice perspective.

The objective of Rutten (1995) is finding terminal locations that will attract sufficient freight to run daily trains. He studies the effect of adding terminals on the performance of existing terminals and of the overall network. Van Duin & van Ham (1998) identify optimal locations while incorporating the perspectives and objectives of shippers, terminal operators, agents, consignees and carriers. For each level, an appropriate model is developed. The location of large potential customers seems to be one of the most decisive factors. Meinert et al. (1998) investigates the location of a new rail-terminal in a specific region in which three rail terminals already have been located. They specifically consider the impact of the location of the new terminal on drayage length and time. Arnold & Thomas (1999) minimises total transport costs to find the optimal location for intermodal rail-road terminals in Belgium. Groothedde & Tavasszy (1999) minimises generalised and external costs to optimize the location of intermodal rail-road terminals.

At the tactical level, the configuration of the train production system is determined. This includes decisions about train scheduling and routing, consolidation of flows, frequency of service and train length. Especially in Europe, there is a need for efficient and qualitative attractive production systems, and various plans to (re)introduce train production systems with complex bundling of flows have been proposed. Janic et al. (1999) evaluates complex bundling networks by means of a multi-criteria analysis of most promising layouts. Kreutzberger (1998; 1999a; 2000) and Terminet (1999) study the consolidation of flows to assess and quantify the basic principles of complex consolidation networks. Janic et al. (1998) formulate mathematical representations for various consolidation models, but no computations have yet been reported. In the USA, however, Newman & Yano (2000a, 2000b) performed calculations on point-to-point versus hub-and-spoke networks. Newman and Yano developed a model for determining a train schedule for both direct and indirect trains and allocating containers to these trains.

The operational level involves the day-to-day management decisions about the load order of trains, redistribution of railcars and load units (fleet management). The literature reviewed deals with:
- *the development of decision support applications.* The problems dealt with are: 1) the planning of the repositioning of empty trailers and containers (Chih & Van Dyke, 1987), 2) routing of container, sizing up of trains and optimal distribution of double-stack rail cars (Chih et al., 1990), 3) assigning trailers and containers to flatcars (Feo & González-Velarde, 1995; Powell & Carvalho, 1998);
- *the development of an efficient heuristic method to solve more complex planning problems* than mentioned above (Nozick & Morlok, 1997);
- *minimising terminal transfers* by determining the optimal load order on trains at an intermediate rail-rail transhipment terminal (Bostel & Dejax, 1998).

The review shows a need for more insight into service network configurations. First, it is not evident which would be more efficient, a few large terminals, or many small terminals. Second, research in optimal location modelling could be extended. Models could be improved in the sense that they represent more accurately the real world. Models could be improved by including for example also the problem of balancing in- and outgoing flows. Also models which incorporate multiple stakeholder objectives are needed. In the area of barge terminals, some multi-criteria analysis models have already been developed (Declercq & Verbeke, 1997, 1999; Macharis & Verbeke, 1999). The three-level modelling approach of van Duin & van Ham (1998) explicitly considers the different goals of stakeholders. In addition, research is needed into optimal location modelling for rail-rail terminals. Hub location models (see for a review Campbell, 1994; Klincewicz, 1998) are quite applicable to the problem of the location of rail-rail terminals. According to Nagy & Salhi (1998), hub location models are connected with routing models (optimizing routes) to get a more realistic approach of the problem. Third, the intermodal network could be extended with more complex consolidations production systems, allowing the integration of smaller flows in the network. Consequently, the number of access points could be increased. Research into intermodal train production system has just begun. We still know little about the relationship between consolidation model, frequency, train length, and costs. Finally, with respect to day-to-day management problems the scientific challenge is threefold. First, to develop techniques to deal with the immediate planning problem. Second, to develop heuristics optimize as much as possible for broad planning problems. Third, to develop fast heuristics for real-time application.

2.5.3 Transhipment: road-rail terminals and rail-rail terminals

Manufacturers regularly develop new transhipment techniques, which researchers then evaluate and compare with existing rail-road transhipment. Héjj (1983) compares eight new handling techniques with conventional transfer by gantry crane. Ferreira & Sigut (1995) investigates and compares the RoadRailer[8] concept. Woxenius (1998) evaluates 72 small-scale transhipment technologies and gives a method to evaluate them.

In subsection 2.5.2, we identified the possibility of intermediate, rail-rail transhipment within the rail haul. Traditionally in rail transport, shunting is used for this. However, in intermodal transport, load units can be separated from the rail wagons. As a result, terminals can be used instead of shunting yards. The use of such rail-rail terminals is a new phenomenon. Meyer (1998) specifically addresses the design process of an optimal terminal layout and optimal operating strategy for such terminal. Bontekoning (2000a) compares several rail-rail terminal designs with a conventional terminal. Bontekoning (2000b) described an explorative case study into operational and performance differences between rail-rail terminals and shunting.

Evaluating and comparing new transhipment techniques with existing technology requires a systemic approach. Ferreira & Kozan (1992), Ferreira & Sigut (1993) and Zografos & Giannouli (1998) stress the lack of systematic methodologies that can be used to quantify impacts of changes in intermodal freight terminal operations. They propose the use of a standard set of performance measures and an integrated methodological framework.

New terminals are developed and evaluated while fundamental insights into their functioning still lack. For instance, the impact of arrival and departure dynamics and synchronised schedules on terminal layout and operations strategy remain unresolved. Bontekoning (2000a, 2000b) illustrates that terminal performances depend on the type of network they are part of. Another issue is that has not been studied is the impact of multi-actor chain co-ordination in performances. Terminals must serve the demands of shippers, truckers, rail operators, as well as those of the terminal operator itself. These objectives can be contradictory. Finally, we want to mention the need to obtain more insight in the impact of standardisation or the lack thereof on terminal costs and performances.

---

[8] RoadRailer uses trailers with the capability of being hauled on road as well as on rail. The trailers are connected to each other by means of detachable bogie.

2.5.4 Standardisation

Despite existing standardisation, there still is a great deal of variation among load units, rail cars and truck-trailer skeletons. The efficiency in the chain can still be improved by more standardisation. Betak et al. (1998) identified a number of unresolved issues related to container standardisation and interoperability in information technology. A study by Johnston & Marshall (1993), who examined the perceptions of intermodal shippers towards equipment types, shows that intermodal shippers tend to favour intermodal containers over piggyback and RoadRailer trailers. The study shows that each type of load unit has its typical advantages, but intermodal containers score the best overall.

More research into the effects of standardisation on intermodal efficiency and the decision process of standardisation agreements is needed. More standardisation in the intermodal chain could save costs. These cost savings will appear only when all actors participate in the agreements. As long as one actor continues to use own sized equipment, load units and information, cost savings will not be apparent. In the process of standardisation, all actors must be convinced of the benefit for the whole system. If the individual actor does not benefit from it, how can they be motivated to participate in changes? In addition, how should the decision making process on standardisation and the implementation phase of agreements with this multitude of actors be organised?

2.5.5 Multi-actor chain management and control

A number of actors are responsible for organising and controlling the transport chain. However, each controls a part of the chain. Together they have to ensure that a synchronised and seamless journey is offered to shippers. Multi-actor chain management and control of the intermodal transport chain is related to drayage, rail haul, transhipment and standardisation. The general problem is to gear all activities in the chain to one another, to provide timely information and communicate the right things at the right time. This is related to the daily management of transport activities, but also to strategic choices such as standardisation or use of information technology. Information and communication technology (ICT) provides new possibilities to support the complex chain co-ordination and control task. Hengst-Bruggeling (1999) and Dürr (1994) developed ICT based chain management design decision support systems. Hengst-Bruggeling did this for the strategic co-ordination level and Dürr for the operational co-ordination.

However, who will take the lead for changes in the chain? Woxenius (1994) and Taylor & Jackson (2000) examined the role and market power of each actor in the intermodal system. They argue that a chain leader, the actor with most power in the intermodal chain, can generate overall chain steering. Both studies concluded that in the international chain, ocean carriers have taken a leadership role, but in the domestic chain, such leadership is lacking. Wiegmans et al. (1999) takes the perspective of the terminal operator and identifies his economic power in the intermodal chain.

Another problem is the liability. Who is responsible for what, especially when things go wrong? Asariotis (1998) and the European Commission (1999) investigated the problems with respect to liability arrangement. The present legal framework determining an intermodal carrier's liability for delay, loss of, or damage to goods consists of a confused jigsaw of international conventions designed to regulate unimodal carriages, diverse national laws, and standard term contracts. Kindred & Brooks (1997) wrote a comprehensive text about liability and the complex legal regimes governing intermodal transport.

Multi-actor chain management is related to all aspects of the intermodal chain and to all other research categories. From the review, we know that no single actor fulfils the role of chain leader. Consequently, other chain co-ordinating structures are needed. However, what is required still needs to be determined. How are decisions taken about issues such as ICT or load unit standards? What is best for the chain is not necessarily the best for the individual actors. How can costs and benefits of changes be redistributed when this does not take place automatically via market mechanisms? What are the consequences for individual organisations when they have to give up some autonomy for the sake of chain objectives?

2.5.6 Mode choice and pricing strategies

The general problem of intermodal transport is its competitiveness in relation to other modes. With respect to the development of marketing measures it is relevant to know for which markets intermodal transport is attractive, how intermodal performs compared to other modes, how market share can be increased, and which pricing strategy to follow. There is a vast body of literature on mode choice determinants and the sensitivity of mode choice when price or quality changes (Winston, 1983; Zlatoper & Austrian, 1989). Several studies specifically deal with mode choice and intermodal transport.

Morash et al. (1977) identified the manufacturing commodities most susceptible to trailer or container on flat car movement in the USA. Harper & Evers (1993), Evers et al. (1996), Murphy & Daley (1998), Ludvigsen (1999) and Tsamboulas & Kapros (2000) assessed shippers' perceptions of various cost-quality determinants of intermodal rail-truck service and other transport mode(s). Most relevant to overall perception for all modes are timeliness and availability. It appears that in general, shippers give the intermodal rail-truck mode lower marks than road transport, but higher marks than unimodal railroad transport. In addition, Tsamboulas & Kapros (2000) show that actors who decide almost exclusively on cost criterion, are intensive users of intermodal transport transportation, while intermodal transportation is a minor portion of an actor's total transport for actors who decide according both quality and cost criteria. Evers & Emerson (1998), who measured the influence of an actor's perception of a mode on the mode choice, found that the more highly a firm perceives motor carrier service, the less likely it is to use intermodal transportation. In addition, as a firm's awareness of third party intermodal providers increases, its intermodal usage also increases. The studies by Harper & Evers (1993) and Murphy & Daley (1998) indicate that non-users of intermodal transport have a lower perception of its performance than users. This suggests that image of characteristics of a transport mode is very relevant in mode choice. Actors do not decide on rational arguments only.

Beier & Frick (1978) and Fowkes et al. (1991) investigate the conditions under which shippers using road transport would switch to piggyback transport. Both studies indicate that the loss of quality by using intermodal transport would only be acceptable for shippers when (large) discounts on intermodal transport are provided. Niérat

(1997) defines zones around a terminal for which intermodal is more competitive than road transport. He shows that the size of these zones highly depends on the efficiency of drayage (number of empty hauls, number of operations per driver-day), cargo weight, discounts, rail haul traffic imbalance and distance. Schijndel (2000) assessed the impact of congestion on the decision to switch from road to intermodal by Dutch transport operators. The study indicates that a majority of the transport companies is able to switch to intermodal transport, but that they prefer other solutions such as driving during the night and dedicated lanes for trucks. Plunkett & Taylor (1998) developed a tool set to support cost analysis and mode selection for motor carriers.

Part of the competitiveness problem is the determination of the right tariff for intermodal transport services, which is called pricing strategy. This pricing strategy plays at two levels. First, at the level of the individual actor in the intermodal chain, each actor must estimate his negotiation power. Horn (1981) and Yan et al. (1995) evaluate various alternative pricing strategies for the rail haul. Spasovic & Morlok (1993) investigates the pricing strategy of drayage operators. Second, a pricing strategy could also be determined for the whole door-to-door intermodal transport service. Tsai et al. (1994) examines several approaches for such pricing strategy.

Mode choice studies reveal the most important mode choice determinants and provide insight in the sensitivity of the mode choice to a change in the cost or quality. However, the results are not generally applicable, but are specific to a certain data set, research population and geographical area. We would like to know how the differences in studies could be explained and overcome. We expect that the mode choice decision-making process is much more complicated than is assumed in current approaches. With respect to cost calculations and pricing strategy, we observe that very little is known about costs in the intermodal chain or appropriate cost calculation methods. Accurate cost calculations are needed to support multi-actor management structures, standardisation decisions and pricing strategies of individual actors and the intermodal chain as a whole.

We did not find studies dealing with macro-economic impacts of intermodal transport, except for Slack (1996) and some economic studies with a clear policy and planning focus. Slack investigates whether the establishment of inland rail hubs affects the number of businesses related to intermodal transportation in the area of the hub. It appears that many of the small firms were newly established. The economic studies with a policy and planning focus are discussed in subsection 2.5.7.

2.5.7 Transportation policy and planning

The policy context in the USA and Europe differs. In Europe, intermodal transport has been a policy objective for years, while it is still new as a policy objective in the USA. A problem in the USA is how to integrate intermodal freight transportation policy in federal, state, and local government transportation programs. The growth of intermodal freight transport has been a private-sector development, but the public sector is now looking to intermodal freight as a means of controlling government highway costs, reducing pollution and stimulating local employment. The literature reviewed investigates how and in which policy issues public bodies could and should become involved (Morlok, 1997; TRB, 1998; Eatough et al., 2000; Zavattero et al., 1998; Anderson & Walton, 1998). In European countries, particularly those belonging to the European Community, all levels of government have supported intermodal freight transportation policy planning and program development for several years already. Various policy and planning documents exist, but with the search strategy applied, no scientific papers dealing with European intermodal policy were retrieved.

A general problem in transport policy is the formulation of effective measures that support policy objectives such as reducing congestion and pollution, and improving safety, but also with respect to spatial and economic objectives, and infrastructure planning. Clarke et al. (1996) shows that American society will benefit in socio-economic terms from a shift from truck transport to intermodal transport. They analyse the impact of a shift of truck traffic to railroad intermodal service on highway safety. It appears that intermodal transportation has reduced fatal highway accidents by about 1%. In Europe, Fonger (1993) and Engel (1996) show that society is better off with road transport. They compare the societal costs of intermodal rail-truck, truck, and rail transport in Germany. However, Jensen (1990) shows the opposite. He designed a rail-truck intermodal system that can compete with long haul domestic road transport on heavy transport links in Sweden, both for private costs, quality aspects and external costs.

With respect to spatial and economic policy objectives, in Europe it is common practice to evaluate a new intermodal terminal not only on business economic merits but also on its contribution to regional economic development. Often terminal related activities are planned around the terminal (freight village). Konings (1996) proposes a specific kind of freight village with a high level of automation of internal transport on the site. Höltgen (1996) argues that the impact of intermodal terminals located in freight villages on regional development has, on the whole, been overrated. In the USA, new intermodal terminals are evaluated on their business economics merits. Slack (1995) compares the role of intermodal terminals in the spatial planning in Europe and the USA. He suggests that the planning practice in the USA could incorporate regional economic development objectives. That this planning practice starts to be incorporated is shown by Stank & Roath (1998) and Barton et al. (1999). Stank & Roath (1998) argues that a survey among manufacturers and shippers/consignees should be carried out before starting to build an intermodal terminal with a freight village with government involvement in order to assess their perceptions regarding the potential development on such facilities. Barton et al. (1999) evaluates the need and possibilities for new or expanded intermodal terminal facilities in the Chicago area. Both studies show limited support for the freight village among potential users.

With respect to infrastructure planning, policy makers search for effective measures. They would like to know the effect of a certain measure. For instance the impact of limited accessibility of trucks on motorways on the use of intermodal transport services (use of rail infrastructure). For this type of problems, spatial price equilibrium models and network models have been developed in the past. Most models, however, have been developed for one mode only and cannot deal with intermodal flows. Crainic et al. (1990), Loureiro (1994), D'Este (1995), Jourquin et al. (1999) and Southworth & Peterson (2000) have developed network models which are capable of dealing with intermodal flows, which implies that freight can be transferred from one mode to another in the model via transfer points.

The main problem in intermodal policy and planning is the lack of insight in effective policy measures. The studies reviewed address a limited number of policy issues. In general the results of these studies reveal that the measures are not effective. Much more policy research is required, for instance into the effect of financial support of the intermodal transport on its attractiveness; the impact of road pricing on the competitiveness of intermodal transport; the impact of the so-called Rail Freeways in Europe; dedicated rail infrastructure on the performance of intermodal transport and the level of sustainability of intermodal transport.

2.5.8 Miscellaneous

This eighth and last research category is reserved for studies which cannot be assigned to any of the other seven categories. Even within the miscellaneous category, some groupings can be made. First, there is a group of studies that deal with decision support tools for shippers in their selection of the optimal intermodal routing for a specific shipment (Min, 1991; Barnhart & Ratliff, 1993; Boardman et al., 1997; Bookbinder & Fox, 1998). Second, there is a group of studies which describe the development of intermodal transport from a historical and or geographical perspective (Charlier & Ridolfi, 1994; Thuong, 1989; Slack, 1995; Bukold, 1996). Lastly, we should mention four different studies. Jones et al. (2000) propose a standard intermodal definition (see also subsection 2.4.3). Evers & Johnson (2000) investigates the relationship between a shipper's perception of intermodal railroad-truck services provided by specific railroads and his perception of the overall performance of that railroad. Evers (1994) examines the extent to which statistical economies of scale[9] occur for four terminals. Norris (1995) analyses the nature of the process by which intermodal innovations diffused on USA railroads.

2.5.9 Applied methods and technique

In the previous subsections we investigated the problems dealt with in the literature. We did not discuss the theoretical embedding of the research nor the methods and techniques used to investigate the problems. In this section applied theories, methods and techniques will be briefly addressed.

Operations Research techniques are used for the analysis of drayage, rail haul and terminal operations, terminal location decisions, transhipment, infrastructure planning, intermodal route selection and intermodal pricing. Different techniques have been applied, among which linear programming, integer programming, non-linear programming, network analysis (sometimes GIS-based) and simulation.

Social science methods and techniques have been used for studies into mode choice, standardisation, multiple actor chain co-ordination, and transport planning and policy. Applied techniques are case studies, surveys, interviews, observation, literature research, expert panel and analytical approaches. To a very small extent the studies reviewed applied theoretical approaches from geography, marketing, economy or policy science. The applied theories are: market area theory, marketing channels theory, location theory, system analysis, welfare economic theory and cost-utility theory.

Intermodal transport research requires a multidisciplinary approach. The review shows that the structure and complexity of intermodal problems demand further development of operations research techniques. Especially, models which can deal with

---

[9] Statistical economies of scale can be defined as advantages that result from the pooling of uncertainty.

larger and more complex problems are required. We see a strong division between quantitative and qualitative approaches between research categories, which mainly is the consequence of the nature of the research problem. However, a more balanced mixture of both approaches towards each problem is needed. Intermodal research could rely much more on logistic, economic, management and policy theory and methods than it does now, also with respect to the operational parts of the intermodal chain.

2.6 Towards an intermodal research agenda

Research performed to date has led to insights into the complex relationships in the intermodal transport chain. It has also provided ideas about how to improve the efficiency, profitability and level of competitiveness of intermodal transport. However, the development of knowledge is quite scattered and is not integrated into an overall framework. We propose the following integrative research agenda that is directed towards the improvement of the efficiency, profitability, and competitiveness of the intermodal transport:

- Development of more efficient and sustainable drayage operations. Drayage causes a relatively large portion of the overall intermodal costs. In addition, the external effects of short distance road transport are considerable (Fonger, 1993).
- Design of networks and consolidation production system for the rail haul. Still very little is known about the relationship between the number, size and location of terminals and the geographical coverage of intermodal transport. This also applies to the relationship between consolidation model, frequency, train length and costs.
- Design and evaluation of terminals in order to obtain a fundamental understanding of the impact of arrival and departure dynamics of trucks and trains, terminal lay-out and operations strategy on terminal performance (handling time and costs). This is especially relevant for the development of new consolidation production systems.
- Analysis of the effects of standardisation on intermodal efficiency and into the decision-making process on standardisation agreements.
- Analysis of cost structure and development of pricing strategies.
- Analysis and development of multiple-actor co-ordination structures and (re)distribution strategies for (investment) costs and benefits among actors.
- Research is needed into the underlying factors of the usually selected mode-choice determinants. The mode choice decision-making process seems much more complicated than is currently assumed.
- Analysis of the impact of information and communication technology (ICT), automation and robotisation on the performance of intermodal transport.
- Policy formulation and evaluation studies in order to design and identify effective and efficient policy measures with respect to sustainability, liveability, accessibility and regional economic objectives.
- Development of methods and techniques to apply to intermodal research the problems.

2.7 Conclusions

A consequence of our search strategy is that we reviewed English scientific publications which could mainly be traced by a computerised research. We are aware that much more literature on intermodal transport exists; non-published scientific literature, scientific literature in national languages and professional publications. Referring to 92 publications we investigated the characteristics of the intermodal freight transport research field.

We contend that intermodal research is emerging. It could and should be a research field in its own right, as it has some distinctive characteristics by which it distinguishes itself from other transport research fields. The problems in intermodal transport are complex and require new methodologies to solve them. We found evidence that the intermodal research field is still in pre-paradigmatic phase. However, we foresee that it should be possible for the intermodal research field to evolve over a short period of time to a stage of 'normal' science. In this review, we identified a number of common research problems and an integrative research agenda. Furthermore, we identified a variety of small research communities. A second step needed to evolve to a period of normal science is the integration of these communities into one or two large research communities. This review may be a starting point for that integration.

A final point we would like to address is the transferable nature of our findings to intermodal transport chains with barge or short sea as long haul mode. The research issues identified in section 2.5 and integrated in section 2.6 also apply to road-barge and road-short sea intermodal transport. The dimensions of the transport units, infrastructure, and terminals are different, but the general problem, the too low level of efficiency, profitability, and competitiveness, remains the same due to the identical distinguishing characteristics of intermodal transport.

3 Hub exchange operations: a system description

3.1 Introduction

A simulation approach was chosen to achieve the main objective of this thesis: *to develop a model to identify favourable operational conditions for new hub terminals to be implemented, and to quantify their operational performances in relation to alternative hub exchange facilities.*

Simulation may be defined as a technique that imitates the operation of the empirical (real-world) system. The empirical system is captured in a model in a set of assumptions about the operation of the system, expressed as mathematical or logical relations between elements in that system (Winston, 1994, Chapter 23). In this study the system is a hub-and-spoke system that consists of features of the hub-and-spoke networks, hub exchange facilities and hub exchange operations (see section 1.2 for definitions). A first step towards the construction of a simulation model is to describe the empirical system, which is the objective of this chapter. In this thesis the empirical system consists of one proposed (not existing) hub-and-spoke system with new hub terminals and three existing ones with hump shunting and flat shunting yards and road-rail terminals.

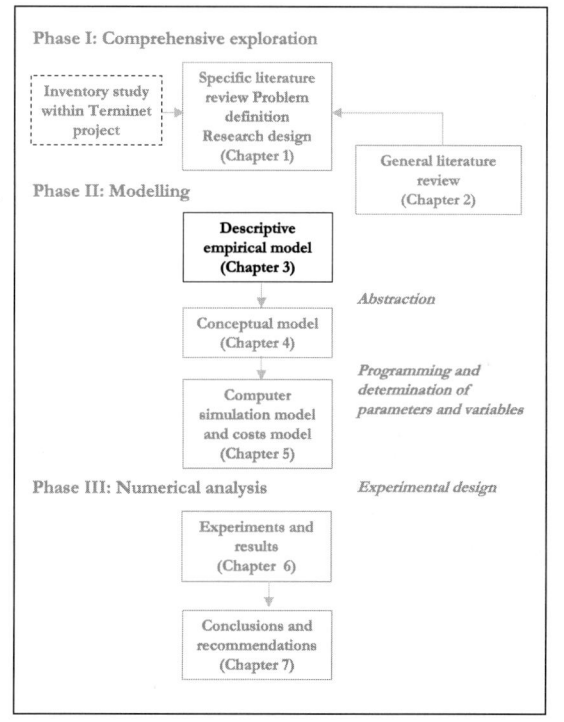

The outline of this chapter is as follows. In section 3.2 the research approach, a system analysis, is described. An analytical framework was developed in order to carry out a uniform assessment of different hub-and-spoke systems and to identify the most relevant system components and elements that needed to be modelled. Three system components were identified. In section 3.3 the elements of the component Demand are described, section 3.4 covers the elements of the component Resources and in section 3.5 the elements of the component Process are described. Next, the relationships between hub exchange operations and their environment are identified in section 3.6. Section 3.7 relates the system description with performance criteria. Lastly, in section 3.8 the system description is summarised in an integrated overview of the elements of hub exchange operations and their relationships with the environment and performance criteria. In addition, conclusions are formulated.

3.2 Approach

3.2.1 System analysis

A system analysis was carried out for the description of the empirical system. System analysis is a technique by which objectives, components and elements of the system, and interactions between components and elements, and between the system and its environment are systematically unravelled. The distinction between a component and an element is that components describe the system at a higher aggregated level than elements. A component consists of several related elements (Clementson, 1988; Flood & Carson, 1990). Components and elements of the system may be assessed from certain viewpoints (Clementson, 1988) of the researcher and be in line with research objectives. This leads to a selection of features of the system to be described and analysed that excludes system components and elements that are not relevant for the purpose of the study. This system analysis is carried out from two viewpoints.

The first viewpoint that directs the system analysis is the perspective on the system, which is taken from the viewpoint of the hub exchange facility. This implies that network elements of the system are perceived from the standpoint of an observer who figuratively is positioned at the hub exchange facility and observes what is happening at and around the exchange facility. Figure 3–1 provides the generic perception of this study on how the hub-and-spoke system is studied. In general the whole process can be described as follows. There is an incoming flow of trains. Trains are allowed access to the exchange facility according to an operations schedule. If they are too early, trains wait at the side yard. When a train is allowed access, load units or rail wagons in that train are processed at the exchange facility. Next, the train leaves the hub exchange facility. In the event that trains cannot re-enter the rail network yet, they wait at the side yard until their departure time.

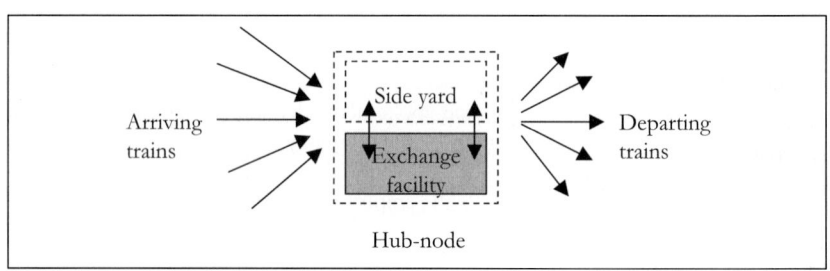

Figure 3–1: Viewpoint on the whole system from the perspective of the exchange facility

The second viewpoint that directs the system analysis is the focus on system elements that influence the performance (time and costs) of hub exchange facilities. Exchange operations must meet certain performance criteria defined by the customer(s) of a hub exchange facility. Although in reality this is much more complex, for the purpose of this analysis hub-and-spoke network operators are defined as the customers of a hub exchange facility. It is assumed that these network operators set up rail services between origin and destination terminals which require the exchange of load units at an exchange facility based on the transport demand of shippers and forwarders. The network operators have to fulfill the performance requirements of these shippers and forwarders. Survey results (Cardebring et al., 2002; Harper & Evers, 1993; Ludvigsen, 1999; Murphy & Daley, 1998) indicate that reliability, risk of loss or damage, flexibility, transport time and costs are considered as the most important performance requirements for shippers and forwarders. Network operators most likely translate these requirements into performance requirements for an exchange facility and add them to or integrate them with performance requirements that they derive from their own business goals. The most general business goal is maximisation of profits in the short or long term. The goal of a network operator may then be formulated as meeting shippers' and forwarders' requirements while maximising utilisation rates of resources such as trains and locomotives. Next, shippers' and forwarders' requirements and network operators' goals may result in the following performance criteria for a hub exchange facility:

- Safe and secure operations: operations should be carried out in such a way that no damage is done to load units, their contents or rail wagons.
- Reliable and timely operation: operations do not necessarily have to be fast. For shippers and forwarders it is more important that operations are carried out carefully, avoiding the exchange of load units to the wrong train. In addition, operations should not cause delayed departure of trains that may lead to delayed arrival of load units at their destination.
- Low/reasonable costs: exchange costs per load unit should preferably be low. Higher costs may be acceptable when they reflect a higher service level.
- Speed of operations: for network operators fast turnaround times for trains (rail wagons) and locomotives at the exchange facility may lead to high utilisation rates and consequently efficient rail haul operations.
- Flexibility of operations: an exchange facility must be capable of catering for variety in demand with regard to volume, arrival and departure times, delayed trains, etc.

These requirements will be kept in mind when investigating relevant system elements.

3.2.2 Analytical framework

An analytical framework was developed in order to carry out a uniform assessment of different hub-and-spoke systems and to identify the most relevant system elements that needed to be modelled. The intermodal hub-and-spoke system may be systematically described by the following three interrelated components:

- features of demand, or component *Demand*;
- technical features of hub exchange facilities, or component *Resources*;
- features of hub exchange operations, or component *Process*.

The component *Demand* consists of system elements such as types and number of trains and load units, batch composition and arrival schedules of trains. The component *Resources* consists of the physical means needed to process transport and load units, or to deal with elements of *Demand*. The component *Process* consists of operations control principles with respect to the component *Resources*. Description of the operational activities of the various *Resources* is part of this component *Process*. In the course of this chapter for each of the three components the relevant elements and their relationships with other elements are determined and described for four hub exchange facilities:

- new hub terminals;
- hump shunting yards;
- flat shunting yards;
- road-rail terminals.

3.2.3 Data collection

Input for the system analysis was a mixture of empirical data and assumptions related to concepts and ideas for new hub terminals and hub-and-spoke networks. To obtain information and data the following approaches were used:
- Desk research on scientific journals, informal reports, professional magazines and commercial documentation.
- (Telephone) interviews with facility manufacturers and facility and network operators.
- Site visits to shunting yards, rail-road terminals, pilot plants for new hub terminals.
- Observation of scale models and animations of new hub terminals.
- Case studies.

3.3 Description of the system component Demand

The component *Demand* consists of elements that specify the features of the daily demand to be processed at a hub exchange facility. These elements are batches and exchange relations, number of batches and trains per day, number of load units/rail wagons per train, type/size of load unit or rail wagon, load order, train length, train arrival and departure schedule and type of traction. These elements are defined and described in the course of this section.

Batches and exchange relations
Explicitly mentioned in the documentation on proposed new hub terminals (summarised in Bontekoning & Kreutzberger, 1999) is that operations imply the exchange of load units between a group of related trains called a batch and that arrivals of trains belonging to the same batch are synchronised within a certain time window. A batch contains two or more trains between which load units have to be exchanged. The term 'batch' is not further defined in the documentation on proposed new hub terminals. Therefore I propose the following definition. A batch is a group of trains that exchange load units (or rail wagons) with each other with the requirement that 1) no train can be removed from that batch without affecting the exchange to any of the other trains, and 2) all departing trains receive load units (or rail wagons) only from trains in the batch. Trains that exchange load units (or rail wagons) have a so-called exchange relation. There may be an exchange relation between all trains as illustrated in Figure 3–2, or between a limited number of trains as illustrated in Figure 3–3. In the case of the latter, a minimum number of exchange relations is required, such that there exists at least one exchange relation with any of the other trains in the batch. Which exchange relations exist in a batch is relevant to work planning and resource control.

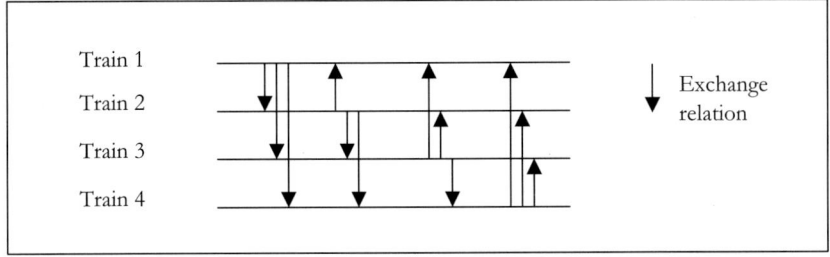

Figure 3–2: Exchange relations between all trains in a batch of four trains

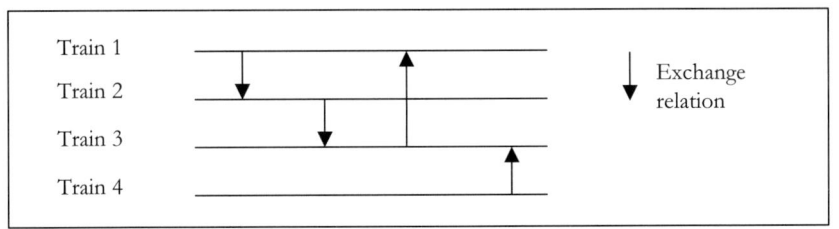

Figure 3–3: An example of a batch of four trains with a minimum number of exchange relations

Number of batches and batch size per day

Insight into the number of batches and batch size in combination with the number of load units or rail wagons is relevant for the dimensioning of infrastructure capacity, work planning and the input of resources. The projected daily demand for a new hub terminal near Paris, France, was 60 trains divided into various batches of between eight and eleven trains and for a new hub terminal near Hanover, Germany, it was four batches of six trains (Bontekoning & Kreutzberger, 1999).

The demand at existing (or former) hub-shunting operations[10] in intermodal hub-and-spoke networks is not organised into structured batches as projected for new hub terminals. Studying the exchange relations of trains at these hub-shunting yards and applying the batch definition as provided above gives the impression that all trains belong to one (large) batch. The demand can be characterised as a batch with a limited number of exchange relations per train as illustrated in Figure 3–3, such that no train can be removed from that batch without affecting the exchange to any of the other trains. The daily demand at the hub at Muizen consists of one batch of 7 or 8 trains (Vleugel et al., 2001), at the Metz hub it is one batch of 25 to 28 trains (Terminet, 2000), and at Herne it is one batch of 5 to 8 trains (Biggler, 2003). Vogtmann & Franke (2000) and Bosschaart (2003) tried to structure the demand volume at the Metz hub into batches. They were unable to do this successfully without violating arrival and departure schedules and some exchange relations.

Exchange operations at existing road-rail terminals are not organised into structured batches as projected for new hub terminals, either. Exchange at road-rail terminals implies that a part of the load units of international trains are exchanged with national trains and vice versa. The other part of the load units involves road-rail and rail-road transhipment. This is called the Gateway concept (Rotter, 2002; 2003). The

---

[10] *QualityNet* with a hub in Metz (France), *X-Net* with a hub in Herne (Germany), *North European Network* (NEN) with a hub in Muizen (Belgium).

batch terminology cannot be applied to the Gateway concept. The road-rail terminal does not function as a hub, but must be seen as an origin-destination terminal with some rail-rail transhipment.

Train length

Train length is important with respect to the dimensions of the infrastructure of the hub exchange facility and the number of load units or rail wagons to be processed. Common train lengths in intermodal transport in Europe, including existing hub-and-spoke networks, are between 400 metres and 600 metres (Biggler, 2003; Fritsch, 2003; Rotter, 2002; 2003; Vleugel et al., 2001). In Europe the maximum permissible train length varies according to country. For instance, in Belgium it is 600 metres, in the Netherlands it is 700 metres and in France it is 750 metres (Impulse, 1997; Rutten, 1995).

Type and size of load unit or rail wagon

Load units or rail wagons are the objects that are handled in exchange operations. Their type and size may affect the dimensioning of handling equipment and infrastructure. The most common types and sizes of load unit are indicated in Table 3–1. Intermodal rail wagons come in lengths of 14, 18, 20 and 34 metres. Occasionally, old flat wagons with a siding length of 12.5 metres are used. The effective loading space is about 1 metre less than the length of the rail wagon (www.stinnes-freight-logistics.de, 2003). Of particular relevance when dimensioning a shunting yard is not really the size of rail wagons, but their axle width. These are standard. Type and length of rail wagon are more relevant with respect to which type and size of load unit can be loaded onto one rail wagon and how many. This is relevant for the re-loading operation of load units at a hub exchange terminal.

Table 3–1: Most common types and sizes of intermodal load units

	Maritime container	Swap body	(Semi-)trailer
Length	20' (6m), 40' (12m) and 45' (13.72m)	7.15m, 7.45m, 7.82m, 13.6m	16.5m, 18.35m
Width	2.44m	2.5m	2.55m
Height	2.44m, 2.54m	2.67m	2.6m, 3.0m

Source: (Impulse, 1997; Rutten, 1995)

Number of load units or rail wagons per train

Load units or rail wagons are the objects handled by the resources at hub terminals and shunting yards respectively. Insight into their number per train and number per batch, and into the exchange relations between trains is relevant for work planning and resource control. The number of rail wagons naturally depends on the length of a train and the length of individual rail wagons. As the lengths of rail wagons vary by train as well as the length of trains, the number of rail wagons will lie somewhere between 12 wagons (400m/34m) and 43 wagons (600m/14m).

The number of load units per train varies widely. In addition to the length of the load units, the weight of the load determines how many load units can be loaded onto one rail wagon. For example, a 14 metre rail wagon may hold two 20' containers weighing a maximum of 35 tonnes, or one 40' container or one swap body, or one heavy 20' container. A common way to estimate the average number of load units per train is to multiply the train length by the load factor. Load factor is defined as the number of load units per rail wagon. The average load factor per rail wagon is 1.6 (Rutten, 1995; Fritsch, 2003; Rotter, 2003). However, the load factor very much depends on the transport relation. The trade determines the mixture of 20' and 40' maritime containers, swap bodies and trailers. Consequently, on some relations the load factor may be closer to 1.4 and on others closer to 1.8.

Load order
Load order is defined as the way in which load units are assigned to load positions on a train at an origin terminal. Various rules may apply when assigning load units to load positions on a train, depending on the optimisation objective. In daily practice, the following issues are generally considered:
- the weight of containers in relation to the maximum load to be carried by a rail wagon;
- the length of containers in relation to the length of a rail wagon;
- the destination of load units (which should be the same) on the same rail wagon (should intermediate shunting take place);
- location of a container at the terminal.

Another aspect that may be considered in load position assignment at the origin terminal is the minimisation of handling operations at the hub facility. With respect to terminals, a study by Bostel & Dejax (1998) showed that the number of exchange handling operations at a hub terminal can be significantly reduced when the load order at the origin terminal is pre-planned and optimised. This type of planned load order, as I like to define it in this thesis, can at a hub terminal exchange facility result in a higher number of direct train-to-train moves. With respect to shunting, a planned load order implies that load units with the same destination terminal are loaded onto rail wagons adjacent to one other (in blocks), such that wagons do not need to be shunted individually, but may be shunted in so-called wagon groups. In this thesis planned load order is distinguished from random (not planned) load order. Hence, a planned load order in this thesis implies that load units are loaded at the origin terminal according to a strategy that optimises exchange operations at the hub exchange facility. Random load order means that the consequences of exchange operations are not considered while a train is being loaded. The type of load order is relevant for the required resource capacity, and work planning and control of resources at the hub exchange facility.
Both planned and random load order occur in shunting practice (Biggler, 2003). With respect to new hub terminals, the studies by Meyer (1998) and Alicke (1999) assume a random load order (worst case scenario).

Train arrival schedule
The arrival schedule is relevant for the required resource capacity, and work planning and control of resources. At a hub exchange facility trains arrive according to a fixed daily and weekly arrival schedule. Modifications of these schedules occur gradually. Batch-structured operations are typical at new hub terminals. As a consequence a synchronised arrival schedule for the trains in a certain batch is assumed. I propose that synchronised arrivals may be defined as an arrival schedule in which trains belonging to the same batch arrive with short train interarrival times such that trains belonging to the same batch can be processed within a similar restricted period of time. An example of a synchronised arrival schedule is provided in Figure 3–4.
A typical arrival schedule proposed for new hub terminals is that first all the trains in the first batch arrive. When the first batch has finished operations, all the trains in the second batch arrive. Then, when the second batch has finished operations, all the trains in the third batch arrive, etc. The interarrival time between trains at new hub

terminals is projected at between 6 and 8 minutes (European Commission, 1997; Bontekoning & Kreutzberger, 1999).

Arrival schedules in hub-shunting practice are far from synchronised as Table 3–2 illustrates for a specific busy day at the Metz hub and a specific day at the hub at Herne. The arrival times are provided in minutes relative to the arrival of the first train.

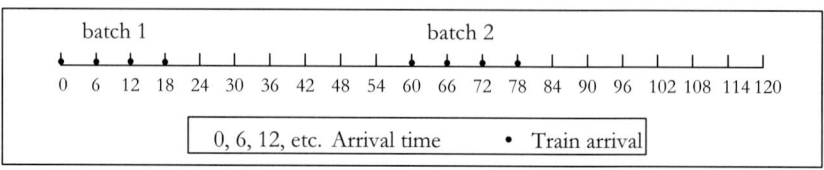

Figure 3–4: **An example of a synchronised arrival schedule**

Train departure schedule

In the same way as for train arrivals, trains leave according to a fixed departure schedule. Each train is allocated a slot on the rail network, which means that a certain part of the rail infrastructure is assigned to that train for a certain (short) period of time. When a train misses its time slot, its journey must be rescheduled and the train must wait until its new departure time. The departure schedule is relevant for the required resource capacity, and work planning and control of resources.

Table 3–2: Relative arrival schedule (interarrival times) in minutes on a busy day at the Metz (18 trains) and Herne (9 trains) hubs

Trainnumber	1	2	3	4	5	6	7	8	9	10	11	12	13	14	15	16	17	18
Metz	0	49	89	130	84	21	37	339	43	6	61	22	19	82	4	187	165	15
Herne	0	15	150	69	140	267	232	8	100	-	-	-	-	-	-	-	-	-

Source: Based on train arrival schedules (Terminet, 2000; Biggler, 2003).

Type of traction

Type of traction of the network locomotive is important with respect to the required resources at the hub exchange facility, and also in terms of operations. There are two types of traction: electric and diesel locomotives. In Europe, electric traction is the most common type of traction for rail haulage. This has certain implications for when the train arrives at the hub exchange facility. Either the exchange facility and side yard need to be electrified, or the electric locomotive must be replaced by a diesel locomotive, or a diesel locomotive must be coupled to the electric locomotive at the front or rear of the train.

3.4   Description of the system component Resources

In this section the elements of the component *Resources* are described. Such elements cover physical means such as facility and side yard infrastructure, and equipment and labour that is needed to process transport and load units, in other words to deal with elements of *Demand*. In addition, resources are relevant with respect to costs calculations. The description of elements of the component *Resources* is carried out for four hub exchange facilities:

- new hub terminal;
- hump shunting yard;
- flat shunting yard;
- road-rail terminal.

Although existing rail-rail operations at road-rail terminals cannot be defined as hub exchange operations (see above), the road-rail terminal is still considered in this chapter, because road-rail terminals may carry out hub exchange operations. A description of the functioning of the various exchange facilities (operations) is part of the component *Process*, and is described in section 3.5.

3.4.1 New hub terminal infrastructure and resources

This section is based on Bontekoning & Kreutzberger (1999) and Terminet (2000) in which the new hub terminal concepts Noell Megahub and Commutor are described, based on various documentations on these concepts. An example of a new hub terminal, the Noell Megahub, is depicted in Figure 3–5. In general, the infrastructure of a new hub terminal consists of a storage area for the temporary stacking of load units, a track area where trains are served and a transport system that moves load units from one crane to another. Load units may be stored to a maximum of three units' height. The storage area may consist of elevated platforms. Each area may consist of one or more lanes or tracks. The terminal layout may comprise any combination of the three different areas. The length and width of a new hub terminal depends on its required capacity. Furthermore, for proposed hub terminals it is assumed that the hub exchange facility is electrified with a moveable catenary and that trains have direct access in order to avoid changes between diesel and electric locomotives. Equipment may include (automated) rail-mounted gantry cranes, bridge cranes and storage cranes. Transport means may be automated, e.g. AGVs (automated guided vehicles), self-lifting AGVs, linear driven roller pallets or cross conveyors or manually driven vehicles such as terminal trucks. Labour may consist of crane drivers (unless automated), drivers for transport (unless automated), inspectors/pin setters[11] and staff for control, planning, management and maintenance.

At this point I must comment on the projected arrival and departure procedure. If this procedure does not work in practice, a shunting locomotive and possibly a detour track around the terminal may be needed to pull and push trains in and out of the terminal.

---

[11] Person who puts pins on rail wagons up or down so pin positions match the corner posts of load units.

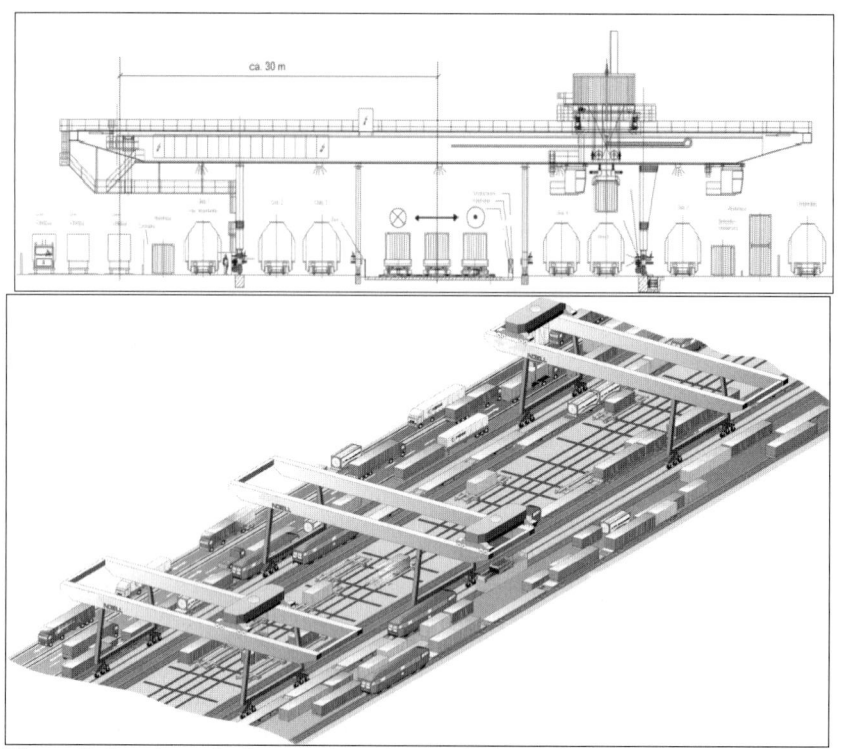

Figure 3–5: **An artist impression of a new hub terminal: at the top a cross-section of the Noell Megahub, at the bottom a top-view (partly)**
Source: Noell GmbH, 2000.

3.4.2 Hump shunting yard infrastructure and resources

This section is based on Sussman (2000), Petersen (1977) and interviews with Bruins (2003) and Fritsch (2003). A hump shunting yard contains an arrival yard, a shunting hill area, a sorting yard and a departure yard. Joint arrival and departure or joint sorting and departure yards are very common. In addition, there is a detour track which is used to reposition locomotives. A general layout of a hump shunting yard with an arrival yard and a joint sorting and departure yard is depicted in Figure 3–6. Most hump shunting yards are one-directional, meaning that trains can only enter the facility from one direction, as in Figure 3–6. The number and length of tracks may vary in each yard depending on the required capacity. The shunting hill area most often consists of one track leading to the shunting hill. A very large yard may have two shunting hills. Downhill there are automated switches leading to the sorting and departure yard. Tracks at the beginning of the sorting yard and the middle of the sorting yard are equipped with automated braking equipment. Large yards may have installed automated equipment between the tracks in the sorting yard for train assembly. Arrival yards and sorting/departure yards are equipped with one or several locomotives. Labour employed includes inspectors/cablemen[12], (un)couplers[13], pin-

---

[12] Person who detaches and attaches air tubes on the brake systems of rail wagons.

[13] Person who loosens or tightens couplings, consisting of a hook on one side and an eye on the other, between rail wagons.

pullers[14] at the shunting hill, locomotive drivers, shunting locomotive assistants and staff for process control, planning, maintenance and management.

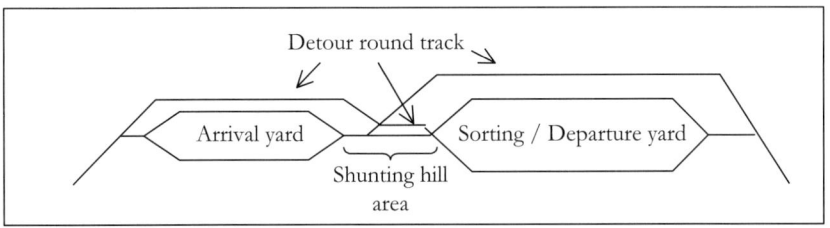

Figure 3–6: General layout of a hump shunting yard with joint sorting and departure yard
Source: Modified from Terminet, 2000.

3.4.3 Flat shunting yard infrastructure and resources

This section is based on Petersen (1977) and an interview with Biggler (2003) and a site visit to the flat shunting yard at Herne. A flat shunting yard consists of an arrival yard, a sorting yard and a departure yard, but in a different configuration to hump shunting yards. Joint arrival and departure or joint sorting and departure yards are very common. A general layout is depicted in Figure 3–7. The number and length of tracks may vary in each yard depending on the required capacity. In contrast with hump shunting yards, there is no shunting hill in flat shunting yards. Instead there is one lead track that leads from the arrival yard to the switches in the sorting area. Flat yards are often one-directional, meaning that trains can only enter the facility from one direction. Locomotives are used at the various yards. Labour employed includes locomotive drivers, locomotive assistants and staff for process control, planning, maintenance and management.

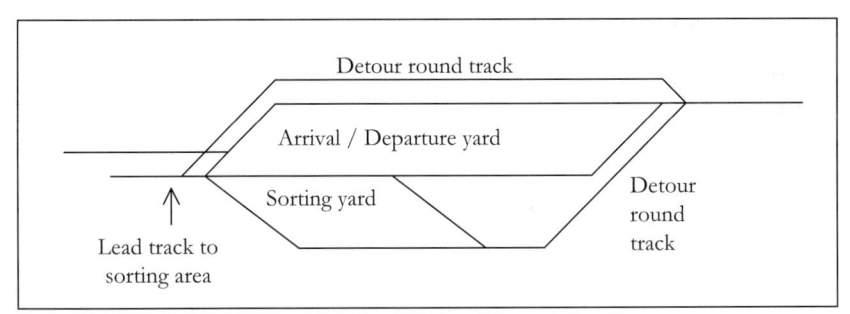

Figure 3–7: General layout of the flat shunting yard at Herne
Source: Modified from Biggler (2003).

3.4.4 Road-rail terminal infrastructure and resources

This section is based on an interview and questionnaire with Rotter (2002; 2003) and Wesseling (2003). The infrastructure of a road-rail terminal consists of a storage area for temporary storage of load units, a track area to serve trains and a truck area to process trucks, most often located parallel to one another. The parallel position of the three areas may be in any order and even mixed. Each area may consist of one or

---

[14] Person positioned at the shunting hill who hits loose couplings between wagons.

Hub exchange operations in intermodal hub-and-spoke networks

more lanes or tracks. A rather common layout is that of four tracks, two road lanes and two storage lanes. The truck area is not in fact relevant for hub exchange operations. It is only mentioned here in the interests of illustrating at what type of terminal hub exchange operations are carried out in practice. Load units may be stored to a maximum of three units' height.

A very common road-rail terminal is depicted in Figure 3–8. Commonly used equipment includes rail-mounted gantry cranes that cover all three areas. Labour employed includes crane operators, inspectors/pin setters[15], and staff for control, planning, management and maintenance.

Figure 3–8: An example of a road-rail terminal: KombiVerkehr terminal in Ludwigshafen

Source: KombiVerkehr.

3.4.5 Side yard infrastructure

At a functional level a distinction can be made between a period of time that a train is processed and a period of time in which it is waiting to be processed and/or waiting to depart. These activities may also be separated spatially. During operations trains are at the exchange facility, while in waiting periods they are parked in a side yard adjacent to the exchange facility. In practice the side yard and the exchange facility may be physically integrated. For instance, when capacity at the exchange facility is not needed for exchange operations trains can wait at the exchange facility. The layout of a side yard consists of a set of tracks connected with the exchange facility and the main rail network. The side yard's dimensions depend on the required capacity.

3.5 Description of system component Process

In this section elements of the component *Process* are described for the four exchange facilities studied in this thesis. The component *Process* consists of exchange activities carried out at and by elements of the component *Resources* and of process control principles. Process control principles determine the order in which these exchange activities are carried out. A distinction is made between strategic and operational process control principles. Strategic control principles are discussed in subsection

---

[15] Person who detaches and attaches air tubes on the brake systems of rail wagons.

3.5.1. Operational control principles are integrally discussed in subsections describing the exchange activities.

3.5.1 Strategic process control principles

With the introduction of new hub terminals two types of strategic process control have been proposed: synchronised and non-synchronised operations (see e.g. European Commission, 1997; Meyer, 1998), although no clear definition is provided. I propose that synchronised operations may be defined as operations in which trains belonging to the same batch are processed within a restricted period of time such that the time it takes to exchange load units (or rail wagons) is minimised. Synchronised arrivals are no precondition for synchronised operations, but are most likely.
Two ways to carry out synchronised operations have been proposed. In the first, synchronised operations may start immediately as soon as the first train of the batch arrives. In the second, operations start at the moment that all the trains in a batch are available, in other words when the last train of a batch has arrived. For the new Noell Megahub terminal the first strategy was proposed, for the new Commutor hub terminal the second was proposed (European Commission, 1997; Meyer, 1998; Alicke, 1999, 2002; Bontekoning & Kreutzberger, 1999).

Non-synchronised operations may be defined as operations during which trains belonging to the same batch are processed, spread out over the total duration of operations and may be alternated with trains from other batches. Non-synchronised operations were studied for new hub terminals in European Commission (1997). These exchange operations imply that a train delivers load units for later trains and picks up load units from earlier trains so long as they belong to the same batch. This means that load units are unloaded and temporarily stored in the storage area until the destination trains arrive, while load units to be collected from earlier trains are loaded from the storage area. Not all of the exchange can be completed in one day, as load units are passed on to later trains. This means that some load units are passed on to trains the next day, to a new but similar batch.

With respect to shunting practice, respondents did not apply synchronised or non-synchronised operations terminology. However, similar definitions as above may also be applied to shunting. If we do so, shunting can be characterised as non-synchronised operations, because the processing of trains is spread throughout the day and not within a restricted period of time.

3.5.2 Hub exchange operations at new hub terminals

This section describes the proposed exchange operations at new hub terminals as described in various documentation on new hub terminals and summarised in Bontekoning & Kreutzberger (1999). Trains may arrive in synchronised or non-synchronised order. It is assumed that no change of locomotives is required, because the facility is electrified with a moveable catenary and trains can directly enter and leave the facility. However, I must comment on this assumption that, if in practice this projected arrival and departure procedure does not work, a different type of operation involving a shunting locomotive may be needed to pull and push trains in and out of the terminal. However, if the technique fails or when trains cannot enter directly the facility because it is occupied, entering the terminal with own traction may not be possible. If the technique fails a diesel shunting locomotive must pull and push trains in and out of the terminal. If a train cannot enter directly the terminal, the side yard must be electrified or the train must be pulled into the terminal by a diesel shunting locomotive.

For each train it is determined whether it may proceed to the exchange facility or whether it must wait in the side yard. In the event of synchronised operations only trains belonging to the batch in operation are allowed to proceed to the exchange facility. In the event of non-synchronised operations trains may proceed to the exchange facility as long as there are empty tracks available. When a train is granted access, resources can be assigned to it to process the load units. Because the course of operations is different for synchronised and non-synchronised operations, they will be discussed separately.

The course of operations in synchronised operations is as follows. All trains are processed at the same time. Each crane serves a part of all trains. As such, the operational area is divided into crane sections. The transport system moves load units from one crane section to another. Cranes and transport systems are operated simultaneously. Load units can be processed in three ways:
- Direct, which means that a crane picks up a load unit from a train and puts it directly (in a single action) onto another train.
- Via the storage area, which means that a crane picks up a load unit from a train and puts it in the storage area. After some time the same crane picks up the same load unit from the storage area and puts it onto another train. This type of handling is often used to free up space on trains, mostly at the start of operations.
- Via the transport system, which means that a crane picks up a load unit from a train and puts it on the transport system. The load unit is transported to another crane section. When the transport system has positioned the load unit near the desired load position, another crane picks up the load unit and puts it onto another train.

The precise sequence of handlings a load unit undergoes depends on its load position at arrival and its planned load position on the destination train. Hence, there is a relation with the element load order, which was discussed in section 3.3.

The course of operations in non-synchronised operations is as follows. First, all load units requiring exchange are unloaded into the storage area. Next, load units dropped off by previous trains are loaded from the storage area. This can be done in two ways:
- Direct, which means that a crane picks up a load unit from the storage area and puts it onto the train.
- Via the transport system, which means that a crane picks up a load unit from the storage area and puts it on the transport system. The load unit is transported to another crane section. When the transport system has positioned the load unit near the desired load position, another crane picks up the load unit and puts it onto the train.

The way load units are loaded depends on their storage position and their planned load position on the destination train. Hence, there is a relation with the element load order, which was discussed in section 3.3.

Trains can be processed in two ways: one after another or simultaneous. The capacity of the operational area allows for several trains, but this does not mean that they must be served at the same time. The allocation of cranes to trains is determined by operational process control routines. In a similar way to synchronised operations, each crane serves a part of a train, the transport system takes care of moving load units from one crane section to another, and cranes and transport system are operated simultaneously.

3.5.3 Hub exchange operations at hump shunting yards

This section, which describes exchange operations at hump shunting yards, is based on Sussman (2000), Petersen (1977a), and interviews with Bruins (2003), Fritsch (2003) and Wesseling (2003). Arriving trains either arrive at a side-yard that is (partly) electrified or enter directly the arrival yard if it is (partly) electrified. When the train arrives at the side-yard, the network locomotive is replaced by a shunting locomotive, which takes the train to the arrival yard. From trains that directly enter the arrival yard, the network locomotive is decoupled. Shunting activities can be divided into sorting-related activities and assembly-related activities. Sorting-related activities take place at the arrival yard and the shunting hill, assembly-related activities at the (joint sorting) departure yard. A description of these two clusters of activities follows.

Sorting-related activities consist of the following sequence of handling operations:
- Uncoupling rail wagons, which involves detaching air tubes, releasing the air and loosening couplings between wagons.
- Coupling of the shunting locomotive to the uncoupled train.
- Pushing the uncoupled train from the arrival siding to the shunting hill at very low (nearly walking) speed.
- Just before a wagon or wagon group passes over the hill, the coupling between wagons is detached, and the wagon (group) rolls under the force of gravity towards the sorting/departure yard. Rail wagons are sorted by correctly set switches, which direct wagons with the same destination to the same track. Various train-to-sorting-track assignment strategies exist, but often a fixed one-train-to-track assignment is used (Kraft, 2002). Since their rolling speed increases while rolling down the hill, automatic brakes must be used to slow wagons to a safe speed before they reach the end of the sorting track or the previous wagon on that track. Meanwhile the locomotive continues pushing the remaining rail wagons over the hill.
- Locomotive returns to the arrival yard to pick up the next train to be sorted.

From the perspective of the shunting locomotive these activities are carried out in a sequential order, except for the uncoupling of rail wagons. Yard personnel can already start uncoupling the next train, if available, while the shunting locomotive is busy pushing the wagons over the hill.

Assembly-related activities consist of:
- Pushing rail wagons together. Since not all wagons or wagon groups are precision-braked a locomotive pushes wagons at the sorting yard together. At large yards this is carried out by special automated equipment installed between the tracks.
- Correcting so-called 'false runners'. Due to badly set switches, incorrect information on wagons or wagons overtaking the preceding one on the way downhill wagons can move into the wrong departure track. This tends to happen in one wagon every ten trains. This is remedied by moving wagons in and out of the departure tracks using a locomotive.
- Attaching air tubes and tightening couplings between wagons.

These three activities are carried out simultaneously for various trains being assembled at the same time. The following assembly activities are related to trains, and can only be started when a new train has been assembled:
- Coupling the network locomotive.
- Filling air tubes with air, brake test and inspection.

This implies that various trains should have finished sorting. It is quite common for a shunting locomotive to be coupled first to take a newly assembled train to the side yard and for these two activities to be carried out in the side yard since there is no electricity facility for trains in the departure siding.

The shunting activities described here are similar to those of classic shunting. The difference, however, lies in the structuring effect of batches and exchange on the course of hub exchange operations.

3.5.4 Hub exchange operations at flat shunting yards

This section is based on an interview with Biggler (2003) and a site visit to the flat shunting yard at Herne. In a similar way to hump shunting, arriving trains either arrive at a side-yard that is (partly) electrified or enter directly the arrival yard if it is (partly) electrified. When the train arrives at the side-yard, the network locomotive is replaced by a shunting locomotive, which takes the train to the arrival yard. From trains that directly enter the arrival yard, the network locomotive is decoupled. These shunting activities may also be divided into sorting-related activities and assembly-related activities. However, these activities are different, basically because there is no shunting hill.

The sorting cycle of a shunting locomotive is as follows:
- pulling train out of track. The first time the locomotive pulls out the complete train from the arrival track, in the course of the sorting process the remaining parts of the train are pulled out of the sorting tracks;
- pushing train to sorting track;
- pushing train into sorting track until the first wagon (group) reaches the end of the track or until it reaches previously shunted wagons (group);
- coupling wagon (group) to rail wagon already standing in sorting track (except where there is no other wagon group yet). This involves attaching air tubes and tightening the coupling;
- uncoupling shunted wagon group from the train.

When the whole train is being shunted, the locomotive drives to the next train in one of the arrival tracks. The whole train is moved back and forth over the tracks; each time a wagon (group) is dropped off at one of the sorting tracks. Consequently, during the course of each shunting cycle the train becomes shorter and so do the distances being travelled by the locomotive.

The assembly activities consist of:
- Coupling the network locomotive.
- Filling air tubes with air, brake test and inspection.

Just like hump shunting, it is quite common for a shunting locomotive to be coupled first to take a newly assembled train to the side yard and for these activities to be carried out in the side yard.
I found no supporting literature on this type of flat shunting operation.

3.5.5 Hub exchange operations at road-rail terminals

As hub exchange operations as defined in section 3.3 do not exist at road-rail terminals in practice, this section contains a description of how they may be carried out. Exchange operations at road-rail terminals may be considered similar to new hub terminal operations, due to their similar parallel infrastructures. To avoid repetition, we shall focus solely on the differences. The first difference is that the electric network locomotive is replaced by a diesel locomotive in the side yard. As such, trains cannot directly enter the exchange facility from the network.

Secondly, road-rail terminals do not have a transport system. The longitudinal movement of load units from one crane section to another is taken care of by the cranes. This can be described as follows. One crane picks up a load unit and puts it in the storage area at the edge of its crane section. The load unit is picked up by the crane in the adjacent crane section and moved to its load position on the destination train or to the other edge of the crane section to be passed on to the next crane section.

Thirdly, when a train has finished service, a diesel locomotive takes it to the side yard. At the side yard the network locomotive is coupled, and a brake test and inspection are carried out. However, these terminals could be equipped with moveable catenaries.

3.6 Relationship between elements and environment

In the previous sections hub exchange operations have been described as a system. This section focuses on the environment of that system. The purpose of this section is to identify elements outside the system of hub exchange operation that may have an impact on elements and performance of hub exchange operations. The most relevant elements are described below:

- *Transport geography and trade volumes*. This concerns the number and location of origin and destination terminals that may be connected by a hub exchange facility and the volume of flows between terminals. Transport geography influences exchange demand in terms of batch size and number of batches per day.
- *Organisation of train services*. Intermodal operators set up train services to meet transport demand. Train service decisions made by the intermodal operator may influence exchange operations. Firstly, they make decisions about the type of bundling they will implement: point-to-point, hub-and-spoke or otherwise. These are strategy decisions, but they may affect the demand at the hub exchange facility. Secondly, intermodal operators make decisions at a tactical and operational level with respect to all elements of the component *Demand*, such as batch composition, number of batches and length of trains. The intermodal facility operator has to deal with fluctuations in demand and the wishes of intermodal operators.
- *Operational planning restrictions*. There are issues that must be considered when organising a transport service and which may influence the arrival, operations and departure schedule at the hub exchange facility. This involves for example train path availability, operational time window at origin and destination terminals and pick-up, delivery times of freight at shippers and receivers, etc.
- *Delays*. Delays may affect the arrival and operations schedule and therefore the performance of an exchange facility. Delays can be caused amongst other things by giving priority to passenger trains on the network, rail track construc-

tion and maintenance work, technical breakdowns of trains or locomotives, strikes, accidents and delayed departure at origin terminal, weather and climate.
- *Government or union policy and regulations.* Working conditions and safety regulations may have an impact on working routines, use of equipment and labour input at an exchange facility.
- *Weather and climate.* Very extreme conditions such as storms or freezing weather may disturb operations. This may lead to slower operations or temporary interruption of operations.

Not all of these elements have to be included in the simulation model, only the ones that mostly affect time and costs performances. Trains service organisation, network geography and operational planning restrictions are relevant, but are already indirectly incorporated into the simulation model, because demand reflects these elements. Arrival delays are very relevant, because they may have significant consequences on the course of operations. The effect of arrival delays must be assessed in order to understand hub exchange operations and therefore incorporated into the simulation model.

3.7 Relationship elements and performance criteria

In this section the relationship between system elements and the performance criteria, determined in subsection 3.2.1, is described. In order to be able to identify these relationships the performance criteria first need to be operationalised into measurable units. The structure of this section is that per performance criterion, first the measurable unit is described, followed by a description of the relationship(s) with the elements.

The performance criterion *safe and secure operations* is defined as $(1- x)\%$; x being the percentage of load units, their contents and rail wagons that is damaged during exchange operations over one year. Damage may be caused by personnel operating equipment wrongly. In terminals, incorrect operation of cranes may damage load units and/or rail wagons. In shunting, poor control of brake systems resulting in braking too late may cause damage to rails and/or load units as rail wagons collide too forcefully with each other in the sorting/departure yard. Incorrect uncoupling or coupling of rail wagons may also cause damages.
One could also define safe operations in terms of safety of facility personnel. Although very relevant, in this section only performance criteria relating to customers of the exchange facility are considered.

The performance criterion reliable and timely operations is split into two measurements. Reliable operations is defined as the percentage of load units that arrive at a wrong destination during a certain period of time due to a fault at the exchange facility. Wrong scheduling of operations or personal mistakes in carrying out the work order may be the cause. Mistakes caused by wrong input data provided by the network operator (such as data on load positions and destination) are not the responsibility of the facility operator.
The performance criterion *timely operation* is defined as the percentage of trains with a delayed departure time due to problems at the exchange facility. Such departure delays are often the result of planning mistakes and/or equipment failure during a certain period of time. Departure delays caused by arrival delays are excluded.

The performance criterion *low/reasonable costs* may be measured as total costs per load unit.
Costs per load unit is defined as the total annual investment and operational costs of an exchange facility divided by the annual hub-and-spoke network volume (= number of trains * the number of load units on these trains). Total costs are related to all elements of the component *Resources*. The annual volume is determined by elements of the component Demand. The annual network volume is used for two reasons. Firstly, door-to-door intermodal transport prices are offered in costs/load unit. Secondly, rail haul costs are also distributed over a (projected) annual volume.

The performance criterion *speed of operations* is defined as the train and batch service and sojourn time. Train service time is defined as the time spent in operations. Train sojourn time is defined as the total time spent by a train at an exchange facility. It includes a train's service time and its waiting time in the side yard.
Batch service time is defined as the period of time from which the first train of a batch enters service operations until the moment the last train of a batch leaves the service area. Batch sojourn time is defined as the period of time from which the first train of a batch enters the side yard until the moment the last train of a batch leaves the service area. Service times are determined by a complex interaction between all elements of all three components.

The performance criterion *flexibility of operations* can be expressed by three measurements. The first is the utilisation rate of equipment over a certain period of time. This measurement could provide an indication of spare capacity and is related to demand and capacity over a certain period of time. The second measurement is defined as the additional capacity jump expressed as the increase of handling capacity due to one additional crane or locomotive, including personnel required to operate it. The third measurement is defined as the capacity of a facility to process traffic other than intermodal trains in a hub-and-spoke network.

A simulation modelling approach cannot incorporate all performance criteria identified in the previous section. Simulation is suitable for determining service times, utilisation rates of equipment and delayed departures. Other criteria should be determined in another way or be excluded. Additional capacity jump and costs per load unit are included in the study, because they can easily be derived from simulation input and output data and some additional data. Percentage at wrong destination and percentage damaged load units and rail wagons are excluded. These seem to be criteria that do not have much to do with the type of facility, but more with the quality of personnel.

3.8 Summary and conclusions

This last section summarises the system descriptions of previous sections in one integrated figure and draws conclusions on hub exchange operations. System analysis was applied to unravel the complexity of hub exchange operations and to obtain a better understanding of the problem area. The most relevant elements of hub exchange operations, their environment and performance criteria as described in various sections of this chapter may be summarised in an integral overview as depicted in Figure 3–9. Elements for all three components, *Demand, Resources* and *Process* are included in the overview. In addition, the most important relationships between elements are indicated, as well as the relationships between elements and components and performance criteria.

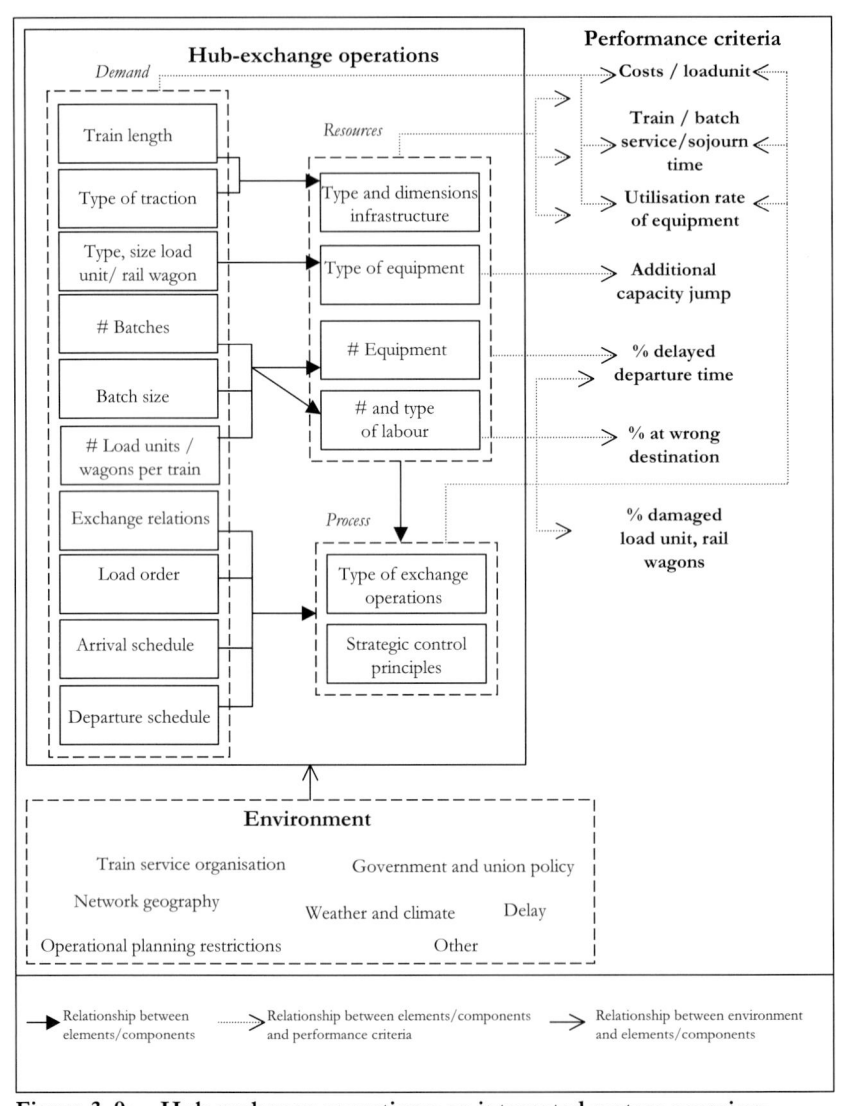

Figure 3–9: Hub exchange operations: an integrated system overview

The assessment of empirical hub-and-spoke systems leads to the following conclusions. New hub terminal operations assume certain demand conditions such as batch-wise structure, synchronised arrivals and synchronised operations. This terminology is not common in existing hub-shunting and road-rail hub terminal operations, but could be applied. These conditions do not seem to equate with practice. As such, it is unclear whether these demand conditions are realistic and can be implemented. On the other hand these demand conditions may also be favourable for hub-shunting practice and road-rail hub terminal operations today. Consequently, modelling should include comparison of various sets of similar demand conditions for shunting, new hub terminals and road-rail terminals.

Train arrival and departure procedures at the proposed new hub terminals may not be realistic and as a consequence handling time and costs performance may be underestimated. It is assumed that the hub exchange facility is electrified with a moveable catenary and that trains can directly access and leave the exchange facility. However, if this procedure does not work in practice, a shunting locomotive and possibly a detour track around the terminal may be needed to pull and push trains in and out of the terminal.

In addition to a large choice of demand variables, there are various variables related to the components *Resources* and *Process* that may be varied in the experiments with the simulation model. A systematic approach towards the experiments is required in order to control the number of experiments to be carried out and to assess the effect of certain variables on performances.

Finally, with respect to the elements of the environment of the system, only arrival delays are included in the simulation models.

4 Conceptual modelling of hub exchange operations

4.1 Introduction

This chapter deals with the conceptualisation of the hub-and-spoke system as was described in the previous chapter (Chapter 3). The real system will be presented in a more abstract and general way. This implies leaving out certain details and focusing on the essential features of the real system.

The objective of the modelling is to develop a transparent generic model that is as aggregated as possible which may be used for different types of hub exchange facility. Distinctive features of each facility may be represented in the model by different parameter and variable settings, but without losing typical features. In this case various, but very similar-structured models should be considered. It turned out that one conceptual model could not sufficiently represent all variations of exchange operations. As a result six conceptual models were constructed, which are all based on a similar general framework and modelling principle.

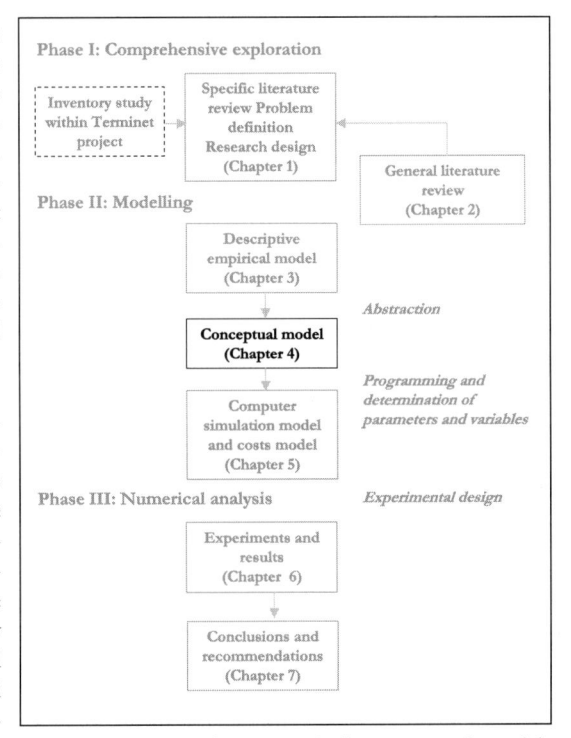

The topic of this chapter, conceptualisation of the real system, is the second step in the simulation approach chosen to achieve the main objective of this thesis. In the next chapter (Chapter 5) the conceptual models presented in this chapter are transformed into simulation models.

The outline of this chapter is as follows. In section 4.2 the approach towards conceptualisation is presented. This section also covers the general model for hub exchange operations, which is the basis for six exchange facility specific models. In section 4.3 the modelling of the component *Demand* is discussed. *Demand* is modelled in a similar way for each specific exchange facility. However, the components *Resources* and *Process* differ for each exchange facility, except for train flow control. Train flow control routine, which applies to all models, is covered in section 4.4. In section 4.5 the modelling of the components *Resources* and *Process* is described for new hub terminals, both shunting facilities are covered in section 4.6 and section 4.7 concerns road-rail terminals. Section 4.8 contains a summary and conclusions.

4.2 Approach

The development of conceptual models is directed by the objective stated in Chapter 1: to keep the models as transparent and as aggregated as possible without losing typical features. Transparent models have some advantages. Firstly, black boxes may be avoided such that each step in the model is logical and can be followed. Secondly, they allow greater control of variables and parameters in numerical experiments. This is important in order to obtain better insight into the typical behaviour of exchange operations at different hub exchange facilities. The disadvantages naturally include a loss of details.

To achieve the modelling objective an abstraction of the system description in Chapter 3 had to be made. Logistics and queuing theory were used as a theoretical modelling framework. Logistics theory regards thinking in flows, stationary points and flow control (De Vaan, 1998, in: Goor et al., 2000). In queuing theory servers process jobs according to a certain service time. Queues may occur in front of servers when the number of jobs exceeds server capacity. A group of similar servers is defined as a workstation. Jobs arriving as a group in the system are defined as batch arrival and jobs leaving as a group as batch departure (Hall, 1991). As such, the conceptual models are the result of an assessment of the components *Demand, Resources* and *Process* described in the previous chapter, from the viewpoint of logistics and queuing theory.

A general model, which is the basis for the six exchange facility specific models that are described in this chapter, is presented in Figure 4–1. In the model, load units and rail wagons are perceived as jobs that arrive and depart as a batch (on a train) and equipment and labour as stationary points or servers, or in the case of a group of servers a workstation (e.g. cranes). Infrastructure such as tracks, side yard and storage area are modelled as queues. Flow control applies to the flow of arriving and departing trains (access control to exchange facility and/or network) and the flow of jobs (routing along servers). Hub exchange operations are perceived as a process consisting of batch arrivals, a flow of jobs along servers or workstations and batch departures.

The general model presented in Figure 4–1 could not sufficiently represent all variations of exchange operations due to:
- different types of resources and routing of flows along these resources at the different hub exchange facilities. This implies different modelling of servers and routings at shunting yards, road-rail terminals and new hub terminals. However, the difference between hump shunting and flat shunting could be incorporated by parameter settings;
- differences between strategic process control principles – synchronised and non-synchronised. This implies different modelling of train access and departure control routines to and from operations for synchronised and non-synchronised operations, as well as different modelling of routings (operations control routines) for terminal facilities.

As a consequence, the components *Demand* and *Resources* to a large extent allow generic modelling, but the component Process requires more specific modelling.
The general model presented in this section is further elaborated for the different exchange facilities in the next sections.

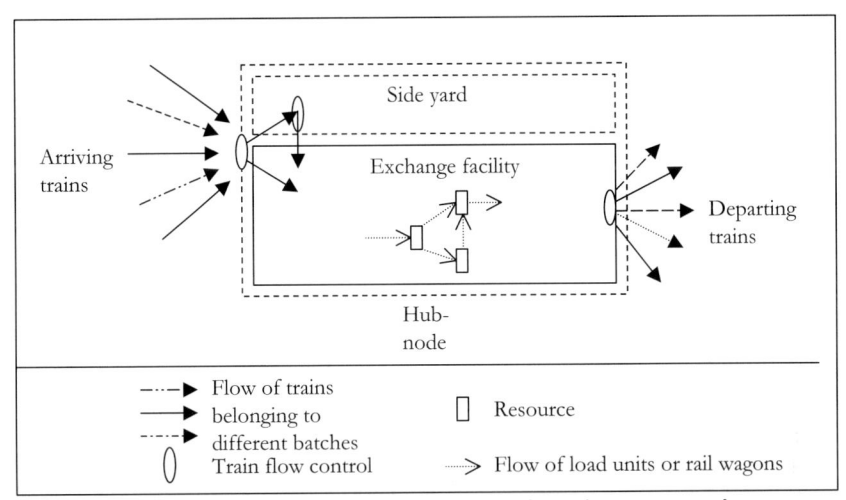

Figure 4–1: A general conceptual model for hub exchange operations

The transparency of the model was obtained, because dimensions of infrastructure, exact origin and destination trains and exact unload and load positions on trains, in the storage area, on the transport system, or exact wagon positions are not specified. Instead, the spatial characteristics of exchange operations are expressed in the service time distribution functions of the servers. This requires accurate data on locomotive and crane cycles, which could be obtained and validated. Furthermore, modelling of allocation problems related to trains and tracks or to equipment and jobs was minimised. As such, the precise relocation of load units or rail wagons was not modelled.
The model output I am particularly interested in is the train and batch service time and the train and batch sojourn time. The train sojourn time consists of the time needed to change a network locomotive, the side-yard waiting time, the shunting time between side-yard and exchange facility and the train facility time (see Figure 4-2). The train facility time is defined as the moment a train enters the exchange facility until the moment the train leaves the facility. The train service time is defined as the train facility time plus the time needed to change network and yard locomotive. Waiting time at the side yard after arrival is not further considered, because its duration is largely influenced by the availability of a trains paths.
Batch sojourn time is defined as the period of time from which the first train of a batch enters the hub node until the moment the last train of a batch leaves the exchange facility. Batch sojourn time minus the waiting time at side yard of the train in a batch with the longest waiting time.
Hence, in my modelling approach load units or rail wagons "flow" through the hub exchange node and are faced with time resistances that accumulate into train and batch service and sojourn times.

```
                    Moment train enters                              Moment train leaves
                    hub node                                         hub node
                          ↓                                                ↓
     |____1____|__2__|_3_|_4_|___5___|___6___|___7___|
                              ↑         ↑
                    Moment train enters exchange  Moment train leaves
                    facility                      exchange facility
```

1 Rail haul time
2 Time for changing locomotives
3 Side yard waiting time if facility is occupied
4 Shunting time between side-yard and exchange facility   } Train sojourn time
5 Train facility time
6 Side yard waiting time for train path
7 Rail haul time

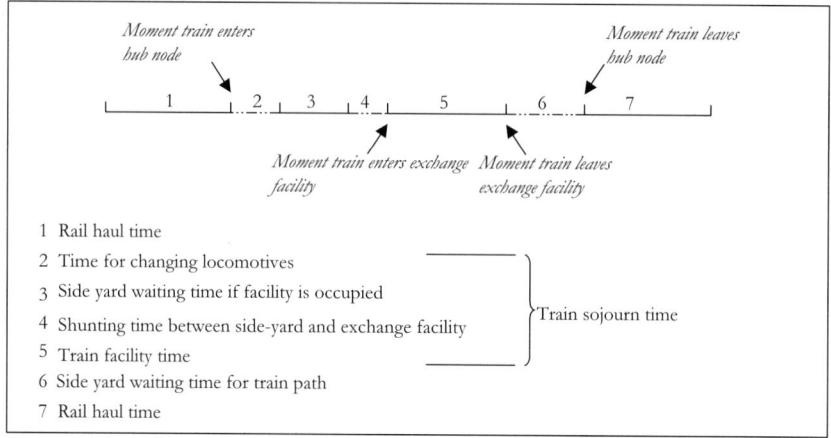

Figure 4-2: **Overview of various time components in hub-and-spoke operations**

4.3 Modelling Demand

In Chapter 3 the following elements were identified for the component *Demand*: train arrival schedule, batches and exchange relations, number of batches and batch size per day, number of load units or rail wagons per train, load order, train length, type and size of load unit or rail wagon, type of traction and train departure schedule. The modelling of these elements is discussed in this section.

Hub exchange operations involve the processing of batches, trains and load units or wagons. As a consequence modelling takes place at three levels. Trains are the objects that enter and leave the system, so their arrival in and departure from the system are modelled. However, load units or rail wagons are the main objects processed at the servers. Consequently, trains have to be dispatched in load units or rail wagons upon arrival and load units or rail wagons have to be regrouped before departure. The batch processing level implies the modelling of exchange relations between trains in the same batch.

Train arrivals are modelled according to a deterministic arrival schedule. As a consequence of the three-level modelling the arrival schedule contains, for each train, information on train arrival time, number and size of the batch the train belongs to, train order in a batch, and number of load units, rail wagons or wagon groups to be exchanged. The number of load units to be exchanged at terminal facilities is smaller than the number of load units on the train. $1/n^{th}$ of the load units remains on the train; n being the number of trains in a batch. A deterministic approach allows for controlled variation of this train information and supports a better analysis and comparison of the performances of different hub exchange facilities. With respect to the exchange relations within a batch it is assumed that the load units of one train have the same destination as other trains in the batch. In practice, however, exchange relations and the number of load units per exchange relation may be different and may vary. In addition, it is assumed that each train in a batch carries an equal number of rail wagons and load units. In practice, there may be much more variation. The arrival schedule contains information for one day of exchange operations. Train length is not specifically modelled, since the number of exchange load units or rail wagons indirectly models it.

Train departures are modelled as trains that exit the system as soon as hub exchange operations have been completed. In the model a train departure implies a batch departure of load units or rail wagons (jobs). After exchange operations and before departure in the model regrouping of load units or rail wagons takes place. Exactly when hub exchange operations are completed depends on the strategic process control principles and the type of exchange facility. This is further explained in sections 4.5 to 4.7.

The modelling of train departure involves a crucial abstraction of the real system for two reasons. First, in practice trains leave according to a departure. Second, trains may not leave directly, since they often have to wait for a train path. Since departure schedules are not considered in the model process priority rules based on due date or tardiness could not be applied in the model. Since the study does not aim to investigate departure punctuality this is no problem, since the performance measure flow time is sufficient adequate to compare the performances of the different exchange facilities. However, the effects of the delays still can be investigated with the models, but not in relation to a departure schedule, only in relation to flow time.

The elements load order[16], type and size of load unit or rail wagon and type of traction are modelled in an indirect way and are sometimes incorporated into the modelling of other components. For shunting the element load order is incorporated into the number of rail wagons. A planned load order implies fewer individual rail wagons to be shunted and more wagon groups, leading to a reduction in the number of rail wagons to be processed. For terminals the type of load order influences the routing of flows through the exchange facility. This effect is incorporated in the modelled hub exchange operations: see subsections 4.5.2 and 4.7.2.

The size and type of a load unit are not modelled, but indirectly reflected in the specification of the load factor (number of load units per rail wagon) in the experiments. As such, all load units are identical in the model. As a consequence crane service time distribution functions (see section 5.4) reflect the average service time for various types of load units. The type and size of rail wagons are not modelled, but indirectly reflected in the specification of the number of rail wagons per train.

The type of rail traction is incorporated into the service time of resources; see section 5.4.

4.4 Modelling train access control to the exchange facility

The component *Process* consists of 1) the exchange activities carried out by the resources and 2) strategic and operational process control routines. Process control routines can be divided into strategic routines, involving access control routines to the exchange facility (called train flow control in Figure 4–1) and operational routines, involving work order control routines for servers. This section only covers the modelling of train flow control, because it applies to all models in a similar way. The modelling of exchange activities and work order control routines for servers is covered in subsequent sections because they are different for each exchange facility.

---

[16] Load order is defined as the way in which load units are assigned to load positions on a train at an origin terminal: this can take the form of planned or unplanned (random) load order (see section 3.3).

There are two strategic process control routines: *synchronised and non-synchronised* operations (see subsection 3.5.1). Access control to the exchange facility is modelled differently for synchronised operations and non-synchronised operations. The train access control routine is modelled as a set of priority rules.

Priority rules for *synchronised* operations are defined as follows. Trains are given priority to proceed to the exchange facility according to their batch number. Only one batch at a time can be processed at the exchange facility. An arriving train pro-ceeds directly to the service process when its batch number matches with the batch number of the train being processed. It is assumed that all facilities are electrified. Various shunting yards have electrified arrival tracks (e.g. Herne) and electrification with moveable catenaries of new (road-rail) terminals is proposed. However, most existing road-rail terminals are not electrified. When trains can directly enter the facility network locomotives do not need to be changed for diesel locomotives before enter the facility. But if a facility is not electrified, changing locomotives before entering the facility is required.

If direct access is not possible, the train queues at the side yard. When all trains of the batch that has been granted access to the service process have been served, the service process is freed up for the next train in the queue at the side yard. If there are other trains queuing at the side yard, all trains belonging to the same batch as the first train are allowed access. The time it takes to shunt a train from the side yard (queue) to the exchange facility can in the model be defined by a service time distribution function or by a constant. At shunting yards and road-rail terminals a diesel locomotive is coupled to the train and takes the train to a track at the exchange facil-ity. For the new hub-terminal it is projected that a train can enter the exchange facil-ity with its own traction, because it is assumed that the network locomotive stays at-tached to the train. The literature does not say how the operations go when a train cannot enter directly the facility and has to wait at the side yard. We may assume that either the train must also be shunted or in case side yard tracks are electrified that the train can still move into the terminal on own power (however, the tracks at the exchange facil-ity are not electrified).

If there are no trains in the queue, the service process remains idle until the next train arrives. These rules also apply in the case of delayed trains.

Priority rules for *non-synchronised* operations are defined as follows. Contrary to synchronised operations, trains instead of batches are served on a first come, first served basis. Trains can access the exchange facility as long as there is track capacity available. If the number of arriving trains exceeds track capacity, trains wait at the side yard. Capacity at the exchange facility is freed up for the next train in the queue at the side yard when a train has finished service, at which time it exits the system. The time it takes to shunt a train from the side yard (queue) to the exchange facility can in the model be defined by a service time distribution function or by a constant. At shunting yards and road-rail terminals a diesel locomotive is coupled to the train and takes the train to a track at the exchange facility. For the new hub-terminal it is projected that a train can enter the exchange facility with its own traction, because it is assumed that the network locomotive stays attached to the train.

An exception to the first come, first served rule applies in the case of delayed arrivals at a terminal facility. At a terminal facility trains within a batch should be handled in order of train number. Therefore, train 1 is handled before train 2, and train 4 before train 5. In a normal arrival schedule this is the case, but in the case of delayed arrivals the arrival order may be changed. If for instance train 5 arrives before train 4 in a certain batch, train 5 queues until train 4 has arrived and has been served. Then train 5 is served. Should more trains have to queue train 5 is then given priority over all the other trains in the queue.

4.5 Modelling Resources and Process for new hub terminals

4.5.1 Modelling infrastructure, equipment and labour

The two different types of resources at new hub terminals, cranes and transport systems, are modelled as two workstations with multiple servers in both the *synchronised* and non-synchronised model. Figure 4–3 illustrates the conceptual model for synchronised operations; Figure 4–4 the conceptual model for *non-synchronised* operations. Workstation 1 contains multiple cranes that can carry out all types of transhipment tasks, from train to train, from train to storage area, from train to transport system, etc. In the model it is assumed that each crane can process any load unit. However, in the proposed system a crane can only process load units in its own crane section. A crane section has a length equal to the length of the facility divided by the number of cranes. This abstraction from reality reduces modelling complexity considerably because scheduling problems such as assigning load units to cranes and decisions about which load unit to handle next are avoided. Work order scheduling aims at a balanced utilisation of cranes. With the use of scheduling heuristics workloads per crane can be equalised as best as possible. However, results by Meyer (1998, p. 139) and Alicke (1999, p. 135) demonstrate that a 100% balanced utilisation of cranes cannot be achieved. The minimum, average and maximum differences in workload between cranes, expressed in time for a batch of 6 trains, compared to the crane with the longest workload are respectively 3, 8 and 15 minutes in Alicke's study (for 8 cranes), and 9, 11 and 19 minutes in Meyer's study (10 cranes). One may have expected the outer cranes to have the lowest productivity, but this was not the case. My model assumes 100% balanced utilisation of cranes, which may lead to an underestimation of generated train service and sojourn times. After all, the crane with the longest workload expressed in time determines when a batch is completed. This must be kept in mind when the model is validated, and deviation may be overcome by applying a correction factor to the crane cycle time.

The crane time taken to complete each task is stochastic, because it depends on the pick-up and drop-off position of a load unit. The crane cycle time for a task is represented by a service time distribution function in the model, which is specified in section 5.4. Workstation 2 contains multiple units of a discrete transport system (e.g. trucks, AGV, roller pallets). Each transport unit can carry out any type of transport task. The transport service time is stochastic. It depends on transport distance and is in the model also represented by a service time distribution function (see section 5.4 for a specification). Interaction between cranes and transport systems is discussed in subsection 4.5.2 about exchange processes.

Infrastructure such as side yard, tracks and storage area is not modelled as such, but is reflected in the models by queues. I have distinguished several queues. The side yard is modelled as an unlimited queue of trains that are waiting to be granted access to the exchange facility. In Figure 4–3 and Figure 4–4 this queue is identified as Y. Tracks at the exchange facility are modelled as a maximum number of trains that can be allowed access to the exchange facility. When trains enter the exchange facility, trains are no longer modelled but load units instead. As Figure 4–3 and Figure 4–4 show, the flow of load units is divided over three routings due to a different sequence of crane handlings that load units require (more about the exchange process in subsection 4.5.2). As a result, queues of load units appear at different locations, but with respect to work order form a joint queue with jobs for the cranes. First, there is an *entrance queue* with load units, still on the train, waiting to be unloaded by one of the servers at workstation 1. In Figure 4–3 and Figure 4–4 this queue is identified as E. This queue is limited, because as mentioned above the number of tracks at the exchange facility is modelled as a maximum permissible number of trains. Second, there is a *storage queue* which reflects the storage area infrastructure. In Figure 4–3 and Figure 4–4 this queue is identified as S. This queue has unlimited capacity. Third, there may be a transport queue of load units that have finished transport service at workstation 2, but have to wait for a server at workstation 1. Note that these load units remain at the transport unit while they wait. As a consequence the queue length is limited to the maximum number of transport units. In Figure 4–3 and Figure 4–4 this queue is identified as T. Finally, there is a *departure queue* comprising load units that have completed exchange operations and have to wait to be regrouped into a departing train. Load units wait on the train. In Figure 4–3 and Figure 4–4 this queue is identified as D.

How the cranes select their next job from these queues is discussed in subsections 4.5.2 and 4.5.3.

4.5.2 Modelling exchange operations –synchronised

Exchange operations at new hub terminals may be perceived as a batch arrival of load units that are divided into various flows that follow different routes along workstations. The routes represent different sequences of crane handlings that load units require. The distribution of jobs over the routes depends on the *Demand* element load order. Although in practice the distribution of jobs over the routes is stochastic and varies according to train, the distribution in the model is deterministic and similar for all trains. A deterministic approach provides a better control of input variables. Three flows of jobs are distinguished (see Figure 4–3):

- Route 1, representing direct transhipment from train to train by a crane.
- Route 2, representing a sequence of activities: (2a) transhipment from train to storage by a crane and (2b) transhipment from storage to train by a crane.
- Route 3, representing a sequence of activities: (3a) transhipment from train to transport system by a crane, (3b) transport job from one crane section to another crane section by the transport system and (3c) transhipment from transport system to train by a crane.

With a planned load order there will be more route 1 jobs, and with an unplanned load order there will be more route 3 jobs. The number of route 2 jobs is limited because only a few load units need to be put into storage to free up space to start operations. The distribution is modelled as a percentage of the load units per train that follow a certain route and determined in advance.

In the previous section various queues were explained. In the proposed system how cranes select their next job from these queues is coordinated by operational process control routines, which depend on the crane handling strategy. A crane handling strategy is defined as a set of rules applied to determine the next load unit to be served. Two types of priority rules exist: 1) rules related to due time of a train, 2) rule related to minimising throughput time.

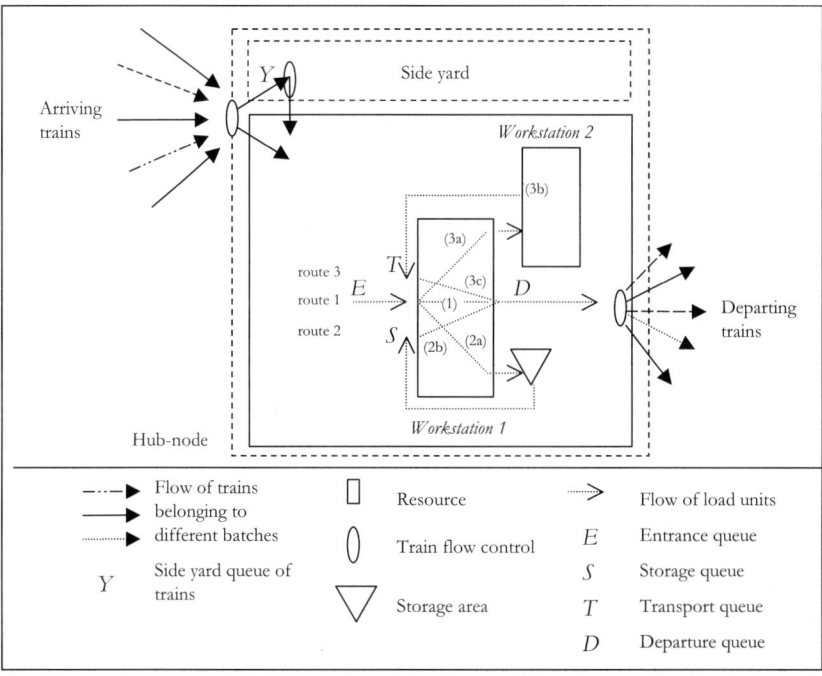

Figure 4–3: A conceptual model for synchronised operations at new hub terminals

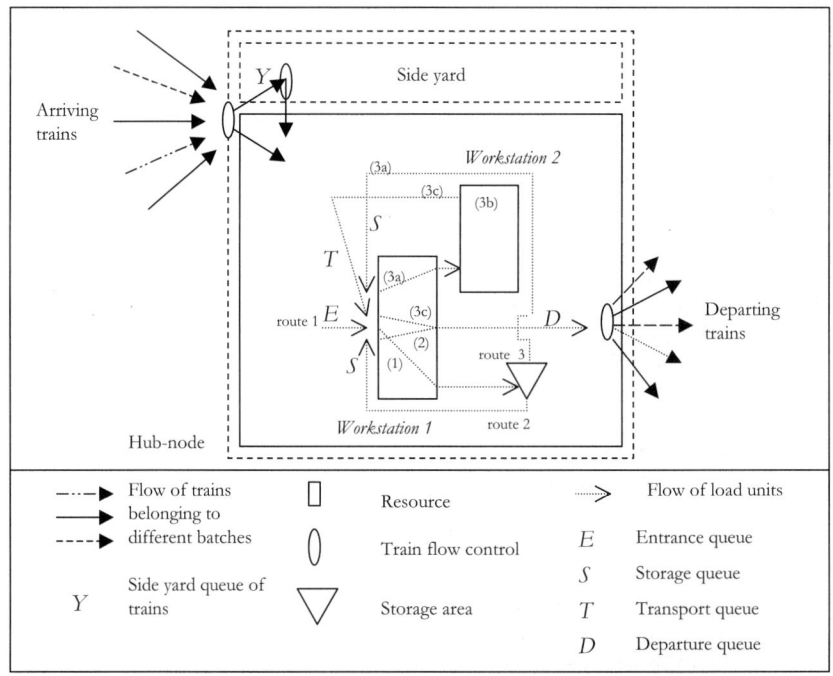

Figure 4–4: A conceptual model for non-synchronised operations at new hub terminals

Hub exchange operations in intermodal hub-and-spoke networks

In the model these routines are reflected on one side by priority and hold rules and on the other side by the crane service time. Priority and hold rules are discussed in this section and crane service times in section 5.4.

Despite the fact that jobs follow different routes and physically queue at different locations, they all queue for service at workstation 1. In principle jobs are served on a first come, first served basis, but some priority rules apply. With respect to jobs in the *entrance* queue jobs following routes 2 and 3 entering workstation 1 for the first time (2a and 3a respectively) have first priority in order to free up train space to get the exchange started. This first priority is overruled at the moment when load units in the transport queue wait longer than a certain deterministic period of time. When this situation occurs, jobs in the *transport* queue get first priority. Otherwise jobs in the transport system (transport queue) have low priority, just like jobs following route 1 as well as jobs in the *storage* queue (2b).

The change of priority with respect to load units in the *transport* queue prevents a situation in which cranes are unable to put load units onto the transport system any more due to saturation of the transport system. This priority rule guarantees a continuous throughput of the transport system. This is important, because the direct interface between cranes and transport system requires finely-tuned operations: a load unit is handed over directly from crane to transport unit and from transport unit to crane. There is no buffer in between crane and transport unit that can control fluctuations in the handling speed of the cranes versus the transport system.

Hold rules apply to two situations. Firstly, load units are held in the *entrance, storage* and *transport* queue if their destination train has not yet arrived. In synchronised operations exchange operations can only be completed when destination trains have arrived. Jobs following route 1 can only be processed when the destination train has arrived. Until that moment jobs remain in the *entrance* queue. Jobs following routes 2 and 3 can start being processed, but the final service step can only be carried out when the destination train arrives. Until that moment jobs remain in the *storage* queue and the *transport* queue respectively. If a job is put on hold to wait for its destination train, succeeding jobs in the *entrance, storage* and *transport* queues are served. However, if all jobs are on hold, operations can only continue when the next train has arrived.

Secondly, load units are held in the *departure queue* prior to departure. Load units can only leave the system grouped as a train. In the model, load units in the same batch are held after they have completed service until all load units in the same batch have completed exchange operations.

4.5.3 Modelling exchange operations –non-synchronised

It should be remembered that non-synchronised operations imply that one train delivers load units for later trains and that it picks up load units from earlier trains in the same batch. Trains in the same batch never meet at the terminal, so all exchange goes via the storage area. For the modelling it is assumed that the system is already in some kind of steady state; there is no start-up phase involving filling the storage area. Consequently, the storage area is filled with load units dropped off by previous trains in a batch. In this case, exchange operations may also be perceived as a batch arrival of load units that may also be divided into three classes based on the routing the jobs follow along workstations (see Figure 4–4). However, the routings and their interpretation differ from synchronised operations:

- Route 1 represents transhipment from train to storage (drop-off) and applies to all load units of arrival trains.
- Route 2, representing transhipment from storage to train (pick-up).
- Route 3, representing a sequence of activities: (3a) transhipment from storage to transport system, (3b) transport job from one crane section to another crane section and (3c) transhipment from transport system to train (pick-up).

Route 2 and route 3 apply to load units dropped off by previous trains in the batch. The number of load units picked up (route 2 and route 3) equals the number of load units dropped off (route 1).

The distribution of jobs over routes 2 and 3 depends on the load order of load units on the train. With a planned load order, there will be more route 2 jobs; with an unplanned load order there will be more route 3 jobs. Although in practice the distribution of jobs over the two routes is stochastic and varies according to train, a deterministic approach is used. A deterministic approach provides a better control of input variables. The same distribution is used for all trains and all batches.

Work order control routines are defined according to priority rules. Despite the fact that jobs follow different routes, they all queue for service at workstation 1. In principle, jobs are served on a first come, first served basis, but some priority rules apply. Jobs in the entrance queue (route 1 jobs only) and route 3 jobs in the storage queue (3a) have equal and first priority. This means that unloading and loading of trains is executed simultaneously. This first priority is overruled at the moment when load units wait in the transport queue longer than a certain maximum deterministic period of time. When this situation occurs, jobs in the transport queue get first priority. Otherwise jobs in the transport queue have low priority, just like route 2 jobs.

4.6 Modelling Resources and Process for hump shunting and flat shunting yards

4.6.1 Modelling infrastructure, equipment and labour

The resources at shunting yards are modelled as two sequential workstations. Figure 4–5 illustrates the conceptual model for both *synchronised* and *non-synchronised* operations. Workstation 1 represents one or two servers that combine all sorting-related activities into one handling operation. These activities are as follows (see subsection 3.5.3):
- Uncouple network locomotive.
- Uncoupling rail wagons and releasing air from brake air reservoirs.
- Coupling switch locomotive to train and pushing train to shunting hill.
- Pushing one wagon over the hump.
- Return trip of switch locomotive to next train to be shunted.

The sorting operation is stochastic because it includes variable locomotive driving distance and labour handling speed. The combined locomotive-labour sorting cycle time is represented in the model by a service time distribution function, which is specified in section 5.4. Workstation 2 represents one or two servers that combine all assembly-related activities into one handling operation. These activities are as follows (see subsection 3.5.3):
- Correcting false runners using the yard engine.
- Assembly.

- Coupling the network locomotive to the departing train.
- Brake test and inspection.

Assembly handling is stochastic, because it also includes variable locomotive driving distance and labour handling speed. The assembly locomotive-labour cycle time is also represented in the model by a service time distribution function (see section 5.4 for a specification). A typical aspect of workstation 2 is that trains are served and not rail wagons, such as is the case for workstation 1. As such, the regrouping of rail wagons into trains takes place earlier than is the case for terminals.

Although the conceptual model has a similar set-up for hump shunting and flat shunting, the service time distribution functions for the servers at the workstations are different for hump shunting and flat shunting due to differences in sorting and assembly activities.

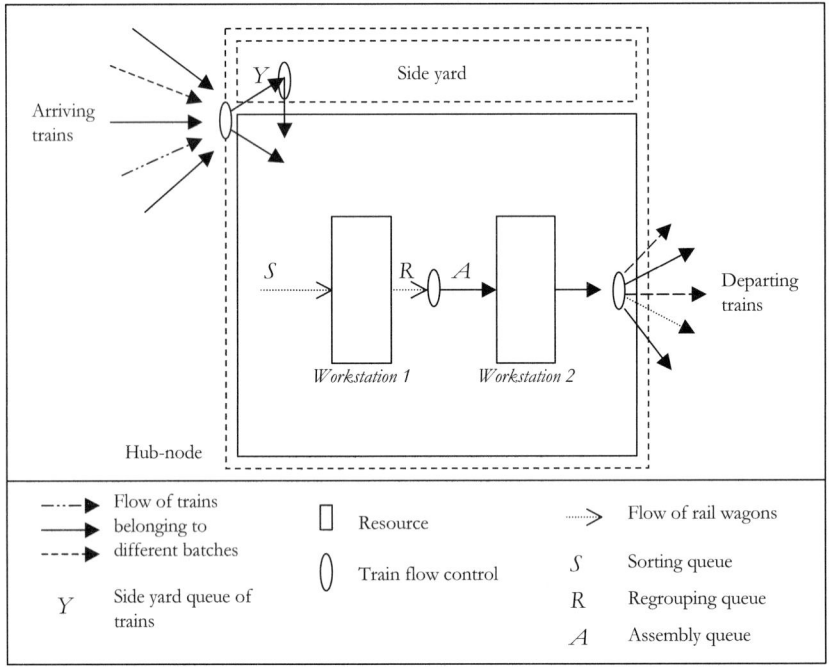

Figure 4–5: A conceptual model for both synchronised and non-synchronised operations at both hump shunting and flat shunting facilities

Infrastructure such as side yard and tracks is not modelled as such, but is reflected in the model by queues. I have distinguished several queues. The side yard is modelled as an unlimited queue of trains waiting to be granted access to the exchange facility. In Figure 4–5 this queue is identified as Y. When trains enter the exchange facility, trains are no longer modelled but rail wagons or wagon groups are modelled instead. Once they have been granted access to the exchange facility, rail wagons must wait for a server to become available at workstation 1. Physically, rail wagons remain at their arrival track, but in the model rail wagons enter the *sorting* queue. In Figure 4–5 this queue is identified as S. This queue has unlimited capacity. Since workstation 2 serves trains and not rail wagons, a *regrouping* queue is modelled after workstation 1.

This is not really a queue, but rather a hold of the flow (more about this in subsection 4.6.2). In Figure 4–5 this queue is identified as R. Once rail wagons have been regrouped, they proceed to the *assembly* queue in front of workstation 2. In Figure 4–5 this queue is identified as A. Physically, the *regrouping* queue and *assembly* queue are located at various sorting/departure tracks, one for each train, but in the model they are modelled as two queues.

4.6.2 Modelling exchange operations –synchronised

Exchange operations at a shunting facility may be perceived as a batch arrival of rail wagons that follow a similar route along two workstations, albeit regrouped as a train at workstation 2. This process is conceptualised in Figure 4–5 and applies both to synchronised and non-synchronised operations. However, there are some fundamental differences in the operational control routines.
In synchronised operations, only one batch at a time is allowed access to workstation 1. Rail wagons are served on a first-come, first-served basis. Rail wagons cannot proceed, regrouped as trains, to workstation 2 if the last rail wagon of the batch has not finished service at workstation 1. In practice, assembly operations may start while a part of the rail wagons still have to be shunted, but in the model it is assumed that parallel execution of sorting and assembly activities do not take place for the train within the same batch. Hence, once the last rail wagon has finished service, rail wagons proceed regrouped to workstation 2 and capacity at workstation 1 is freed up for trains in the next batch. A first-come, first-served rule also applies at workstation 2.

4.6.3 Modelling exchange operations –non-synchronised

In non-synchronised operations, trains from different batches are served on a first-come, first-served basis at workstation 1. Just as for synchronised operations, rail wagons cannot proceed to workstation 2 if the last rail wagon of the batch has not finished service at workstation 1. However, capacity at workstation 1 is already freed up as soon as all the rail wagons of a train have finished service at workstation 1. A consequence of non-synchronised operations is that there are more rail wagon queues waiting for the batch to be completed at workstation 1 than for synchronised operations. A first come, first served rule also applies at workstation 2. The trains in a batch that first completes service at workstation 1 proceed to workstation 2.

4.7 Modelling Resources and Process for road-rail terminals

4.7.1 Modelling infrastructure, equipment and labour

The resources at road-rail terminals are modelled as one workstation with multiple servers in both the synchronised and non-synchronised model. Figure 4–6 illustrates the conceptual model for *synchronised* operations; Figure 4–7 the conceptual model for *non-synchronised* operations. This workstation contains multiple cranes that can carry out all types of transhipment tasks, from train to train, from train to storage, from train to transport system, etc. Since there is no transport system the cranes also take care of the transport task, which is to transport load units from one edge of a crane section to the other edge. The crane cycle time for a task is represented in the model by a service time distribution function, which is specified in section 5.4.
Just as for the new hub terminal model it is assumed that each crane can process any load unit. However, in the proposed system a crane can only process load units in its

own crane section. With the use of scheduling heuristics workloads per crane can be equalised as best as possible. However, a 100% balanced utilisation of cranes cannot be achieved. My model assumes 100% balanced utilisation of cranes, which may lead to an underestimation of generated train service and sojourn times. The crane with the longest workload expressed in time determines when a batch is completed. This must be kept in mind when the model is validated, and deviation may be overcome by applying a correction factor to the crane cycle time.

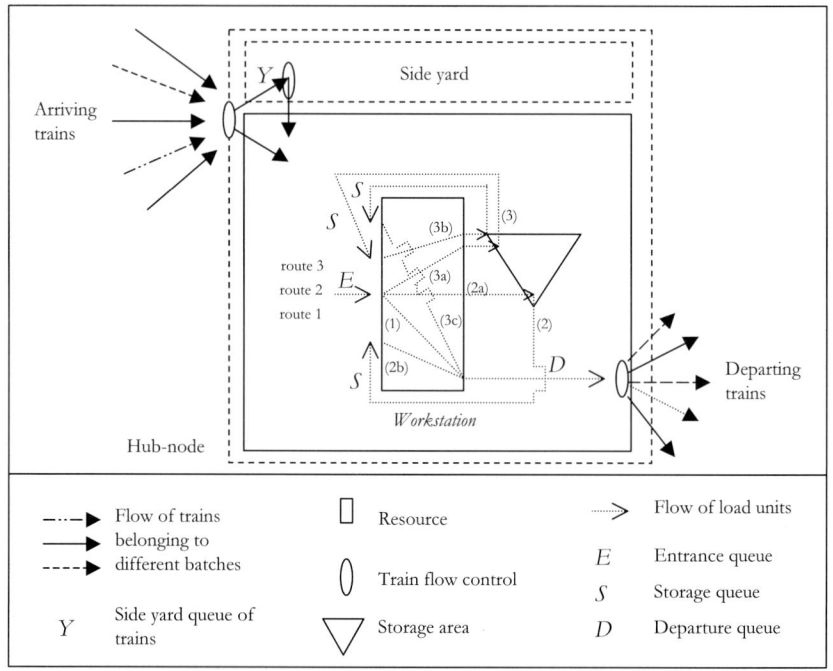

Figure 4–6: A conceptual model for synchronised operations at a road-rail terminal

Just like shunting yards and new hub terminals, infrastructure such as side yard, tracks and storage area is not modelled as such, but is reflected in the models by queues. I have distinguished several queues. The side yard is modelled as an unlimited queue of trains waiting to be allowed access to the exchange facility. In Figure 4–6 and Figure 4–7 this queue is identified as Y. Tracks at the exchange facility are modelled in a similar way as for the shunting and new hub terminal models; as a maximum number of trains that can be allowed access to the exchange facility. When trains enter the exchange facility, trains are no longer modelled but load units are modelled instead. As Figure 4–6 and Figure 4–7 show, the flow of load units is, just as in the new hub terminal model, divided over three routings due to a different sequence of crane handling operations that load units require (more about the exchange process in subsection 4.7.2). As a result, queues of load units appear at different locations, but with respect to work order form a joint queue with jobs for the cranes. At the exchange facility similar queues may occur to those at new hub terminals (see subsection 4.5.1), except for the *transport* queue, since there is no transport system. Load units that have to be transported between crane sections queue in the *storage* queue (indicated in Figure 4–6 as S related to route 3).

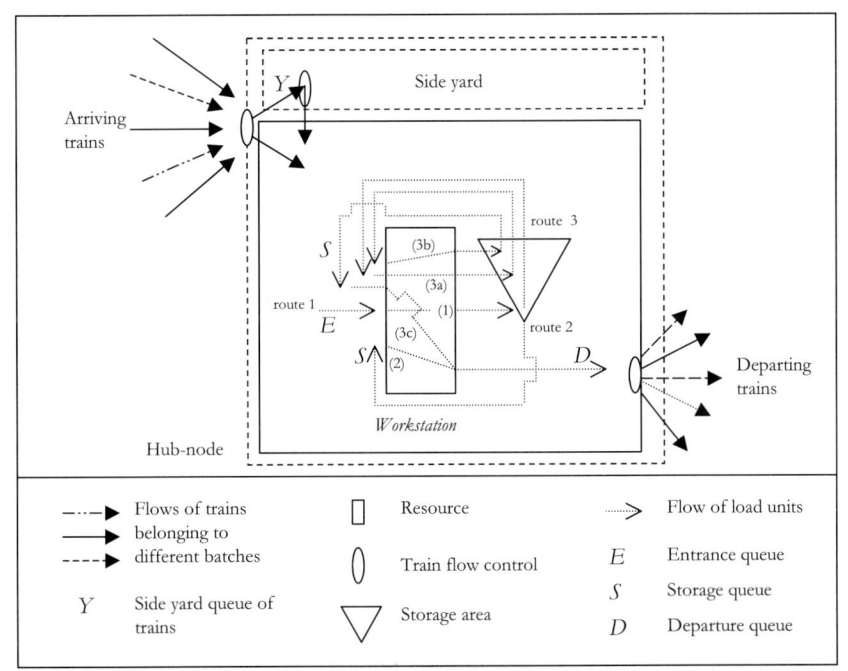

Figure 4–7: A conceptual model for non-synchronised service process at a road-rail hub terminal

4.7.2 Modelling exchange operations at road-rail terminals –synchronised

Modelling of exchange operations at road-rail terminals is rather similar to modelling operations at new hub terminals, except for modelling jobs following route 3 due to the lack of a second workstation. This difference affects route 3 and has a slight effect on priority rules. All other aspects remain the same, and are therefore not repeated in this section.

Route 3 for road-rail terminals represents the following sequence of activities: (3a) transhipment from train to edge of storage, (3b) transport job from edge of storage to other edge of storage, and (3c) transhipment from edge of storage to train.

With respect to the priority rules, the difference applies to the rule when the first priority of jobs in the entrance queue—jobs following routes 2 and 3 entering workstation 1 for the first time (2 and 3a respectively)—is overruled. In the new hub terminal model this first priority is overruled at the moment when load units wait in the transport queue longer than a certain maximum deterministic period of time. In the road-rail model the first priority is overruled when load units following route 3 wait longer than a certain maximum deterministic period of time in the storage area.

4.7.3 Modelling exchange operations at road-rail terminals –non-synchronised

Modelling of non-synchronised exchange operations at road-rail terminals is also rather similar to modelling operations at new hub terminals, except for modelling jobs following route 3 due to the lack of a second workstation. This difference affects route 3 and has a slight effect on priority rules. All other aspects remain the same, and are therefore not repeated in this section.

Route 3 for road-rail terminals represents the following sequence of activities: (3a) transhipment from storage to edge of storage, (3b) transhipment from edge of storage to other edge of storage and (3c) transhipment from edge of storage to train.

With respect to priority rules, the difference applies to the rule when the first priority of jobs in the entrance queue (route 1 jobs only) and jobs following route 3 in the storage queue (3a) is overruled. In the new hub terminal model this first priority is overruled at the moment when load units wait in the transport queue longer than a certain maximum deterministic period of time. In the road-rail model the first priority is overruled when load units following route 3 wait longer than a certain maximum deterministic period of time in the storage area.

4.8 Summary and conclusions

In this chapter one generic conceptual model and five derived models for hub exchange operations have been presented. The objective was to elaborate and to differentiate one generic model. This was not possible due to differences between exchange facilities. Due to differences between synchronised and non-synchronised operations two models needed to be constructed for each hub exchange facility under investigation. However, one model could represent both hump shunting and flat shunting. Differences between these two exchange facilities and exchange operations can be brought out by using different values for model parameters and variables.

Logistics and queuing theory were used as theoretical inspiration for the abstraction from the real system, described in Chapter 3. As a result, exchange operations are perceived as a batch arrival of load units or rail wagons that flow through different routes along servers (e.g. cranes). When demand exceeds server capacity queues occur. Hold rules, which do not exist in queuing theory, are applied in order to control flows of load units and rail wagons. As such, exchange operations cannot be modelled using queuing theory. After operations, load units or rail wagons depart as a batch.

This approach leads to the following significant abstractions from the real system:
- Dimensions of infrastructure are not modelled. Infrastructure such as tracks, side yard and storage area are modelled as queues with unlimited capacity.
- Exact unload and load position on trains, in the storage area and on the transport system and exact wagon position are not accounted for. Neither are the exact origin and destination train, or details on type and size of load unit and rail wagon.
- Each crane can process any load unit, while in reality a crane can only process load units in its own crane section. A 100% balanced utilisation of cranes is assumed.
- Each train in a batch consists of an equal number of load units or rail wagons.
- Between batches the number of load units or rail wagons of a train may vary.
- In the exchange operation load units or rail wagons of one train are equally redistributed among the other trains in a batch.
- Train departure times are not modelled. After operations the train leaves the system.
- Type of equipment and dimensions of facility infrastructure are reflected in the service time distributions of servers.
- The modelling is carried out for one day of exchange operations.

- Priority and hold rules determine the work order of servers.
- Network effects are not considered.

The modelling approach in this chapter leads to transparent conceptual models with sufficient distinction between exchange facilities. The models focus on the interaction between train arrival schedule characteristics and strategic process control principles and the effects on batch and train service time performance. A crucial element of the models is the service time of servers, which are represented by distribution functions. The estimation of these distribution functions is of crucial importance for the numerical modelling output as well as the translation of the conceptual models into computer models. In the validation phase of the terminal models the assumption of a 100% balanced utilisation of cranes must be kept in mind. This assumption may lead to an underestimation of generated train service and sojourn times.

5 Computerised modelling

5.1 Introduction

This chapter reports on the six computer models that were the result of programming the conceptual models of the previous chapter (Chapter 4) into simulation software and specifying parameters and variables. It reports on the final steps of the modelling phase. The computerised modelling approach, model construction, the verification and validation process and specification of parameters and variables are discussed. The models described in this chapter are used for numerical analysis, the results of which are reported in the next chapter (Chapter 6). Since a simulation model does not include a cost evaluation module, a separate cost model was constructed. This cost model is also reported in this chapter.

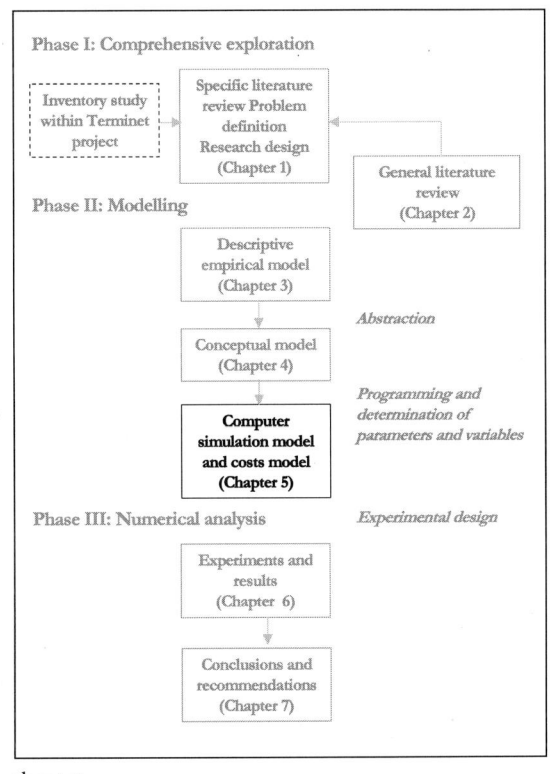

The outline of this chapter is as follows. In section 5.2 the transformation from the conceptual models in the previous chapter to computer models is described. The section covers reasons for choosing ARENA for the simulation language, a brief description of the computer model construction phase, and a justification of model verification and validation activities. In section 5.3 the constructed computer models are specified. The models contain six modules. For each module its functionalities, specific programming features (solutions) and programming deviations with respect to the conceptual models are discussed. Section 5.4 reports on the estimation of service time distribution functions for the servers in the various models. In the previous chapter it was concluded that the service time of servers is a crucial element of the models, because they express the spatial characteristics of exchange operations. This section also reports on a special tool that was developed in order to estimate crane cycle times for the terminal facilities. Section 5.5 describes the costs model that was constructed in a spreadsheet. This chapter ends with a summary and conclusions in section 5.6.

5.2 Approach

The transformation from conceptual model to computer simulation model consists of various steps. The following steps were carried out:
- Choice of simulation language.
- Computer model construction (programming).
- Specification of variables and parameters (data collection).
- Model verification.
- Model validation.

ARENA was chosen as the simulation software. Choosing simulation software is an important aspect of simulation studies. In practice many different simulation software packages exist for constructing simulation models (Swain, 1999). Packages can be evaluated either on their own merits or in comparison with other packages. The task of evaluating and selecting simulation software, which involves multi-criteria decision-making, is usually time-consuming (Nikoukaran et al., 1999). Based on past experience I chose to construct the simulation models using ARENA after carrying out an evaluation of ARENA based on its own merits. Nikoukaran et al. (1999) provide a comprehensive list of criteria for the selection of suitable simulation packages. Law & Kelton (1991) provide a list of desirable features for simulation software. The criteria offered by Nikoukaran et al. (1999) and Law & Kelton (1991) are general criteria for selecting simulation software. When choosing simulation software, case-specific criteria play an equally important role. Three criteria mentioned by Nikoukaran et al. (1999) were especially important in justifying our choice of ARENA. Firstly, ARENA has a flow-oriented paradigm that closely represents the flows of load units and rail wagons. Secondly, ARENA offers features for two-dimensional animations to represent the dynamic behaviour of the system. Thirdly, the simulation model builder and the author already had experience working with ARENA.

Danielle Stekelenburg, a systems engineering student, constructed the computerised models under the supervision of Dr. Ir. C. Versteegt of the Faculty of Technology, Policy and Management and the author herself. Six models were constructed and are presented in section 5.3. For the specification of model parameters and variables data collected for the system analysis in Chapter 3 were used. This data was collected through desk research, interviews, site visits, observation of scale models and animations of new hub terminals. In addition, representatives of the flat shunting yard at Herne (Germany), the hump shunting yard at Metz (France), the hump shunting yard at Kijfhoek (The Netherlands) and the Kombi-Verkehr Gateway terminals (Germany) and a railway expert on flat shunting and hump shunting yards and road-rail terminals filled in questionnaires about specific detailed information needed for the estimation of service times of servers.

During model verification checks were made to see whether the simulation models behaved as the modeller intended (Law & Kelton, 1991; Shannon, 1975). Verification is a continuous process that starts at the very beginning of simulation model construction (Balci, 1998). Two verification techniques were used to test the models during development. First, a structured walk-through in which the program developer explained her computer program code statement by statement to the author was carried out. The author verified that the computer model resembled the conceptual model. Second, the author carried out various dynamic tests. Data input files with a limited and traceable amount of data were used. The order and time of events was verified with a low simulation running speed.

Correspondence of the model with the real system was checked in the validation process (see Balci, 1998). Eight[17] computerised models had to be validated: one per type of hub exchange facility model and for both synchronised and non-synchronised operations. Four validation techniques were used. First, model outputs were compared with real performances or other model outputs. Second, animation was used. Third, structured walk-throughs of the model were carried out. Fourth, all models were tested for extreme conditions such as very short interarrival times, lengthy service times, many load units or rail wagons and many trains.

Since a simulation model does not include a cost evaluation module, a separate cost calculation model was constructed in a spreadsheet. The common business economic perspective on costs evaluation is used. Total annual costs and costs per load unit for greenfield situations are evaluated. Hence, costs calculations imply a total costs approach, implying that both capital (depreciation and interest) and operational costs are included.

Cost data was data collected from the literature (Terminet, 2000; Impulse, 1999; Black et al., 2003; Gruppo Clas, 2002; ZEW et al., 2000; European Commission, 1997) and questionnaires (Rotter, 2003; Biggler, 2003; Fritsch, 2003; Wesseling, 2003). More about the model in section 5.5.

5.3 Specification of the computer models

The final modelling step was to translate the conceptual models of the previous chapter into computer models. This implies programming train arrivals, servers, flows, priority rules, train departures and output values. In addition, values for model parameters and variables had to be specified. Service time distribution functions were the most important parameters to be determined. The next section (section 5.4) is devoted to the estimation of service time distributions functions. This section presents the main features of the computer models. As a result of the generic approach in the conceptualisation phase, the computer models have a similar modular structure and content. The models contain six modules. For each module its functionalities, specific programming features (solutions) and programming deviations with respect to the conceptual models are discussed.

5.3.1 Module: Train arrivals

In this module train arrivals are generated (read) from an input file with deterministic data. A sample file is provided in Table 5–1. The input file contains the following demand data: train number, arrival time, interarrival time, batch number, number of trains in a batch, train number in a batch and number of load units or rail wagons to be processed[18]. This data is specified by the researcher and may be based on empirical data or be hypothetical. The exchange relation between trains is not specified in

---

[17] Although six main models were constructed, the shunting models had to be validated for parameter and variable settings for both hump shunting and flat shunting.

[18] Remember that for terminals the number of load units to be processed is lower than the number of load units on the train. 1/n load unit remains on the train; n being the number of trains in a batch (see Section 4.3).

the input file, because it is assumed that load units or rail wagons of one train are equally redistributed among the other trains in a batch. The programming of this redistribution is discussed in the module *Operations* and *Operations Control*. In the experiments different input files could be generated. By varying arrival times, different arrival patterns as well as delayed trains could be analysed. By varying the number of batches, trains and load units or rail wagons, different demand volumes could be analysed. This construction provides the required control for numerical experiments for different train arrival time and demand volumes.

In the terminal models the module differs slightly from the shunting models. In the terminal models the distribution, which resembles a certain load order[19], of load units over the various routes is specified in this module. The distribution is modelled as the percentages of load units per train that follow a certain route through the terminal. Although in practice the distribution of jobs over the routes is stochastic and varies according to train, the distribution in the model is deterministic and similar for all trains. A deterministic approach provides a better control of input variables. Per run the distribution may be different, but once set the distribution applies to all trains of the input file. The shunting models do not have this feature.

Table 5–1: Example of the input file for the generation of train arrivals

Train number	Arrival time (minutes)	Interarrival time (minutes)	Batch number	Number of trains in a batch	Train order in batch	Number of load units or rail wagons*
1	0	0	1	4	1	30
2	6	6	1	4	2	30
3	12	6	1	4	3	30
4	18	6	1	4	4	30
5	110	92	2	3	1	30
6	116	6	2	3	2	30
7	122	6	2	3	3	30
8	150	28	3	5	1	30
9	156	6	3	5	2	30
10	162	6	3	5	3	30
11	168	6	3	5	4	30
12	174	6	3	5	5	30

* To be exchanged.

5.3.2 Module: Operations access control

In this module the priority rules based on the type of strategic operations control principle are programmed. In the synchronised models checks are made to ascertain whether the exchange facility is idle. If it is, the train proceeds; if not, the batch number of the train is checked against the batch number of the train(s) at the exchange facility. If the batch numbers are the same, the train proceeds; if they are different, the train queues at the side yard. When the exchange facility becomes idle again, the first train in the queue proceeds and the batch number checking procedure is applied to all other trains in the queue.

---

[19] With a planned load order, there will be more route 1 jobs; with an unplanned load order more route 3 jobs. The number of route 2 jobs is limited, because only a few load units need to be put in storage to free up space to start operations (see 4.5.2).

In the non-synchronised models checks are made to ascertain whether the maximum number of trains at the exchange facility has been reached. If it has not, the train proceeds; if it has, it queues. Consequently, the maximum number of trains at the exchange facility must be specified. When a train leaves the exchange facility, the next train in the queue enters the exchange facility.

In this module the researcher can specify a distribution function for the service time to shunt a train from side yard to exchange facility.

In this module the researcher can specify a distribution function for the service time to shunt a train from side yard to exchange facility. Due to the three modelling levels and our specific interest in train and batch service and waiting time, a separate throughput time registration for batches and trains was programmed. Therefore in this module time attributes and variables are assigned to trains and batches in order to be able to measure train waiting, service and sojourn time and batch service and sojourn time and duration of operations.

5.3.3 Module: Generation of load units and assignment of job classes/rail wagons

The transformation from trains to rail wagons or load units is programmed in this module. The number of rail wagons/load units generated equals the number stated in the input file. Each rail wagon or load unit is given a sequence number, ranging from 1 to the number of units on the train involved indicated in the input file. This sequence number is used in conjunction with the train and batch number to identify the rail wagon or load unit throughout the process.

In addition, in the terminal models load units are assigned to different routes in this module. Each load unit of a certain train is given a number from 1 to the number of load units to be exchanged as specified in for that train in the input file. This sequence number in combination with the train and batch number is used for identification of the rail wagon or load unit. The assignment rules to job classes are as follows:
- job class 1: sequence number $\leq$ total number of containers on train * distribution percentage;
- job class 2: total number containers on train * 0.2 > sequence number $\leq$ total number of containers on train * distribution percentage;
- job class 3: sequence number > total number of containers on train * distribution percentage.

The distribution percentage must be carefully selected in order to realise an equal number of jobs before and after the job class assignment. Using tens as percentages is recommended.

No time registration is carried out at the level of rail wagons or load units.

5.3.4 Module: Exchange operations

In this module workstations and servers, handling of rail wagons or load units, routing of flows, priority rules and the freeing up of track capacity at the exchange facility are programmed. This module differs for each exchange facility and for synchronised and non-synchronised operations. However, the module is structured in a similar way. The flow-oriented paradigm of ARENA means that each flow (sequence of service activities) is programmed separately, as well as each handling operation a load unit or rail wagon undergoes at a workstation. As a result, the researcher can specify the service time distribution function and the priority for each handling operation. In addition, the researcher must specify the number of servers per workstation. Hence, the number of servers, service time distribution functions and priority rules may be modified for different analyses.

A typical feature of shunting is that rail wagons are processed at workstation 1, but trains at workstation 2. The regrouping of rail wagons of trains is programmed in the module Operations Control, which is discussed in the next subsection. The first come, first served priority rule that applies for rail wagons and trains matches with the default programming routine of ARENA. ARENA works with a so-called "job list". An idle server selects the first job at the top of this list, while new jobs are added to the bottom.

Priority programming for the terminal models is more complicated and slightly different to the conceptual modelling. Priority rules based on flow time are applied. In the shunting models the simple priority rule first in queue adequately resembles real operations. But in the terminal models certain handling operations have higher priority than others. Priorities should be assigned such that the objective that different flows finish service at about the same time is achieved. Priorities are basically programmed as fixed priorities: high, medium and low, but with respect to the flows along route 3 priorities are dynamic.

The job list is divided into these three priority categories. Idle servers select the first job from the top of the high priority list as long as there are jobs, the next jobs are selected from the medium priority list and, lastly, jobs are selected from the low priority lists. As soon as a higher priority job is added to an empty list, this job is served as soon as a server becomes idle. Priority rules for crane handling operations in synchronised operations determined in subsection 3.5.2 are programmed as follows:

- route 1: (1) transhipment from train to train: low;
- route 2: (2a) transhipment into storage area: medium;
- route 2: (2b) transhipment from storage to train: low;
- route 3: (3a) transhipment into storage (road-rail terminal model)/onto transport system (new hub terminal model): medium;
- route 3: (3b) transhipment from storage to storage (only applicable in the road-rail model): more than x jobs in storage: high, otherwise medium;
- route 3: (3c) transhipment onto train: more than y jobs in storage/z jobs on transport system: high, otherwise low.

Although the priorities are programmed as proposed in the conceptual model, the result is not quite as intended. Jobs are not put on the job list randomly but in the order they are "administratively" and/or physically processed. For instance, in the module "generation of load units", load units for route 1 are generated first, then units for route 2 and finally for route 3. When jobs for two different routes have equal priority, jobs from the route generated first are put earlier on the job list and thus served first. Consequently, some routes are served before others, despite having equal priority.

Furthermore, with respect to route 3, the switch of priority from medium to high is programmed differently from the conceptual model. The priority switch has been made conditional upon a certain number of load units in the storage area or on the transport system instead of a certain period of time as was stated in the original priority rules in Chapter 4. When this point of saturation is reached all load units put in the storage area or on the transport system are given high priority status. Therefore load units already in storage or on the transport system do not switch priority status. Model validation proved that these deviations from the conceptual model are acceptable, because they do not affect the moment that a complete train or batch is served.

Similar programming problems apply to priority rules for crane handling in non-synchronised operations. These priorities are programmed as follows:
- route 1: (1) transhipment from train to storage: medium;
- route 2: (2) transhipment from storage to train: medium;
- route 3: (3a) transhipment from train into storage (road-rail terminal)/onto transport system (new hub terminal): medium;
- route 3: (3b) transhipment from storage to storage (only applicable in the road-rail model): more than x jobs in storage: high, otherwise medium;
- route 3: (3c) transhipment onto train: more than x jobs in storage/y jobs on transport system: high, otherwise low.

In contrast to the synchronised models, validation showed that this specific model behaviour should be taken into account when designing scenarios for numerical analysis. As long as trains arrive just in time to succeed each other, the model works fine. If the order of trains differs from this, interpretation of the simulation results should be carried out with a certain amount of care.

With respect to non-synchronised operations there is another programming problem: that of programming an incoming and an outgoing flow of load units. This problem is resolved as follows. The same load units as generated in the module "generation of load units" are used for the outgoing flow. Once generated, load units follow route 1 (incoming flow). When finished, they are directly redistributed over routes 2 and 3 (outgoing flows). As such, storage (= time gap) is left out of the simulation. This approach is allowed, because the fact that in reality different load units are unloaded then loaded is not important here. The main objective of the modelling is to model the duration of activities in order to determine train and batch service times.

5.3.5 Module: Operations control

This module is part of all models except for the non-synchronised terminal models. *Operations control* manages the hold rules. In the (synchronised) terminal models it controls the fact that load units in a certain train are kept in hold queues (one per train) when the destination train has not yet arrived. Jobs following route 1 only start being processed when the destination train has arrived. Until that moment jobs are held in hold queues. All route 1 jobs are distributed equally over the queues of the destination trains. Jobs following routes 2 and 3 start processing, but service is only completed when the destination train has arrived. After initial processing these load units are kept in hold queues. All jobs are distributed equally over the queues of their particular destination trains. When the next train arrives, load units in that particular hold queue are released, and merge on a first come, first served basis in the flow (queue) they were separated from.

A different hold rule is modelled for shunting models. In these models the regrouping of rail wagons into a train before they can proceed to workstation 2 is programmed. The moment that trains can proceed to workstation 2 is programmed as follows. Rail wagons with the same train number are first regrouped into trains. Next, trains with the same batch number are grouped together. Once the batch is formed the service of the batch (trains and rail wagons) at workstation 1 is considered completed. This programming approach implies that the exchange between trains is not programmed as such. Only the duration of exchange activities is simulated. This method of programming assumes that trains cannot be assembled before the last rail wagon of a batch is processed at workstation 1.

5.3.6 Module: Train departures

The purpose of this module is to register the end of train and batch waiting, service and sojourn times and file this information in an output file. This module is different for terminal and shunting models. In the terminal models regrouping of load units into a train has yet to take place, while in the shunting models this regrouping of rail wagons has already taken place in the module *Operations*.

In the terminal models the regrouping of load units into a train marks the end of the service time of a train, and the grouping of trains with the same batch number into a batch the batch service time. A similar programming approach as described in the previous subsection for regrouping of rail wagons applies. The exchange of load units between trains as such is not programmed. Only the duration of exchange activities is simulated. As a result, load units with the same train number are regrouped into a train. This regrouping can only take place when the last load unit of a train has completed service. Next, trains with the same batch number are grouped when the last train of that batch has been regrouped.

In the shunting models the train service time is automatically kept track of after the regrouping of rail wagons before workstation 2. However, the end of the batch service time is programmed in a similar way as for the terminal models.

All registered train and batch arrival, waiting and service times are written to a data file, which can be read in Excel. These data are: train number, entrance time model, entrance time file, train waiting time due to operations access control, batch service time, train service time, batch departure time, batch sojourn time, train sojourn time and start of operations. An example of such an output file is provided in Table 5–2.

To conclude, in this module only administrative handling operations, which do not add any time to load units, trains or batches, are programmed before trains exit the system.

Other output statistics such as maximum and average length of queues, maximum and average time of jobs in queues and server utilisation rate are registered automatically by ARENA.

Table 5–2: An example of an output file (average time in minutes)

Train number	Entrance time model	Entrance time file	Train waiting time entrance	Train service time	Train sojourn time	Batch departure time	Batch sojourn time	Start of operations
1	0	0	0	57	66	66	66	0
2	1	1	0	59	65	-	-	1
3	2	2	0	61	64	-	-	2
4	3	3	0	63	63	-	-	3
5	65	65	1	45	50	116	51	66
6	66	66	0	47	50	-	-	66
7	67	67	0	49	49	-	-	67
8	150	150	0	98	116	266	116	150
9	151	151	0	100	115	-	-	151
10	152	152	0	102	114	-	-	152
11	153	153	0	104	113	-	-	153
12	154	154	0	106	112	-	-	154

5.4 Estimation of service time probability distributions

Crucial variables of the models are the service times of servers. Service times are stochastic and are generated according to theoretical distribution functions. These distribution functions must be determined for each type of server and for each sort of handling operation. For the shunting models the service time distribution functions for the sorting of one wagon and the assembling of one train were estimated; for the terminal models the service time distribution functions for various transhipments for different routes were estimated. In addition, for the new hub terminal model the service time distribution function for the transport system had to be estimated. The following subsections explain how distribution functions were estimated. Subsection 5.4.1 covers the estimation of service time distributions for the terminal models, subsection 5.4.2 covers those for the hump shunting models and subsection 5.4.3 those for the flat shunting models.

5.4.1 Estimation of service time distributions for servers in terminal models

Servers at workstation 1 can carry out various types of transhipments, train to train, train to storage or transport system to train. Due to differences in crane and trolley travel distances, each type of transhipment has a different service time distribution function. Distribution functions for the following seven categories of transhipment were estimated:
- direct transhipment from train to train;
- transhipment from train to storage and transhipment from storage to train;
- transhipment from train to transport system and transhipment from transport system to train (new hub terminal models only);
- transhipment from storage to transport system (new hub terminal models only);
- transhipment from storage to edge of storage (road-rail terminal models only);
- transhipment from train to edge of storage and from edge of storage to train (road-rail models only);
- transport from one crane section to another crane section (road-rail models only; in the new hub terminal models workstation 2 carries out this function).

The sequence of crane and trolley activities that need to be carried out in order to complete one transhipment is defined as a crane cycle. Crane cycles for the different types of transhipment could not be observed and measured because no new hub terminal is operational and hub exchange operations at road-rail terminals are integrated with road-rail transhipment. However, kinematics data for cranes in combination with layout data were available from the literature and could be obtained through the questionnaires that were sent out to network and node operators and rail experts. This made it possible to simulate crane cycles.

5.4.1.1 A tool for simulating crane cycles
In a spreadsheet a tool was developed that simulates crane cycles. A crane cycle consists of the following movements:
- Driving crane to right row of load units (L_t).
- Driving trolley to right lane of train/transport system/buffer (W_t).
- Adjusting spreader to size of load unit (A).
- (Un)folding grip arms (for swap body or trailer) (U).
- Letting down spreader (empty) (LD_e).

- Positioning and attaching load unit (P_1).
- Hoisting spreader (full) (H_f).
- Driving trolley to right train/transport system/buffer (W_2).
- Driving crane to right row of load units (L_2).
- Turning container to get doors on the right side (T).
- Letting down spreader (full) (LD_f).
- Positioning and detaching load unit (P_2).
- Hoisting spreader (empty) (H_e).

End of cycle.

The crane cycle time S_t is determined by adding up the times taken for each movement, except for movements that can be carried out in parallel. These movements are: crane driving, trolley driving, adjustment of the spreader, turning containers and (un)folding grip arms. In this case only the maximum time of any of the movements carried out in parallel is included in the addition. Thus,

$$S_t = Max\{L_1;W_1;A;U\} + LD\_e + P_1 + H\_f + Max\{L_2;W_2;T\} + LD\_f + P_2 + H\_e \quad (1a)$$

It is assumed that A, U and T take less time than L_1, W_1, L_2 and W_2, and are therefore not considered further in the crane cycle simulation tool. Thus, in the tool the cycle time is determined by the following:

$$S_t = Max\{L_1;W_1\} + LD\_e + P_1 + H\_f + Max\{L_2;W_2\} + LD\_f + P_2 + H\_e \quad (1b)$$

In the tool L_1, W_1, L_2, W_2, LD_e, H_f, LD_f and H_e are distance- (d) dependent time values in any of the following three directions:
- longitudinal (x) by crane driving;
- latitudinal (y) by trolley driving, and
- vertical (z) by hoisting/letting down.

P_1 and P_2 are constants.

The time for each distance-dependent movement depends on the parameters for acceleration (a), full speed (s), deceleration (a) and distance (d). This data was obtained in the data collection as well as the constant time values for P_1 and P_2. Travelling a certain distance (d) requires a time ($T(d)$) that can be calculated as in Hee (1988):

$$T(d) = \begin{cases} 2\sqrt{\dfrac{d}{a}}, & d \leq \dfrac{s^2}{a}, \\ \dfrac{d}{s} + \dfrac{s}{a}, & \text{otherwise} \end{cases} \quad (2)$$

This formula is applied in the tool to calculate L_1, W_1, L_2, W_2, LD_e, H_f, LD_f and H_e.

The tool also determines d_x and d_y, while d_z is determined outside the tool and used as an input parameter. d_x, d_y and d_z depend on the crane handling strategy applied. A crane handling strategy is defined as a set of rules applied to determine the next load unit to be served. The crane handling strategy is on one side modelled as priority rules and on the other side incorporated as assumptions about the range of crane movements in the crane service time. Priority rules were discussed in section 5.4; the assumptions on ranges of crane movements are discussed in this section. In the next subsections the way in which d_x, d_y and d_z were determined is explained. The tool functions independently of the load order. The effect of load order is incorporated in the distribution of load units over the different types of transhipment.

The x-coordinate of the crane *initial* position (position in which the crane ends after the previous job) is any value (in metres) between zero and the length of the crane section (see bottom part of Figure 5–1). Cranes covers the complete with of the facility and each crane serves a particular longitudinal section. The length of this section is determined as the length a train or the length of the facility divided by the number of cranes.

In the tool, a random number generator generates the value of this initial position. The x-coordinate of the crane *pick-up* position (at track, storage lane or transport lane) is also any value between zero and the length of the crane section, while the x-coordinate of the crane *drop-off* position is assumed to be within a certain range from the *pick-up* position. Such a range could be, for instance, 30 metres left or right of the *pick-up* position. The tool draws a random number for *pick-up* and *drop-off* positions. Four examples of *pick-up* positions (x_1, x_2, x_3 and x_4) and ranges for *drop-off* positions for the x-coordinates are illustrated in Figure 5–1. The y-coordinates are not yet specified. In the tool, a random number generator generates these x-coordinate *pick-up* and *drop-off* positions. The range for the *drop-off* position can be specified in the tool. The tool corrects for *drop-off* positions that fall outside the borders of a crane section. Values for x-coordinates that fall outside the crane section are corrected to a value that equals the x-coordinate of the left or right border of the crane section. This cut-off range applies to examples x_1 and x_4 in Figure 5–1.

The tool determines the longitudinal crane driving distances to respectively pick up ($d_{x(L1)}$) and drop off ($d_{x(L2)}$) a load unit as follows. If the initial position of the crane is denoted by x_i and its pick-up position by x_p then:

$$d_{x(L1)} = | x_i - x_p | \tag{3}$$

and, then:

$$d_{x(L2)} = | x_p - x_d | \tag{4}$$

Next, $d_{x(L1)}$ and $d_{x(L2)}$ are inserted into the formula (2) in order to calculate L_1 and L_2.

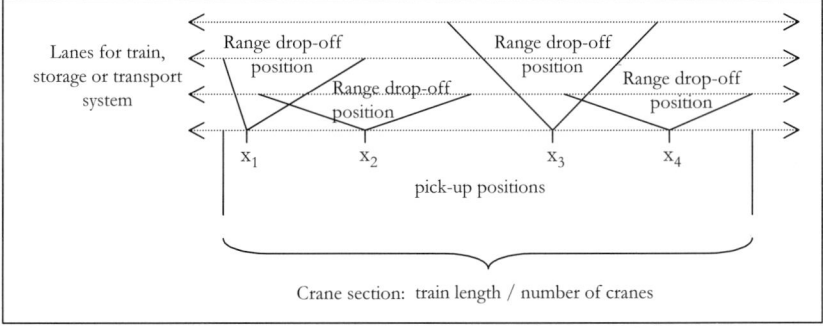

Figure 5–1: Four examples of initial x-coordinates (x_1, x_2, x_3 and x_4) and the search range of the tool for a drop-off position

The y-coordinate of the *initial, pick-up or drop-off* trolley position is the value for the centre of any lane (track, storage, transport) at the terminal. The distance between these centres is on average 5 metres. The centre of the first lane is determined at 0 metres and the centres of the other lanes at multiples of 5 metres. Figure 5–2 shows a cross-section of a sample terminal layout in which the *y*-coordinates are indicated. The *initial*, *pick-up* and *drop-off* trolley positions depend on the type of transhipment (direct, via storage, etc). So, in the tool for each type of transhipment the search range for the random number generator to select lanes for *initial*, *pick-up* and *drop-off* positions is specified.

The tool determines the latitudinal trolley driving distances to respectively pick up $(d_{y(W1)})$ and drop off $(d_{y(W2)})$ a load unit as follows. If the initial position of the trolley is denoted by y_i and its drop-off position by y_d, then:

$$d_{y(W1)} = |y_i - y_p| \tag{5}$$

and, then:

$$d_{y(W2)} = |y_p - y_d| \tag{6}$$

Next, $d_{y(W1)}$ and $d_{y(W2)}$ are inserted into the formula (2) in order to calculate W_1 and W_2.

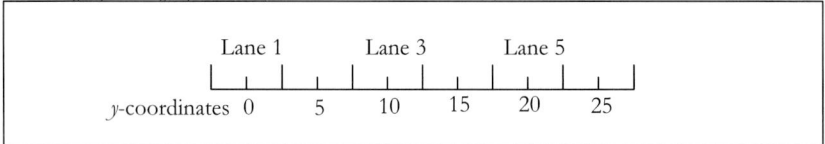

Figure 5–2: *Y*-coordinates specifying trolley pick-up and drop-off position

Contrary to the *x*- and *y*-coordinates, the tool does not generate *z*-coordinates. Instead, two parameters for d_z must be specified and are used as input for the simulation. One parameter is for letting down/hoisting an empty spreader $(d_{z(E)})$, the other for letting down/hoisting a full spreader $(d_{z(F)})$. These values, however, may vary for different jobs.

A typical *z*-coordinate is the safety zone, which is the initial position of the spreader. The safety zone is determined at 4.5 metres above ground level for movements within the area with track and transport system lanes. For movements between the area with track and/or transport system lanes and the storage area, and within the storage area, the safety zone is 5.5 metres, allowing containers to be stacked in two stories[20]. This implies that the bottom of every load unit and the empty spreader have to be hoisted to 4.5 metres or 5.5 metres respectively before any crane or trolley movement can be carried out. Other typical *z*-coordinates, such as ground level, top of load unit, top of rail wagon or transport system are specified in Figure 5–3. Using these z-coordinates values for $(d_{z(E)})$ and $(d_{z(F)})$ for different jobs were determined. For jobs that are moved between trains or between a train and the transport system the average hoisting distance $(d_{z(E)})$ is 1.75 metres[21], and for $(d_{z(F)})$ 3.5 metres[22]. For jobs that are moved between train or transport system and storage the average hoisting distance $(d_{z(E)})$ is 1.75 metres[23], and for $(d_{z(F)})$ 4.25 metres[24].

---

[20] Swap bodies cannot be stacked up.

[21] The safety zone is 4.5 metres. 1 metre (maximum hoisting distance) plus 0.5 metres (minimum hoisting distance) divided by 2 is 1.75 metres.

[22] The safety zone is 4.5 metres. The hoisting distance is always 3.5 metres.

[23] The safety zone is 5.5 metres. 3 metres (maximum hoisting distance empty) plus 0.5 metres (minimum hoisting distance) divided by 2 is 1.75 metres.

[24] The safety zone is 5.5 metres. 5.5 metres (maximum hoisting distance) plus 3 metres (minimum hoisting distance) divided by 2 is 4.25 metres.

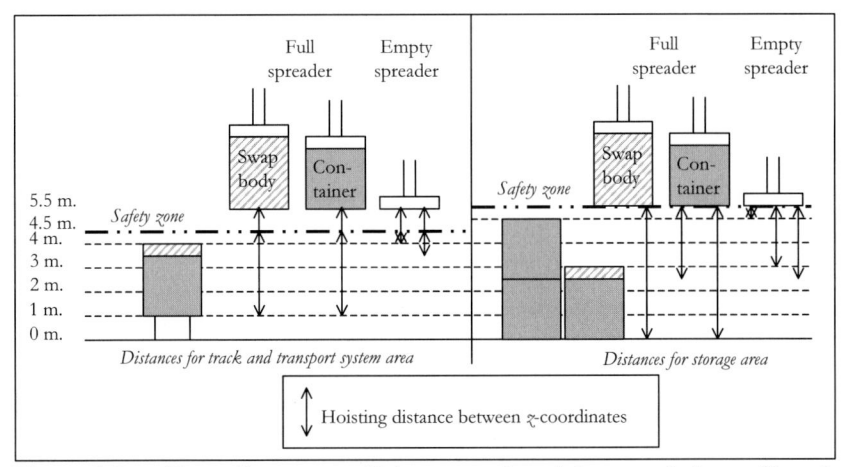

Figure 5–3: Z-coordinates specifying spreader pick-up and drop-off positions

For jobs that are moved within the storage area the average hoisting distance ($d_{z(E)}$) is 1.75 metres[25], and for ($d_{z(F)}$) 4.25 metres[26]. Next, these parameters were inserted into formula (2) in order to calculate LD_e, H_f, LD_f and H_e for various jobs.

Table 5–3: Kinematics data new hub terminal (in seconds)

Crane cycle component	a (m/s²)	s (m/s)	Crane cycle component	Constant
Crane driving	0.54	3	Positioning and attaching/detaching load	8
Trolley driving	0.54	3	Adjustment of spreader	15
Hoisting/letting down empty	1	1.5	(Un)folding grip arms	10
Hoisting/letting down full	1	0.75	Turning container 180°	30

Source: Meyer (1998, p. 110)

5.4.1.2 Application of the simulation tool to generate crane service times

To generate crane service times for new hub terminals kinematics parameters were specified with the data presented in Table 5–3. For crane services for road-rail terminals kinematics parameters were specified with the data presented in Table 5–4. Variables indicating the dimensions of the terminal were based on the layouts depicted in Figure 5–4 and Figure 5–5 respectively. These layouts were chosen, because, firstly, the road-rail terminal represents very common dimensions in intermodal practice. Secondly, using dimensions of the new hub-terminal made it easier to validate the synchronised new hub model. However, a layout may have serious impacts on the crane cycles, and the chosen layouts may not be the most optimal. Whether different layouts, especially with respect to the new hub-terminal, affects significantly the crane cycle distribution functions may be subject to further studies. Detailed specifications are provided in Appendix A. The average distance between the centre of tracks and

---

[25] The safety zone is 5.5 metres. 3 metres (maximum hoisting distance) plus 0.5 metres (minimum hoisting distance) divided by 2 is 1.75 metres.

[26] The safety zone is 5.5 metres. 5.5 metres (maximum hoisting distance) plus 3 metres (minimum hoisting distance) divided by 2 is 4.25 metres.

lanes was specified at 5 metres and the longitudinal length of the terminal at 600 metres (a common train length – cf Chapter 3).

Table 5–4: Kinematics data rail-mounted gantry crane rail-road terminal (in seconds)

Crane cycle component	a (m/s²)	s (m/s)	Constant
Crane driving	0.4	1.8	
Trolley driving	0.4	1.8	
Hoisting/letting down empty	0.3	0.67	
Hoisting/letting down full	0.3	0.33	
Positioning and attaching/detaching load			8

Source: Rotter (2003), Terminet (2000), Meyer (1998), Wesseling (2003), SIMET (1994b)

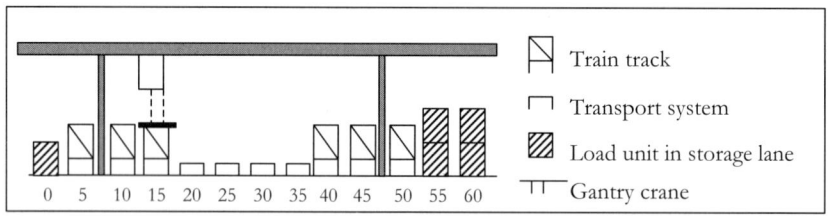

Figure 5–4: Schematic cross-section layout new hub terminal (distance in meters)

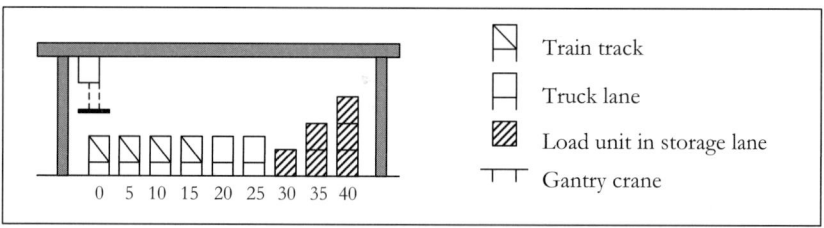

Figure 5–5: Schematic cross-section layout road-rail terminal (distance in meters)

The simulation tool was used to generate 100 cycle times for each type of transhipment for each type of terminal (see Appendix B for a justification) and for a different number of cranes. Since the number of cranes influences the *x*-coordinate, for each number of cranes separate service times had to be generated. Variables related to the cross-directional crane distances had to be adjusted per type of transhipment, because trolley travelling distances vary according to type of transhipment. For the road-rail terminal the tool was validated for a terminal with two cranes; for the new hub terminal it was validated for a terminal with ten cranes. Data on terminal dimensions and crane kinematics was collected from literature and questionnaires. Validation included the following:

1. A comparison of the average of 100 generated $d_{x(L1)}$, $d_{x(L2)}$, $d_{y(W1)}$ and $d_{y(W2)}$ values with the hand-estimated account of expected average values. This was done for each type of job and for both types of terminal.
2. A comparison of the average of 100 generated crane cycle times with cycle times obtained in the data collection.

For more details about the validation, see Appendix C.

Generated maximum, mean and minimum crane cycle times for various types of transhipment are provided in Table 5–5 for the new hub terminal, and in Table 5–6 for the road-rail hub terminal. The crane cycles are bounded due to minimum and maximum crane and trolley travel distances. Stochastic disturbances are not included. The general tendency is that the cycle times reduce with an increasing number of cranes as a consequence of shorter crane driving distances, but that the cycle times converge to one average value. The exception to this tendency is road-rail terminal transport transhipment, because this involves a different type of transhipment. It was expected that crane cycle times would vary significantly for different types of transhipment due to different trolley travel distances. As Table 5–5 and Table 5–6 indicate, this is the case for the road-rail terminal cycle times, but it does not really apply to new hub terminal cycle times.

Table 5–5: Maximum, mean and minimum crane cycle times generated by the tool for various types of transhipment for new hub terminals with different numbers of cranes (in seconds)

Type of transhipment		Number of cranes			
		2	4	6	10
Direct transhipment from train to train	Max	149	93	82	74
	Mean	86	68	64	61
	Min	53	48	47	46
Transhipment from train to storage and from storage to train	Max	139	97	83	76
	Mean	85	70	66	61
	Min	52	47	49	47
Transhipment from train to transport system and from transport system to train	Max	138	96	80	68
	Mean	82	67	62	59
	Min	47	48	49	47
Transhipment from storage to transport system	Max	138	98	81	74
	Mean	85	71	67	64
	Min	54	52	52	52

5.4.1.3 Estimation of crane service time probability distributions

ARENA's Input Analyser (see for example Kelton et al., 1998, p. 132-139) was used to fit a theoretical probability distribution for each 100 generated service times per type of transhipment and number of cranes. A crane cycle is bounded due to minimum and maximum crane and trolley travel distances. As a consequence only bounded Beta and Triangular distributions could be fitted and tested for their goodness-of-fit. The Input Analyser calculates the mean square error value and carries out two standard statistical hypothesis tests: the Chi Square test and the Kolmogorov-Smirnov test. The Input Analyser calculates the corresponding p-value, which is an indication of goodness-of-fit. Conventionally (and arbitrarily) a p-value of 0.05 is generally regarded as a fair degree of confidence for the theoretical distribution to represent the data (Kelton et al., 1998). The distribution with the highest p-value, equal to or greater than 0.05, was selected. In the event that neither Beta nor Triangular distribution met this p-value, an empirical distribution was selected.

Table 5–6: Maximum, mean and minimum crane cycle times generated by the tool for various types of transhipment for road-rail hub terminals with different numbers of cranes (in seconds)

Type of transhipment		Number of cranes		
		2	3	4
Direct transhipment from train to train	Max	222	180	146
	Mean	122	105	99
	Min	78	69	71
Transhipment from train to storage and from storage to trains	Max	219	187	158
	Mean	134	117	112
	Min	74	72	78
Transhipment from train to edge of storage and from edge of storage to train	Max	237	172	143
	Mean	207	158	132
	Min	72	74	70
Transhipment from storage to edge of the storage	Max	227	168	147
	Mean	201	159	130
	Min	75	76	78

The crane service time distributions determined for the new hub terminal models are presented in Table 5–7 and the road-rail models in Table 5–8. For the purposes of clarity the empirical distribution for road-rail cranes is presented in a separate table (Table 5–9).

Table 5–7: Estimated service time distributions for cycle times at new hub terminal models (in seconds)

Number of cranes	Transhipment from train to train	Transhipment from train to storage or from storage to train	Transhipment from train to transport system or from transport system to train	Transhipment from storage to transport system
2	52.5+97* BETA(1.07, 2.04)	TRIA (51.5, 64.2, 140)	TRIA (46.5, 60, 139)	TRIA (53.5, 64, 139)
4	47.5+46* BETA(1.92, 2.46)	47.5+46* BETA(1.92, 2.46)	47.5+49* BETA(1.79, 2.8)	47.5+43* BETA(1.81, 2.7)
6	46.5+36* BETA(2.9, 3.13)	48.5+35* BETA(2.77, 2.65)	48.5+32* BETA(1.64, 2.35)	TRIA (51.5, 68.8, 81.5)
10	45.5+29* BETA(2.04, 1.75)	TRIA (46.5, 63, 76.5)	46.5+22* BETA(2.26, 1.8)	TRIA (51.5, 67.7, 74.5)

The parameters of the Beta, Triangular and empirical distributions should be read as follows. The standard Beta distribution is bounded between 0 and 1, but can be transformed to other values. The values 52.5 and 97 in 52.5+97*BETA(1.07, 2.04) determine the location of the distribution. The value 52.5 indicates the lower bound of the distribution. The values 1.07 (α) and 2.04 (β) determine the shape of the distribution.

$\alpha > 1$ and $\beta > 1$ lead to asymmetric variants of a Normal distribution. When $\alpha > \beta$, the distribution is weighted to the left side; when $\beta > \alpha$, it is weighted to the right side.

The values in TRIA (51.5, 64.2, 140) indicate, from left to right, the minimum value, the most likely value and the maximum value. The distribution has a triangular shape. The values in the empirical distributions in Table 5–9, presented in two columns, read as a histogram. The left column indicates probability, the right column the borders of the intervals with cycle times.

Table 5–8: Estimated service time distribution functions for cycle times at road-rail model (in seconds)

Number of cranes	Type of transhipment			
	Transhipment from train to train	Transhipment from train to storage or from storage to train	Transhipment from train to edge of storage and from edge of storage to train	Transhipment from storage to edge of storage
2	67+156* BETA(1.14, 2.02)	TRIA (78, 102, 236)	See Table 1 9	101+249* BETA(1.9, 2.48)
3	TRIA (65.5, 86.5, 162)	TRIA (72, 88.5, 182)	See Table 1 9	See Table 1 9
4	TRIA (64.5, 78, 156)	TRIA (73.5, 93.5, 154)	See Table 1 9	See Table 1 9

It is possible to deduce from Table 5–7 and Table 5–8 that the distributions for a terminal with 4 cranes or fewer are weighted to the right side. This implies a longer curve on the right side, due to longer crane cycles (greater maximum) as a result of larger crane sections. When the number of cranes is increased, the maximum value decreases, resulting in a switch in weighting to the left side. Hence, the more cranes, the shorter the crane cycles and the faster the terminals become.

Table 5–9: Overview of empirical continuous distributions for road-rail cranes (in seconds)

Transhipment from train to edge of storage and from edge of storage to train			Transhipment from storage to edge of the storage	
2 cranes	3 cranes	4 cranes	3 cranes	4 cranes
0.000, 79.999,	0.000, 80.999,	0.000, 74.999,	0.000, 84.999,	0.000, 81.999,
0.070, 110.599,	0.090, 100.399,	0.080, 95.399,	0.050, 98.999,	0.100, 96.899,
0.160, 141.199,	0.220, 119.799,	0.160, 115.799,	0.150, 12.999,	0.220, 111.799,
0.300, 171.800,	0.380, 139.200,	0.270, 136.200,	0.310, 127.000,	0.400, 126.700,
0.450, 202.400,	0.530, 158.600,	0.510, 156.600,	0.620, 141.000,	0.560, 141.600,
0.750, 233.000,	0.760, 178.000,	0.710, 177.000,	0.760, 155.000,	0.790, 156.500,
0.850, 263.600,	0.900, 197.400,	0.760, 197.400,	0.850, 169.000,	0.830, 171.400,
0.910, 294.200,	0.930, 216.800,	0.820, 217.800,	0.910, 183.000,	0.900, 186.300,
0.920, 324.801,	0.960, 236.201,	0.900, 238.201,	0.970, 197.001,	0.940, 201.201,
0.970, 355.401,	0.990, 255.601,	0.960, 258.601,	0.980, 211.001,	0.970, 216.101,
0.970, 386.001	0.990, 275.001	0.960, 279.001	0.980, 225.001	0.970, 231.001

5.4.1.4 Estimation of transport service time distributions in terminal models

In the new hub terminal model a separate workstation 2 represents the transport system; in the road-rail model the cranes carry out this longitudinal transport operation between crane sections.

In the new hub terminal model each transport unit (automated roller pallet) is considered a server. The service time of a roller pallet was determined as a constant value of 2.5 minutes. This value was generated in the simulation study by Meyer (1998, p.

131) for a hub terminal with 10 cranes and 45 roller pallets as the average cycle time of a roller pallet (full and empty transport and waiting time).

In the road-rail model, the transport time by a crane is also determined as a constant. There is one constant per capacity variant. The constants were determined on the basis of the following:
- the average transport cycle time as indicated in Table 5–10, and ;
- the probability that a load unit is transhipped one, two or three crane sections along the transport system from its pick-up position.

The crane cycle time simulation tool was used to generate the transport cycle times per crane section in Table 5–10. Transport cycle time varies with the number of cranes, because the number of cranes determines the size of the crane section and therefore the transport distance per crane. In the case of two cranes transport time is zero, because transhipment to the neighbouring crane section is modelled as one "transhipment from train to edge of storage" and one "transhipment from edge of storage to train". In this situation the constant is also zero. There is no separate transport task undertaken by a crane.

Table 5–10: Maximum, mean and minimum cycle times for a road-rail crane to transport a load unit one crane section ahead (in seconds)

	Number of cranes		
	2	3	4
Maximum	0	284	228
Mean	0	230	187
Minimum	0	176	147

When a load unit has to transfer two crane sections, the total transport time is twice the transport cycle time mentioned.

However, in the case of three or four cranes, probability with respect to transport distance plays a role. The transport time of a load unit that has to be transported to another crane section depends on its pick-up and drop-off position. This is illustrated in Figure 5–6 for a situation with four crane sections and a load unit in crane section 2. There are three possible directions in which to transport the load unit. Only the movement to the fourth crane section involves crane transportation. The other movements can be achieved by "transhipment from train to edge of storage" and "transhipment from edge of storage to train".

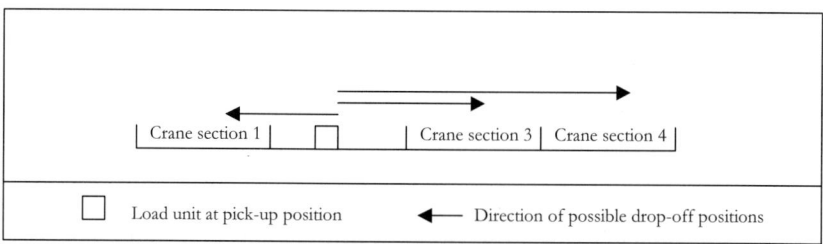

Figure 5–6: The transport time of a load unit that has to be transported to another crane section depends on its pick-up and drop-off position

In the road-rail model the pick-up positions of a load unit are not specified. Therefore the constant should reflect the average expected transport time of a random load unit following the route with transport. It is assumed that load units have an equal probability of having a pick-up position in any of the crane sections and a drop-off position in any of the crane sections. By calculating all possible situations the probability of each situation can be determined. In the case of three cranes, in four situations a load unit must be transhipped to a neighbouring crane section (no transport system) and in two situations a load unit has to be transhipped from one of the outer crane sections to the other outer section. In the case of four cranes, in six situations a load unit must be transhipped to a neighbouring crane section (no transport system), in four situations a load unit must be transported one crane section and in two situations a load unit has to be transported two crane sections (from one of the outer crane sections to the other outer section).

Next, the probability (P) can be determined. Table 5–11 summarises the procedure for determining the constant for the situation with two, three and four cranes. In the case of three cranes there are six possible situations. There is a probability of 4/6 that a load unit does not have to be transported, and a probability of 2/6 that it is transported one crane section. Multiplying the probabilities with the average crane transport time from Table 5–10 and adding them up gives the average expected transport time. The constants are zero seconds for a terminal with two cranes, 77 seconds for three cranes and 125 seconds for four cranes.

Table 5–11: Determination of constant value for transport function (in seconds) for road-rail terminal models

Number of cranes	2	3	4
Number of crane sections to cross: number of times the situation may occur	0: 2 occasions	0: 4 occasions 1: 2 occasions	0: 6 occasions 1: 4 occasions 2: 2 occasions
Sum of each probability (for occasions) multiplied by average transport time is average expected transport time (= constant)	No transport by crane	$P = 4/6 * 0$ (no transport) $+P = 2/6 * 230$ (mean transport time see Table 5–10)	$P = 0.5 * 0 +P = 1/3 * 187$ (mean transport time see Table 5–10) $+P = 1/6 * 374$ (twice mean transport time see note Table 5–10)
Constant (seconds)	0	77	125

5.4.2 Estimation of service time distributions for servers in hump shunting models

For the hump shunting model two service time distribution functions were estimated, one for servers at workstation 1 (sorting) and one for servers at workstation 2 (assembly). As each workstation represents a combination of activities, their service times are composed of the summation of the durations of these activities. The durations of the separate activities were obtained through questionnaires and interviews. For each activity the minimum, the most likely and the maximum duration were requested. The data obtained (see Appendix D for an overview) was not very consistent. As a consequence the duration of individual activities for workstation 1 (in seconds/rail wagon) and workstation 2 (in minutes/train) had to be estimated. The resulting time values of these estimations are presented in Table 5–12 and Table 5–13. Next, the estimates for minimum, most likely and maximum values for the separate activities were summed up into an estimate for the service time for each workstation (see row "Total" in Table 5–12 and Table 5–13.) The distribution function for workstation 1 is estimated as Triangular [50, 74, 146] (parameters in seconds) and for workstation 2 as Triangular [30.5, 49, 72] (parameters in minutes).

Table 5–12: Estimated duration of various activities related to workstation 1 at a hump shunting yard

Sorting-related activities	Time* (seconds/rail wagon)		
	Minimum	Most likely	Maximum
Uncouple network locomotive	4	5	6
Uncoupling rail wagons and releasing air from brake air reservoirs	20	30	60
Coupling switch locomotive to train and pushing train to shunting hill	6	13	20
Pushing one wagon over the hump	10	14	30
Return trip of switch locomotive to next train to be shunted	10	12	30
Total	50	74	146

* Operators were asked to state the duration of sorting-related activities per rail wagon or for a train with 30 wagons (600 metres), which is a common length in intermodal operations. The duration of activities related to a complete train have been translated into a duration per rail wagon.
Source: Wesseling (2003), Terminet (2000), Fritsch (2003), Bruins (2003)

A few remarks. Firstly, some of the activities involve only labour and others labour and a locomotive. To guarantee smooth operation the labour and equipment input of the various activities should be finely tuned. Based on the working speed of the locomotives we were able to determine how much labour was required to carry out labour activities to keep up with the locomotive. The amount of labour required is provided in Appendix K. Secondly, with respect to sorting strategy it is assumed that one track is allocated to one crane. This strategy does not require any assembly of wagon groups before departure and is commonly applied. Other strategies exist, but are more complex (see for example Kraft, 2002). Thirdly, the activity of pushing automated wagons at the combined sorting/departure yard is not included in the parameters because this activity is automated and is carried out in parallel with other activities.

Table 5–13: Estimated duration of various activities related to workstation 2 at a hump shunting yard

Activities related to assembly	Time* (minutes/train)		
	Minimum	Most likely	Maximum
Correcting false runners using the yard engine	0.5	1	2
Coupling rail wagons**	10	20	30
Coupling the network locomotive to the departing train	5	8	10
Brake test and inspection	15	20	30
Total	30.5	49	72

* Operators were asked to state the duration of assembly-related activities for a train with 30 wagons (600 metres), which is a common length in intermodal operations, or per rail wagon. The duration of activities related to one rail wagon have been translated into a duration for a train of 30 rail wagons.
** For wagon groups: 4, 8 and 12 minutes respectively.
Source: Fritsch (2003), Bontekoning & Trip (2004) and Bruins (2003)

5.4.3 Estimation of service time distributions for servers in flat shunting models

For the flat shunting model two service time distribution functions were estimated, one for servers at workstation 1 (sorting) and one for servers at workstation 2 (assembly). Data obtained on sorting-related activities were not as detailed as for hump shunting. However, with the data collected the behaviour of a shunting locomotive in the sorting process could be simulated. The data obtained consists of yard layout and distances, speed of a shunting locomotive and the duration of sorting-related activities such as (un)coupling wagons (see Table 5–14). Using this data, an imaginary sorting scenario was simulated, and for each wagon group the duration of the sorting process was calculated. The design of the simulation is discussed in detail in Appendix E. The simulation resulted in 39 service time observations. Just as for the generated crane service times ARENA's Input Analyser was used to analyse the data set and to select the best-fitting distribution functions (see previous subsection 5.4.1.3 for more information on this procedure). The service time distribution is estimated as Triangular [7, 9.22, 15.9] – (parameters in minutes per wagon).

Table 5–14: Duration of sorting-related activities at flat shunting yards

Activity	Value
Coupling shunting locomotive (incl. filling air tubes)	12 min
(Un)coupling wagon group	2 min
Speed of locomotive	125m/min.

Source: Biggler (2003), Wesseling (2003)

The service time for servers at workstation 2 is composed of the duration of a combination of assembly-related activities. Data on these activities is limited to the minimum, most likely and maximum duration of each activity. The service times of individual activities (in minutes/train) for workstation 2 are presented in Table 5–15. Due to the limited data the distribution function is estimated as Triangular [44, 54, 68] – (parameters in minutes per train).

Table 5–15: Duration of activities related to workstation 2

Activities included in Assembly module	Time (minutes/train)		
	Minimum	Most likely	Maximum
Coupling the network locomotive to the departing train	5	8	10
Assembly of 2 groups to one train	24	26	28
Brake test	15	20	30
Total	**44**	**54**	**68**

Source: Biggler (2003), Wesseling (2003), Bontekoning & Trip (2004), Fritsch (2003)

5.4.4 Estimation of service time distribution function for shunting from side yard to exchange facility

In Section 4.4 it was discussed that in some situations trains cannot enter the exchange facility directly, with the consequence that the train must be shunted between side yard and exchange facility. Also when the facility is not electrified shunting between side yard and exchange facility is needed. It is assumed that all facilities are electrified. Various shunting yards have electrified arrival tracks (e.g. Herne) and electrification with moveable catenaries of new (road-rail) terminals is proposed, such that all trains can directly enter the facility when tracks are not occupied. Travel time

from the moment a train leaves the main line to full stop at the facility was accounted as network time. Hence, no time is accounted to trains entering the facility directly.
In analogy, the time it takes to travel from side yard to full stop at the side-yard was also accounted as network time and determined at 0 minutes. 0 minutes was applied for all facilities, due to similar distances from yard and facility distances and train speed, the service time is assumed to be more or less the same duration for all facilities.

Afterwards reflecting on these assumptions, I realised that it would have been better to apply a stochastic shunting time of between 3 to 6 minutes. These times are based on track lengths of 1000 and 2000 meters respectively and a driving speed of 20 km/hour. So the consequence, with respect to the simulation results is that the train service and sojourn times are underestimated with 3 to 6 minutes.

5.5 A cost model

Since a simulation model does not include a cost evaluation module, a separate cost model was constructed in a spreadsheet. The cost model is a tool that can be used to easily calculate costs per cost category, total annual costs and costs per load unit for the four hub exchange facilities for greenfield sites. Hence, costs calculations imply a total costs approach, implying that both capital (depreciation and interest) and operational costs are included.
Cost categories included in the model are defined below. In addition, a classification of cost items per category included in the model is provided.
The effects of different amounts of investment, cost parameters and volume levels on capital and operational costs and cost per load unit can be studied using the cost model. However, in this study about the performance comparison of new hub terminals with the three other hub exchange facilities, the costs indicator "costs per load unit" is the most relevant. A comparison of "costs per load unit" for greenfield sites was chosen, because the study involves a general comparison of four hub exchange facilities. Since the comparison is not related to any specific hub-node with specific characteristics, facilities with different capacity levels are compared for various demand volumes. This approach helps to avoid comparing apples with pears.

I used a simple valuation technique: average costs. The main purpose of the cost model is to provide a transparent comparison of the costs of the four facilities and several capacity levels of each facility. Future evaluation techniques for costs and benefits, such as the basic discounted cash flow models net capital value and internal rate of return (see for example Hirsch, 1994), were not applied for two reasons.
Firstly, the objective of this study is a general performance comparison between four facilities. The simulation and cost models are used for a what-if analysis, since volumes and capacity levels of the various facilities are variable. The purpose of my investigation is to obtain insight into the facility with the best costs-quality ratio from the perspective of the intermodal hub-and-spoke network. The investor's perspective on the investment with the greatest benefits and lowest risks is not considered. The investor's perspective would be relevant when considering alternative facilities for a specific hub node. The discounted cash flow technique assumes virtual certainty about all parameters and variables. This is not the case for the general comparison made between facilities in this thesis, but would be for a concrete case. Indispensable data for a discounted cash flow technique are, among others, location, realistic vol-

ume forecasts, projected selling price, rest value equipment, the node operator's capital structure and finance options, actual and expected interest and inflation rates.

Secondly, the use of basic discounted cash flow models in this thesis would give the impression that calculated costs are more accurate, while actually this introduces more uncertainty. Most of the abovementioned required data are not known. Missing data could be estimated, but will not lead to better costs calculations.

In conclusion, due to the generality of the comparison between facilities essential data for the application of discounted cash flow techniques are lacking. The average costs technique applied suits the purpose of the investigation and the valuation technique is very transparent and easy to understand.

Cost categories and the classification of cost items per category are defined as follows:

Capital costs

Depreciation costs: amount of investment divided by lifetime. Classification of cost items for which depreciation costs are calculated:
- Infrastructure such as rail tracks, storage areas and surfaces (pavement);
- Buildings;
- Equipment: cranes, shunting locomotives, terminal transport system;
- Software terminal operational control system;

Interest costs: interest rate multiplied by (total amount of investment divided by 2). Classification of cost items for which interest costs are calculated:
- Infrastructure such as rail tracks, storage areas, land, surfaces (pavement);
- Buildings;
- Equipment: cranes, locomotives, terminal transport system;
- Land: surface of terminal or shunting yard;
- Software terminal operational control system.

Operational costs

Labour costs: salaries, social security, pensions and bonuses for evening and night work. Classification of cost items for which personnel costs are calculated:
- Terminal/shunting yard workers;
- Overhead (control, management, administration);
- Replacement personnel (holidays and illness).

Consumption costs: fuel and electricity. Classification of cost items for which consumption costs are calculated:
- Diesel for shunting locomotives;
- Electricity for cranes and trains in terminal.

Maintenance costs: repair and ongoing maintenance of terminal and shunting yard infrastructure and equipment. Classification of cost items:
- Equipment;
- Infrastructure;
- Buildings;
- Software terminal operational control system.

Other operating costs: costs that are not provided for in the other categories such as insurance, administrative and organisational costs such as marketing, public relations, legal advice/consulting, software, telephone, taxes, etc.

In order for the model to calculate the total annual costs and the cost price per load unit, unit prices per cost item, number units and annual exchange volume need to be specified. Specification of unit prices is difficult. Data of sufficient detail in the literature is scarce and questions in the questionnaires sent to network and node operators often remained unanswered. The reasons for this are twofold. Firstly, operators claimed to have difficulties extracting unit costs from balance sheets. Secondly, terminal and shunting yard operators are reluctant to provide sensitive data to researchers. For most costs items data could be obtained, but seldom be compared with other data sources. Data was obtained from Terminet (2000), Impulse (1999), Black et al. (2003), Gruppo Clas (2002), ZEW et al. (2000), European Commission (1997) and from questionnaires (Rotter, 2003; Biggler, 2003; Fritsch, 2003; Wesseling, 2003). An overview of the specification of unit prices is provided in Appendix F.

Specification of the number of equipment and infrastructure units is easy and follows from the case analysed with the simulation models. Annual volume, defined as the number of load units multiplied by the number of working days multiplied by 52 weeks, can also be derived from the inputs of the simulation model.

All costs calculated in the model are costs directly related to the exchange facilities and their operations. However, there may be certain demand, arrival schedules and delays that affect the rail haul operations to such an extent that rail haul costs are affected, too. A thorough analysis of rail haul costs is beyond the scope of this thesis. The thesis focuses on node operations and costs, but some insight into the potential effects on rail haul costs is required. I therefore carried out some rough estimations of the impacts on rail haul costs.

Costs related to network locomotives, network locomotive drivers and rail wagons are considered as rail haul costs. Exchange operations may affect costs related to network locomotives (capital costs) and driver costs. After all, they stay attached to the train during operations (new hub terminals) or are uncoupled and become (theoretically) available for other tasks (other facilities). Based on existing practice (uncoupling network locomotives) I am not convinced that keeping the locomotive attached to the train leads to significant changes in rail haul costs. I put forward two arguments. First, the average productivity of a network locomotive is rather low, while train sojourn times at new hub terminals are relatively short. Until a certain train sojourn time, we may question whether the network locomotive productivity calculated is really affected. In rail haul costs calculations the average annual distance covered by the network locomotive is assumed to be 150,000km (600km per day over 250 operating days) (Gruppo Clas, 2002, p. 48). If we assume an average speed of 60km per hour, it implies that the locomotive is only busy 10 hours a day. In around one quarter of the experiments train sojourn times remain under 30 minutes and in around 50% of the experiments they are under 60 minutes. In just under 20% of the experiments, all experiments with two cranes, train sojourn times exceed two hours. But these cases are not considered as favourable options. Hence, compared to the large number of non-productive hours, the time locomotives have to wait is rather limited.

Second, as the productivity of network locomotives is low, I also expect locomotive driver productivity to be low. As a consequence, I think that waiting time of locomotive drivers at the new hub terminal is limited compared to the non-productive hours, and therefore does not seriously affect rail haul costs.

Lest I underestimate rail haul costs effects, it would be interesting to know to what extent rail haul costs may be affected. Locomotive waiting costs would lead to an increase in the costs per load unit of 2.45 euro for a train sojourn time of 60 minutes. Locomotive driver salary costs would lead to an increase in the costs per load unit of 0.83 euro cents for a train sojourn time of 60 minutes. In total, costs per load unit may increase by 3.28 euro when the train sojourn time is 60 minutes. If the train so-

journ time is shorter, additional costs are less; if it is longer, additional costs are higher.
See Appendix G for detailed costs calculations.

Besides the direct effect of different hub exchange operations, there are also the impacts of delays. Delays may have consequences for other trains, and thus also on the availability of locomotives and locomotive drivers (e.g. rescheduling issues). In this thesis only cost effects related to the node itself are included in the analyses; costs related to rail haul are not. Based on the outcomes of the simulations costs effects on rail haul costs may be an issue for further research.

5.6   Summary and conclusions

This chapter reported on the transformation of the conceptual models of the previous chapter into computer models. ARENA was chosen as the simulation software. Six computer models were constructed: a synchronised and a non-synchronised model were specified for each exchange facility. The shunting models can be applied to simulate hump shunting as well as flat shunting. The simulation models function as intended by the conceptual models. However, there are a few aspects that should be kept in mind with regard to the numerical analysis:

- Exchange relations are not specified. Hence, in the model load units or rail wagons do not really switch between trains in the exchange operation in the model. At the end, load units or rail wagons in the same train are regrouped into a train. The purpose of the simulation is to generate a realistic accumulated duration of exchange activities at train and batch level. It is stated that registration of the last load unit or rail wagon of a train or batch is sufficiently accurate to determine train and batch service times.
- The terminal models are sensitive for the following combination: number of load units per train stated in the input file and the percentages representing the distribution of load units over the various routes through the terminal. Some combinations lead to unclarified rounding-up problems.
- Work order priorities with respect to route 3 are not programmed as proposed in the conceptual model. The priority switch is conditional upon a certain number of load units in the storage area or on the transport system instead of a certain period of time as was stated in the original priority rules in Chapter 4. When this point of saturation is reached all load units put in the storage area or on the transport system get high priority status. Load units already in storage or on the transport system do not switch priority status. For the synchronised models this does not affect train and batch service times. However, with respect to the non-synchronised terminal models arrival times of trains should be specified with care. As long as interarrival times are equal to or longer than the train service time, the model works as intended.
- Other work order priorities are programmed as intended, but do not work as intended. In ARENA jobs are not put on the job list randomly but in the order they are "administratively" and/or physically processed. When jobs for two different routes have equal priority, jobs of the route that were generated first are put earlier on the job list and are thus served first. Consequently, some routes are served before others, despite having equal priority. For the synchronised models this does not affect train and batch service times, but may affect the course of

operations and therefore the train and batch service times of non-synchronised terminal models.
- Afterwards reflecting on the assumed times for entering the facility from the network and for shunting trains between the side yard and the facility, I realised that it would have been better to apply a stochastic shunting time of between 3 to 6 minutes. These times are based on track lengths of 1000 and 2000 meters respectively and a driving speed of 20 km/hour. So the consequence with respect to the simulation results is that the train service and sojourn times are underestimated with about 3 to 6 minutes.

Crucial variables of the models are the service times of servers. Therefore special attention was paid to the data collection on service times and the estimation of theoretical service time distributions. Distributions were estimated for each type of server and each type of handling operation. To estimate distributions for cranes a crane cycle time micro simulation tool was developed. With this tool crane cycle times can be simulated for each type of transhipment.

Since a simulation model does not include a cost evaluation module, a separate cost model for greenfield sites was elaborated in a spreadsheet. With the costs model total annual costs (capital plus operational costs) and costs per load unit can be calculated.

6 Experiments and results

6.1 Introduction

This chapter reports on the application of the six constructed computer models and four cost models presented in the previous chapters. A wide variety of experiments were carried out with the models. The main objective of these experiments was to identify favourable operational conditions for new hub terminals. Questions to be answered in the experiments were as follows:

- What are favourable combinations of demand and capacity input for new hub terminals in order to offer an attractive time and cost performance for new intermodal markets?
- What are the effects of changes in demand with respect to the number of trains per batch, number of batches per day, number of load units/rail wagons (load factor) per train and load order on the time and cost performance of new hub terminals compared to other hub exchange facilities?
- What are the effects of changes in cost parameter values on the cost performances for various hub exchange facilities?
- What are typical levels of synchronisation of arrivals and operations for new hub exchange operations that will help to attract new markets?
- What is the effect of delays on the time performances of new hub terminals?
- What changes in the design and resources of new hub terminals could make the new hub terminals more favourable?

Alongside the main objective, the experiments contribute to broadening insight into the characteristics of and differences between all hub exchange facilities.

The outline of this chapter is as follows. In section 6.2 I discuss the design of the experiments. Three main sets of experiments were carried out: an initial set with variable demand, a sensitivity set for the variables load order, load factor and costs, and a final set with variable arrival times, delays and type of operations. In order to be able to identify favourable conditions an evaluation framework with two benchmark criteria for speed of operations and costs was developed. This framework is presented in section 6.3.

In sections 6.4 to 6.6 the results are discussed. Section 6.4 covers the impacts of changing demand on handling time and costs. In subsection 6.4.1 favourable options, which are facilities in combination with a certain demand that meet the benchmark criteria, are identified. Next, in subsection 6.4.2 train service and sojourn times are analysed. In subsection 6.4.3 the required minimum network volume in order for a facility to be economically feasible is determined. Subsection 6.4.4 focuses on the cost structures of the various hub facilities. Section 6.5 discusses the impacts of different settings for the variables load order, load factor and costs on the set of favourable options identified in the previous section. In section 6.6 the impacts of various arrival schedules including delays are analysed. In section 6.7 a final interpretation of the results with regard to the research questions and some conclusions are formulated.

6.2 Approach

From the previous chapters (3–5) we have learned that many variables may be included in the experiments. To focus the search for the most favourable operational conditions for new hub terminals, experiments were carried out in a controlled and structured manner. Controlled experiments imply that the effect of a single variable on certain performance indicators was studied. Structured experiments imply that the experiments in which single variables were studied were carried out in a specific order. Table 6–1 provides an overview of all variables of which the effects were included in the experiments. The general design of the experiments is described in the following subsections.

Table 6–1: Overview of single variables (per system component) included in the experiments

System components	Demand *Volume*	*Arrival*	Resources and Process	Environment
Variables	- Number of load units/rail wagons per train* - Number of trains per batch - Load order - Load factor (number of load units per rail wagon)	- Arrival time - Extent of synchronisation of arrivals	- Number of equipment - Service times (type of equipment) - Strategic operations principle	- Delays

* Composed of the variables train length, size of rail wagon and load factor.

6.2.1 Initial set of experiments

We started our experiments by studying three volume variables: number of load units/rail wagons per train, number of trains per batch and number of batches per day. The purpose of these experiments was to identify favourable demand, the required minimum demand volume for facilities to be economically feasible and to obtain general insight into cost structure and train sojourn times. The exchange volume in the experiments was increased gradually as indicated in Table 6–2.

Table 6–2: Initial experimental design to determine favourable volume conditions for new hub terminals

Set of experiments	Number of load units (LU)/train; rail wagons/train	Number of batches	Number of trains in a batch
I – increase length of train	32 LU; 20 wagons	1	3
	48 LU; 30 wagons		
II – increase number of trains	48 LU; 30 wagons	1	4, 6, 8
III – increase number of batches	48 LU; 30 wagons	3	3, 4, 6

Other variable values in the experiments were determined as presented in Table 6–3. Values were based on data obtained on real systems and the projected new hub terminal operations as described in Chapter 3 and Chapter 5. Values applied were as follows:

- The most common applied load factor is used.
- Load order is determined as random (unplanned), because it can be considered as worst case and is realistic (see section 3.3). The random load order for terminals is (based on Meyer, 1998), expressed as a distribution of flows with 10% direct from train to train, 10% via the storage area and 80% via the transport system in this study. For shunting it is assumed that the random load order implies that individual rail wagons are shunted, therefore there are no wagon groups.
- The values for variables related to arrival follow from proposed new hub terminals, which assume synchronised arrivals. Meyer (1998) calculated that with an interarrival time of 8 minutes none of the trains at the Noell Megahub would be delayed with respect to their scheduled departure time.
- The effect of variables was studied in combination with differentiating the capacity input. This is further explained below.
- The number of load units to be exchanged at terminal facilities is fewer than the number of load units on the train. $1/n^{th}$ of the load units remain on the train; n being the number of trains in a batch (see section 4.3).
- The service time distribution functions are given in Chapter 5.
- The strategic control principles are defined as synchronised operations, based on the proposed new hub terminals.
- The operational control principles were transformed into priorities in Chapter 5.
- Delay is the only environmental element included in the analysis, because it has an impact on operations on an almost daily basis. However, the initial experiments are carried out without the inclusion of delay.
- No equipment breakdowns.

Table 6–3: Values of various variables in the initial experiments with variable demand

System component	Variables	Values
Demand – *Volume*	Load factor	1.6 load unit per rail wagon
	Load order	Unplanned
Demand – *Arrival*	Arrival time	Train interarrival time is 8 minutes
	Extent of synchronisation of arrivals	Synchronised
Resources and Process	Number of equipment	See Table 6–4, Table 6–5, Table 6–6
	Service times (type of equipment)	See section 5.4.1.3.
	Strategic control principle	Synchronised (see section 3.5.1)
	Operational control principles (service priorities)	Priorities as defined in section 5.3.4
Environment	Delays	None

Variables were studied in combination with differentiating the variable number of equipment for the new hub terminal and the three alternative hub exchange facilities hump shunting, flat shunting and road-rail terminals. However, flat shunting was not included in the initial set of experiments, since this facility "by nature" is used for shunting wagon groups, which is defined as planned load order in this thesis. Hence, flat shunting is included in the set of experiments carried out after the initial experiments.

For the new hub terminal four capacity levels as indicated in Table 6–4 were selected. The choice of capacity levels was derived from the proposed Noell Megahub which was studied by Meyer (1998) and in the Terminet project (2000). The choice of the number of cranes is as follows. Ten cranes are projected as the optimal number of cranes for the Noell Megahub for the specific node Hanover-Lehrte (Meyer, 1998). In Terminet (2000), megahubs with four and six cranes were designed for potential hub nodes in Venlo (The Netherlands) and Metz (France). For the purposes of comparison with a very common road-rail terminal capacity level a new hub terminal with two cranes was added.

Based on a simulation study by Meyer (1998), the manufacturer Noell determined the number of units in the transport system at 33 for a terminal with 10 cranes (Bontekoning & Kreutzberger, 2001, p. A24). The numbers of transport units for other capacity levels were estimated based on extrapolation of values applied in case studies in Terminet (2000).

Table 6–4: Capacity levels in experiments with new hub terminal models

Capacity level	Number of cranes	Number of transport units
C2	2	13
C4	4	18
C6	6	23
C10	10	33

For the experiments with hump shunting and flat shunting yards, four capacity levels (see Table 6–5) were chosen. The respondents (Biggler, 2003; Fritsch, 2003) indicated that at their shunting yards one locomotive is employed at the arrival yard and one at the departure yard. This may be considered as the basic capacity level. By increasing the capacity level by one unit at a time, three other capacity levels were obtained. We know from interviews (Bruins, 2003; Wesseling, 2003) that only very large yards employ two locomotives at the arrival yard.

Table 6–5: Capacity levels in experiments with hump shunting and flat shunting yard models

Capacity level	Number of locomotives at workstation 1 (arrival yard)	Number of locomotives at workstation 2 (departure yard)
H11; F11	1	1
H21; F21	2	1
H12; F12	1	2
H22; F22	2	2

H = hump shunting yard; F = flat shunting yard.

Three capacity levels were determined for experiments for road-rail terminals (see Table 6–6). A typical number of cranes for Gateway road-rail terminals is two or three (Rotter, 2003). For the purposes of comparison with new hub terminals a variant with four cranes was added. I am not aware of any road-rail terminal with four cranes per track bundle. To my knowledge most terminals have one or two cranes per track bundle. In the case of larger terminals an additional track bundle with storage and truck lanes is added with another one or two cranes.

Table 6–6: Capacity levels in experiments with road-rail models

Capacity level	Number of cranes
RR2	2
RR3	3
RR4	4

Based on the outcomes of the aforementioned initial experiments only favourable demand conditions and capacity levels were further explored. To determine favourable conditions, benchmark criteria for maximum train sojourn time and costs per load unit for time-sensitive flows were applied. The way in which these benchmark criteria were determined is discussed in section 6.3.

6.2.2 Experiments to test sensitivity of initial results for variables: load order, load factor and costs

Once favourable options for variable demand were determined, the sensitivity of the results for changes in the variables load order and load factor as well as for different cost levels was studied. I expected that different conditions might be more favourable for other hub facilities, or at least that performance differences would become less striking, because the initial conditions were derived from the conditions proposed for new hub terminals. These initial conditions may be much more in favour of new hub terminals than the alternative facilities. In addition, from Chapter 3 we learned that the proposed conditions for new hub terminals deviate largely from common practice. In these sensitivity analyses, but also in the experiments related to arrival times and level of synchronisation of arrivals, I was looking for conditions that might call into question the new hub terminal as the most favourable option for the time-sensitive freight market. I investigated the three variables independently:
- Load order.
- Load factor.
- Costs.

These sensitivity analyses were carried out for a selected number of cases. Cases included were those that may become favourable options under the condition of planned load order, different load factor or lower costs. Based on an educated guestimate, time and costs per load unit criteria were determined. Values for the volume variables: number of load units/rail wagons per train, number of trains per batch and number of batches per day were determined as indicated in Table 6–7 and were selected on the basis of the results of the previous set of experiments. In addition, Table 6–7 gives an overview of the experiments carried out for the sensitivity analyses.

Table 6–7: Experimental design sensitivity analyses for load order, load factor and costs

Set of experiments	Alternative value(s) sensitivity variable	Number of load units (LU)/train; rail wagons/train	Number of batches	Number of trains in a batch
V – Sensitivity load order	Planned	48 LU; 30 wagons	Depending on demand selected cases	Depending on demand selected cases
IV – Sensitivity load factor	1.4 1.8	42 LU; 30 wagons 54 LU; 30 wagons	Depending on demand selected cases	Depending on demand selected cases
VI – Sensitivity costs	- +25% investment equipment - +25% investment infrastructure - 3% and 6% interest rate - Cheaper, but slower cranes	48 LU; 30 wagons	Depending on demand selected cases	Depending on demand selected cases

Experiments with different load orders
In a first set of experiments I experimented with different load orders. The initial experiments were carried out for unplanned load orders, because this is what was assumed in studies on the Noell Megahub (Meyer, 1998; Alicke, 1999). However, research shows (Bostel & Dejax, 1998) that faster exchange operations can be achieved at a new hub terminal when load orders at origin terminals and at the hub terminal are planned. In addition, Biggler (2003) and Fritsch (2003) commented that on average trains at the flat shunting yard at Herne consist of between 10 and 12 wagon groups of two to three rail wagons.

A planned load order would be more favourable for all hub facilities. A planned load order implies fewer handling operations at terminals, because fewer load units have to switch crane sections. It means fewer handling operations at shunting yards, because fewer wagon groups need to be handled. In the sensitivity analysis the effects of a planned load order consisting of 12 wagon groups instead of 30 individual rail wagons was investigated. I was required to make an assumption about the distribution of flows for the terminals, because trains with load units for transhipment at an intermediate node instead of shunting may be loaded differently at the origin terminal. In addition, a part of the load units remain on the train at the intermediate node. And the number of load units that remain on the train depends on the number of trains in a batch. To avoid weighting in favour of new hub terminals over shunting yards I assumed a distribution of flows of 50% direct from train to train, 10% via the storage area and 40% via the transport system. This distribution guarantees that the reduction in rail wagons to be handled remains greater than the reduction in load units to be handled for the various demand levels investigated.

Experiments with different load factors
In a second set of experiments I varied the load factor (number of load units on a rail wagon). In the initial experiments the most commonly used load factor was applied. However, system analysis in Chapter 3 showed that the load factor very much depends on the transport relation. Consequently, on some relations the load factor may be closer to 1.4 and on others closer to 1.8.

Experiments with different cost levels
In a third set of experiments I tested the sensitivity of the cost performance of the facilities for the following:
- higher investment costs;
- higher interest rates;
- cheaper but slower cranes at the new hub terminal (time effects were also studied).

Higher investment costs
In Chapter 5 I stated that specification of costs in the cost model is difficult. Data problems concern availability, actuality, level of detail and variability (interest rates, for instance). In literature, cost data are scarce and questions about costs in the questionnaires sent out to network and node operators often remained unanswered. Furthermore, we know from practice that investments in (new) infrastructure are often underestimated. Two sets of experiments were carried out to investigate sensitivity for higher investment:
- A 25% increase in investment in equipment;
- A 25% increase in investment in infrastructure.

Higher interest rates
Another two sets of experiments were carried out to investigate the effects of higher interest rates. In the initial experiments a yearly interest rate of 2.3% (12-month Euribor rate as at 01/01/04 (http://www.euribor.org/html/content/euribor_data.html)) was applied. This interest rate was chosen rather arbitrarily and should be considered as a minimum rate. Interest rates vary over time and from country to country. In some countries the government, which may borrow money at lower rates than private companies, finances infrastructure. In such cases an alternative interest rate may be the 10-year state bond interest rate (between 3% and 3.5% in 2004). In the case of private investment a long-term private capital loan (between 6% and 8% in 2004) must be chosen for the interest rate. In the two sets of experiments the effects of interest rates of 3% and 6% on the cost per load unit were investigated. I expected new hub terminals to be most sensitive to increases in costs, because their costs are already much higher than those of alternative facilities.

Cheaper, but slower cranes
In the last set of experiments, cheaper but slower cranes at the new hub terminal were investigated. These experiments were carried out because of the relatively high costs per load unit and the very fast handling time compared to other facilities. In addition, the new hub terminal cranes applied in the models are much faster than any other rail gantry crane for which data was obtained (Bontekoning & Kreutzberger, 2001; SIMET, 1994). As a consequence these new terminal cranes are also very ex-

pensive. In the experiments the road-rail terminal included in this study replaced the new hub terminal cranes. New service time distribution functions, based on kinematics data for a road-rail terminal crane, were estimated for the new hub terminal model. In addition, total annual costs were recalculated, based on the investment costs of a road-rail terminal crane.

I anticipated that cheaper cranes would benefit the new hub terminal, because the costs per load unit could be brought down considerably. I also anticipated that the decrease in crane handling speed would not really harm the time performance of the new hub terminal because of the crane-supporting transport system and the higher number of cranes employed.

6.2.3 Experiments to test the sensitivity of initial results for variables arrival time, delay and strategic control principle

In a third and final set of experiments variations in arrival times, delays and strategic operations control principle were studied. Three main sets of experiments, each consisting of various subsets of experiments, were carried out. An overview of the values of variables is provided in Table 6–8. Variables not mentioned remain unchanged from the initial experiments.

Experiments with arrival time
With respect to the variable arrival time three subsets of experiments were carried out. First, the ideal interarrival time was determined. From the initial experiments it became clear that the chosen train interarrival time of 8 minutes was not ideal, meaning that trains had to wait at the side yard, leading to a longer stay at the hub. A *just-in-time* arrival schedule would lead to a situation in which the train sojourn time equals the train service time. Trains do not have to wait for service, and equipment does not have to wait for trains. Although ideal circumstances are seldom achieved, I carried out an analysis to determine ideal train interarrival times. The purpose of this was for the results to function as points of reference that could be used for comparison with any realistic arrival schedule, such as those of the hubs at Metz and Herne.

The exploration into ideal interarrival times started off with an arrival schedule that was determined by a preliminary manual calculation of the duration of operations per train. Next, the course of the operation was observed using the animation module of the simulation model. Based on the observed behaviour of the system the arrival schedule was adjusted. Finally, the arrival schedule was fine-tuned based on the information generated by the simulation model for, among other things, utilisation rate of resources, queuing time of trains at the side yard and number of trains queuing at the side yard.

Analysis of train arrival schedules was carried out for new hub terminal cases and "competitive" facilities that appeared and remained among the favourable options in the initial and sensitivity experiments.

Next, for the same cases, train sojourn times were calculated for modified arrival schedules of former shunting hubs at Metz and Herne. The Herne arrival schedule was modified from one batch of 9 trains into 3 batches of 3 trains and the Metz arrival schedule from one batch of 19 trains into 3 batches of 6 trains.

Due to very long interarrival times in the Metz and Herne schedules, a third set of experiments was carried out with reduced (improved) train interarrival times (to be implemented through better network planning and inter-organisational communication, for instance).

Table 6–8: Experiments with arrival time, delay and strategic operations control principle

Set of experiments	Alternative value(s) sensitivity variable	Load order	Number of batches	Number of trains in a batch
VII – Arrival time	- Ideal schedule	Unplanned/	3	3; 4; 6
	- Herne/Metz schedule	Planned*	3	3; 6
	- Herne/Metz improved schedule		3	3; 6
VII – Delay	- Ideal schedule - Random national - Random international	Unplanned/ Planned*	3	3; 6
IX – Strategic operations control principle	- Non-synchronised operations: - Metz/Herne schedule - Delayed ideal schedule	Unplanned/ Planned*	3	3; 6

* Planned load order applies to new hub terminals, unplanned load order to alternative facilities.

Experiments with delay

In the second set of experiments the effects of delayed trains on the train sojourn time were studied. In previous experiments it was assumed that trains arrive according to schedule. However, in international hub-and-spoke intermodal traffic around 30% of trains are delayed each day. In national hub-and-spoke intermodal traffic 10% of trains are delayed each day. Delayed arrival time of trains varies from several minutes to over 24 hours (Biggler, 2003; Fritsch, 2003; Rotter, 2003; Bosschaart, 2003).

As for all experiments a deterministic approach was applied. Six instances with realistic random delays were analysed for a selected number of hub exchange facilities and two demand levels. In the first set with three instances, the impact of delays on a national network was studied. In the second set, the impact of delays on an international network was investigated. The impacts of delays were studied for ideal arrival schedules. Different durations of train interarrival times were selected, because it was expected that the duration of the arrival delay might have different impacts due to different durations of the train interarrival times.

Delays occur randomly. In order to determine in the experiments which trains to delay and by how long, a delay generator was constructed in Excel. The delay generator draws a random number for each train in an arrival schedule. Based on the number drawn and the cumulative distribution of delays, the generator determines whether a train is delayed and by how long. The cumulative distribution is based on the estimated probability as indicated in Table 6–9. The delay time is rounded up to the maximum of the delay category as indicated in Table 6–9. Although in practice delay has a continuous scale and may exceed the four hours, this deterministic approach seems adequate for understanding the effects of delays of different durations.

Based on the outcome of the delay generator, the arrival schedules in the input files of the simulation model were adjusted. For each arrival schedule studied, three delay schedules were generated. The generated schedules had to fulfill a number of requirements. First, the schedule must meet the average number of delayed trains per day. Second, in order to be able to study different situations, there must be some variation in which trains are delayed and by how long.

Table 6–9: Percentage delayed trains for international and national hub-and-spoke traffic

Delay	International traffic (%)	National traffic (%)
On time	70.00	90.00
< 30 min.	7.50	2.50
30 min. – 1 hour	7.50	2.50
1-2 hours	3.75	2.50
2-3 hours	3.75	1.25
3-4 hours	7.50	1.25

Adjusted from Biggler (2003), Fritsch (2003), Rotter (2003) and Bosschaart (2003).

Experiments with non-synchronised operations
All experiments so far have focused on synchronised operations. However, at some level of non-synchronisation of arrivals or delays, train sojourn times may be better off with non-synchronised operations. In this last set of experiments the impact of non-synchronised operations on Herne and Metz, and a few selected delayed arrival schedules from the previous experiments were studied.
For these experiments different models were applied to a few selected cases from the previous experiments with arrival times and delays.

6.2.4 Simulation output, replications and confidence intervals

In summary, the initial experiments are based on variable values derived from data from the projected new hub terminals, while in the sensitivity experiments values of the most relevant variables are varied one by one. Alternative values are derived from intermodal hub-and-spoke practice. The objective of the sensitivity analysis is to search for conditions that might call into question the new hub terminal as the most favourable option for the time-sensitive freight market. In addition, the sensitivity analysis aims to investigate the conditions under which alternative hub exchange facilities are competitive with new hub terminals.

With respect to the results presented in the course of this chapter one should be aware of the following. Time results are generated by the simulation models and presented as average train service and/or sojourn time. The output of the simulation model is stochastic, because server service times are stochastic. In order to reduce variance in the output performance values as far as possible 20 replications of each simulation run were carried out. One simulation run consists of one day of operations. Twenty replications appeared to lead to sufficiently small half-width confidence intervals for the output variable train sojourn time (of 95%) for most experiments. Table 6–10 provides the average half-width confidence interval for each facility. The half-width confidence intervals presented are the average taken over all capacity and demand levels. The absolute (in minutes) and relative (in % of the average train sojourn time) size of the half-width confidence are provided. Absolute and relative half-width confidence intervals per case (per combination of capacity and demand level) is provided in Appendix H. The half-width intervals turned out to be on the large side, especially for the hump shunting yard experiments with one locomotive at workstation 2 (assembly server). Increasing the number of replications, however, did not lead to smaller confidence intervals.
Cost performances were calculated in a spreadsheet and are not stochastic. The costs results are general and based on a greenfield situation for each exchange facility. All costs, capital and operational, are included.

Table 6–10: Average half-width confidence interval for output variable train sojourn time based on twenty replications for different facilities

Facility	Absolute (in minutes)	Relative (in %)
New hub terminal	0.4	0.3
Hump shunting yard	16.6	5.0
Flat shunting yard	11.0	3.0
Road-rail terminal	2.1	0.8

6.3 Evaluation of performances: time and cost benchmark criteria

The expectation is that new hub terminals may be suitable for new, more time-sensitive, intermodal markets because of their fast transhipment. To determine favourable operational conditions for new hub terminals, but also to identify favourable facilities and conditions in general, I constructed a general options portfolio. This is illustrated in Figure 6–1. It should be remembered that in section 3.7 train sojourn time and costs per load unit were identified as performance indicators from the perspective of hub-and-spoke network operators. These two indicators are plotted on the x- and y-axis respectively.

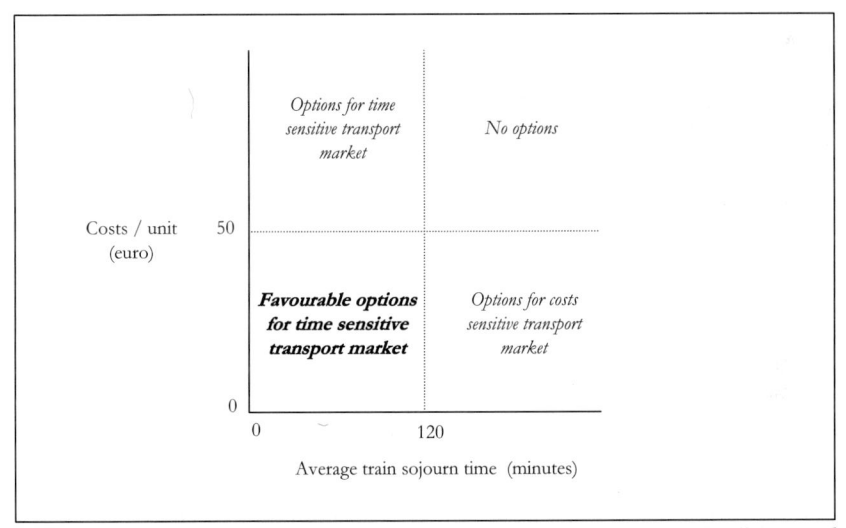

Figure 6–1: General options portfolio to identify favourable facilities and conditions

Train sojourn time is defined as the total time spent by a train at an exchange facility. It is composed of the train service time and waiting time at the side yard. The train service time is defined as the time spent in operations. The train waiting time is defined as the time a train spends at the side yard waiting to be granted access to operations. The simulation models keep track of the time spent by trains at the side yard and in operations.

Costs per load unit (LU) is defined as the total (capital plus operational) annual costs of an exchange facility divided by the annual network volume. Costs are therefore divided over all load units in a hub-and-spoke network and not simply over the actual transhipped or shunted load units. Such an approach would imply a node operator's perspective, while in this study the perspective of the node customer (network operator) is applied. In practice, network operators are mostly charged a price per train. Although from a commercial point of view network operators use different pricing strategies for their customers, the total costs to operate a hub-and-spoke network divided by the expected transported volume (average total costs per load unit) serve as a point of reference.

A general options portfolio was constructed by plotting the benchmark criteria for train sojourn time and costs per load unit in a graph (see Figure 6–1). Somewhat arbitrarily I argue that these benchmark criteria may be valued at:
- 120 minutes for train sojourn time, and
- 50 euros per load unit for costs.

Arguments to support these values are discussed in the course of this section.
The two dotted lines indicating the benchmark criteria generate four quadrants that can be used to classify simulation results. Each quadrant stands for a certain qualification of time and cost performances. The lower left quadrant represents favourable hub exchange facilities for time-sensitive flows, namely due to short sojourn time at low to reasonable costs. The upper left quadrant also represents options for time-sensitive flows, due to short sojourn times, but at less attractive costs. The question is which sector of the time-sensitive market is prepared to pay more than the benchmark costs criterion. The lower right quadrant represents hub exchange facilities for cost-sensitive flows. Short sojourn times are less important than low costs. Lastly, the upper right quadrant represents a situation that is not attractive to any transport market, due to long sojourn times and high costs.
The conclusion is that the objective of the simulations and cost calculations is to identify cases in the lower left quadrant.

In this section it is argued why the benchmark criterion for sojourn time is determined at a maximum of 120 minutes. Little is known about acceptable and preferred sojourn times of trains at hub exchange facilities by hub-and-spoke network operators. I therefore followed two lines of reasoning from which a benchmark criterion may be derived.
First, we can determine a value for the time benchmark criterion based on train sojourn time in existing hub-and-spoke networks. In Chapter 1 it was explained that existing hub-and-spoke networks basically serve cost-sensitive flows. As such, compared to existing train sojourn times we may assume that for time-sensitive flows significantly shorter train sojourn times are expected. Existing hub-and-spoke networks apply flat shunting or hump shunting yards as the hub exchange facility. For flat hub-shunting a minimum planning rule of thumb is that three hours should be allocated for train disassembly, and another three hours for train assembly. However, a critical connection can be realised in three hours (Biggler, 2003). Analysis of arrival and departure schedules and exchange relations showed for the hump hub-shunting yard at Metz that the critical connection time is 2.5 hours (ICF, 1999). The critical connection time is the available time window between scheduled arrival time of an inbound train and the scheduled departure time of an outbound train. Within this critical time window, rail wagons from the same inbound train and with similar destinations must be processed in order to make their connection with their outbound train. The critical connection time is not the same as train sojourn time, because it only applies to processing of a part of a train. However, it could be used as a point of reference for the determination of a benchmark criterion. After all, processing a complete train in

the critical connection time instead of a part of a train may be perceived as a significant improvement of the train sojourn time. I therefore argue that the upper limit of the benchmark criterion is 2.5 hours, the critical connection time, but is preferably lower to reflect an improvement in minimum exchange time.

Second, we may determine a value for the time benchmark criterion by taking the duration of an intermodal journey in a point-to-point network or truck trip as points of reference. These points of reference apply to a situation in which a new hub-and-spoke network is implemented. If total transport time is important for time-sensitive flows, the total transport time in a hub-and-spoke network should be about equal to that of the points of reference. However, the implementation of a hub-and-spoke network implies additional transhipment time and additional transport time due to detours. Therefore, to minimise the increase in total transport time in hub-and-spoke networks, the train sojourn time at the hub should be minimised.

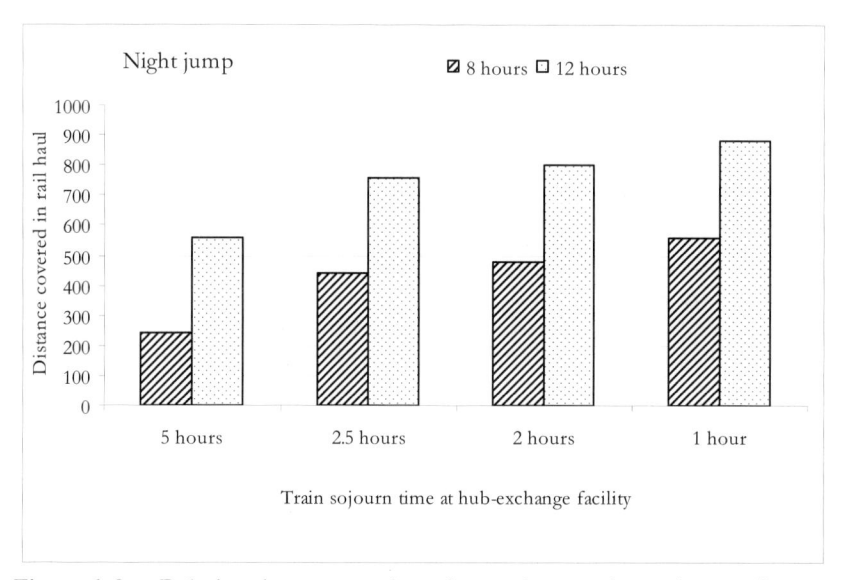

Figure 6–2: Relation between train sojourn time and maximum distance covered with a train speed of 80kph

A typical transport duration in intermodal transport is the so-called "*night-jump*". Many intermodal trains depart in the late afternoon or early evening and arrive at night or in the early morning (also known as A/B connection). A rail operator wants to cover as much distance as possible during the night. As such, he wants to spend as little time as possible at hub exchange nodes. Common "*night-jump*" durations are between 8 and 12 hours. Figure 6–2 shows for two "*night jump*" cases the distance that can be covered by a freight train with an average speed of 80 kilometres per hour for four possible train sojourn times at a hub-node. From Figure 6–2 it may be concluded that the longer the train sojourn time at an exchange facility, the less time, and therefore less transport distance, remains available for the actual transport. Typical transport distances in Europe are between 500 and 1200 kilometres. Figure 6–2 suggests that for new hub-and-spoke networks with distances between 500 and 800 kilometres the maximum allowed train sojourn time is 2 hours. However, when distances exceed 800km or the average train speed is lower than 80kph, the maximum allowed train sojourn time must be set at 1 hour or less. Based on this analysis I determined the time benchmark criterion at 2 hours.

The reasons why I determined the benchmark criterion for costs per load unit at 50 euros are put forward in this section. Little is known about acceptable price levels for new, time-sensitive markets. I used existing knowledge on costs and prices for shunting in hub-and-spoke networks and for road-rail transhipment as my benchmark. Existing prices for intermodal shunting are between 15 and 40 euros per load unit (Black et al., 2003, p. 41). The problem with existing shunting prices is that often they do not always reflect the underlying total costs due to investment subsidies or cost calculations based on operational costs only. Another point of reference that may be used is price per load unit for road-rail transhipment. These are between 16 and 40 euros (Terminet, 2000; Black et al., 2003, p. 41). However, a similar problem applies as with shunting prices: prices often do not reflect the underlying total costs. The following example illustrates this. Total annual cost calculations for optimal annual throughput indicate a total costs per load unit of between 25 and 35 euros for road-rail terminals (Ballis & Golias, 2002; Impulse, 1997) and between 20 and 44 euros for new hub terminals (European Commission, 1997; Terminet, 2000). No total cost calculations for shunting could be obtained.

If new hub exchange terminals provide a higher-quality (faster) service than shunting yards or road-rail terminals, I argue that a higher price per load unit can be charged for the new hub terminal. If we assume the abovementioned 40 euros per load unit as a price for shunting and road-rail transhipment that more or less reflects total costs, the price per load unit at a new hub terminal may exceed it. How much higher the price may be depends on how shippers and network operators value the fast exchange service. Their willingness to pay a higher price is strongly related to the cost savings the fast service offers. If, for instance, due to time savings at the node rolling equipment and labour may be used more efficiently (additional roundtrips), a network operator will be willing to pay more than when time savings do not lead to a more efficient use of equipment or labour.

Kreutzberger (2002) calculated the potential costs reduction per load unit in the case of a hub-and-spoke network replacing direct trains in a point-to-point network with two origin and two destination terminals (600 to 1200 kilometres apart). The potential costs reduction for rail haul transport lies between 60 and 135 euros per load unit. Due to bundling economies of scale (larger loading degree and/or larger transport unit) can be achieved. However, a hub-and-spoke network implies additional transhipment costs, which must be covered by the cost savings. Therefore, for situations in which a hub-and-spoke network is implemented, the 60 to 135 euros transport cost reduction may be perceived as a price accepted by the market to pay for the service. For networks that are larger than two origin and two destination terminals, no cost savings were documented by Kreutzberger. Nevertheless, we would expect larger savings due to larger bundling advantages.

Considering the documented prices of 40 euros per load unit, existing total cost calculations and the minimum calculated cost savings of 60 euros for new hub-and-spoke networks, and in the knowledge that margins in transport are very small, I chose a cost (not price!) benchmark criterion of 50 euros. This benchmark value reflects both a value that may represent an acceptable cost level for existing hub-and-spoke networks with a fast exchange service and for new hub-and-spoke networks.

6.4 Impact of the variable demand on handling time and costs

The design of the experiments is such that through a sequence of experiments, conditions for favourable options for the time-sensitive market are identified. The results of the various experiments are grouped into three clusters. In this section the results of what I call the initial experiments are discussed. The initial experiments contain various demand and capacity levels, which are described in Table 6–2 to Table 6–6. The main variable features are the following: train arrivals every 8 minutes, non-planned load position of load units, synchronised arrivals and synchronised operations (see further Table 6–3).

In addition to the presentation of favourable demand conditions for favourable options (subsection 6.4.1), this section aims to provide analyses of the train service/sojourn time (subsection 6.4.2), minimum required annual volume (subsection 6.4.3) and cost structures (subsection 6.4.4) for various demand and capacity levels. Although in the end the objective of the thesis is to identify favourable operational conditions specifically for new hub terminals, the contents of these analyses have a more general character. Sections 1.5 and 1.6 focus on the sensitivity of favourable options for changing conditions identified in subsection 6.4.1. As explained in 6.2.2, the objective of the sensitivity analyses is to find conditions that may call into question new hub terminals, which in the initial experiments are identified as the most favourable options for the time-sensitive freight market.

Note that since the experiments involve a non-planned load order, flat shunting yards are excluded from the experiments. Flat shunting basically involves shunting of wagon groups as was described in Chapter 3. However, flat shunting is included in subsection 6.4.4 in which the cost structures of the various facilities are discussed.

6.4.1 Identification of favourable options

The results of the experiments for all different configurations of variable demand and capacity levels are plotted in Figure 6–3. It should be noted that the average train service time is presented instead of the average train sojourn time, which was suggested and defined in section 1.3. As such, waiting time at the side yard is excluded. I shall discuss this further in the next subsection.
If we take the length of the 95% confidence intervals into account (see Appendix H), we may conclude that each case may have a train sojourn time which is slightly shorter or longer than the average. This does not imply that it might end up in a different quadrant for any of the cases. Some hump shunting cases with one locomotive at the assembly workstation have rather lengthy 30- to 45-minute half-width intervals (see Appendix H). However, due to the lengthy average service times, the lower border of the confidence interval will never fall below the 120 time benchmark criterion.

Figure 6–3 shows two things. Firstly, the faster the facility (shorter average train service times), the higher the costs per load unit. Secondly, the new hub terminal clearly dominates in quadrants I and II with short train service times to attract time-sensitive flows. Three other facilities show up in quadrant II: a hump exchange facility with 2 x 2 locomotives, a road-rail terminal with 4 cranes and a road-rail terminal with 3 cranes. For a demand of one batch with three short trains they meet the time benchmark criterion. The new hub terminal cases showing up in quadrants II and IV relate to cases with a new hub terminal with two cranes and one case with a new hub terminal with four cranes.

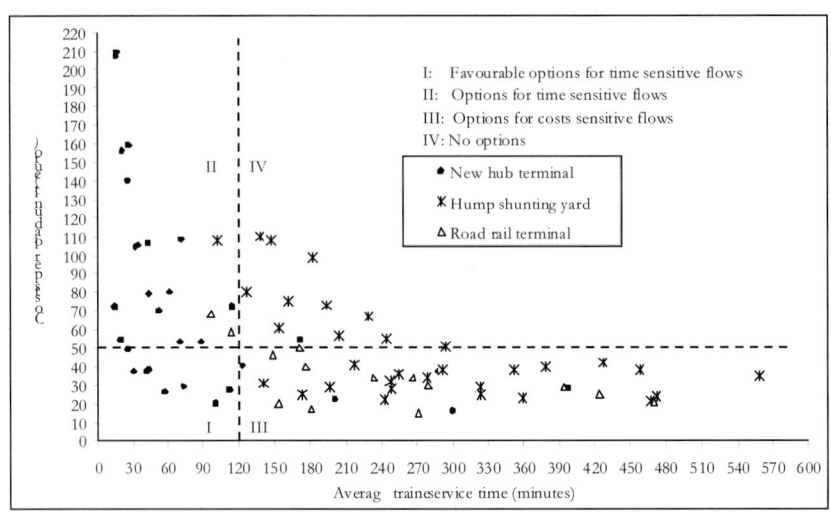

Figure 6–3: Time and cost performances related to the general option portfolio for all initial experiments

Demand as described in Table 6–2 and Table 6–3 and capacity levels as described in Table 6–4 to Table 6–6. Flat shunting is excluded, because flat shunting commonly only involves shunting of wagon groups, implying a planned load order. In this figure, results of an unplanned load order are presented.

The lower left quadrant (I), indicating favourable options for the time-sensitive transport market, includes eight new hub terminal cases. These favourable cases are specified in Table 6–11. In addition to the train service time, Table 6–11 also provides information on the batch service time and duration of the total daily operation. Batch service time is defined as the period of time from which the first train of a batch enters the exchange facility until the moment the last train of a batch leaves it. Duration of total daily operation is the period of time between the start of service of the first load unit or rail wagon and the end of service of the last load unit or rail wagon of the daily demand.

Table 6–11 shows that the new hub terminals with four (C4) and six (C6) cranes perform well for all three multiple-batch volume levels. The variant with two cranes (C2) is too slow to deal with larger batches. When the number of trains is greater than three, the train sojourn time exceeds the benchmark criterion. The variant with ten cranes (C10) is too expensive for small batches. Only for the highest volume level investigated in the experiments does this variant meet the benchmark criterion for costs per load unit. For a specification of the cases in other quadrants the reader is referred to Appendix J.

Table 6–11: Specification of favourable options for time-sensitive transport markets

Demand*	Facility and capacity level	Train service time (minutes)	Batch service time (minutes)	Duration total operation (minutes)	Costs per load unit (euros)
3*3	C6	26	32	97	49
3*3	C4	44	49	147	38
3*3	C2	113	118	353	27
3*4	C6	42	55	166	37
3*4	C4	74	87	260	29
3*6	C10	31	55	163	37
3*6	C6	58	84	250	26
3*6	C4	101	213	388	20

* Number of batches * number of trains/batch
Daily network demand: 3*3 = 432 LU's; 3*4 = 576 LU's; 3*6 = 864 LU's
Daily exchange demand: 3*3 = 289 LU's; 3*4 = 432 LU's; 3*6 = 717 LU's
See also Appendix I.

These initial results suggest that, as proposed for the new hub terminal concept, new hub terminals outperform the alternatives for given conditions. A part of the performance difference may be explained by the fact that the fast and very fast new hub terminal variants have very high capacity. This raises the question of whether existing hub facilities could meet the time benchmark criterion with additional equipment to the equipment levels involved in the experiments. The experiments include existing equipment levels and one to three higher capacity levels (see section 6.2). I argue that additional equipment cannot be added to the existing infrastructural layout of shunting yards in order to meet the benchmark time criterion due to their typical dimensions. This can be explained as follows. There is only one lead track to the shunting hill at the hump shunting yard studied, compared with the sorting tracks at the flat shunting yard studied. This allows for a maximum of two shunting locomotives at the arrival yard. While one locomotive is busy pushing rail wagons over the shunting hill and pushing them into the sorting tracks, the other is busy with its return trip to pick up a new train. This locomotive must wait until the lead track is empty to continue processing a train.

With respect to adding capacity at the departure yard, capacity may be increased to improve the service time, but since the processing time of a train at the arrival yard already exceeds the service time of new hub terminals, this would not lead to competitive service times. As such, it makes sense to increase the amount of equipment and labour at shunting yards only through additional (parallel) infrastructure such as a lead track, a shunting hill and sorting tracks. But still, no matter how much extra equipment and infrastructure is added, shunting (as studied in this thesis) has a performance backlog of between 20 and 40 minutes, due to the need to couple a network locomotive, fill air tubes and carry out a lengthy brake test.

With respect to the rail-road terminal the number of cranes may be increased to meet the time benchmark criterion. A quick assessment of the performance of a road-rail terminal with six cranes demonstrated that a demand of one or several batches of three trains results in train service times just below the benchmark time criterion of 120 minutes. However, the more cranes there are, the more they will hinder each other at the border of their crane sections, especially if a large part of the load unit has to switch crane sections. This hindrance may incur crane waiting time with respect to the passing on of load units that have to switch between crane sections.

Nevertheless, hindrance of cranes is not included in the crane service time distribution functions. Furthermore, the more cranes there are, the more time it takes to transfer load units from one crane section to another. This is illustrated in Table 6–12 (refer to subsection 3.5.5 for an explanation of the passing on of load units by cranes). To compare, the average transport time at the new hub terminal is 150 seconds. Technically speaking, therefore, the road-rail terminal may meet the benchmark criterion for a certain demand, but functionally speaking adding more cranes results in a more complicated exchange process with decreasing output per crane due to longer crane driving times.

Table 6–12: Increasing average time to transport load units from one crane section to another at the road-rail terminal

Number of cranes	2	3	4	5	6
Average transport time (seconds)	150	223	262	314	340

Now that we have identified the most favourable new hub terminal facilities under favourable conditions (see Table 6–11), the question is what will happen to their performance when conditions change. In other words, which of the cases in Table 6–11 will still be favourable after all sensitivity experiments have been carried out? Under which conditions can alternative facilities move into quadrant I? This will be studied in sections 6.5 and 6.6. Prior to that, we will take a closer look at the preliminary results.

6.4.2 Analysis of train service times and sojourn times

In this section we take a closer look at average train service and sojourn times. As mentioned above, in this section I chose to present average train service times instead of the train sojourn times. I will explain why.

Analysis of train sojourn and service times for multiple batch demand shows that the initial train interarrival time of eight minutes (see section 6.2) may lead to waiting time at the side yard for trains of the second batch and onwards. This especially accounts for the slower facilities at hump shunting yards and road-rail terminals, leading to significant differences between the sojourn and service times. This is illustrated for four facilities, C6, C2, H22 and RR4 in Table 6–13. Table 6–13 shows that for a demand of one batch of three trains (1*3) the train service time equals the train sojourn time. For instance, for C6 the train service and sojourn time is 26 minutes. For a demand with three batches Table 6–13 shows that train sojourn times are longer than train service times. Table 6–13 also shows that the differences between train service and train sojourn times are greater when the facilities are slower. See for instance the difference between C6 and C2. Obviously, when a facility is slower, trains have to wait longer at the side yard, leading to longer sojourn times. Furthermore, Table 6–13 shows that the difference between train service and train sojourn time is greater when the number of trains in a batch is increased. This can be explained by the fact that the more trains there are, the more units there are to be handled, and the longer the time that a batch is in operation. In the meantime trains from succeeding batches still arrive every eight minutes and have to wait at the side yard for the duration of the operation.

At this stage of the analysis insight into the capability of each facility with respect to the potential speed of operations (service time) is most important and not the sojourn time. With respect to multiple demand, Table 6–13 shows that the train sojourn time would lessen the performance potential of certain facilities. However, in the end the train sojourn time is most relevant with respect to the benchmark time criterion. After all, the train sojourn time reflects the duration that a train is at the node and not out in the network. In a later stage, when the ideal interarrival time for each facility has been determined (see subsection 6.6.1), the train sojourn time is used as performance indicator.

Table 6–13: Differences between train service and train sojourn time for a selected number of cases for an arrival schedule with 8-minute train interarrival times (in minutes)

Demand*	C6 Train service time	C6 Train sojourn time	C2 Train service time	C2 Train sojourn time	H22 Train service time	H22 Train sojourn time	RR4 Train service time	RR4 Train sojourn time
1*3	26	26	109	109	127	127	149	149
3*3	26	31	113	202	141	178	153	281
3*4	42	59	210	370	173	222	245	456
3*6	58	84	-	-	242	314	-	-

* Number of batches of trains per batch.
Cx: new hub terminal with x number of cranes.
Hxy: hump shunting yard with x number of locomotives for sorting and y number of locomotives for assembly.
RRx: road-rail terminal with x number of cranes.

We can learn two things from the analysis of train service and train sojourn times for the experiments with an 8-minute train interarrival time. First, train sojourn times can still be improved, especially for the slower facilities, when trains of a succeeding batch do not arrive earlier than the service capacity becomes available. In other words, waiting time at the side yard can be avoided if the time between the arrival of the first train of a batch and the first train of the succeeding batch equals the service time of the complete first batch. I define this period of time as the batch interarrival time.

Second, optimising batch interarrival times may also lead to a reduction in train service times. This may be derived from Figure 6–4 where train service times of single batch demand are compared with the service times of multiple batch demand for three, four or six trains per batch. The train service time for a single batch demand is, for various facilities and capacity levels, shorter than a multiple batch demand. Aside from some stochastic variation in the results, the time differences between one and three batches are related to the 8-minute train interarrival time. This can be explained as follows. Trains in succeeding batches must wait at the side yard until the previous batch has finished. Next, waiting trains in the next batch proceed all at once to the exchange facility, instead of gradually, with 8-minute time intervals. As a result, trains remain in operation for longer because load units or rail wagons have to queue for service.

With respect to the hump shunting variant with 2 locomotives at workstation 2 (H22 and H12), there is an additional factor that leads to time differences between one batch and multiple batch demand. Due to a capacity difference between workstation 1 and workstation 2, there is an accumulation of waiting time due to queuing in front of workstation 2.

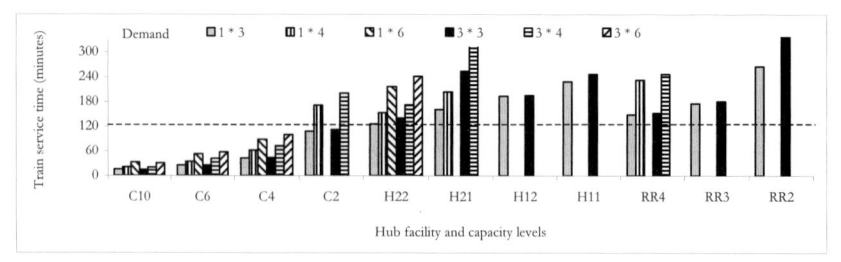

Figure 6–4: Train service time in relation to demand and capacity level of various hub facilities

Demand: number of batches * number of trains per batch (see for specification Table 6–3).

C*x*: new hub terminal with *x* number of cranes.

H*xy*: hump shunting yard with *x* number of locomotives for sorting and *y* number of locomotives for assembly.

RR*x*: road-rail terminal with *x* number of cranes.

The two exceptions to this general trend are (see Figure 6–4):
- The new hub terminal with 10 cranes, for all demand levels, and
- The new hub terminal with 6 cranes, for a demand level with a single or multiple batch of 3 trains.

For these capacity and demand levels there is no time difference between single and multiple batch demand. Analysis of the new hub terminal operations showed two factors as the cause. First, due to the relative speed of operations, fewer or no trains accumulate at the side yard in cases with multiple batches. Consequently fewer or no trains proceed at once to the exchange facility. Thus all or a part of the trains continue to arrive with an 8-minute time interval. As a result there is no or a limited extension of the train service time. Second, due to the speed of operations, cranes face waiting time during the handling of the first two to three trains. This is explained as follows. At terminal facilities load units can only continue to be processed when the destination train has arrived at the terminal. Therefore, the number of load units to be processed is limited with respect to the first two to three trains of a batch, but increases with every succeeding train that arrives. As a consequence, at facilities with a large capacity, cranes must wait for the next train to arrive to continue operations with respect to the first two to three trains. The effect on the train service time is that for single batch demand the service time includes crane waiting time, while for multiple batch demand the service time includes waiting time of trains taken in operations. The total effect is that this results in similar train service times.

In addition, Figure 6–4 shows a general trend that the train service time increases when the number of trains in a batch increases. For terminal operations there are two factors influencing the increase in train service time. First, the more trains there are in a batch, the more load units there are to be processed. Second, the more trains there are in a batch, the higher the number of load units per train to be exchanged. In the simulation it is assumed that $n-1/n$, n being the number of trains in a batch, is the share of the total amount of load units of each train that is exchanged. So, the greater the value for n, the larger this share.

With respect to hump shunting operations only the first factor applies: the more trains there are in a batch, the more rail wagons there are to be processed at workstation 1 and the more trains there are at workstation 2.

These findings suggest that, from the perspective of the hub-node, it may be better to organise hub-and-spoke networks in various small batches than several larger batches. Whether this is possible depends on the geographical location of the origin and destination terminals, transport volumes and the possibilities and willingness of rail operators to add their services to a hub-and-spoke network (where one operator does not have sufficient volume).

With respect to identifying favourable conditions we may conclude the following. Ideally, in order to minimise train sojourn times, train and batch interarrival times should be determined such that trains do not have to wait at the side yard, and equipment does not have to wait for trains. A *just-in-time* arrival schedule would lead to a situation in which the train sojourn time equals the train service time. In addition, in preferable conditions demand is structured into various small batches, because this leads to shorter train sojourn and service times than demand structured into several large batches.

6.4.3 Required minimum network volume

Minimum network volume is defined as the required annual number of load units to be transported in a hub-and-spoke network in order to achieve a costs per load unit equal to the cost benchmark criterion. This value is used to identify, for each hub exchange facility, the scale of hub-and-spoke networks for which it is suitable. In this section we take a closer look at the required minimum network volume for each facility and capacity level.

To estimate the minimum required network volume the demand level and the costs per load unit of all initial experiments were plotted into a graph (see Figure 6–5). For each capacity level of an exchange facility, daily demand expressed as for instance three batches of three trains (3*3) is now expressed as annual volume (as it is used in the cost model). Next, a trend line was drawn through the observations per facility and capacity level by means of a spreadsheet (Excel) functionality. In addition, a (horizontal dotted) line representing the value of the cost benchmark criterion was added. The point where the trend line and the line for the benchmark criterion cross is identified as the required minimum. The required minimum volume can be read from Figure 6–5 when a vertical (dotted) line is drawn from this point to the x-axis.

The minimum network volumes derived from Figure 6–5 are specified in Table 6–14. The new hub facilities with 10, 6 and 4 cranes (C10, C6 and C4) require the greatest minimum network volume: 192,000, 134,000 and 99,000 load units per year respectively, to achieve a maximum costs level of 50 euros per load unit. Expressed in terms of number of trains per day, this implies 13, 9 and 7 trains per day respectively.

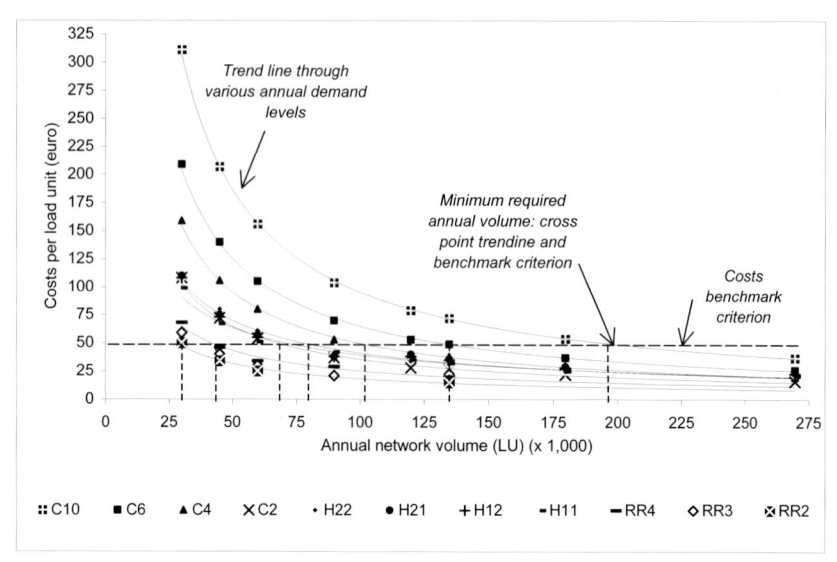

Figure 6–5: Illustration of the estimation of the minimum required annual network volume

C*x*: new hub terminal with *x* number of cranes.

H*xy* or F*xy*: hump shunting yard or flat shunting yard with *x* number of locomotives for sorting and *y* number of locomotives for assembly.

RR*x*: road-rail terminal with *x* number of cranes.

It is difficult to qualify these volumes as very large, large or intermediate or as realistic or unrealistic. In other words, are there regions with a terminal landscape, trade volume and trade relations such that a minimum of 7 to 13 trains (minimum 600 metres) per day can be accumulated at the hub-node? Table 6–15 provides various data for comparison, derived from Chapter 3. With respect to former (Metz) and proposed (Paris, Hanover) locations for hub facilities the required minimum volumes seem realistic. Kreutzberger (2002) studied the relationship between type of network and the number of origin and destination terminals, area, train length, loading degree, train service frequency and annual network volume. For regions with 6 to 10 origin terminals connected by a hub-and-spoke network with 6 to 10 destination terminals in another region a hub-and-spoke network is much more efficient than a point-to-point network. On the basis of a frequency of one departing train per origin terminal per working day this type of hub-and-spoke network generates an annual network volume of between 150,000 and 250,000; that is, between 8 to 10 trains to be exchanged at the hub facility.

Table 6–15 also shows that there may be a need for hub facilities for smaller demand. Existing (Muizen) and former (Herne) hub locations suggest a demand of 5 to 8 trains. In the same study Kreutzberger (2002) suggests that a hub-and-spoke network is more efficient than a point-to-point network where there are 2 or 4 origin terminals in a certain region connecting with 2 or 4 destination terminals in another region. These hub-and-spoke networks generate an annual volume of 50,000 and 100,000 load units respectively.

Table 6–14: Estimated required annual minimum network volume to achieve a cost per load unit of 50 euros per hub facility and capacity level

Hub facility and capacity level	Annual network volume (LU)	Daily volume (LU)	Daily number of trains* (600 metres)	Train service time (x batches of 3 trains) (minutes)
C10	192,000	615	13	16
C6	134,000	417	9	26
C4	99,000	317	7	43
H21	79,000	253	6	162
H22	75,000	240	5	127
H12	75,000	240	5	194
H11	69,000	221	5	229
C2	67,000	215	5	109
RR4	40,000	128	3	206
RR3	35,000	112	3	222
RR2	30,000	96	2	266

* All rounded upwards.

Taking into account the train service times, the new hub terminal with 2 cranes seems to be most suitable for small hub-and-spoke networks. However, if the market does not accept a price based on costs of 50 euros per load unit and requires a service time below 120 minutes, alternative solutions are needed for small hub-and-spoke networks. Solutions may include reducing costs at new hub terminals or improving operations at alternative facilities.

Cost reduction at new hub terminals may be achieved by attracting road-rail flows or by using cheaper equipment and/or infrastructure. To obtain insight into options for cost reduction, insight into the cost structure of new hub terminals is needed. The next section focuses on the cost structure of new hub terminals and compares it with those of alternative facilities.

Exploring solutions to improve operations at alternative facilities is beyond the scope of this thesis. With respect to shunting one could investigate measures for reducing the performance backlog due to the need to couple a network locomotive, (un)couple rail wagons manually, fill air tubes and carry out lengthy brake tests.

Table 6–15: Daily volume at existing, former and proposed hub facilities

Case*	Number of trains** per day
Proposed hub terminal near Paris	60
Former hump shunting yard at Metz	25-28
Proposed hub terminal Hanover-Lehrte	24
Suggested for situation with 8 to 10 origin terminals by Kreutzberger (2002)	6-8
Existing flat shunting yard at Muizen	7-8
Former flat shunting yard at Herne	5-8
Suggested for situation with 2 to 4 origin terminals by Kreutzberger (2002)	2-4

* Refer to Chapter 3.
** Minimum length 600 metres.

6.4.4 Cost structures

Analysis of the required minimum annual volume in the previous section already suggested that the total annual cost level of the new hub terminal is higher than that of the other facilities. In this section I analyse the various cost categories of each facility, including the flat shunting yard. The analysis comprises two parts. Firstly, the cost structure is analysed for what I call the basic capacity of each facility. The basic capacity consists of a fixed basic infrastructure for the exchange facility, no side yards, and required equipment and labour related to the capacity level. The dimensions of the basic capacity for each facility are described in Appendix K and summarised in Table 6–16. The costs of the basic capacity apply to the single batch demand levels (1*3, 1*4, 1*6) investigated in this study. However, the demand of one batch of 6 trains for the road-rail terminal is excluded because the terminal only has capacity for four trains. For the demand of 1*8 additional infrastructure at the exchange facility itself is included in the cost calculations. For multiple demand (3*3, 3*4 and 3*6) costs are calculated to include the basic capacity and the required side yard capacity. It is assumed that side yard capacity equal to the batch size should be available at the arrival yard and also at the departure yard. To provide general insight into cost structures a selection of the calculated cost cases is presented in this section. Cost structures are presented for a demand of 1*6, 3*3 and 3*6.

Table 6–16: Summary of infrastructural features of basic capacity

	New hub terminal (C)	Hump shunting yard (H)	Road-rail terminal (RR)	Flat shunting yard (F)
Tracks (700 metres)	6	6 arrival 6 departure	4	3 arrival 3 departure 6 sorting*
Switches	10	24	6	24
Detour track (metres)	-	3400	-	2400
Tracks with brake system	-	9	-	-
Tracks with assembly system	-	6	-	-

* 350 metres.

In Figure 6–6, we can see that total annual costs for terminal equipment (cranes, roller pallets and the operations control system) are responsible for the wide variance in costs between most new hub terminals and other facilities. The relatively high investment in very fast cranes and the transport system results in high annual capital costs (depreciation and interest). As a consequence, maintenance and operating costs are also higher than for the other facilities, because those costs are expressed as a percentage of the investment costs. Labour costs are lower, except for the variant with ten cranes. Labour costs are related to the total duration of a daily operation. In Figure 6–6 labour costs are related to the duration of an operation of one batch with six trains. For the new hub terminal and the hump shunting yard variants this demand implies labour costs for one shift (8 hours), and for the other facilities for two shifts. Note that in the simulations it is assumed that trains arrive every eight minutes, while in reality demand may be spread out over the day, leading to different labour (shifts) needs during any given day.

Figure 6-6 also shows why a hump shunting yard requires a higher minimum volume than the road-rail terminal and the flat shunting yard. Annual infrastructure costs are much higher, while other costs are more or less the same.

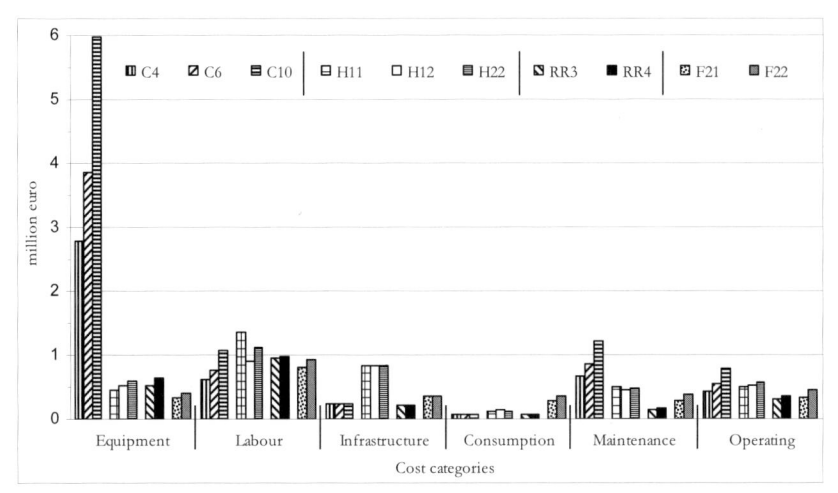

Figure 6–6: Annual costs per cost category for various hub exchange facilities at basic capacity and a demand of one batch of 6 trains (based on cost data from 2000-2003)

The basic capacity consists of a fixed basic infrastructure for the exchange facility, no side yards, and required equipment and labour related to the capacity level. For details see Appendix K.

Costs categories:
- Equipment and infrastructure costs: depreciation and interest costs.
- Consumption costs: fuel and electricity.
- Labour costs: salaries, social security, pensions and bonuses for evening and night work.
- Maintenance costs: repair and ongoing maintenance of terminal and shunting yard infrastructure and equipment.
- Operating costs: insurance, administrative and organisational costs such as marketing, public relations, legal advice/consulting, software, telephone, taxes, etc.).

Until now, costs related to the basic capacity of a facility and a single batch demand have been considered. For a demand of more than one batch per day, side yard capacity is needed for trains that have to wait for operations, and trains that have to wait to enter the network. In the experiments it is assumed that infrastructure capacity at both the arrival side yard and the departure side yard matches the number of trains in a batch in the case of multiple batches. Infrastructure costs are therefore increased, as are variable costs. This is illustrated in Figure 6–7. Figure 6–7 shows the development of costs for one batch with six trains, three batches of three trains and three batches of six trains for a new hub terminal with two cranes and a hump shunting yard with 2 x 2 locomotives. These facilities were selected because they both require a minimum demand volume of 5 trains per day to meet the benchmark criterion of 50 euros per load unit (see Table 6–14). Figure 6–7 shows the increase in annual infrastructure costs due to additional track and switch capacity required at the side yard. The increase in these costs is greater at the hump shunting yard, because in addition to tracks and switches there are additional investments to be made in braking and pushing systems. Labour costs increase at both facilities for a demand of three batches of six trains, because the duration of operations exceeds one shift. As consumption costs are also related to the duration of shunting operations, these increase as well. At the new hub terminal, the increase in consumption costs is related to the increase in the number of load units. Maintenance and operating costs increase at both facilities, because they are related, among other things, to the amount of investment in infrastructure, which is increased.

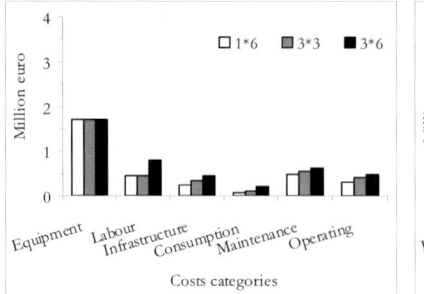

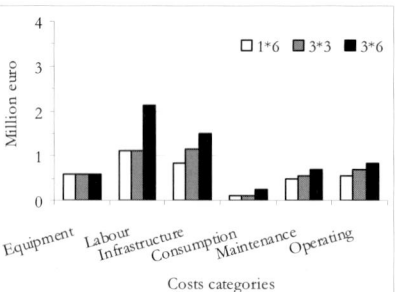

Figure 6–7: Effect of different demand levels on annual costs per cost category for two facilities

In subsection 6.4.3 it was suggested that a reduction in costs at the new hub terminals might improve their attractiveness. Most effective cost reductions may be obtained by using fewer roller pallets or cheaper cranes. Such measures may naturally affect the speed of operations. The effect of cheaper but slower cranes was studied in the sensitivity analysis and is discussed in subsection 6.5.4.

A final but important remark is that we should be aware that costs in general, but especially those for the new hub terminal, may be underestimated. In Chapter 5 it was noted that cost data sources are limited or even not available. In addition, with respect to the new hub terminal, it was noted that building costs for new infrastructure often exceed their forecasts. Furthermore, in Chapter 3 it was mentioned that the proposed infrastructure and operations seem to present the ideal situation. This is especially the case with respect to the arrival and departure of trains. If the projected arrival and departure procedure does not work, a shunting locomotive may be needed to pull the train into the terminal. In the case of operations involving multiple batches that fill up all the tracks at the terminal, a detour track may be needed for this locomotive. Such measures naturally lead to higher investment costs and annual total costs.

A sensitivity analysis to investigate the impact of significantly higher costs on the results was carried out. The results are reported in subsection 6.5.3.

6.4.5 Conclusions

From the results presented in this section it may be concluded that under the given conditions for load order, load factor, interarrival time, synchronisation of arrivals and operations, only the new hub terminal is able to meet the time and benchmark criteria, albeit under the conditions of sufficiently large volume, which is determined as a minimum of between 5 and 13 trains per day, depending on the required speed of operations. The faster the operations, the more equipment is required and the higher the minimum demand will be. If costs lower than 50 euros per load unit are required, the minimum volume must be higher, or else cheaper or fewer items of equipment should be employed so as to reduce costs.

Alternative hub facilities are limited with respect to applying additional capacity in order to improve their handling times. Their train service and sojourn time may be improved under different conditions such as planned load order (fewer handling operations) and just-in-time train and batch interarrival times, or technical modifications with respect to infrastructure and equipment.

Model outputs were validated, but that is no guarantee that model assumptions do not significantly affect the results. Therefore, it is good to reflect on the model assumptions in relation to the results. In this paragraph I try to identify and quantify under- or overestimation of the results as result of certain model assumptions.

Assumption: job assignment to cranes
In the model each crane can process any load unit, while in reality a crane can only process load units in its own crane section. As a consequence in the model each crane has an equal load unit, which is seldom reached in practice. In practice the use of scheduling heuristics supports to equally divide workloads over cranes, but a 100% balanced utilisation of cranes is seldom reached. Meyer (1998, p. 139) demonstrated for a batch of 6 trains and a facility with 10 cranes that the crane with the longest workload is 19 minutes longer occupied than the crane with the shortest work. With an average crane cycle time of 60 minutes (see Table 5–5) this implies an additional workload of 19 load units. The smaller the number of cranes, the longer the average crane cycle times (see Table 5–5) become. However, we may assume that by increasing lengths of crane sections differences in workload level off. As a result maximum differences in total handling time between cranes may stay about 19 minutes. When we consider the train service time as average duration that cranes are busy, some cranes will be busy for a shorter period of time, some longer, with a maximum difference of 19 minutes. Most likely the difference between the train service times and the crane with the longest workload will be less than 19 minutes. Hence, most likely the train service time in the terminal models are underestimated with about 10 minutes to a maximum of about 19 minutes.

Assumption: volume per exchange relations
In the model a batch consists of an equal number of load units or rail wagons (each train has the same length) and it is assumed that load units or rail wagons of one train are equally redistributed among the other trains in a batch. In practice some transport relation may have more volume than others. This implies that trains to some destination will be longer and that more load units will be loaded to that train than from that train. The total throughput in the model compared to practice remains the same. However, model assumptions may affect the results of the terminal models. Different train lengths imply that some cranes (sections) have fewer trains to serve than other cranes. As a result workload between cranes may vary. Since Meyer (1998) studied a batch of 6 trains of equal train length (see above), batches with different trains length may imply additional underestimation of the train service time.

The combination of the underestimation due to differences in crane work load and the volume per exchange relations makes that the facilities C4 and C2 in combination with the demand 3*3 and 3*6 respectively fall outside quadrant I. But, although the underestimation of the service time has a considerable impact on some train service times of the new hub-terminal, the performance difference between new hub-terminal and other facilities is too large to affect the ranking.

Assumption: train entrance time and shunting time between side yard and facility
Afterwards reflecting on the assumed times for entering the facility from the network and for shunting trains between the side yard and the facility, I realised that it would

have been better to apply a stochastic shunting time of between 3 to 6 minutes. These times are based on track lengths of 1000 and 2000 meters respectively and a driving speed of 20 km/hour. So the consequence with respect to the simulation results is that the train service and sojourn times are underestimated with about 3 to 6 minutes.

Further it is assumed that trains can enter the facility with own traction, due to electrification of arrival yards and terminals. If facilities are not electrified, a diesel locomotive must be attached to the train outside the facility, which implies an underestimation of the service time of about 12 minutes (see Table 5–15).

Assumption: no equipment breakdowns
Results are provided for the situation that cranes, locomotives, software, etc. do not break down. However, in any operation equipment fails. So compared to reality the train service times are underestimated. With respect to the comparison of facilities I assume that operations are equally sensitive for equipment break down, implying that the ranking of the results will not be affected when breakdowns are included.

It was stated in Chapter 5 that specification of unit prices is difficult. Data of sufficient detail in the literature is scarce and questions in the questionnaires sent to network and node operators often remained unanswered. Consequently, costs most likely may be underestimated. Therefore, cost sensitivity analyses were carried out. See section 5.5.

In this section the impact of variable demand on time and cost performances was presented, keeping other variables constant. In the next section, the sensitivity of the results presented in this section is discussed for different load order, load factors, annual costs and arrival times.

6.5 Sensitivity of favourable options for load order, load factor, annual costs and arrival times

In the previous section it was concluded that sensitivity of the results for load order, load factor, cost levels and train and batch interarrival times should be investigated. This section describes the results of various sensitivity analyses for a selected number of cases. The initial experiments were carried out with an unplanned load order, a load factor of 1.6, a certain cost level and a train interarrival time of eight minutes. With the sensitivity analysis I wanted to investigate under which conditions cases which in the previous section scored just outside the time and cost benchmark criterion, move within the benchmark boundaries, in other words, the conditions under which facilities other than the new hub terminal may become favourable options. Furthermore, I intend to study the conditions under which new hub terminal cases lose their status as a favourable option. In addition, with the sensitivity analysis I intend to study the impact of different conditions on the time and cost performance of new hub terminals as presented in the previous section.

Variables studied in the sensitivity analysis were as follows (see subsections 6.2.2 and 6.2.3 for details):
- a planned load order (subsection 6.5.1);
- a load factor of 1.4 and 1.8 respectively (subsection 6.5.2);

- an increase in total annual costs due to a higher amount of investment in equipment and infrastructure or higher interest rates of 3% and 6% respectively (subsection 6.5.3);
- cheaper, but slower cranes at the new hub terminal (subsection 6.5.3), and
- ideal train and batch interarrival times (section 1.6).

The cases included in the sensitivity analysis are all cases that meet the time criterion of 240 minutes and the costs per load unit criterion of 60 euros per load unit (see Appendix L for a specification). These criteria were determined based on an educated guestimate on potential cases to meet the time and cost criterion. In the sensitivity analysis with the planned load order the four variants of the flat shunting yard were also included.

6.5.1 Impact of a planned load order on the set of favourable options

In the experiments with a planned load order the parameter setting for the distribution of flows in the terminal models was changed from 10% direct from train to train to 50% and 80% via the transport system to 40%. For shunting, the number of wagons shunted was changed from 30 individual rail wagons to 12 wagon groups (see subsection 6.2.2 for an explanation). I expected that hump shunting yards would benefit more from planned load order than the terminals, because shunting yards involve fewer handling operations as well as longer service times. Based on the server distribution functions for flat shunting I expected flat shunting to be slower (but cheaper) than hump shunting. Furthermore, I expected that the road-rail terminals would benefit more from the planned load order than the new hub terminal due to the longer crane service times of road-rail cranes.

The results presented in Figure 6–8 confirm these expectations. The relatively slower facilities benefit the most from a planned load order. This is indicated by the larger arrows. While the train service time for new hub terminal cases is reduced by 2 to 24 minutes, hump shunting and road-rail cases show a reduction of between 40 and 105 minutes. As a consequence an additional number of cases move into quadrant I.

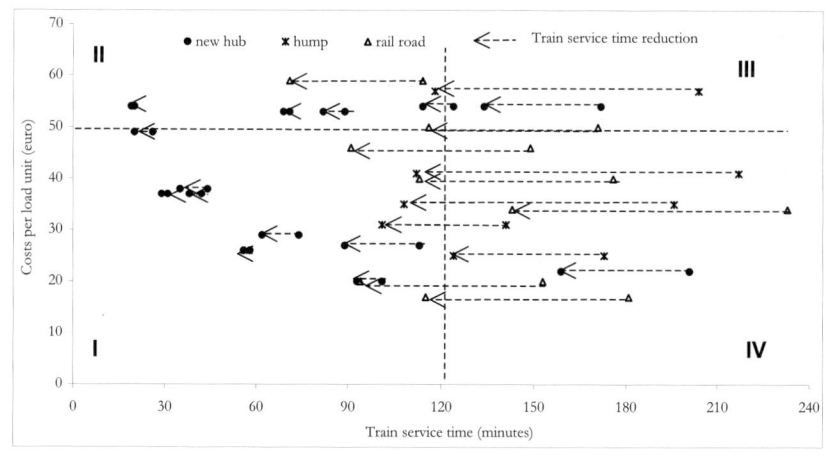

Figure 6–8: Reduction of train service time due to a planned load order

The parameter settings for the distribution of flows in the terminal models were changed from 10% direct from train to train to 50% and 80% via the transport system to 40%. For shunting, the number of wagons shunted, which was changed from 30 individual rail wagons to 12 wagon groups, was investigated.

Figure 6–8 presents the favourable options under the condition of the abovementioned planned load order. Taking the size of confidence intervals of the output into account, train service times may vary slightly, but this does not affect the quadrant in which the case appears. The top half of Figure 6–8 shows the cases that move into the quadrant with favourable options. The bottom half of Figure 6–8 shows the new hub terminal variants which were already identified in subsection 6.4.1 as favourable options.

Figure 6–8 suggests three issues. First, under the condition of a planned load order, hump shunting yards and road-rail terminal facilities have become an alternative for new hub terminals for a demand of three batches of three trains. Although these facilities meet the time benchmark criterion, the new hub terminals remain (much) faster. On the other hand, the alternatives perform better in terms of costs per load unit. Note that the road-rail terminal performs better, faster and at lower cost than the hump shunting yard. See Table 6–17 for a specification of cases that move into the quadrant for favourable options.

Second, under the condition of a planned load order, hump shunting yards and road-rail terminals also show up as options for small hub-and-spoke networks.

Third, for larger volumes than three batches of three trains, the new hub terminal remains the only choice.

Table 6–17: Specification of cases that move into the quadrant for favourable options under the condition of planned load order

	Demand	Facility	Service time (minutes) Planned load order	Service time (minutes) Not planned load order	Costs per load unit (euro)
New favourable options	400m*1*3	RR2	116	171	50
	1*3	RR4	91	149	46
	1*3	RR3	113	176	40
	1*6	H22	112	217	41
	3*3	RR4	94	153	20
	3*3	H22	101	141	31
	3*3	H12	108	196	35
	3*3	RR3	115	181	17
Existing favourable options	3*3	C6	20	26	49
	3*3	C4	35	44	38
	3*3	C2	89	113	27
	3*4	C6	38	42	37
	3*4	C4	62	74	29
	3*6	C10	29	31	37
	3*6	C6	56	58	26
	3*6	C4	93	101	20

The parameter setting for the distribution of flows in the terminal models was changed from 10% direct from train to train to 50% and 80% via the transport system to 40%. For shunting, the number of wagons shunted, which was changed from 30 individual rail wagons to 12 wagon groups, was investigated.

Cx: new hub terminal with x number of cranes.

Hxy: hump shunting yard with x number of locomotives for sorting and y number of locomotives for assembly.

RRx: road-rail terminal with x number of cranes.

Flat shunting variants were also included in the analysis, but for reasons of clarity these are not presented in Figure 6–8. Flat shunting alternatives can be found in quadrants III and IV of the benchmark graph. However, the shortest train service time in quadrant III turned out to be 263 minutes and the longest 815 minutes. The performances of the simulated flat shunting cases that appear in quadrant III (options for cost-sensitive flows) are presented in Table 6–18. The alternatives that are not options (quadrant IV) are presented in Appendix M.

Table 6–18: **Specification of flat shunting alternatives in quadrant III: options for cost-sensitive flows**

Demand*	Facility and capacity level	Train sojourn time (minutes)	Costs per load unit (euros)
1*3	F22	263	50
1*3	F21	301	41
1*3	F11	492	44
1*4	F22	331	38
1*4	F21	385	31
1*4	F12	588	40
1*4	F11	642	34
1*6	F22	480	31
1*6	F21	564	26
3*3	F22	434	23
3*3	F21	471	19
3*3	F12	815	23

* Number of batches * number of trains per batch.

Although a planned load order that results in a 12-wagon group is rather realistic, the reduction in train service times for alternative facilities raises the question of "what would be the impact of ideal planned load orders?" I carried out a few additional simulation runs for a demand of one batch of three trains in order to answer this question. The ideal planned load order for a batch of three trains leads to three wagon groups to be shunted, one for each destination. Service time distributions were adjusted for this specific situation. For the terminals I assumed a distribution of flows of 70% direct from train to train instead of 50% and 20% via the transport system instead of 40%. The results are presented in Figure 6–9.

Figure 6–9 clearly shows that the alternative facilities benefit the most from planned load orders. See Appendix N for a specification of the performances of all cases. Under the conditions of an ideal load order and a demand consisting of one or several batches of three trains, the performances of hump shunting yards and road-rail terminals are similar to the train service time for the new hub terminal with four cranes (C4). The flat shunting yard variants benefit the most from an ideal load order, but the performance improvement levels off at a higher level than the other alternatives. For flat shunting (F11) I simulated two additional variants in order to see whether performance could be further improved. I assumed that the network locomotive remains attached to the train and is used to drop off two wagon groups and to pick up two others. I also distinguished between a normal brake test and a short brake test. These two variants show improvements in the performance of flat shunting, but this is not sufficient enough, however, to reach the time benchmark criterion of 120 minutes.

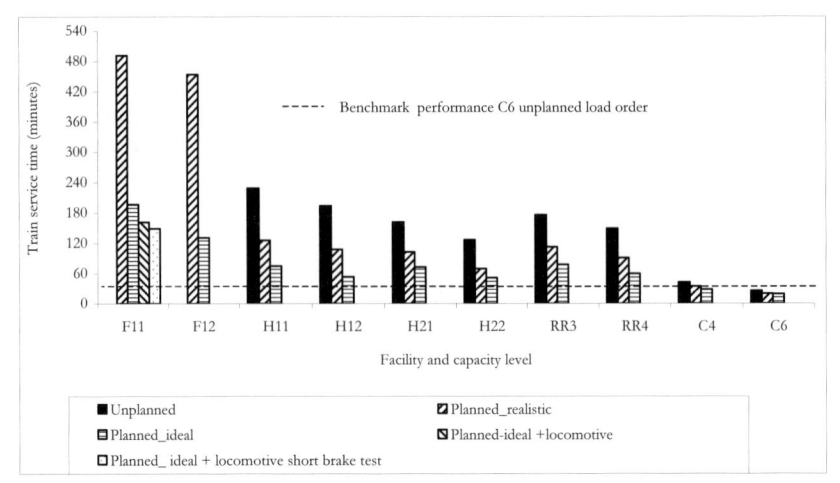

[Figure: bar chart showing train service times across facilities F11, F12, H11, H12, H21, H22, RR3, RR4, C4, C6 with five load order categories]

Figure 6–9: **Train service times for a demand of one batch of three trains for different load orders for a few selected facilities (in minutes)**

Cx: new hub terminal with x number of cranes.
Hxy or Fxy: hump or flat shunting yard with x number of locomotives for sorting and y number of locomotives for assembly.
RRx: road-rail terminal with x number of cranes.

6.5.2 Impact of a smaller and larger load factor on the favourable options

In the experiments with variable demand the load factor was 1.6 load units per rail wagon. However, system analysis in Chapter 3 showed that the load factor very much depends on the transport relation. Consequently, the load factor on some transport relations may be closer to 1.4 and others closer to 1.8. A lower or higher load factor influences the number of load units per train, but it only influences time performances of terminals. In the shunting process it does not matter how many load units are on a shunted rail wagon. With respect to costs per load unit, however, the load factor affects all facilities. The results of the sensitivity analysis are presented in Figure 6–10. Per facility and capacity level the costs per load unit and train service for each of the three load factors are plotted in Figure 6–10. The results are specified in Appendix O.

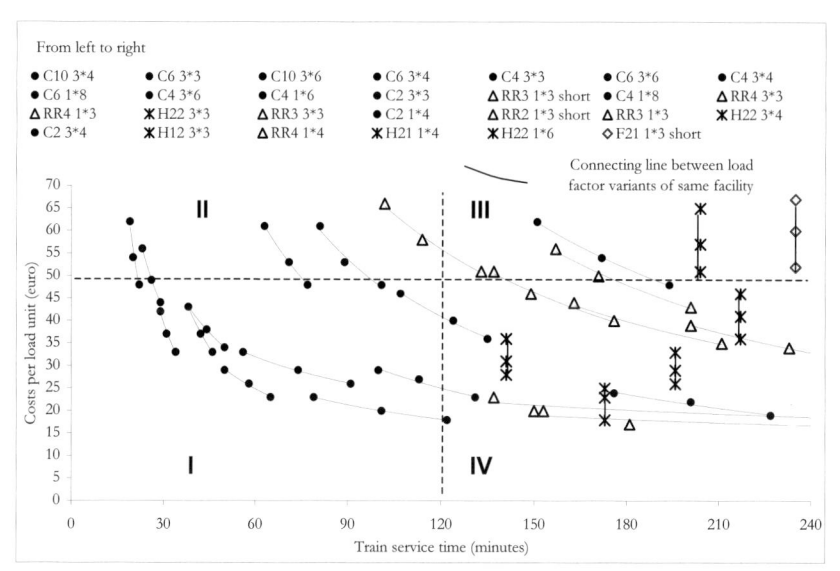

Figure 6–10: Variation in train service time and costs per load unit due to three load factors, 1.4, 1.6 and 1.8

The legend should be interpreted as follows. C10 3*4: new hub terminal with 10 cranes and a demand of 3 batches of 4 trains each.

Cx: new hub terminal with x number of cranes.

Hxy or Fxy: hump or flat shunting yard with x number of locomotives for sorting and y number of locomotives for assembly.

RRx: road-rail terminal with x number of cranes.

Per facility and capacity level the costs per load unit and train service time for each of the three load factors are plotted. The upper cost value of a set of three marks is related to a load factor of 1.4, the middle to a load factor of 1.6 and the lower mark to a load factor of 1.8.

Figure 6–10 indicates four things. First, the load factor (obviously) does not affect the train service time of shunting yards (* or H and ◊ or F marks in Figure 6–10), because the load factor does not affect the number of rail wagons. The shunting facilities can be easily distinguished from the terminals because they have vertical connecting lines. However, the load factor does affect the train service time of terminals. For new hub terminals a load factor of 1.4 leads to shorter train service times of between 2 (for instance C10 (3*6)) and 25 minutes (for instance C2 (3*4)). A load factor of 1.8 leads to increases in train service times of between 1 (for instance C10 (3*4)) and 27 minutes (for instance C4 (3*4)). The reduction or increase in train service time may be slightly affected (by several seconds to a few minutes) when the length of the 95% confidence intervals is taken into account.

In general, the results show that fast facilities with 10 or 6 cranes, C6 and C10, are less sensitive to changes in load factor than the facilities with less capacity, C4 and C2. The fact that crane service times decrease as the number of cranes is increased explains this. We can derive this from the varying steepnesses of the connecting lines in Figure 6–10. The new hub terminal facilities basically appear to the left of the time benchmark criterion line in Figure 6–10. The connecting lines left of 60 minutes have steeper slopes than the ones between 60 and 120 minutes. The steeper the slope, the less sensitive the train service time is to changing load factors. The steepest slopes are mostly related to facilities with the highest numbers of cranes.

The slopes of connecting lines for the road-rail terminals (marked as RR and Δ) are less steep than those for C4 and C2. This indicates again that the slower the facility the larger the differences in train service time under changing load factor conditions. In addition, in Figure 6–10 we can see that there is a clear difference between the slope of the connecting line for road-rail facilities with single batch demand (upper right part of Figure 6–10) and multiple batch (lower right part of Figure 6–10). The road-rail terminals are especially sensitive to an increase in load factor with multiple batch demand. The explanation for this is the accumulation of longer duration of operations due to additional load units and longer waiting times at the side yard for trains of the second and third batches. After all, despite more load units per train, the interarrrival times were (purposefully) not adjusted in these experiments. In later experiments the interarrival time was varied.

Secondly, load factor (naturally) affects the costs per load unit. The minimum costs increase per load unit due to smaller load factor (1.4) is 2 euros. This applies for instance to the facilities H22 (3*4) and C4 (3*6). The maximum costs increase per load unit is 8 euros. This applies for instance to the facilities RR3 (1*3 short), C4 (1*6) and C10 (3*4). The minimum costs decrease per load unit due to a larger load factor (1.8) is 1 euro. This applies for instance to the facility RR3 (3*3). The maximum costs decrease per load unit is 8 euros. This applies for instance to the facility F21 (1*3 short).

Since new hub terminals require the highest investments, I had expected that the costs per load unit at new hub terminals would be more sensitive to differences in the total number of load units on a train than at other facilities. However, Figure 6–10 indicates that cost sensitivity is related to demand volume in combination with the capacity level of a facility. In general, it applies that the connecting lines in the top half of Figure 6–10 relate to single batch demand and the lines in the bottom half to multiple batch demand. The distance between the upper and lower markers connected by the lines is large for the lines in the top half of Figure 6–10. This implies greater sensitivity to changing load factor conditions.

Thirdly, under the condition of a higher load factor, cases C2 (3*3) and C4 (3*6) fall outside 'favourable options' quadrant I due to a longer service time, while cases C10 (3*4), C6 (1*8) and C4 (1*6) benefit from it due to a reduction in costs per load unit and move into quadrant I.

Fourth, under the condition of a lower load factor, case C6 (3*3) falls outside quadrant I due to higher costs, but case C4 (1*8) benefits from it, resulting in a shorter train service time, which falls inside this quadrant I.

Cases that fall into quadrant I under the condition of a different load factor are specified in Table 6–19. The outcomes with respect to cases that fall in or outside quadrant I do not change when the length of the 95% confidence intervals is taken into consideration.

Table 6–19: Specification of new favourable options under the condition of a lower and higher load factor

Demand*	Load factor	Facility and capacity level	Train service time (minutes)	Costs per load unit (euros)
1*6	1.8	C4	101	48
1*8	1.4	C4	107	46
1*8	1.8	C6	77	48
3*4	1.8	C10	22	48

* Number of batches * number of trains.

The general conclusion is that alternative hub exchange facilities are not affected by different load factors to such an extent that they become a competitive alternative. However, four new hub terminal variants, under the condition of a different load factor, fall into the 'favourable options' quadrant. This applies to smaller (single batch) demand levels, and also to a new hub facility that, due to a large input of cranes, is able to generate a very fast train service time.

Generally speaking, due to a large input of cranes train service times of fast new hub facilities are less sensitive to changes in load factor than facilities with less capacity. The time difference compared to the initial load factor can increase from around 2 minutes for the faster facilities to around 30 minutes for the slower facilities. The result is that cases C2 (3*3) and C4 (3*6) fall outside quadrant I with the favourable options.

6.5.3 Impact of an increase in costs on the favourable options

Since there is some uncertainty in the applied cost data in the initial experiments, the sensitivity of the initial results to changing costs was investigated (see subsection 6.2.2). For these experiments only the cost model was used to recalculate the costs per load unit for:
- A 25% increase in investments in equipment and infrastructure, and
- Interest rates of 3% and 6%.

Of the selected cases for the sensitivity experiment (see Appendix L), only cases with costs of 50 euros or lower were included in the experiments pointed out above. The results are presented below.

Impact of higher amounts of investment

With respect to increases in investment, I expected a higher increase in costs per load unit due to higher equipment investment than infrastructure investment. Furthermore, I expected the new hub terminals to be most sensitive to higher equipment investment and the hump shunting yards most sensitive to increases in infrastructure investment. I explain these expectations as follows.

The analysis of cost structures in subsection 6.4.4 showed that high equipment costs dominate the annual costs of a new hub terminal, while infrastructure costs dominate hump shunting yard costs. Furthermore, equipment costs of the new hub terminals are higher than infrastructure costs of the hump shunting yards. A 25% increase in investments leads to higher depreciation costs per year, as well as higher interest costs. In absolute terms the increase in depreciation and interest costs is greater for an amount of investment of 1 million than for an amount of 100,000. So, costs for hub terminals increase more than costs for hump shunting yards. However, the sensitivity of the costs per load unit also depends on the demand. For a large demand (e.g. multiple batch demand) these additional costs are spread out over more units than for a small demand (e.g. single demand), resulting in a lower increase in the costs per load unit.

As such, with respect to the results presented in Figure 6-11 and in Figure 6-12 I expected to find the following:
- on the left side of the x-axis, shunting facilities (in absolute terms, low increase in costs);
- on the right side of the x-axis, new hub terminals, especially those with 6 and 10 cranes (in absolute terms, high increase in costs) and relatively small demand levels (single batch and 3*3), and
- in the middle, mostly road-rail terminals and new hub terminals with 2 and 4 cranes.

However, in Figure (infrastructure) I expected to find the following:
- on the left side of the x-axis, terminals (in absolute terms, a low increase in costs), especially those with relatively large demand compared to capacity, and
- on the right side of the x-axis, hump shunting yards (in absolute terms, high increase in costs).

Figure 6–11 and Figure 6–12 show the absolute and relative increase in costs per load unit for an increase in the amount of investment of 25% for equipment and infrastructure respectively. The cases are sorted on absolute costs increase in the first place and relative costs increase in the second place.

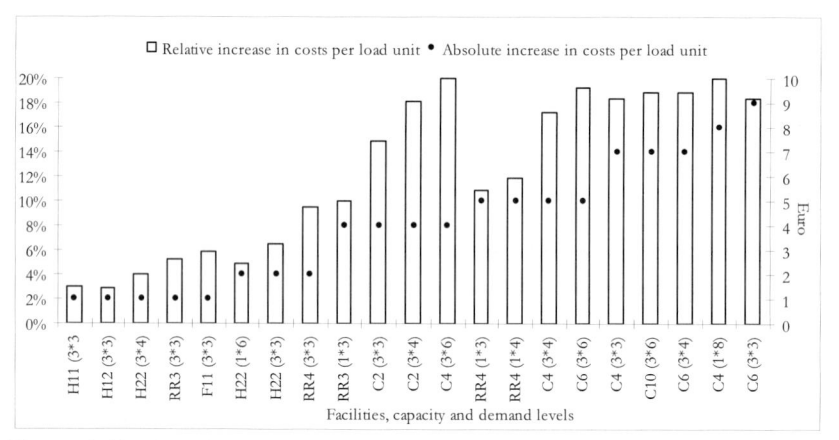

Figure 6–11: Relative and absolute effects of a 25% increase in investment in equipment on the costs per load unit

Figure 6–11 and Figure 6–12 confirm my expectation that the impact of higher equipment costs is greater than that of higher infrastructure costs. If we compare Figure 6–11 and Figure 6–12, we see first that the additional costs per load unit varies between 1 and 10 euros for an increase in equipment investment, and between 1 and 4 euros for an increase in infrastructure investment. Second, the ranking of facilities in Figure 6–11 and Figure 6–12 largely equates with my expectations: the new hub terminal is on the right side and the shunting facility on the left side of Figure 6–11 and hump shunting facilities on the right side of Figure 6–12. However, the ranking of facilities on the left side of Figure is less pronounced than expected. Apparently, due to relatively small costs increases, the absolute costs increases are relatively small also and for many cases are rounded up to one euro. As a consequence, the distinction between cases is less clear.

In addition to the absolute costs increase per load unit, Figure 6–11 and Figure 6–12 also present the relative increase of the costs per load unit. The lower the initial costs per load unit, the greater the relative costs increase becomes. Within each category of absolute costs increase per load unit, cases are sorted by increasing relative costs. The relative costs increase due to an increase in equipment investment lies between 3% and 20%; due to an increase in infrastructure investment this is between 2% and 13%.
See Appendix P for a specification of the results.

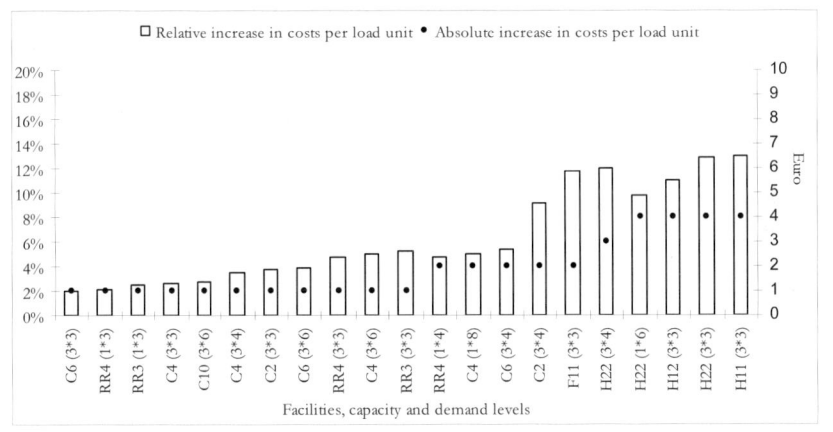

Figure 6–12: Relative and absolute effects of a 25% increase in investment in infrastructure on the costs per load unit

Impact of higher interest rates
With respect to higher interest rates I expected the 3% interest rate, compared to the initial 2.3%, to have a marginal cost-increasing effect of a few euros. I naturally expected a greater increase with an interest rate of 6%. Interest costs are calculated over the average amount of investment (see Chapter 5). The greater the total amount of investment in equipment and infrastructure, the greater the average amount of investment. Since new hub terminals require the greatest total investment, I expected the new hub terminal to be the most sensitive to higher interest rates. With regard to the results presented in Figure 6–13 and Figure 6–14, and based on the total amount of investment in equipment and infrastructure I expected the general order of facilities from left to right on the x-axis to read as follows: road-rail terminals, flat shunting yard, hump shunting yard and new hub terminals. I also expected that due to small demand (single batches), cases for different types of facilities might move towards the right side of the x-axis and mix with other types of facilities.

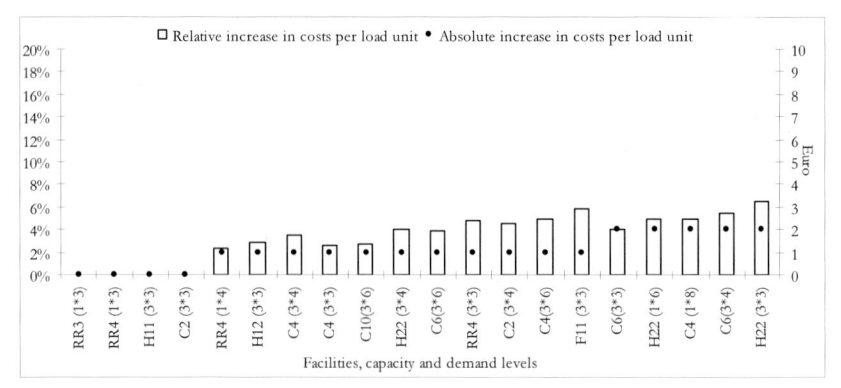

Figure 6–13: Relative and absolute effects of an interest rate of 3% instead of 2.3% on the costs per load unit

Figure 6–13 and Figure 6–14 show the absolute and relative increase in costs per load unit for interest rates of 3% and 6%. The cases are ranked by absolute costs increase in the first place and relative costs increase within an absolute cost category. Figure 6–13, which shows the results for an interest rate of 6%, confirms this expected general trend. However, in Figure 6–14, which shows results for an interest rate of 3%, this general trend is less visible. The slight increase in interest costs (0.7%), leads to less marked differences in absolute costs as a consequence of rounding off costs to whole euros.

The absolute costs increase per load unit for a 3% interest rate is indeed, as expected, small, at between 0 (rounded-up result) and 2 euros per load unit. The absolute costs increase of a 6% interest rate is between 4 and 9 euros per load unit. The relative costs increase per load unit due to an interest rate of 3% is between zero and 6% and for an interest rate of 6% it is between 4% and 20%.

See Appendix P for a specification of the results.

In just two facilities the increase in costs exceeds the benchmark criterion of 50 euros per load unit:
- as a result of a 25% increase in equipment investment costs, the cost per load unit for cases RR4 (1*3) and C6 (3*3) increases to 51 and 58 euros respectively;
- as a result of an interest rate of 3%, the costs per load unit for case C6 (3*3) increases to 51 euros, and
- as a result of an interest rate of 6%, the costs per load unit for case RR4 (1*3) rises to 51 euros, and for C6 (3*3) to 58 euros.

The 25% increase in infrastructure costs does not incur a costs per load unit above 50 euros.

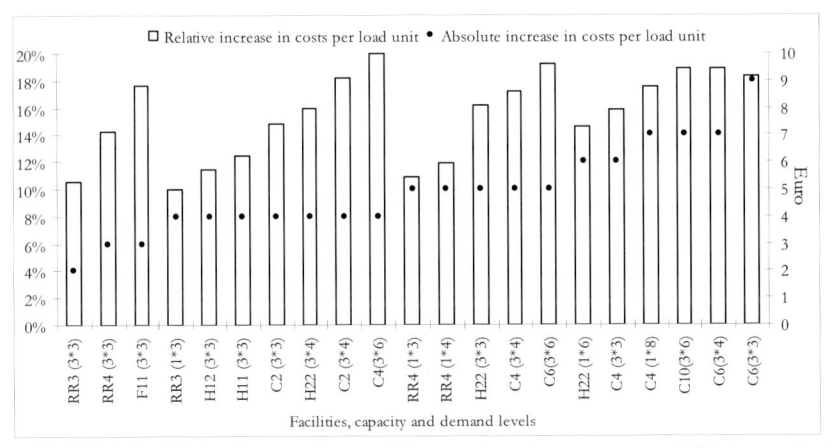

[Figure: bar chart with dots showing relative increase in costs per load unit (bars, left axis 0-20%) and absolute increase in costs per load unit (dots, right axis 0-10 Euro) across various facilities, capacity and demand levels: RR3 (3*3), RR4 (3*3), F11 (3*3), RR3 (1*3), H12 (3*3), H11 (3*3), C2 (3*3), H22 (3*4), C2 (3*4), C4(3*6), RR4 (1*3), RR4 (1*4), H22 (3*3), C4 (3*4), C6(3*6), H22 (1*6), C4 (3*3), C4 (1*8), C10(3*6), C6(3*4), C6(3*3)]

Figure 6–14: Relative and absolute effects of an interest rate of 6% instead of 2.3% on costs per load unit

6.5.4 Impact of cheaper but slower cranes on the favourable options

With respect to solutions for total annual costs reduction using cheaper cranes at the new hub terminal was suggested. Therefore, in one of the sensitivity analyses the effect of replacing the new hub terminal cranes with cheaper and slower road-rail cranes was studied. The crane service distribution functions in the new hub terminal model were replaced by those applied in the road-rail model. This implies an average increase in the crane cycle of about 40 seconds. In the cost model the amount of investment in new hub cranes was replaced by the amount applied for road-rail cranes. This means a reduction in the amount of investment per crane of about 3 million euros. All new hub terminal cases that appeared in the quadrant with favourable options in the initial experiments were included in the analysis. The results are presented in Figure 6–15.

The general trend in Figure 6–15 is that the difference between initial costs per load unit and the costs per load unit due to cheaper road-rail cranes is greatest for cases with a relatively high initial costs per load unit. This applies to the three black dots to the far left in Figure 6–15. In these cases costs are reduced by 14 to 25 euros per load unit (see also Table 6–20). The difference in costs per load unit is smallest for cases with already relatively low costs per load unit. This applies to the two black dots furthest to the right in Figure 6–15. In these cases costs are reduced by 2 and 7 euros per load unit (see also Table 6–20).

Contrary to this, cases with the greatest difference in costs have the smallest difference in train service time due to slower cranes. For the three black dots furthest to the left in Figure 6-15 the increase in train service time is between 12 and 25 minutes, while the increase for the two black dots furthest to the right in Figure 6–15 is between 71 and 107 minutes.

The number of load units in a case in combination with the number of cranes causes the differences. The more load units and the fewer cranes there are, the longer a batch is in operation and the longer the waiting time for trains in the second and third batches at the side yard.

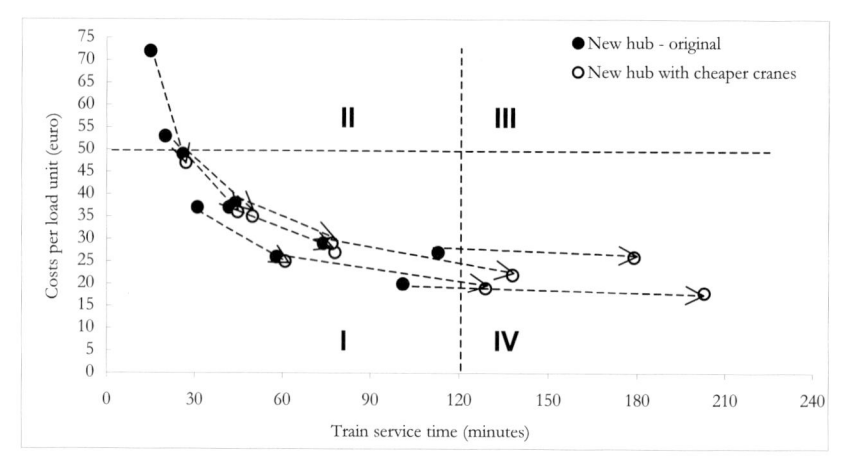

Figure 6–15: Sensitivity of train service time and costs per load unit to cheaper but slower cranes

Results are presented as pairs of black (original situation) and white dots (situation with cheaper cranes) connected by a dotted line.

It is worth noting that in the quadrant with favourable options, facilities with cheaper cranes for a certain demand lead to very similar train service times and costs per load unit as for the facilities with faster but fewer cranes. This is illustrated in Figure 6–15 by the white dots which represent the cases with cheaper cranes, in the quadrant with favourable options that almost fall in the same area as the black dots. For a demand of three batches of three trains C10_rr has similar performance to C6. For a demand of three batches of four trains the facility C10_rr has similar performance to C6 and C6_rr is similar to C4. For a demand of three batches of six trains facility C10_rr is similar to C6 (see also Table 6–20). The exception to this trend is the demand of three batches of three trains for the facility C4_rr. Its performance is not similar to that of facility C2.

Cases that leave quadrant I with favourable options are C6 (3*6), C4 (3*6), C4 (3*4), and C2 (3*3).

At this stage it is interesting to point out the advantages of a transport system such as that applied at the new hub terminals. In Figure 6–16 four capacity levels of the new hub terminal with road-rail cranes and three capacity levels of the road-rail terminal for a demand of 3 batches with 3 trains is presented. Since the same cranes are employed at both terminals, the difference in service time between C6 and RR6, C4 and RR4 and C2 and RR2 can be attributed to the existence of a transport system at the new hub terminal with road-rail cranes. The fewer cranes there are, the greater the advantages of a transport system. In the case of six cranes, the train service time is reduced by 60 minutes due to the transport system. In the case of two cranes the time difference is 92 minutes. The fewer cranes there are, the larger the crane section, therefore the longer the crane driving distances.

Table 6–20: Specification of cases in order of increasing train service time per demand level

Demand	Facility and capacity level	Train service time (minutes)	Costs per load unit (euros)
3*3	C10	15	72
3*3	C6	26	49
3*3	C10_rr	27	47
3*3	C4	44	38
3*3	C6_rr	50	35
3*3	C4_rr	77	29
3*3	C2	113	27
3*4	C10	20	53
3*4	C6	42	37
3*4	C10_rr	45	36
3*4	C4	74	29
3*4	C6_rr	78	27
3*6	C10	31	37
3*6	C6	58	26
3*6	C10_rr	61	25
3*6	C4	101	20
3*6	C6_rr	129	19
3*6	C4_rr	208	18

_rr facility with cheaper and slower road-rail cranes.
Italics: facilities with more but slower cranes with almost similar performances as facilities with fewer but faster cranes.

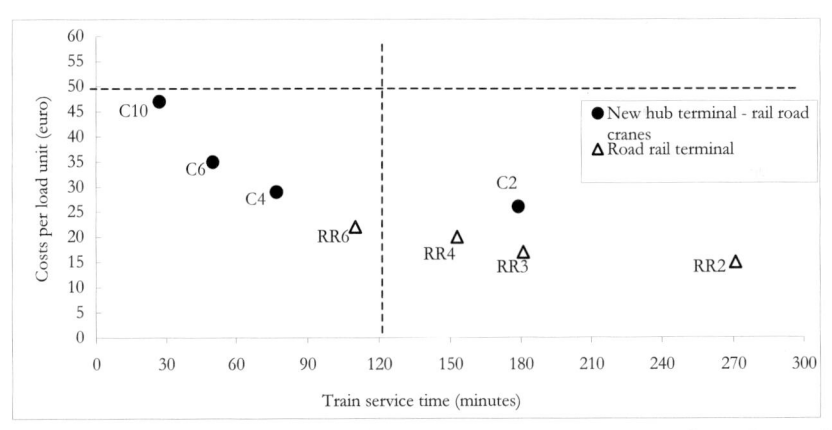

Figure 6–16: Illustration of the advantage of a transport system for a demand of 3 batches with 3 trains: new hub terminals with road-rail cranes versus road-rail terminals

We may conclude from this that cheaper cranes do not really offer new performance alternatives, except for the facility C4_rr. This facility fills a performance gap for the demand three batches of three trains between the facility C4 and C2.
Furthermore, a transport system that supports the cranes longitudinally contributes largely to a fast handling performance compared to a terminal without a transport system.

6.5.5 Conclusions

In this section the main results of the sensitive analyses for the variables load order, load factor and annual costs are summarized. Further, in Section 6.4.5 I tried to quantify the effects of certain model assumptions. In this section I discuss if these effects influence the results.

The sensitivity analyses for the variable load order showed that some of the variants for hump shunting yards and road-rail terminal facilities have become an alternative for new hub terminals for a demand of three batches of three trains. Although the alternative facilities meet the time benchmark criterion, the new hub terminals remain (much) faster. And, for larger volumes than three batches of three trains, the new hub terminal remains the only choice.

Taking the quantified effects of the assumption on crane workload into account, it is concluded that train service times of terminals are underestimated with 10 to 19 minutes compared to shunting. This underestimation slightly affects the ranking of facilities with respect to planned load order train service times. Facility C2 no longer performs faster than H12 and H22, but more or less equals the shunting performance (see Tale 6–17). Facility RR4 no longer performs faster than shunting, but performs about the same. However, batches with different trains length may imply additional underestimation of the train service time. Although the underestimation is not quantified, most new hub-terminal facilities have sufficient slack compared to the benchmark criterion to allow at least about 10 minutes (C4) longer train services times.

The sensitivity analyses for the variable load factor showed that load factor does affect the train service time of terminals, but not for shunting yards. Taking into account the underestimation of train service times due to crane workload differences, two cases, C4 (1*6) and C4 (1*8), would fall outside quadrant I (see Table 6–19), while due to a higher, respectively lower load factor they first moved into quadrant I. But the general conclusion holds: alternative hub exchange facilities are not affected by different load factors to such an extent that they become a competitive alternative that alternative hub exchange facilities are not affected.

The sensitivity analyses for costs showed that the cases RR4 (1*3) and C6 (3*3) would exceed the benchmark criterion of 50 euros per load unit when equipment costs increase by 25% and when interest rates increases. A 25% increase in infrastructure costs does not incur a cost per load unit above 50 euros. A reduction of costs due to cheaper cranes does not really offer new performance alternatives, except for the facility C4_rr. This facility fills a performance gap for the demand three batches of three trains between the facility C4 and C2. Furthermore, a transport system that supports the cranes longitudinally contributes largely to a fast handling performance compared to a terminal without a transport system. Model assumptions do not seem to affect these results. But, I may have underestimated rail haul costs effects, due to locomotives that remain attached to train during exchange operations. In case of underestimation of the rail haul costs effects; costs per load unit may increase by 3.28 euro when the train sojourn time is 60 minutes. If the train sojourn time is shorter, additional costs are less; if it is longer, additional costs are higher (see Chapter 5.5).

The other assumptions, train entrance time and shunting time between side yard and facility and no equipment breakdowns, underestimate the train service times of all facilities compared to reality, but not with respect to their mutual ranking.

6.6 Impacts of variable arrival schedules, delays and non-synchronised operations on handling time

So far all the results presented have been for synchronised arrivals, an arrival schedule with 8-minute interarrival times and synchronised operations. These are typical elements for one of the proposed new hub terminals. However, in subsection 6.4.2 it was demonstrated that 8-minute interarrival times are more or less ideal for a new hub terminal with six or more cranes. These are certainly not ideal for other new hub terminal variants and the alternative facilities. For these facilities longer interarrival times reduce train sojourn times because trains do not have to wait (or they wait less) at the side yard. Furthermore, in Chapter 3 it was concluded that the proposed interarrival times of eight minutes for new hub terminals deviate significantly from arrival schedules of until recently existing hub shunting yards. Finally, in Chapter 3 it was indicated that international trains in particular face serious delays: 30% of trains per day and delays of several hours are not unusual.

Finally, in a third set of experiments the impact of different, less- and non-synchronised and delayed arrival schedules was studied. At some point the arrival schedules may reach such a level of non-synchronisation that the non-synchronised operations strategy (the alternative operations control principle) may lead to better handling times than the initial synchronised operations strategy. Therefore, in this final set of experiments the impact of non-synchronised operations is also investigated. Three main sets of experiments, each consisting of various subsets of experiments, were carried out. An overview of the experiments is given in Table 6–8. Each subsection discusses the results of one of the main sets of experiments.

Analysis of train arrival schedules was carried out for new hub terminal and alternative facilities that appeared and remained in the quadrant of favourable options in the initial and sensitivity experiments. The cases included in the experiments were as follows:
- for a demand level of 3 batches of 3 trains: C2, C4, C4_rr, H22_planned, H12_planned, RR4_planned, RR3_planned
- for a demand level of 3 batches of 4 trains: C4, C6, and
- for a demand level of 3 batches of 6 trains: C4, C6, C10.

The new hub terminals with cheaper road-rail cranes C10_rr and C6_rr were not included, because their performance is rather similar to that of C6 and C4 respectively.

Table 6–21: Features of ideal arrival schedules for different demand under the condition of synchronised arrivals and operations for favourable facilities

Demand	Facility	\multicolumn{7}{c	}{Train interarrival time, ... train in batch (minutes)}	Batch interarrival time (minutes)
		1st	2nd	3rd	4th	5th	6th	7th	
3*3	C4	0	7	10	32	-	-	-	49
	H22_p	0	11	11	38	-	-	-	60
	H12_p	0	20	20	20	-	-	-	60
	C4_rr	0	7	18	56	-	-	-	81
	RR4_p	0	18	36	50	-	-	-	103
	C2	0	12	25	80	-	-	-	117
	RR3_p	0	19	42	63	-	-	-	124
3*4	C6	0	5	5	7	38	-	-	55
	C4	0	7	7	14	59	-	-	87
	C10	0	3	3	3	3	10	28	49
3*6	C6	0	5	5	5	6	7	53	79
	C4	0	8	8	8	11	17	83	133

_p: analysis under the condition of planned load order.
_rr: analysis under the condition of cheaper cranes.

6.6.1 Impact of different arrival schedules

In this subsection the results of three sets of experiments with different arrival schedules are discussed. First, ideal arrival schedules for the selected cases are presented. Ideal means a *just-in-time* arrival schedule in which trains do not have to wait for service, and equipment does not have to wait for trains. In this ideal situation the train sojourn time equals the train service time. Ideal circumstances are seldom reached, but this analysis is carried out for the purposes of comparison. In the second set of experiments arrival schedules based on arrival schedules of the (former) existing hubs at Metz and Herne are analysed.

In Table 6–21 the ideal arrival schedules with just-in-time train and batch interarrival times are presented. An example of how to read the table is illustrated for a demand of 3 batches of 3 trains for the facility C4. The first train arrives at time = 0. After 7 minutes of operations the second train of the batch is expected. After another 10 minutes, which is 17 minutes after operations started, the third and final train of the batch should arrive. The first train of the second batch, the 4th train, is expected to arrive after 32 minutes, which is 49 minutes after the first batch started. The time in between the first train of a batch and the first train of the next batch is called the batch interarrival time, which is the time needed to complete the whole batch.

A typical situation for terminals is an increase in interarrival times between trains in the same batch, while for shunting yards interarrival times are constant. This can be explained as follows. At terminal facilities load units can only continue to be processed when the destination train has arrived at the terminal. Therefore, the number of load units to be processed is limited with respect to the first train(s) of a batch, but increases with every succeeding train that arrives. As a consequence of the limited availability of destination trains in the first part of operations, in larger batches interarrival times of the first trains are shorter and more constant. See for instance the demand of three batches of six trains. With respect to shunting, each train can be processed at the first workstation without requiring the presence of other trains of the same batch.

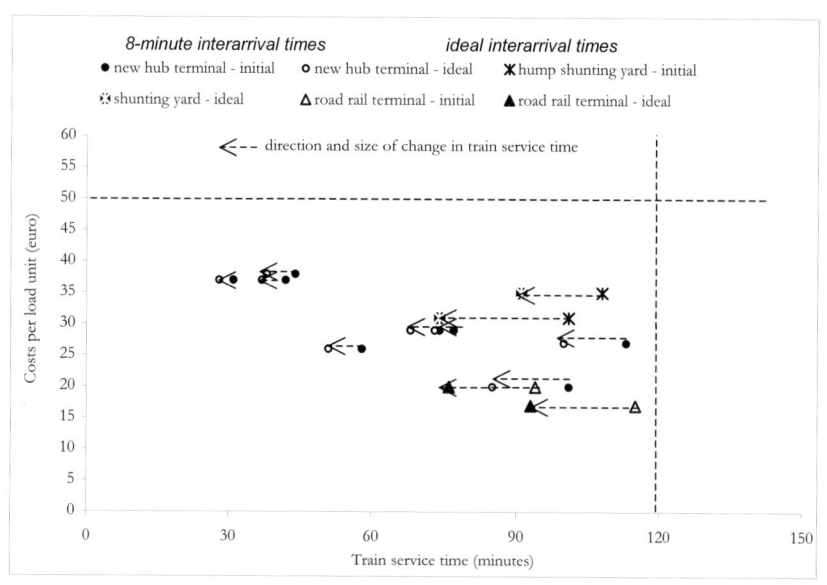

Figure 6–17: Ideal interarrival times lead to a reduction of the train service time compared to the initial 8-minute interarrival time

Results are presented as pairs of black and white marks in a horizontal direction. The right mark of the pair is related to the train service time under the condition of the original interarrival time of 8 minutes, the left mark to the train service time under the condition of ideal interarrival times.

Compared to the initial 8-minute interarrival time, Table 6–21 suggests that such a schedule is only close to ideal for the facility C4 for a demand of three batches of six trains. For other facilities either trains arrive too early and have to wait at the side yard (mainly for a 3*3 demand), or they arrive too late with the consequence that equipment stands idle (principally for all other demand levels). Both situations lead to longer train service times compared to 8-minute train interarrival times.

Figure 6–17 shows the extent to which train service times presented in the previous sections may be reduced under the condition of ideal arrival times. The greatest reduction in train service time is obtained for the facilities with relatively long train service times (marks on the right in Figure 6–17) which include the alternative facilities hub shunting and road-rail terminals. The largest reduction is 27 minutes (for H12_p). See Appendix Q for a specification of the results.

However, as mentioned at the start of this section, ideal circumstances are seldom achieved. When we compare the obtained ideal interarrival times with those of the shunting hubs at Metz and Herne (see Table 6–22), we can see that these real-life schedules deviate widely from the ideal schedules. This raises the question of what the impact of such schedules would be on the train sojourn time. This was analysed in another set of experiments. In these experiments the 8-minute train interarrival times were replaced by the arrival times of the Herne hub for the demand of three batches of three trains and those of Metz for the demand of three batches of six trains. Only the arrival times were taken from the Metz and Herne data. Other variables such as the arrival order of trains and exchange relations remained as was determined for the experiments.

Table 6–22: Interarrival times on a busy day at the Metz hub (18 trains) and the Herne hub (9 trains), in minutes

Train number	1	2	3	4	5	6	7	8	9	10	11	12	13	14	15	16	17	18
Metz	0	49	89	130	84	21	37	339	43	6	61	22	19	82	4	187	165	15
Herne	0	15	150	69	140	267	232	8	100	-	-	-	-	-	-	-	-	-

Source: Based on train arrival schedules (Terminet, 2000; Biggler, 2003).

The results are presented in Figure 6–18. Each facility generates a train sojourn time that (far) exceeds the time benchmark criterion, due to often very lengthy waiting times for the next train to arrive. Figure 6–18 also indicates that long interarrival times have a greater impact on larger batches. After all, time spent waiting to continue operations accumulates more in a large batch than in a small batch.

In another set of experiments an improvement in the interarrival times due to (for instance) better planning, was examined. It was assumed that all train interarrival times of 100 minutes or longer were halved, except for the first trains of a batch. The limit of 100 minutes was rather arbitrary, but was also inspired by the train interarrival times presented in Table 6–21. Interarrival times of about 100 minutes seem to be far beyond the ideal. The arrival times of the first trains in a batch were not reduced, because a reduction in the interarrival time of the first train in a batch does not lead to shorter train sojourn times. The results are also presented in Figure 6-18. For this improved arrival schedule the train sojourn time remains below the benchmark criterion in only three cases: C4, C4_rr and RR4_p for a demand of three batches of three trains.

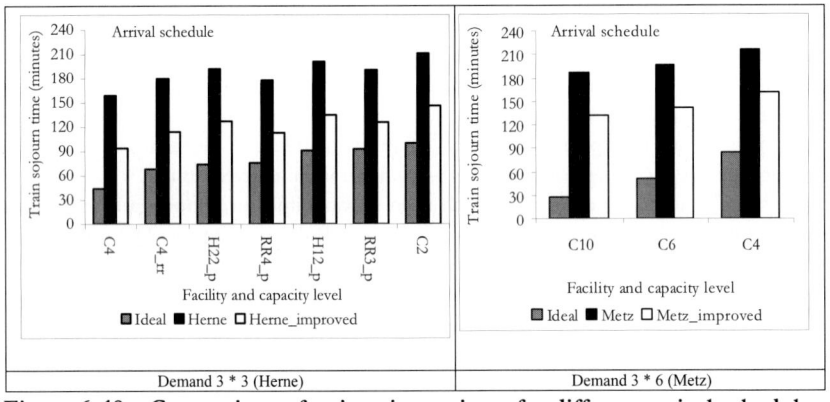

Figure 6–18: Comparison of train sojourn times for different arrival schedules

Not only does the train sojourn time increase for non-ideal arrival schedules, but the duration of daily operations is also affected. For a demand of 3*3 it increases from between 2.5 and 9 hours for an ideal schedule to between 11 and 17 hours for the Herne_improved schedule. For a demand of 3*6 it increases from between 2.5 and 7 hours to about 19 hours for the Metz_improved schedule. The increase in duration of operations may imply an increase in labour costs, because operations last 1 or 2 shifts longer. The increase in labour costs is greater for the shunting cases than for the terminal cases, because shunting yards—especially hump shunting yards—use much more labour (see subsection 6.4.4 about cost structures).

The conclusion can be formulated that ideal (just-in-time) arrival times lead to the lowest train sojourn and service times and vary between exchange facilities. However, reality dictates that train arrival schedules may be far from ideal, resulting in a lot of waiting time in the sojourn times. Since sojourn time consists of service time plus waiting time, faster facilities have an advantage over slower facilities. The faster a facility, the larger the available time window to absorb waiting time before the time benchmark criterion is reached. This can be illustrated with the following example. For a demand of three batches of three trains the train service (= sojourn) time for the new hub facility C4 is 38 minutes for an ideal arrival schedule. For a non-ideal schedule the train sojourn time becomes longer, due to waiting time. This waiting time can accumulate to 120 minutes (benchmark criterion) minus 38 minutes, which is 82 minutes. For the slower H22 facility under the condition of planned load order, the train service time for an ideal arrival schedule is 74 minutes. The benchmark criterion minus 72 minutes allows an accumulation of waiting time of only 48 minutes. When the facilities are faced with non-ideal realistic arrival schedules none of the cases are fast enough to maintain a sojourn time below the time benchmark criterion. Furthermore, non-ideal arrival schedules are another reason to favour several smaller batches over a few larger batches (see also subsection 6.4.2). In smaller batches accumulated waiting time due to non-ideal arrival times of succeeding trains is less because there are fewer trains.

So far, delays have not been considered. In the next section delays are investigated, because they also have an impact on train sojourn time. Furthermore, we may raise the question "if arrival schedules are difficult to synchronise, are non-synchronised operations an alternative?" In non-synchronised operations the processing of trains is less dependent on synchronised arrivals. The effect of non-synchronised operations on train sojourn times is investigated in subsection 6.6.3.

6.6.2 Delays

The results previously presented all apply under the condition that trains arrive according to schedule. In this subsection the sensitivity of some of the previous results for delay is discussed. As for all experiments a deterministic approach was applied. Six instances with realistic random delays were analysed for a selected number of hub exchange facilities and two demand levels. This approach provides good insight into the effects of delays, but does not provide a complete overview. For a complete overview a thorough delay simulation study would be required with a large number of delay experiments.

Since delays differ in national and international networks, in the first set of experiments the impact of delays on a national network was studied. In the second set, the impact of delays on an international network was investigated. The impacts of delays were studied for ideal arrival schedules. Ideal arrival schedules are the most appropriate schedules to use for studying the impact of delays, because they do not include any buffer time that might absorb delays. Studying the impact of delays provides insight into the required buffer time to include in arrival schedules in order to rule out unreliability as far as possible. Different durations of train interarrival times were selected because it was expected that the duration of the arrival delay may have different impacts due to different durations of the train interarrival times.

Table 6–23: Specification of delays in the various experiments

	Demand*	3*3		3*6	
	Experiment	Train(s) delayed	Delay (minutes)	Train(s) delayed	Delay (minutes)
National network	Delay 1	Train 8		Train 6	30
				Train 18	30
	Delay 2	Train 5		Train 1	30
				Train 12	60
	Delay 3	Train 1	30	Train 8	120
				Train 14	30
International network	Delay 4	Train 3	120	Train 3	180
		Train 5		Train 5	30
				Train 9	60
				Train 11	30
				Train 16	60
				Train 17	30
	Delay 5	Train 1	240	Train 3	60
		Train 4		Train 4	60
				Train 5	120
				Train 14	180
				Train 16	60
	Delay 6	Train 2	60	Train 2	240
		Train 7	120	Train 10	30
				Train 11	30
				Train 14	60
				Train 17	120

* Number of batches * number of trains per batch.

Two demand levels were included in the experiments. For a demand level of three batches of three trains the facilities C4, RR4_p and H12_p were included in the experiments; for a demand level of three batches of six trains the facilities C10 and C6 were included. A random number generator was used to determine which trains were delayed and for how long. The way in which the six instances were determined was explained in subsection 6.2.3. The six instances are described in Table 6–23.

Some considerations about delays in practice and in the model
In practice, some delays are somewhat longer than the ideal interarrival time (by more than 1 hour). When delays occur terminal management may decide to deviate from normal operating strategy and priority rules. Depending on the type and duration of a delay or delays, the alternative operating strategy may be different. The purpose of the delay experiments is not to provide an overview of delays and effective delay operating strategies. The model was not constructed to analyse complex delay strategies. The purpose is to provide insight into what happens to train sojourn times under certain conditions. In the next paragraph I will discuss differences between effects of delays in practice and in the model.
As a consequence of long delays, some delays result in a situation in which the delayed train arrives later than the last train of the succeeding batch. As a consequence, in the model, all trains in the succeeding batch are kept waiting at the side yard. Remember that the model does not allow two batches to be in operations at the same time. Instead of the normal batch order (in practice and in the model) a different priority rule may be applied. This could involve, for instance, giving priority to a later

batch when an earlier batch is affected by a delay of a certain length. Possibilities for changing priority are subject to timely and reliable information on delays. If one or a part of the trains in a batch have already gone to operations, it may be more difficult to change the batch order. In practice, possibilities depend on the capacity of tracks at the exchange facility (for two batches to be taken into operations) and/or possibilities for temporarily removing trains in a delayed batch to the side yard. Neither option is possible in the model.

A final remark on the differences between practice and the model is related to capacity at the side yard. In practice deadlocks may occur when various trains are delayed with an unknown delay. It may happen that more trains have to wait at the side yard than there is capacity. Trains may need to be diverted to side yards in the area or trains at the exchange facility (partly served or not served) may be ordered to leave. In the model such deadlocks cannot occur, because track capacity at the side yard is modelled as an unlimited queue.

Explanation on how delays are incorporated in the modelling

In the experiments the extreme delay problem is simplified. Firstly, it is assumed that the delay is known in advance. Secondly, it is assumed that when a delay results in a delayed arrival time later than the last train of a succeeding batch (including delays) or the last train of the second succeeding batch, the succeeding batch(es) is/are served first and the serving order is changed. It should be noted that in the model batches are served in order of arrival. A switch in batch service order must be realised by constructing the correct arrival order of trains in the input file.

The delays were incorporated into the various input files. Arrival times, arrival order and train interarrival times needed to be adjusted manually in the input file (cf explanation of input files with deterministic data - see Table 5–1 in subsection 5.3.1). This is illustrated for train 5 in *Delay 2*.

The switch of batch priority applies to the delay in train 5. If the normal train access control principle was applied, train 4 and train 6 of batch 2 would be allowed access to operations and the whole operation would be held up until train 5 arrived. The delay in train 5 is rather long: it arrives 181 minutes after train 9. In the meantime trains 7, 8 and 9 of batch 3 would be waiting at the side yard. The adjustment of the data in the input files is illustrated for Delay 2 for the ideal arrival schedule of facility C4 and a demand of three batches of three trains (3*3). Table 6–24 provides the initial input file and Table 6–25 the adjusted input file due to the delay of 240 minutes in train 5.

In order to switch the handling order of batches in the model, one train from batch 3 should arrive before trains of batch 3. Manipulation of the train arrival times of trains 4 and 6 in the input file is required to obtain the right handling order of batches. These trains should arrive after train 7, such that batch 3 is the next batch in the handling order and not batch 2. Trains 4 and 6 were given an arrival time one minute later than the first train of the third batch. This change in the input file affects the waiting time of trains 4 and 6 at the side yard and also the train sojourn time. As a result waiting and sojourn times of trains 4 and 6 in the output file were corrected with the time difference between manipulated and real arrival time, 50 and 33 minutes respectively.

Table 6–24: Initial input file with the ideal arrival schedule for a demand of three batches of three trains (3*3) for facility C4

Train number	Arrival time (minutes)	Interarrival time (minutes)	Batch number	Number of trains in a batch	Train order in batch	Number of load units to be exchanged
1	0	0	1	3	1	30
2	7	7	1	3	2	30
3	17	10	1	3	3	30
4	49	32	2	3	1	30
5	56	7	2	3	2	30
6	66	10	2	3	3	30
7	98	32	3	3	1	30
8	105	7	3	3	2	30
9	115	10	3	3	3	30

The impact of the delays on the train sojourn times is presented in various graphs in Figure 6–19 to Figure 6–22. Figure 6–19 and Figure 6–20 present the results of three experiments with random delay for a demand of three batches of three trains (3*3) and the facilities C4, RR_P and H12_p. Figure 6-19 covers the delay probability in a national network and Figure 6–20 presents the delay probability in an international network.

Figure 6–21 and Figure 6–22 present the results of three experiments with random delay for a demand of three batches of six trains (3*6) and the facilities C19 and C6. Figure 6–21 covers the delay probability in a national network and Figure 6–22 shows the delay probability in an international network.

Table 6–25: Adjusted input file for a delay of 240 minutes in train 5 for a demand of three batches of three trains (3*3) for facility C4

Train number	Arrival time (minutes)	Interarrival time (minutes)	Batch number	Number of trains in a batch	Train order in batch	Number of load units to be exchanged
1	0	0	1	3	1	30
2	7	7	1	3	2	30
3	17	10	1	3	3	30
7	98	81	3	3	1	30
4 (manual hold)	49 (+50 = 99)	1	2	3	1	30
6 (manual hold)	66 (+33 =99)	0	2	3	3	30
8	105	6	3	3	2	30
9	115	10	3	3	3	30
5 (delayed)	296 (56+240)	181	2	3	2	30

Each graph in these figures represents one experiment with delayed arrival(s) for one facility.

For all previous experiments the average train sojourn time was presented. For the delay experiments the train sojourn times of all trains of the first simulation run are presented. To study the impact of delay(s) it is better to look into the effects on individual trains.

In addition to the individual train sojourn times, the average train sojourn time (black horizontal line) and the benchmark criterion (dotted horizontal line) are shown in the graphs.

Interpretation of the graphs in Figure 6–19 to Figure 6–23
The graphs in Figure 6–19 are related to a demand of three batches of three trains and a delay probability for a national network. This implies that one train out of nine is delayed. The first graph (upper left corner in Figure 6–19) shows the effect of a 120-minute arrival delay occurring in the third batch in train 8 for facility C4. This delay does not affect the trains in batches 1 and 2: the related square white markers correspond with the straight black line that represents the average train sojourn for an ideal arrival schedule. Besides train 8, trains 7 and 9 are also affected by the delay, because operations can only be completed if all trains are at the facility. The train sojourn time increases by 120 minutes.

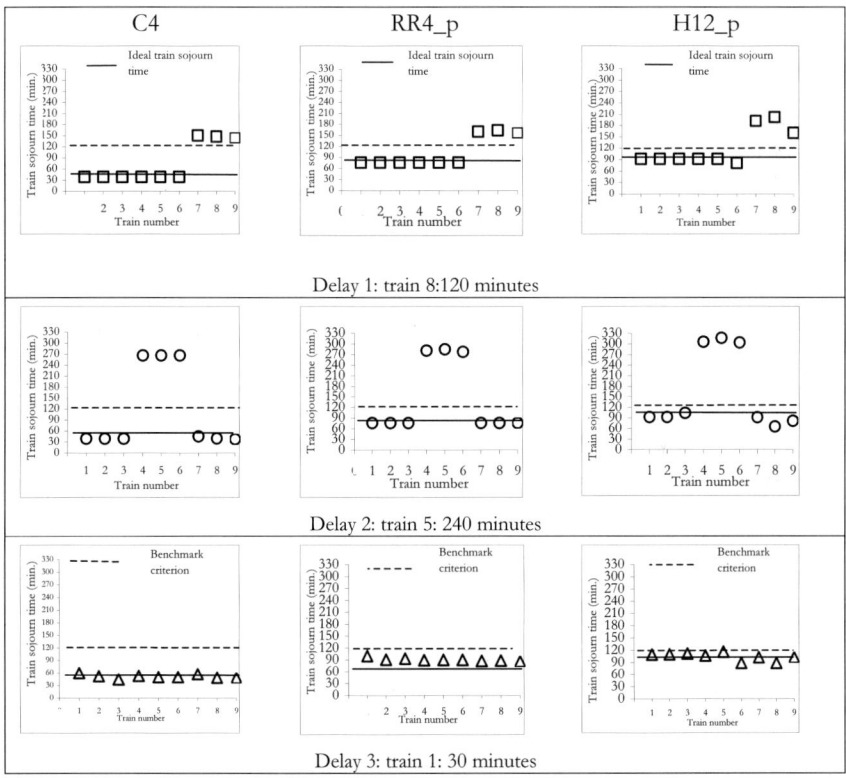

Figure 6–19: Three examples of the impact of a random delay of one train (national network) on train sojourn times for a demand of three batches of three trains (3*3) for three facilities

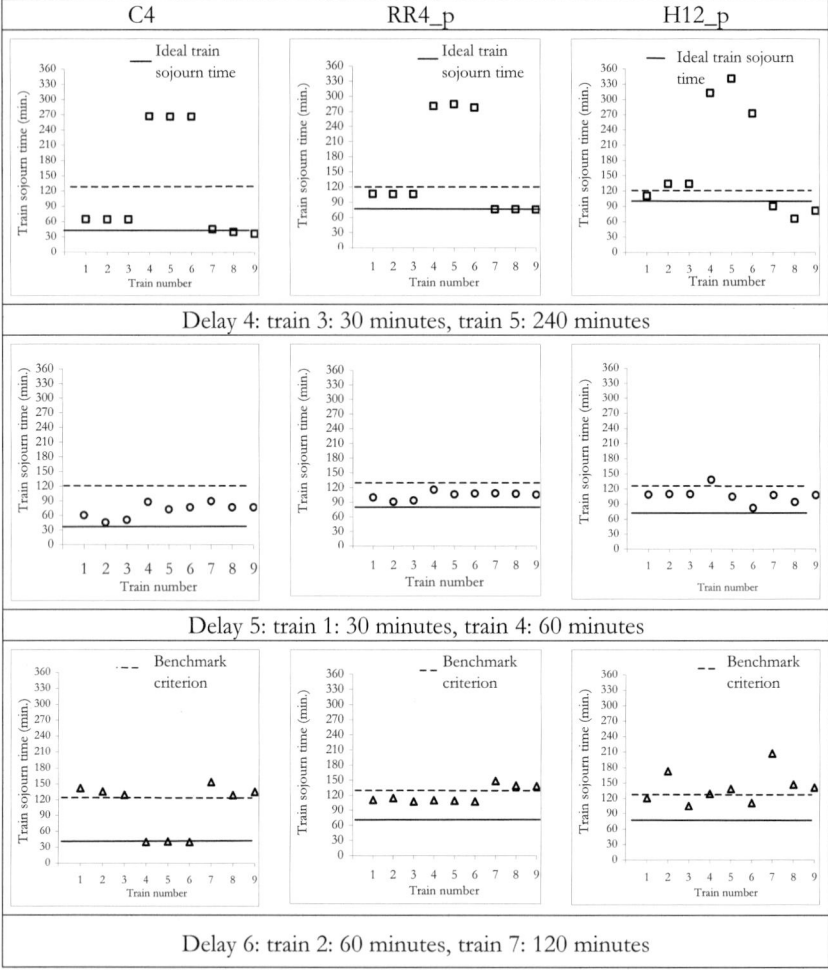

Figure 6–20: Three examples of the impact of a random delay of three trains (international network) on train sojourn times for a demand of three batches of three trains (3*3) for three facilities

Circle markers specify the second delay case. The delay of 240 minutes occurs in the second batch in train 5. For the facility C4 (middle graph in left column) this delay does not affect the trains of the first batch, or the trains in the third batch (the related white square markers correspond with the straight black line). The latter may seem odd, because the common access control principle applied in the models is that batch 3 trains must wait while batch 2 is served and waiting for the delayed train. However, due to the delay priority rules applied (see above), delay 2 in combination with the ideal arrival schedule of facility C4 means that train 5 arrives later than train 9. Consequently, trains in batch 3 are served before trains in batch 2. As a result train sojourn times for batch 3 do not increase. Whether or not batches switch service priority will vary according to each exchange facility, because each facility has its own ideal arrival schedule. However, the longer the arrival delay, the greater the probability that batches will switch service priority. As such, batches 2 and 3 also switch service order for the facilities RR4_p and H12_p for delay 2 in Figure 6–19. But with respect to delay 6 in Figure 6–20 batch 2 and batch 1 at facility C4 switch handling order, but they do not for facilities RR4_p and H12_p. As a result we see that the triangles of batch 2 for C4 correspond with the dark straight line, while they do not for the other two facilities.

The third delay case is specified by triangles. The 30-minute delay occurs for the first train of batch 1. For all facilities this means that the departure delay is shorter than the arrival delay: the train sojourn time increases by less than 30 minutes. This can be explained as follows. A part of the delay coincides with the operations of trains 2 and 3, and as such does not result in 30 minutes' waiting time, but fewer minutes. We can also see that the delay is passed on to batches 2 and 3. Differences in extended train sojourn times are due to stochastic differences in server time, and also to switches in the handling order of trains in a batch. This phenomenon is for instance clearly visible for the 2nd and 3rd trains of batches 2 and 3 at facility H12_p for delays 1 and 2. In the ideal situation the first and second trains of a batch are processed first, while the third train has to wait for the duration of a server cycle. In the delayed cases the order in which trains arrive from workstation 1 to workstation 2 changes. Trains 1 and 3 arrive before train 2. Consequently, the first and third trains are served first, and the second train has to wait. As a result, the sojourn time of the third train is shorter, but the sojourn time of the second train is longer.

Generally speaking, the graphs can be interpreted as follows:
- Train sojourn times are not affected by arrival delays when the related marker for train sojourn times lies on the straight black line that represents the average train sojourn time for an ideal arrival schedule.
- If the (vertical) distance between the train sojourn time marker and the straight black line is shorter than the arrival delay, the arrival delay (partly) coincides with operations time, reducing the actual departure delay.
- Train sojourn times for batches 2 and 3 are not affected by the delay in batches 1 and 2 when the handling order of batches has changed. Train sojourn times of batch 2 and batch 3 fall on the straight black line. In addition, the batch affected by the delay has a train sojourn time of a minimum of the delay time plus the average train sojourn time for an ideal arrival schedule.
- Due to delays within a batch or in any of the preceding batches train sojourn times may vary due to changes in the handling order of trains within a batch.

Similar phenomena as described above apply for results of the experiments with a demand of three batches of six trains for the facilities C10 and C6 (see Figure 6–21 and Figure 6–22).

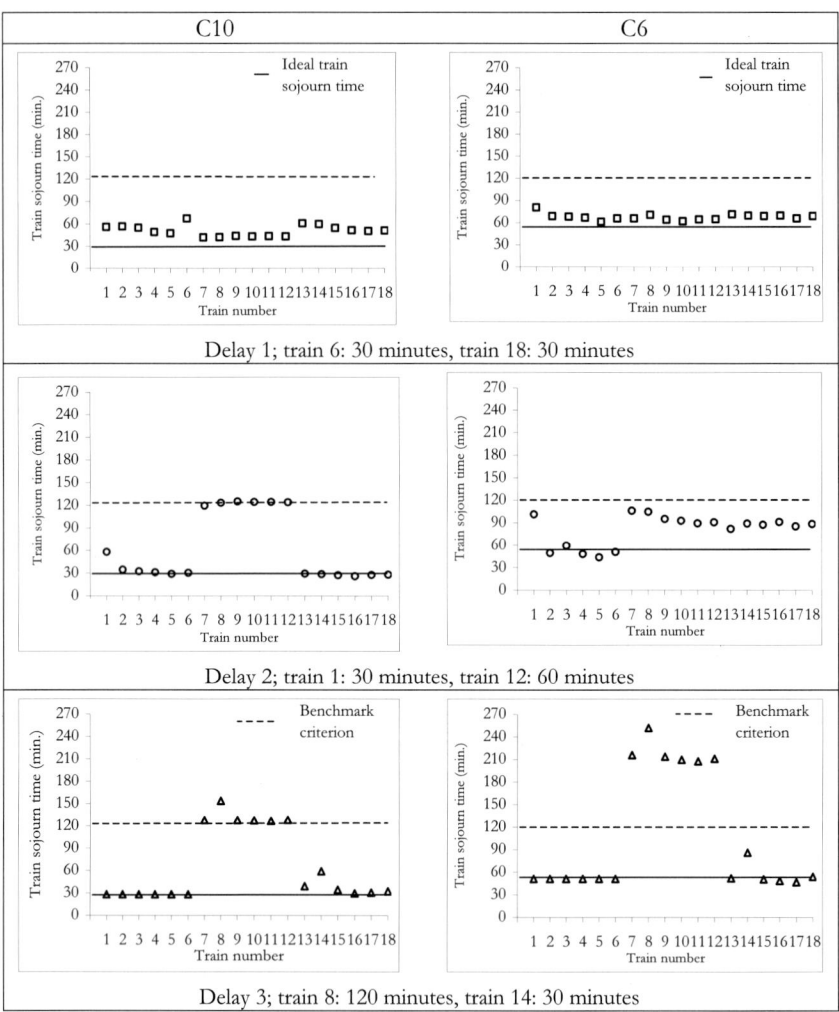

Figure 6–21: Three examples of the impact of a random delay of two trains (national network) on train sojourn times for a demand of three batches of six trains (3*3) for two facilities

General findings based on Figure 6–19 to Figure 6–22
Although the experiments only include a very limited number of (random) delay situations, some general findings may be obtained from Figure 6–19 to Figure 6–22. First, arrival delays that do not result in a switch in batch handling order affect the train sojourn time of all succeeding trains. Handling orders do not switch under the applied delay priority rule for delays of 30 minutes and in some experiments for a delay of 60 minutes (delay 5 for facilities C4, RR4_p and H12_p; delay 2 for facility C6; delays 4 and 6 for facility C10).

	C10	C6

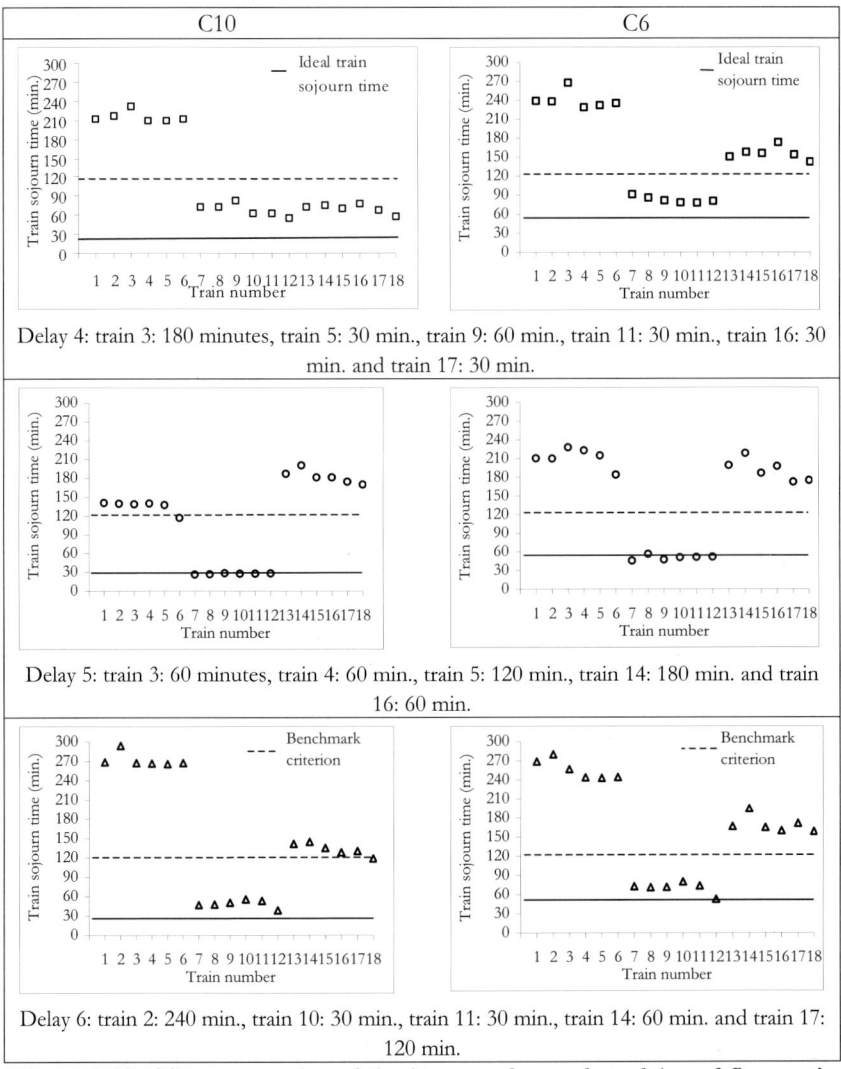

Delay 4: train 3: 180 minutes, train 5: 30 min., train 9: 60 min., train 11: 30 min., train 16: 30 min. and train 17: 30 min.

Delay 5: train 3: 60 minutes, train 4: 60 min., train 5: 120 min., train 14: 180 min. and train 16: 60 min.

Delay 6: train 2: 240 min., train 10: 30 min., train 11: 30 min., train 14: 60 min. and train 17: 120 min.

Figure 6–22: **Three examples of the impact of a random delay of five or six trains (international network) on train sojourn times for a demand of three batches of six trains (3*6) for two facilities**

Secondly, at which duration of arrival delay do batch handling order switches depend on the type of facility and level of demand? I related the priority rule for switching to the arrival time of the last train in a batch. The ideal arrival time of the last train in a batch varies for each facility as was shown in subsection 6.6.1. This may be illustrated with delay 6 at C4 compared to RR4_p and H12_p in Figure 6–20. At C4 batches 1 and 2 switch handling order, but they do not at the two other facilities. This finding also applies to delays 2, 4 and 6 for C10 compared to C6.

Thirdly, delays in the last train of a batch not resulting in a switch of the batch handling order have a larger effect on train sojourn times than other delayed trains in the same batch. The smallest impact has a delay on the first train of a batch, because for the largest part of the delay time the delay does not lead to waiting time. The operations of the succeeding trains can continue for a while. When the last train is affected, the delay time directly results in waiting time. Compare for instance batch 1 for delays 4 and 5 for facilities C4, RR4_p or H12_p; or batch 1 for delays 1 and 2 for facilities C6 or C10.

Fourthly, trains running in international networks seem more sensitive to arrival delays than trains in national networks. After all, in international networks there is a greater probability that trains will be delayed (see subsection 6.2.3). However, in networks with multiple arrival delays, delays may accumulate, but may also be neutralised. Delays are neutralised when a delay coincides with another delay. This mainly applies to smaller delays that fall together with a larger delay. This is, for example, the case for batch 1 and delay 4 or batch 1 and delay 5 for facility C6 and C10.
But delays may also coincide (partly) with operations of other trains in a batch, which also neutralises (a part of) the effect on the train sojourn time. This applies to delays to the first trains in a batch. See for instance batch 1 and delay 6 for C10 or C6: the increase in train sojourn time is smaller than the delay.

Fifth, the gap between the straight black line (average train sojourn time) and the dotted line (benchmark criterion) indicates the available time window for deviations from the ideal arrival schedule. The faster the facility (in relation to demand), the larger the time gap between the ideal train sojourn time and benchmark criterion. For C4 this time gap is about 80 minutes, for RR4_p 45 minutes and H12_p about 30 minutes. For *C10* the time gap is around 90 minutes and for C6 70 minutes. The six instances suggest that new hub terminals can deal with delays of up to 60 minutes without exceeding the benchmark criterion train sojourn time, except sometimes for C4. Compare batch 2 in delay 5 and batch 1 in delay 6. A delay of 60 minutes in the first train of a batch (batch 2 in delay 2) does not lead to a train sojourn time longer than the benchmark criterion. But a similar delay in the second (or third) train does (batch 1 in delay 5), due to a switch in the batch handling order. Some delays might even be longer than 60 minutes, given the time windows of 80, 90 and 70 minutes.
The facility RR4_p is capable of dealing with delays of up to 60 minutes if the delay occurs to the first or second train in a batch (see delay 5 and 6), while the time window is only 45 minutes. A part of the delay is neutralised by the operations of trains 2 and 3. The results do not show whether the train sojourn time remains below the benchmark criterion with a delay of 60 minutes to the third train of a batch.
The time window of the facility H12_p is too small to deal with delays of 60 minutes, but sufficient enough to deal with delays of 30 minutes.

The six instances suggest that, in order to cater for delays of up to 60 minutes (and only 30 minutes for H12_p), ideal arrival schedules should include buffer time. Buffer time is defined as a margin of a certain planned period of time for contingencies in the ideal arrival schedule. Buffer time is time added to the ideal interarrival times such as presented in Table 6–21. Preferably, buffer time is included between the last train of a batch and the first train of the next batch. After all, buffer time between the first trains of a batch cannot neutralise the delays of later trains. This is illustrated in Figure 6–23 for facility C6, a demand of three batches of three trains (3*3) and delay 2. The graph for delay 2 is repeated for the purposes of comparison (graph I in the upper left corner of Figure 6-23).

Impact of buffer time on the effects of delays

Figure 6–23 shows the effect of buffer time on two succeeding batches of 30 and 60 (graphs II and III), and the effect of buffer times of 10 minutes between each train. In the case of the latter a buffer time of 60 minutes between batches is spread out over each batch. Figure 6-23 suggests the following.

First, buffer time between batches in this particular case does not seem to affect the train sojourn times of trains in the first and second batches. Most of the effect of the delay of the first train is neutralised because the delay coincides with operations of other trains in the batch. The buffer time absorbs this delay, such that it does not affect batch 2. However, the delay is so small that it is hardly visible in Figure 6–23.

Second, buffer time between batches leads to a reduction in train sojourn times for batch 3. The dots in graphs II and III are clearly lower than those in graph I. In addition, with a buffer time of 60 minutes between batches, the train sojourn time reaches the level of the ideal train sojourn times (graph III). In graph III the 60-minute delay of train 12 is absorbed by the buffer time of 60 minutes.

Third, a different allocation of for instance a buffer time of 60 minutes leads to different effects. Compare graphs III and IV. In graph IV 10 minutes' buffer time is allocated in between each train, instead of all 60 minutes in between the last train of the batch and the first train of the next batch. In graph IV train sojourn times in general are higher, except for train 1, compared to graph III. They are also higher in comparison with graph I. This is explained as follows. The 10-minute buffer time in between each train arrival postpones each train arrival by an additional 10 minutes onto the ideal interarrival time. As was explained in subsection 6.6.1, ideal interarrival times imply that neither trains nor facilities have to wait. Deviation from the ideal arrival time implies longer train sojourn times (see subsection 6.6.1). However, interarrival times that exceed ideal interarrival times between the last train of a batch and the first train of the next batch do not lead to longer sojourn times. After all, the whole batch starts later, and the train interarrival times between trains in the same batch stay the same.

Finally, the results suggest that the allocation of buffer time between batches is the most effective. Delays of a certain magnitude cannot be passed on to the next batch, resulting in apparently shorter train sojourn times. However, when buffer time between batches is included in the ideal arrival schedule, the average train sojourn time is no longer indicative of the performance of a facility. Buffer time should be added to the average train sojourn time (indicated as dotted line 'minimum departure time'). This is comparable to the effect of buffer time in between trains of the same batch as was discussed above in relation to graph IV. Time is reserved for contingencies. If nothing happens, trains are kept waiting. If a delay occurs, the buffer time absorbs all or part of the effects on later trains, depending on the magnitude of the delay. Hence, for the specific case C6 a buffer time between batches of 60 minutes leads to a minimum departure time of 111 minutes. This is still below the benchmark criterion. The minimum departure time is important for the network operator with respect to planning slots at the network. In many European countries trains cannot freely re-enter the rail network after they have finished operations. Access is strictly planned. Network operators buy slots in advance, often for several months to a year.

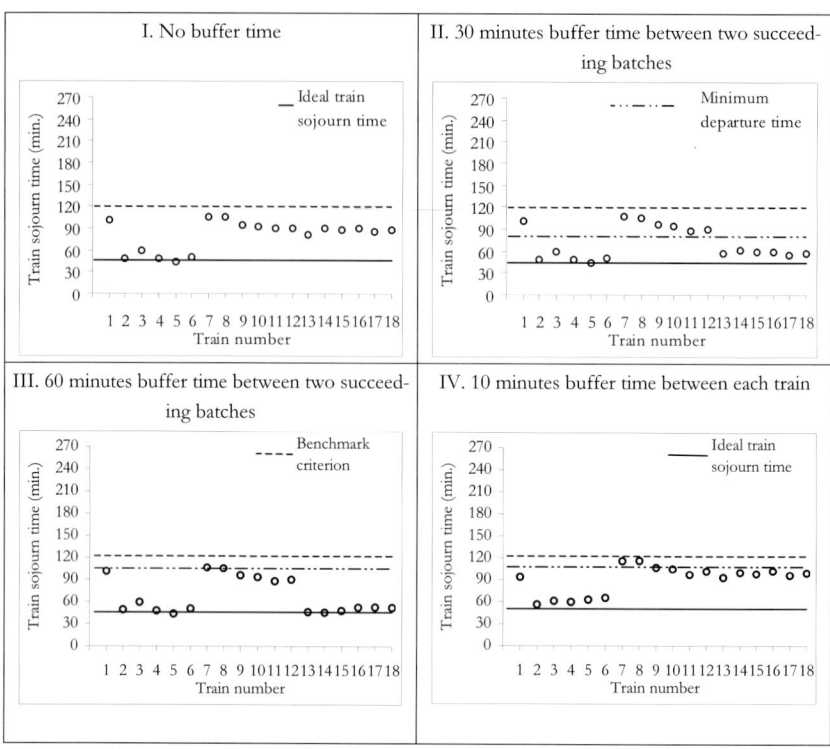

Figure 6–23: Effects of buffer time on train sojourn times for facility C6, a demand of three batches of three trains (3*3) and delay 2

Conclusion

To conclude, as was suggested in subsection 6.6.1, arrival schedules are not always ideal. Consequently, all or part of the buffer time is already allocated, and no longer free to allocate in the schedule where it could be most effective. As a result the buffer time that may be allocated freely in the train arrival schedule is much smaller than the 60 (or 30) minutes. Although buffer time is included in the arrival schedule with the purpose of providing the network operator with a "guaranteed" departure time, the results indicate that node and network operators still face wide unreliability of departure times. This is no small problem because network operators buy network slots in advance. Due to the large probability of arrival delays, they must incorporate longer buffer times into arrival schedules, with the consequence that the minimum departure time exceeds the benchmark criterion or that additional slots have to be planned and bought, leading to higher costs. The fact that ICF abandoned their two shunting-based hub-and-spoke networks Qualitynet and X.net at the end of 2004 due to the increasing unreliability of traction on the railways in recent years (Arndt & Rozendaal, 2004), illustrates how serious this problem is. The wide unreliability of train arrivals in current intermodal practice has serious effects on all hub exchange facilities. Despite the fact that new hub terminals have larger time windows to deal with delays because they are faster, their ideal arrival schedules can only incorporate buffer times of around 60 minutes.

Finally, alternative ways to deal with delays other than those studied may lead to different effects on train sojourn time. Firstly, different priority rules with respect to switching the handling order of batches may be considered. With the synchronised models only the choice to switch or not to switch can be simulated. There is a possibility of more complex handling strategies in which two or more batches are served parallel to each other. In the case of the new hub terminal with six tracks, two batches of three trains can be served parallel to each other. Operations may then start off with trains of a particular batch that are not delayed, continue with trains of a succeeding batch and switch back to the other batch when the delayed train arrives. Alternatively, both batches may be served at the same time.

This strategy is not effective for every facility or demand level. The possibility of servicing two batches in parallel depends on the available track capacity and the batch size. For instance, for a road-rail terminal with four tracks and a demand of three batches of three trains, two trains cannot be served without additional train handling operations. Several trains have to be pushed and pulled in and out of the facility in order to complete exchange operations. For shunting this parallel service strategy may work under the condition that sufficient tracks are available at the assembly yard. Trains may be served by workstation 1 (sorting) upon arrival. Shunted wagons may wait at the departure siding until the last train of the batch has arrived. Next, trains proceed to workstation 2. In actual fact, this is how non-synchronised shunting models work. However, a parallel operations strategy would require modifications to the simulation models for the terminal facilities.

Secondly, the results raise the question of whether non-synchronised operations might deal better with delays. This is investigated in the next subsection.

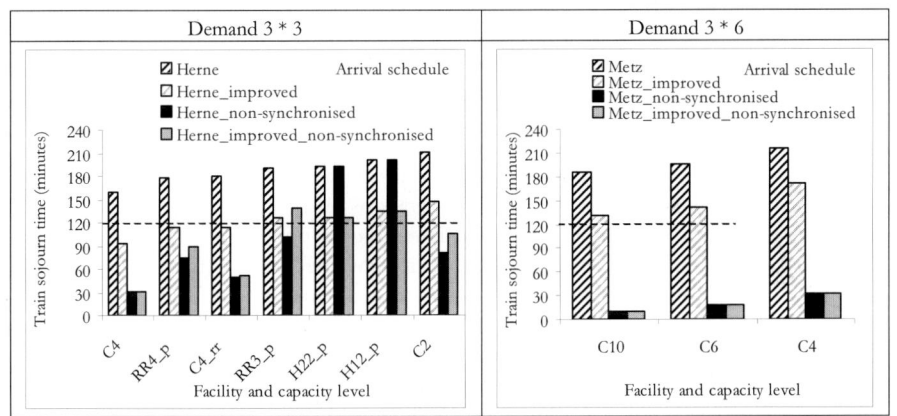

Figure 6–24: Comparison of train sojourn times between synchronised and non-synchronised operations for various facilities, arrival schedules and demand

6.6.3 Non-synchronised operations

The results presented earlier were all based on synchronised operations, which are proposed for new hub terminals. However, in the previous two subsections I suggested that for realistic arrival schedules with non-synchronised arrivals and delays, the option of non-synchronised operations should be investigated. In non-synchronised operations the processing of trains is less dependent on synchronised arrivals. For less synchronised arrival schedules, non-synchronised operations may lead to a reduction in the time that trains wait for each other. As a result the train sojourn time will decrease.

In the first part of this subsection the results of experiments with non-synchronised operations for similar facilities, demand and on the Metz and Herne hubs-based arrival schedules are presented. In the second part of this subsection the results of experiments with non-synchronised operations for one facility C6 and international delays as in subsection 6.6.2 are presented.

Subsection 6.6.1 showed that train sojourn times turned out to exceed the benchmark criterion for train sojourn time for realistic arrival schedules based on arrival times of former shunting hubs at Herne and Metz. With improved arrival times (see subsection 6.6.1 for an explanation) the train sojourn times of new hub terminal facilities remained below the benchmark criterion. These results are repeated in Figure 6–24. Figure 6–24 also shows the train sojourn times for non-synchronised operations. Arrival schedules remained the same, only the strategic control principles were changed. The general difference in non-synchronised operations for terminals is that trains exchange their load units via the storage area. As a result trains do not need to be present at the terminal at the same time. However, the order in which trains of the same batch are served is important for terminals. In the initial train arrival schedule each train drops off load units for succeeding trains. If trains of the same batch are not served in the order of their train number, a part of the load units misses their connection train. This does not apply to shunting, because new trains cannot be assembled as long as not all trains of the same batch have arrived. Hence, trains can only proceed to workstation 2 when all the trains of a batch have been served at workstation 1, just like synchronised operations. For hump shunting non-synchronised operations imply that trains can be served in any order at workstation 1. The batch to which a train belongs is not relevant for obtaining access to workstation 1. Chapter 4 gives a more detailed explanation of non-synchronised operations.

If we compare synchronised results with non-synchronised results, the following can be observed. Firstly, non-synchronised operations lead to much lower train sojourn times for all new hub terminal facilities. Train sojourn times approach those for ideal arrival schedules. However, this significant improvement in the train sojourn time is at the expense of load unit sojourn times. Since load units are exchanged via the storage area and passed on to various later trains, they spend the duration of various train sojourns at the terminal. A part of the load units remain at the terminal until the following day. How many load units remain until the next day depends on the composition of the daily volume. For instance, for a demand of three batches of three trains (3*3), 1/9 of the daily volume (volume of one train) makes its connection the next day in the case that each batch serves the same origin and destination terminals. How load units are passed on to later trains is illustrated in the upper graph of Figure 6–25. However, if each batch serves different origin and destination terminals many more load units will make their connection the following day: around 8/9 of the daily volume. Only the volume of one train can be exchanged on the same day. This exchange is illustrated in the lower graph of Figure 6–25.

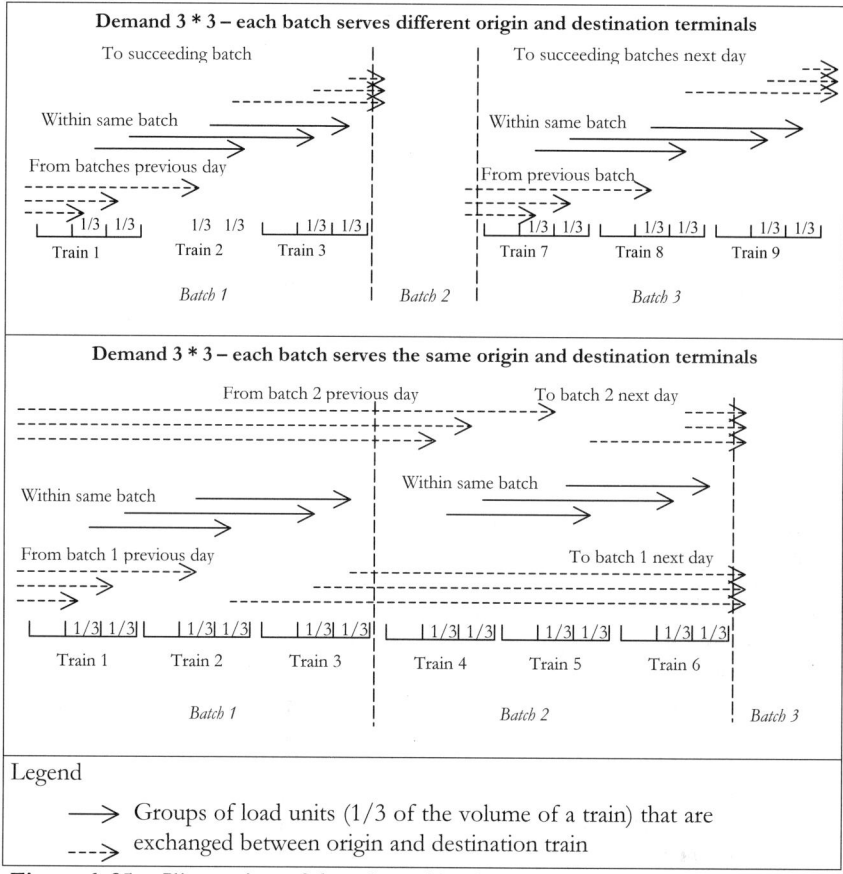

Figure 6–25: Illustration of duration of load unit sojourn times for two different compositions of the daily demand consisting of three batches of three trains (3*3) for non-synchronised operations (but synchronised arrivals)

It may be concluded that load unit sojourn times may vary between the average train sojourn time and about 24 hours. The more train arrivals of trains in the same batch are mixed with trains of other batches, the longer the load unit sojourn times become.

The connection time of the other load units depends on the train interarrival times, which, as shown in Table 6–21, vary from several minutes to several hours. Assuming that most shippers and forwarders are looking for a daily connection, non-synchronised operations do not seem as favourable as seemed at first.

The road-rail terminals also show an improvement in the train sojourn time, except for RR33_p in combination with an improved Herne arrival schedule. This is explained as follows. The non-synchronised model is sensitive to trains that arrive while the previous train has not yet finished operations. When this happens, load units of the first train which has arrived at the end of its operation are put into a low priority queue, while load units of later trains start off in a higher priority queue. Since cranes in the model cannot be allocated to trains, operations are directed by the priority rules. As a result all trains remain longer in operation than they would when they were the only train served, which is the case for the new hub terminal variants. This phenomenon also explains why the train sojourn time of RR4_p and the improved Herne arrival schedule is higher than for the original Herne arrival schedule. Train sojourn times at the shunting facilities do not improve at all with non-synchronised operations, but for different reasons than for the road-rail terminal. At the shunting facilities trains still have to wait for trains in the same batch in order to proceed to the assembly process (workstation 2).

In subsection 6.6.2 I raised the question of whether non-synchronised operations might be an option for arrival schedules that face random delays on a daily basis. Delays affect the arrival order of trains and departure reliability. Experiments were carried out for a demand of three batches of six trains (3*6) and international delay, because in this situation the arrival order of trains is affected the most. Experiments were carried out for the facility C6, because of its lower costs per load unit than C10. Results are presented in the left graph in Figure 6–26. On the right side of Figure 6–26 the graph for non-synchronised operations is repeated.

Figure 6–26 shows the following. First, for some trains, non-synchronised operations lead to shorter train sojourn times than the average train sojourn time in non-synchronised operations. This is the case for all markers below the straight black line. Train sojourn times are shorter, because only one train is served at a time, and not —as in synchronised operations—all trains of a batch in parallel.

Secondly, on the other side there are trains with much longer train sojourn times than for synchronised operations. Compare for instance trains 3 to 5 for delay 4 and trains 2 to 5 of delay 6 in the left graphs (non-synchronised operations) with the right graphs of Figure 6–26. In both cases a delayed train 6 causes the longer train sojourn times. Although trains exchange load units via the storage area, trains must be handled in their planned order of arrival, otherwise load units miss their connection train. When a train is delayed, earlier trains in that particular batch have to wait for service until the delayed train has arrived. This waiting time incurs a longer train sojourn time than in synchronised operations.

Thirdly, Figure 6–26 shows an increasing train sojourn time for some succeeding trains. See, for instance, for delay 1 trains 13 to 16 or for delay trains 4 to 10 (left graphs). This is caused by the fact that the arrival schedule is ideal for synchronised operations, but not for non-synchronised operations. The next train arrives without delay, while the previous train is still in operation. As a consequence the train sojourn time of each succeeding train accumulates waiting time.

Fourthly, in non-synchronised operations fewer trains exceed the benchmark criterion: for delay 1, ten trains versus twelve in synchronised operations, for delay 2, seven versus twelve and for delay 6, six versus twelve. In non-synchronised operations there may be an improvement in the train sojourn time for individual trains, but in general non-synchronised operations do not lead to better train sojourn times. Hence, these results suggest that non-synchronised operations may be a means for dealing with unreliable service networks. However, train sojourn times improve, but the load unit sojourn time increases considerably (see also above).

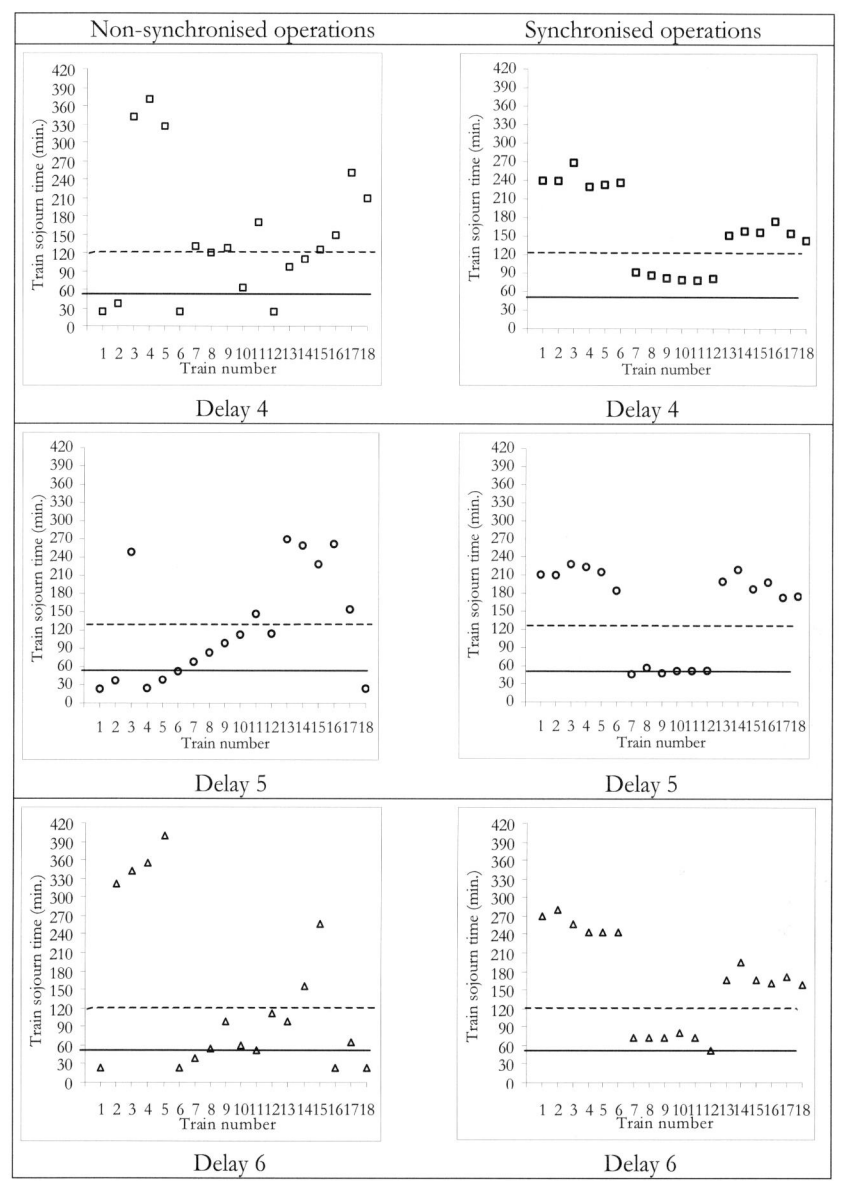

Figure 6–26: Comparisons of train sojourn times between non-synchronised and synchronised operations for facility C6 with a demand of three batches of six trains

Finally, and although this is not investigated, from the results in the first part of this section it may be seen that hump shunting operations could benefit to a certain extent from non-synchronised operations. With non-synchronised operations, workstation 1 at the hump shunting yard will be used more efficiently. After all, trains can be served in order of arrival. However, since trains still have to wait until all trains have been processed at workstation 1 before they can be assembled at workstation 2,

Hub exchange operations in intermodal hub-and-spoke networks

large improvements in train sojourn time cannot be expected. Trains still have to wait for the delayed train, but in the middle of the shunting process and not at the start.

My conclusion is that the results seem to suggest that non-synchronised operations are an attractive solution for non-delayed non-synchronised arrival schedules as well as delay-sensitive synchronised arrival schedules. However, this is only true on the level of the train sojourn time, not on the level of load unit sojourn time. With respect to time-sensitive goods markets, I expect that shippers would not accept a load unit sojourn time that exceeded the benchmark criterion. Hence, non-synchronised operations are not an option for dealing adequately with non-synchronised arrivals and delays. However, train sojourn times at hump shunting yards may benefit slightly from non-synchronised operations.

6.6.4 Conclusions

In this section the main results of the sensitive analyses for the variable arrival time are summarized. Further, in Section 6.4.5 I tried to quantify the effects of certain model assumptions. In this section I discuss if these effects influence the results.

The conclusion can be formulated that ideal (just-in-time) arrival times lead to lower train sojourn and service times than 8-minute interarrival times applied in the initial set of experiments. The greatest reduction in train service time is obtained for the facilities with relatively long train service times which includes the alternative facilities hub shunting and road-rail terminals. The largest reduction is 27 minutes. Taking into account the underestimation of train service times for terminals, it may be concluded that under the condition of ideal interarrival times, facilities C4 (3*6) and RR4_p (3*3) still remain in quadrant I. This was not the case for 8-minute train interarrival times.
However, reality dictates that train arrival schedules may be far from ideal, resulting in a lot of waiting time in the sojourn times. Simulating realistic arrival schedules for previous shunting yards Metz and Herne shows that train sojourn time (far) exceeds the time benchmark criterion, due to often very lengthy waiting times for the next train to arrive.

If ideal arrival schedules could be achieved, they should include buffer time to delay with arrival delays. The six instances simulated suggest that the ideal arrival schedules can incorporate delays up to about 60 minutes, without exceeding the benchmark criterion. However, some of the new hub-terminals can deal with delays up to 90 minutes. The allocation of buffer time between batches is the most effective. The current magnitude of delays require large buffer times with the result that the time benchmark criterion is exceeded. Taking into account the underestimation of train service times for terminals due to differences in crane workloads, it may be concluded that the margin for buffer time becomes smaller with between 10 to 19 minutes. Due to different trains lengths the trains service time may be underestimated with several more minutes. As a results the margin to include buffer time in the arrival schedules becomes even smaller.

Since synchronisation of arrivals seems to be difficult to realise, non-synchronised arrivals and operations were investigated as alternative. Although, this alternative leads to better performance of the train sojourn time, it does not on the level of load unit sojourn time. Hence, non-synchronised operations are not an option for dealing adequately with non-synchronised arrivals and delays. However, train sojourn times at hump shunting yards may benefit slightly from non-synchronised operations.

The other assumptions, train entrance time and shunting time between side yard and facility and no equipment breakdowns, underestimate the train service times of all facilities, but not with respect to their mutual ranking.

6.7 Conclusions

In this chapter the results of nine sets of experiments, each set consisting of various sub-sets, were presented. Each set of experiments focused on a specific variable that influences the performance of an exchange facility. The experiments were carried out in order to find answers to the six research questions that were formulated at the beginning of this chapter. In this section the following research questions are answered.

What are favourable combinations of demand and capacity input for the new hub terminal in order to offer an attractive time and cost performance for new intermodal markets?
In section 6.3 attractive time and cost performances were determined as a train sojourn time of 120 minutes and costs per load unit of 50 euros. The combination of demand and capacity that meet these criteria even under the conditions of an unfavourable load factor or an increase in annual costs of 25% are as follows:
- For a demand of three batches of three trains a new hub terminal with 4 fast cranes and one with four road-rail cranes.
- For a demand of three batches of four trains a new hub terminal with 6 or 4 fast cranes, and
- For a demand of three batches of six trains a new hub terminal with 10 or 6 fast cranes.

The new hub terminal concept in general requires a demand of between 9 to 18 trains per day. The new hub terminal may be part of one large hub-and-spoke network with many origins and destinations such as the former hub at Metz, but could also serve as hub for various smaller hub-and-spoke networks in such a way that the joint demand accumulates into 9 to 18 trains per day. In addition, hub-and-spoke networks may be operated by one network operator, which is mostly the case nowadays, but could also be operated jointly by various operators. From the perspective of the hub terminal, this is not so relevant as long as the total demand meets the minimum required level to realise a costs per load unit below the benchmark criterion.
Under the condition of unplanned load order there are no alternative facilities that meet the performance benchmark criterion.

The second research question is:
What are the effects of changes in demand with respect to the number of trains per batch, number of batches per day, number of load units/rail wagons (load factor) per train and load order on the time and cost performance of new hub terminals compared to other hub exchange facilities?
Preferably, daily demand is structured into various small batches of two or three trains instead of one or a few large batches of, for instance, four or six trains (assuming similar capacity input). The more trains there are in a batch, the more load units there are to be exchanged and the longer it takes for a batch to complete service. As a consequence the train service time increases. For the costs per load unit for the terminal service it does not matter how the demand is structured, as long as the minimum required volume is achieved.

A short train service time has several advantages. First, trains may spend more time in the network. Second, non-ideal arrival schedules are another reason to favour several smaller batches. Smaller batches accrue less waiting time waiting for the next train to arrive into the train sojourn time. Third, short service times provide a larger available time window between the train service time and the benchmark criterion for train sojourn time. This time window can accommodate waiting time due to non-ideal arrival schedules or buffer time to deal with delays.

A planned load order leads to a reduction in train service time, because more load units are directly exchanged between trains and fewer via the transport system. This leads to fewer crane handling operations and saves time. This optimisation of exchange handling operations requires the support of terminal operators of origin terminals and network operators. They must be willing to plan the loading of the train in a certain order. For them, this optimal load order may not be as optimal. For instance, it may lead to longer train handling times at the origin terminal because it cannot minimise crane driving distances. For network operators it may imply more empty slots on the train, which costs money.

Under the condition of a planned load order, hump shunting yards H22 and H12 and road-rail terminal facilities RR3 and RR4 are alternatives for new hub terminals for a demand of three batches of three trains. Although these facilities meet the time benchmark criterion, the new hub terminals C4, C2 and C4_rr remain (much) faster. On the other hand, these alternatives perform better in terms of costs per load unit. However, taking into account that trains service times of terminal are underestimated due to difference in workload and volume difference in exchange relations, RR3 and C2 have service times exceeding the benchmark criterion of 120 minutes.

The train service time of new hub terminals may decrease or increase by a few minutes to 20 minutes for a larger load factor (1.8), or a smaller load factor (1.4). New hub terminals with relatively small capacity (2 and 4 cranes) mainly face larger changes in service time, especially for the larger demand levels (3*4 and 3*6). New hub terminals with a relatively large capacity (6 and 10 cranes) mainly face smaller impacts. Furthermore, load factor (naturally) affects the costs per load unit. The impact on the costs per load unit varies from 2 to 8 euros more (load factor of 1.4) or less (load factor of 1.8) compared to a load factor of 1.6.

Different load factors do not affect alternative facilities in such a way that they meet the benchmark criterion.

The third research question is:
What are the effects of changes in cost parameter values on the cost performances for various hub exchange facilities?

There is a large difference between total annual costs of new hub terminals and the alternative facilities, leading to the relatively large required demand per day. The large investment in terminal equipment (cranes, roller pallets and the operations control system) is behind this large difference in costs. As a consequence, maintenance and operating costs are also higher than for the other facilities, because those costs are determined as a percentage of the investment costs.

Cost reductions may be obtained if fewer roller pallets or cheaper cranes are used. The new hub terminals with cheaper cranes studied do not really offer new performance alternatives, except for the facility C4_rr. For a demand of three batches of three trains (3*3) this facility fills in a capacity and performance gap between facilities

C4 and C2. Therefore, reducing costs by using cheaper cranes leads to almost similar performances as reducing the number of fast cranes.
The effects of fewer roller pallets were not studied.

Specification of costs in the cost model was difficult. As a consequence some data was estimated; others rely on one source. This causes some unreliability in the outputs of the cost model. Furthermore, new-build facilities are often confronted with an underestimation of costs. Idealistic starting points about the concept may lead to underestimation of costs. In the costs model electrified costs are assumed, such that trains can enter the facility without changing locomotives. But what if facilities cannot be electrified? Is a shunting locomotive required?
The effects of a 25% increase in investments in equipment and infrastructure on the costs per load unit was calculated, as well as the effects of interest rates of 3% and 6%.

The results indicate that the additional costs per load unit varies between 1 and 10 euros for an increase in equipment investment, and between 1 and 4 euros for an increase in infrastructure investment. The new hub terminals are more sensitive to equipment costs, while the hump shunting yard is more sensitive to higher infrastructure costs.
The costs per load unit increases by between 0 (rounded-up result) and 2 euros per load unit for a 3% interest rate, and between 4 and 9 euros per load unit. The new hub terminals are most sensitive to a higher interest rate, because they require the largest investment.
Most facilities can bear the costs increase, implying that the costs per load unit does not exceed the benchmark criterion. However, if costs should stay at the same level when investments or interest rates are higher than assumed in this study, additional demand volume is required.

The fourth research question is:
What are typical levels of synchronisation of arrivals and operations for new hub exchange operations that are favourable to attract new markets?
The shortest train sojourn times are achieved for ideal synchronised arrivals and synchronised operations. Ideal means a just-in-time arrival schedule in which trains do not have to wait for service, equipment does not have to wait for trains, and trains are not confronted with network delays. In this ideal situation the train sojourn time equals the train service time. This does not only apply to the new hub terminals. It also applies to the alternative facilities.
Typical ideal train interarrival times were provided in subsection 6.6.1. For new hub terminals ideal train interarrival times lie between 3 and 25 minutes. The faster the hub facility and/or the larger the batch, the shorter the train interarrival times. A typical feature of terminals is that train interarrival times in a batch increase. For shunting, train interarrival times are constant. Ideal shunting interarrival times appeared to be 11 or 20 minutes.
Due to underestimation of train service times due to various assumptions, ideal train interarrival times may be a few minutes longer.

Comparison of these ideal interarrival times with the arrival times for the former shunting yards at Herne and Metz suggests that there is a large gap between intermodal practice and the preferred arrival times. This gap should be bridged before implementation of new hub terminals is considered.

However, for alternative hub facilities the gap between ideal and actual arrival times should also be bridged. The results indicate that actual performances of existing hub facilities can be improved when arrival times are optimised. Furthermore, under the condition of planned load order, these facilities are able to perform better than the benchmark performance criteria for a demand of three times three batches. This leads to the conclusion that the new hub terminal is not the only facility that is suitable for the time-sensitive market. However, it is the only facility that can generate very fast service times under the right conditions.

Non-synchronised operations are not a serious option for terminals, because a part of the load units cannot make their connection on the same day. Train service times may be faster for non-synchronised operations, but service times for load units become longer. With respect to time-sensitive goods markets, I expect that shippers would only accept a load unit sojourn time that did not exceed the benchmark criterion. For shunting, non-synchronised operations provide a bit more flexibility, but do not significantly lead to better performances.

The fifth research question is:
What is the effect of network delays on the time performances of new hub terminals?
New hub terminals are very sensitive to delays, but no more so than the other facilities: for synchronised as well as non-synchronised operations. The advantage of new hub terminals is their short train service times. As was already mentioned above, short service times provide a larger available time window between the train service time and the benchmark criterion for train sojourn time. This time window can accommodate buffer time to deal with delays. However, in general this buffer time can accommodate delays of no longer than 60 minutes and perhaps a little more. But considering underestimation of train service times, the difference between train service time and benchmark criterion becomes smaller and thus the buffer capacity. The advantage of new hub terminals over the other facilities is that they can deal with larger delays. However, current practice indicates a serious probability of delays over 60 minutes. Sound fallback procedures may help to deal with delays, but at what expense? This is also a problem for the other facilities.
I conclude that before implementation of new hub terminals may be considered, in addition to more synchronised arrivals, network delays should be significantly reduced. Current network unreliability is a serious threat to the advantages of new hub terminals, and to the performances of hub exchange facilities in general.

The sixth (and final) research question is:
Which changes in the design and resources of new hub terminals could make the new hub terminal more favourable?
The relatively high required minimum demand volume (due to high investment costs) to achieve a reasonable costs per load unit, is not the main obstacle to implementation as was pointed out with the previous two questions. But when network-related problems are resolved, lower investment costs may make the new hub terminal more attractive.
The greatest effect may be obtained by reducing equipment costs. As mentioned before, reducing costs by using cheaper cranes leads to almost similar performances as reducing the number of fast cranes, except for the facility C4_rr. This facility fills a performance gap for the demand of three batches of three trains between facilities C4 and C2.

The effects of fewer roller pallets were not studied. Under the condition of planned load order using fewer roller pallets is entirely feasible.

Other options for cost reduction may include changes to terminal infrastructure. The number of rail tracks may be reduced, especially if the demand can be structured into small batches. The number of storage areas, transport systems and truck lanes could be reduced. Such possibilities should be investigated in conjunction with a concrete business case.

Instead of reducing costs, one might also consider how to attract additional road-rail transhipment volume. An existing rail-road terminal could be upgraded with a transport system. The results suggest that a transport system supports the cranes longitudinally and contributes significantly to a fast handling performance compared to a terminal without a transport system. In this way, investments and risks may be limited. This suggestion merits further investigation.

With respect to shunting, in addition to network improvements, solutions for reducing performance backlogs of between 20 and 40 minutes due to the need to couple a network locomotive, fill air tubes and carry out lengthy brake tests, merit further investigation. What could automated coupling or self-propelled rail wagons contribute in this sense?

7 Conclusions and recommendations

7.1 Introduction

This final chapter presents the main research findings, conclusions and recommendations for further research. In this chapter I return to the central and secondary objectives formulated in Chapter 1. The central objective was formulated as follows: *"to develop a model that can be used to identify favourable operational conditions for new hub terminals to be implemented and to quantify their operational performances in relation to alternative hub exchange facilities"*. Favourable operational conditions are defined as demand volumes, train arrival schedules and facility capacity levels, which lead to a certain performance level. In Chapter 6 this performance level was determined as a train sojourn time of a maximum of 120 minutes and costs per load unit of a maximum of 50 euros.

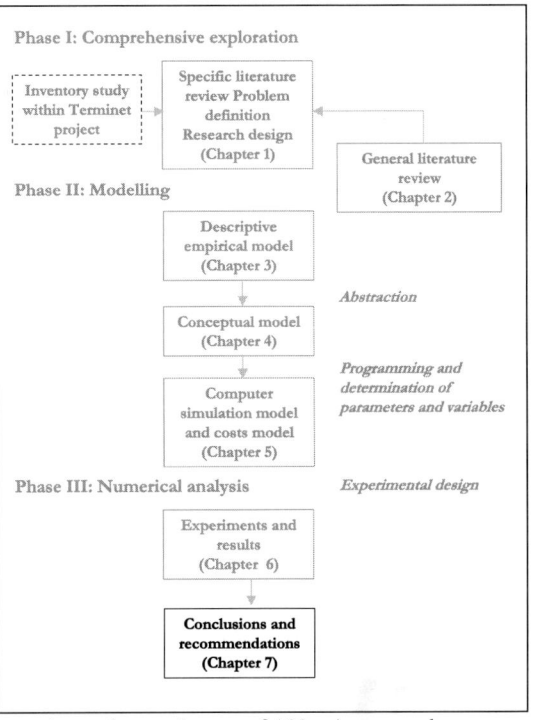

The implementation of hub-and-spoke networks in intermodal transport is suggested as one of the potential solutions for helping to increase the intermodal market share (European Commission, 1997; Kreutzberger, 1999a; 1999b; Cardebring et al., 2002). Three intermodal hub-and-spoke networks became operational in the past decade in Europe. Two of them have been abandoned due to the increasing unreliability of traction on the railways in recent years (Arndt & Rozendaal, 2004). Traditionally, trains are shunted at these hubs, which is a time-consuming process. Since the early 1990s a new type of intermodal terminal, specifically designed for fast transhipment at nodes in hub-and-spoke networks, has been suggested for implementation in Europe. These hub terminals could replace time-consuming shunting. Studies on the new hub terminals suggest that they may perform more efficiently than shunting yards (European Commission, 1997; Jourquin, 1999; Bontekoning & Kreutzberger, 2001; Bontekoning & Trip, 2004). However, a systematic comparison to reveal the operational and costs differences between shunting and these new hub-terminals for a broad range of situations still lacks.

The proposed hub exchange operations differ from current shunting practise, from transfer operations in other freight transport industries and from operations at marine and road-rail terminals. Due to these differences, existing models for transfer operations may be of limited use. As a consequence, a new model had to be developed in order to determine the conditions under which new hub terminals perform better than shunting.

The outline of this chapter is as follows. Firstly, in section 7.2 the main findings and three main conclusions related to the main objective are presented. As a spin-off of the main objective four secondary objectives were formulated in Chapter 1. In section 7.3 findings and conclusions with respect to these secondary objectives are presented. Finally, in section 7.4 several recommendations for further research are formulated.

7.2 Main research findings and conclusions

7.2.1 Model development

One general and six derived similar structured flow-oriented conceptual models for hub exchange operations were developed in this thesis. As a consequence of differences in the operations control between synchronised and non-synchronised operations two types of models had to be constructed. Next, different models had to be constructed due to different features of the exchange facilities. However, differences between hump shunting and flat shunting could not be resolved by different parameter settings in the same model. I therefore constructed four models for the terminals, and two for the shunting yards.

The flow-oriented approach chosen, which was inspired by logistics and queuing theory, led to transparent valid conceptual models with sufficient distinction between exchange facilities. The underlying principle of the models is that trains, load units or rail wagons "flow" through the hub exchange node and are faced with time resistances that accumulate into a train sojourn time. Not specifying dimensions of infrastructure, exact origin and destination of trains, and exact unload and load positions, led to transparent models. The spatial characteristics of exchange operations are expressed in the service time distribution functions of the servers. This requires accurate data on locomotive and crane cycles and could be obtained and validated. A contribution of this thesis is that a special tool for the generation of crane cycle times for different terminal configurations and crane-operating strategies was developed. Other significant abstractions from the real system are as follows:
- Each train in a batch consists of an equal number of load units or rail wagons.
- In the exchange operation load units or rail wagons of one train are equally redistributed among the other trains in a batch.
- In practice deadlocks may occur when various trains are delayed with an unknown delay. It may happen that more trains have to wait at the side yard than there is capacity. Trains may need to be diverted to side yards in the area or trains at the exchange facility (partly served or not served) may be ordered to leave. In the model such deadlocks cannot occur, because track capacity at the side yard is modelled as an unlimited queue.

A typical feature of aggregation is the loss of real details, which, despite model validation, may influence results. Assumptions with respect to job assignment to cranes. volume per exchange relations, train entrance time and shunting time between side yard and facility and equipment breakdowns lead to underestimation of train service and sojourn times. However, the mutual ranking among facilities is not affected. Assumptions with respect to job assignment to cranes and volume per exchange relations only lead to underestimation of service time at the terminals. As a consequence, the gap between new hub-terminals and shunting is expected to be smaller.

Third, in the shunting models I combined the service time of certain activities into one service time. Some activities involve a locomotive plus labour, others only labour. I approached reality with a fixed ratio between a locomotive and labour required for the combined activities. Furthermore, shunting operations with two locomotives at the arrival yard are modelled as parallel activities, while in reality only part of the activities can be carried out in a parallel way. Due to the fact that operations are more complex in reality than in the model train sojourn times estimated for shunting yards may be shorter than in reality.

The transformation of the conceptual terminal models into computer models led to some deviations of the computer models from the intended conceptual models. One major difference is that work order priorities are programmed as intended, but do not work as intended in the terminal models. In ARENA jobs are not put on the job list randomly but in the order they are "administratively" and/or physically processed. When jobs of two different routes have equal priority, jobs of the route that were generated first are put earlier on the job list and are thus served first. Consequently, some routes are served before others, despite having equal priority. For the synchronised models this does not affect train and batch service times, but it does for non-synchronised terminal models where trains are processed at the same time.

Conclusion
The objective to develop several transparent and aggregated models without losing specific features was achieved thanks to the flow-oriented modelling approach. Accurate estimated and validated service time distribution functions are crucial for the accuracy of the models and could be obtained. The result was one generic transport model and six derived models. A typical feature of generality is the loss of real details, which, despite model validation, may influence results. Due to some assumptions train service and sojourn times are underestimated. When applying the models and interpreting the model outputs the specific simplifications of reality applied should be considered. The models may be improved by integrating a few more details

7.2.2 Favourable operational conditions for new hub terminals

The new hub terminal concept requires a minimum daily demand (throughput) of nine trains of 600 metres in length per day. The new hub terminal could be part of one large hub-and-spoke network with many origins and destinations such as the former hub at Metz, but could also serve as a hub for various smaller hub-and-spoke networks, such that joint demand accumulates into nine trains per day. Under preferable conditions the daily demand is structured into small batches of two or three trains rather than large batches of, for instance, four or six trains. Smaller batches lead to shorter train service times. The more trains in a batch, the more load units need to be exchanged and the longer the train service time will be for a similar capacity input.

For the new hub terminal it is less relevant whether the hub-and-spoke networks are operated by one network operator, or via a joint effort between various operators. The main requirement is that the exchange volumes of various operators add up to the minimum required demand level to realise costs per load unit which are acceptable to the network operators. However, joint network operations between various operators are a challenging objective. For instance, trains need to be synchronised and costs and benefits redistributed between network participants.

With respect to the assumed acceptable costs per load unit, facility capacity levels with two or four fast cranes or four road-rail cranes can be applied for a demand of nine trains or more. For a demand of about twelve trains or more a capacity level of six cranes may be considered and for a demand of about eighteen trains or more a facility with ten cranes is an option. These facilities also remain below the cost per load unit benchmark criterion of 50 euros for unfavourable conditions for load factor and total annual costs.

The shortest train service times are achieved for ideally (non-delayed) synchronised arrivals and synchronised operations. Ideal means a *just-in-time* arrival schedule in which trains do not have to wait for service, and equipment does not have to wait for trains. For new hub terminals ideal train interarrival times are between 3 and 25 minutes. Typical features for train interarrival times within a batch are that they increase for each successive train and that the faster the hub facility and/or the larger the batch, the shorter they become.

Table 7–1: **Quantification of performances for favourable operational conditions of new hub terminals under the condition of ideal synchronised train arrivals**

Demand*	Facility and capacity level	Average train service time (minutes)	Average batch service time (minutes)	Average duration total operation (minutes)	Costs per load unit (euro)
3*3	C4_rr	68	77	244	29
3*3	C4	44	49	147	38
3*4	C6	37	55	166	37
3*4	C4	73	87	260	29
3*6	C10	31	49	163	37
3*6	C6	58	79	250	26

* Three batches of three trains.

The various time performances and costs per load unit for ideally (non-delayed) synchronised arrivals and synchronised operations are quantified in Table 7–1. For these ideal conditions train and batch service times are equal to train and batch sojourn times. When train interarrival times deviate from the ideal schedule, which is highly likely due to planning problems and/or delays, train service and sojourn times in most cases increase. The increase in train sojourn times in itself is not problematic so long as waiting time due to deviations from the ideal interarrival times and delays does not amount to a train sojourn time higher than the train sojourn time benchmark criterion. The difference between ideal train service time and the benchmark criterion determines the maximum permissible accumulation of waiting time. The new hub terminal facilities C4, C6 and C10 allow, with respect to a train sojourn time benchmark criterion of 120 minutes, an accumulation of waiting time of around 60 minutes. Assuming ideal interarrival times this time window allows these terminals to deal with delays of up to 60 minutes with no danger of exceeding the benchmark criterion. To deal with delays of up to 60 minutes, 60-minute time buffers are included between the last train of a batch and the first train of the next batch. When in the ideal arrival schedule buffer time is included between batches, the average train sojourn time is no longer indicative of the performance of a facility. The buffer time plus the average train sojourn time gives the so-called minimum departure time. The minimum departure time is important for the network operator with respect to planning slots at the network.

However, even with buffer time in the schedule node and network operators still face wide unreliability with respect to departure times. This is a big problem, because network operators buy slots at the network in advance. Due to the large probability of arrival delays, they must incorporate longer buffer times into the arrival schedules, with the consequence that the minimum departure time exceeds the benchmark criterion or that additional slots have to be planned and bought leading to higher costs.

Results apply for the projected operation in which the network locomotive remains attached to the train during operations. However, if the projected arrival and departure procedures do not work in practice, a shunting locomotive or electrified side yard tracks may be needed. Such measures may naturally lead to slower operations and higher total annual costs.

Conclusion
Average favourable operational conditions for new hub terminals are a minimum daily demand of nine trains organised into several small batches of two or three trains, with train interarrival times within a batch of between 5 and 25 minutes, arrival schedules with a buffer time in between batches of about 60 minutes, and arrival delays with a maximum of about 60 minutes.

7.2.3 Large gap between practice and favourable conditions

A comparison of ideal interarrival times with realistic arrival schedules and delays suggests that there is a large gap between intermodal practice and the preferred arrival schedules for new hub terminals. This gap must be bridged before implementation of new hub terminals is even considered. Train sojourn times at new hub terminals and also at alternative hub exchange facilities are seriously affected by non-synchronised train arrivals and regular (and often lengthy) delays, as is often the case in practice.

In actual fact, in current practice not even the train sojourn time benchmark criterion of 120 minutes can be guaranteed to customers of any of the hub facilities.

A train sojourn time of 120 minutes provides each facility with a relatively small margin in which to deal with waiting time caused by deviations in ideal arrival schedules and delays. Compared to alternative facilities, the advantage of new hub terminals is that they can offer longer waiting times, which implies that new hub terminals have larger margins to include buffer time in the train arrival schedule. After all, the short train service times of new hub terminals provide a larger available time window between the train service time and the benchmark criterion for train sojourn time. The larger the time window, the more buffer time is allowed.

It was expected that non-synchronised operations might be a solution for non-synchronised and delayed arrivals. Simulation showed, however, that non-synchronised operations are not a serious option for terminals, because a part of the load units cannot make their connection on the same day. Train service times may be fast, but service times for load units may be long. For shunting, non-synchronised operations provide a little more flexibility, but do not significantly lead to better performances.

Conclusion

Considerable improvement of service network planning and control is required in order to realise synchronisation of train arrivals and a reduction in the frequency and duration of delays before the implementation of new hub terminals may be considered. Such improvement is of similar importance for performances of alternative hub exchange facilities.

7.2.4 Alternatives for new hub terminals

Under the condition of an unplanned load order there are no alternative facilities that meet the performance benchmark criterion. However, under the condition of a planned load order (which is already sometimes the case in intermodal practice), hump shunting yards with one or two locomotives at the arrival yard and two locomotives at the assembly yard, and road-rail terminal facilities with four cranes also meet the performance benchmark criteria. The performances of alternatives are specified in Table 7–2. Three things may be concluded when the favourable new hub terminal facilities of Table 7–1 are compared with the alternatives in Table 7–2. First, the alternatives are competitive with new hub terminals for a demand of nine trains. The new hub terminals C4, C2 and C4_rr are (much) faster (and would be even faster for a planned load order), but the alternatives perform better in terms of costs per load unit. Second, for a demand of higher than nine trains there are no alternatives for new hub terminals. Third, for a demand of fewer than nine trains there is just one facility that meets the benchmark criteria. A road-rail terminal with three cranes is suitable for small hub-and-spoke networks for up to three trains.

Finally, flat shunting facilities, which were also studied, do not meet the benchmark criteria: neither do they meet the criteria when only three wagon groups are shunted and the locomotive remains attached.

Table 7–2: Alternative hub exchange facilities that meet the benchmark criteria under the condition of planned load order

Demand*	Facility and capacity level	Train service time (minutes)	Batch service time (minutes)	Duration total operation (minutes)	Costs per load unit (euro)
3*3	RR4	94	157	300	21
3*3	H22	101	133	222	31
3*3	H12	108	131	248	35

* Three batches of three trains.

The relatively high required minimum demand volume (due to high investment costs) to achieve a reasonable costs per load unit is not the main obstacle to implementation. Poor network conditions are the main obstacle, as pointed out above. But if network-related problems are solved, lower investments may make the new hub terminal more attractive. After all, relatively large volumes are required to cover the total annual costs. Reducing investment will reduce the required minimum demand volume.

The greatest effect can be obtained by reducing equipment costs. Reducing the number of cranes leads to similar performances as the application of cheaper road-rail cranes, except for the facility C4_rr. This facility fills in a performance gap for the demand of three batches of three trains between facilities C4 and C2.

Other options for reducing costs, which were not investigated, may include reducing the number of roller pallets (especially under the condition of planned load order) and making changes to the terminal infrastructure. The number of rail tracks may be reduced, especially if the demand can be structured into small batches. The number of storage, transport system and truck lanes may also be reduced. This leads to reduced infrastructure costs, and smaller and therefore cheaper cranes can be constructed. These possibilities could be investigated in conjunction with a concrete business case.

Compared to the alternatives, new hub terminals imply a so-called greenfield investment. The question must be asked as to whether investors want to invest in an entirely new terminal. It may be more expedient to follow a gradual path towards innovation. Existing road-rail terminals (already with sufficient base volume) could be upgraded with a transport system. The results suggest that a transport system contributes significantly to a fast handling performance compared to a terminal without a transport system. This option should certainly be further investigated, because road-rail terminals appeared in the results as a solid alternative to new hub terminals and seems to be the only alternative for small demand. Kreutzberger (2002) calculated that networks with a daily volume of between 2 and 4 trains would benefit especially from a hub-and-spoke system. New hub terminals do not offer the right costs-quality for these networks, but road-rail terminals without a transport system do. As such, road-rail terminals with a terminal transport system may be an interesting innovation to advance intermodal transport quality for the time-sensitive market.

With respect to both hump shunting and flat shunting, solutions for reducing the performance backlog of between 20 and 40 minutes due to the need to couple a network locomotive, fill air tubes and carry out a lengthy brake test, are required. Available techniques seem to be automated (un)coupling and self-propelled wagons. These innovations require modification of or investment in rolling stock. Further investigations into the feasibility of such solutions seem to be needed.

Conclusion

If network-related problems are solved, investing in a new hub terminal, even where modified to reduce costs, may still be perceived as too risky for investors. Apart from the high amount of investment required, the success of the new hub terminal depends on a new type of operations, new technology and strict scheduling conditions. Investors may prefer a more gradual path towards innovation. Existing road-rail terminals upgraded with a transport system seem to be an interesting solution to function as hub exchange facility for a demand of up to nine trains per day. This option merits further investigation.

7.3 Main findings and conclusions with respect to secondary objectives

As a prologue to the main objective the first secondary objective was formulated as *"Provide a general assessment of the state of the art of road-rail intermodal transport research"*.

The purpose of this objective was to provide the first comprehensive overview of the field, to define an intermodal research agenda and to select a thesis topic. This first comprehensive review of road-rail intermodal transport with suggestions for a research agenda, based on 92 publications between 1977 and 2000, was published in 2004 in Transportation Research A (Bontekoning et al., 2004).

In the review it is concluded that research carried out prior to 2000 lacks an integrated, systematic approach to these problems. Most research focuses on a single component of the intermodal system, such as pre-haulage and end-haulage, transhipment or the rail haul service network. The research agenda proposed consists of ten items. The contents of this thesis contribute to the following three items of that agenda:

- Design and evaluation of terminals in order to obtain a fundamental understanding of the impact of arrival and departure dynamics of trucks and trains, terminal layout and operations strategy on terminal performance (handling time and costs). This is especially relevant for the development of new consolidation production systems.
- Design of networks and consolidation production system for the rail haul. Still very little is known about the relationship between the number, size and location of terminals and the geographical coverage of intermodal transport. This also applies to the relationship between consolidation model, frequency, train length and costs.
- Analysis of cost structure and development of pricing strategies.

Conclusion

The prologue to this thesis is the first comprehensive review of road-rail intermodal transport. In the review it is concluded that research carried out prior to 2000 lacks an integrated, systematic approach to these problems. Most research focuses on a single component of the intermodal system, such as pre-haulage and end-haulage, transhipment or the rail haul service network.

The second secondary objective was formulated as *"Provide a thorough assessment of the functioning of (former) existing and proposed hub-and-spoke systems"*.

Chapters 3, 4 and 6 contribute to this objective. Chapter 3 describes the major elements of (former) existing and proposed hub-and-spoke systems and explains how these systems function. The intermodal hub-and-spoke system may be systematically described by the following three interrelated components:

- features of demand, or component *Demand;*
- technical features of hub exchange facilities, or component *Resources;*
- features of hub exchange operations, or component *Process.*

The component *Demand* consists of elements that specify the features of the daily demand to be processed at a hub exchange facility. These elements are batches and exchange relations, number of batches and trains per day, number of load units/rail wagons per train, type/size of load unit or rail wagon, load order, train length, train arrival and departure schedule and type of traction. The component *Resources* consists of physical elements such as facility and side yard infrastructure, and equipment and labour that is needed to process transport and load units, in other words, to deal with elements of *Demand*. The component *Process* consists of exchange activities carried out at and by elements of the component *Resources* and of process control principles.

The system description demonstrated the lack of uniform terminology in intermodal hub-and-spoke practice, literature on proposed new hub terminals and literature on intermodal hub-and-spoke networks. Chapter 3 contributes to new or modified terminology in intermodal transport research with respect to terms such as hub exchange operations, batch, synchronisation of arrivals, synchronised operations, hub exchange facility and hub-node.

The assessment of hub-and-spoke systems in Chapters 3, 4 and 6 leads to the conclusion that different hub exchange facilities require the same demand characteristics to achieve efficient hub exchange operations. But due to differences in layout and equipment hub exchange operations are carried out in a different way for the four hub facilities studied, resulting in different time and cost performances.

Conclusion
> *Typical features of train arrivals for efficient hub exchange operations are their batch-wise structure and the synchronisation of arrival times. It is a misconception that shunting (or road-rail terminal) hub-operations do not require synchronised arrivals. For efficient exchange operations the presence of other trains in a batch is required. (Previous) existing hub-shunting seems slow, because a large part of the process time at shunting yards is waiting time due to non-synchronised arrival schedules. Optimisation of arrival schedules would, under the condition of planned load order, lead to competitive hump shunting and road-rail hub terminals compared to new hub terminals.*

The third secondary objective is to "*Provide new and additional performance data for various hub exchange facilities for different operational conditions*".

The purpose of this objective is to provide other studies with values for time and costs parameters for hub exchange operations, which until now have been assumed and seem to be poorly founded with empirical data. Chapter 6 and the appendices provide train sojourn times and related costs for various demand volumes, load order, load factor, batch sizes, arrival schedules, capacity levels and costs. This new data shows that time and costs performance may vary significantly under different conditions.

Conclusion
> *This thesis may contribute to other studies with more precise node time and costs data for hub-and-spoke networks.*

7.4 Recommendations for further research

A first recommendation for further research is to investigate the causes and solutions of poor, unreliable rail network service planning and control. Synchronised arrivals and occasional small delays are important conditions for successful hub-and-spoke networks. If these conditions are not met, fast hub exchange facilities have no reason for existence. In general, railway practice nowadays is not able to meet these criteria. This situation hampers not only the development of hub-and-spoke networks but any advancement of the competitiveness of intermodal transport.

A second recommendation for further research is to investigate among shippers, forwarders and intermodal and railway operators which train sojourn times for intermediate exchange they consider to be acceptable and at what price. Such investigation should be carried out with shippers, forwarders and intermodal and railway operators that handle time-sensitive goods. General demand studies have been carried out in the past (see for example Cardebring et al., 2002; Harper & Evers, 1993; Ludvigsen, 1999; Murphy & Daley, 1998), but I would suggest creating surveys for specific transport relations in specific geographic areas and distinguishing between types of goods and types of actor. Shippers and forwarders may only be interested in total transport time from origin to destination, while intermodal and railway operators may be specifically interested in the duration of the rail haul including transhipment time at intermediate nodes.

As a third recommendation for further research I would suggest investigating the potential and possibilities of upgrading existing road-rail terminals to hub exchange facilities. On the one hand, upgrading implies modifying a facility's function. This means that besides its normal function as a start and end terminal, its function is extended to a hub exchange facility. The possibilities depend on its geographical location and transport relations. The general research question in this respect is: which existing road-rail terminals can be upgraded to a hub?
On the other hand, upgrading implies technical modification of the facility due to the integration of a transport system that supports the cranes. Two research questions apply. First, can a transport system be integrated with existing road-rail facilities? Second, what type of transport system could be integrated and how would it affect the terminal's time and costs performance?

For methodological reasons, as a fourth recommendation I suggest reconstructing the models and incorporating more details into them. The models constructed in this thesis are dedicated especially to the main objective of the thesis. They would be unsuitable for use in other research questions. For instance, in the thesis an alternative strategy for dealing with delays in parallel operations of batches was proposed, but the strategy could not be studied with the models. Modelling suggestions are:
- to include allocation problems such as the allocation of flows to certain cranes, allocation of trains to tracks and the allocation of cranes to trains;
- to model shunting-related activities closer to reality.

In addition, it would be interesting to see whether incorporation of more details leads to significantly different outputs. In this sense the reconstructed models could be used to validate the outputs of the more aggregated models used in this thesis.

As a fifth research theme I propose to further investigate the cost and operational effects of delays. In this thesis only effects related to the node itself were included in the analyses; operations and costs related to rail haul were not. Delays may have consequences on other trains, and thus affect the availability of locomotives and locomotive drivers. As a consequence the input of drivers and locomotives may need to be rescheduled, leading to operational changes and additional costs.

As sixth recommendation I suggest to set up a central public database with accurate and recent data about various costs, accounting rules, investments in equipment and infrastructure for the rail network and nodes.

A seventh line of research I recommend is to investigate the transport relations on which automated (un)coupling or self-propelled rail wagons (see Hansen, 2004) could be implemented and the extent to which time and costs performances at hump shunting and flat shunting yards will be improved.

A last line of research that may be carried out is to investigate how new hub terminals can be modified (fewer tracks, smaller cranes) in order to realise a significant reduction in the amount of investment and at which greenfield locations new hub terminals may be implemented.

Summary   Yvonne Bontekoning

Problem definition
The implementation of hub-and-spoke networks in intermodal transport is suggested as one of the potential solutions for helping to increase the intermodal market share (European Commission, 1997; Kreutzberger, 1999a; 1999b; Cardebring et al., 2002). The advantages that hub-and-spoke networks may offer, compared to point-to-point networks, are a higher frequency of transport services per transport relation, an increase in the number of transport relations (serving small flows) and economies of scale. Various intermodal hub-and-spoke rail networks became operational during the past decade in Europe. Two of them were abandoned at the end of 2004 due to the increasing unreliability of traction on the railways in recent years (Arndt & Rozendaal, 2004). Traditionally, trains are shunted at these hubs; this is a time-consuming process. Since the early 1990s a new type of intermodal terminal, specifically designed for fast transhipment at nodes in hub-and-spoke networks, has been introduced in Europe. These hub terminals could replace this time-consuming shunting.

Studies on the new hub terminals suggest that they may perform more efficiently than shunting yards (European Commission, 1997; Jourquin, 1999; Bontekoning & Kreutzberger, 2001; Bontekoning & Trip, 2004). However, a systematic comparison to reveal the operational and costs differences between shunting and these new hub-terminals for a broad range of situations still lacks.
From 1997 to 2000 I participated in an EU project called Terminet. The findings of the Terminet project gave rise to the idea of further investigating hub-and-spoke networks and new hub exchange facilities with a dynamic approach and including alternative hub exchange facilities. A dynamic assessment would provide better insight into exchange operations at different hub facilities. A simulation approach also allows for the incorporation of different batch and train arrival schedules and delays. In addition, it allows an assessment of the development of the operations. The proposed hub exchange operations differ from current shunting practise, from transfer operations in other freight transport industries and from operations at marine and road-rail terminals. Due to these differences, existing models for transfer operations may be of limited use. As a consequence, a new model should be developed in order to determine the conditions under which new hub terminals perform better than shunting.

Research objectives
The central objective was formulated as follows: "*to develop a model to identify favourable operational conditions for new hub terminals to be implemented and to quantify their operational performances in relation to alternative hub exchange facilities*".
Develop a model implies to develop one or various models in which different parameter and variable settings can represent different hub-and-spoke systems and make the model as transparent and as aggregated as possible without losing specific features.
Favourable operational conditions are defined as demand volumes, train arrival schedules and facility capacity levels, which amount to a certain performance level.

As a spin-off of the main objective, three secondary objectives were formulated. Firstly, as a prologue to the formulation of the main objective the following objective was formulated: *"Provide a general assessment of the state of the art of road-rail intermodal transport research".*

Secondly, as transitional steps towards the main objective: *"Provide a thorough assessment of the functioning of (former) existing and proposed hub-and-spoke systems".*

Lastly, parallel to the main objective and with the purpose of providing other studies on hub-and-spoke networks with values for time and costs parameters, the following objective was formulated: *"Provide new and additional empirical performance data for various hub exchange facilities for different operational conditions".*

Until now time and costs parameters have been based on assumptions and seem to be poorly founded with empirical data.

Research approach

Research consisted of three phases, which are presented in Figure 1. Phase I can be characterised as an exploration into a research topic and problem definition. This phase consisted of three research activities: 1) a general literature study on the state of the art of road-rail intermodal transport research, 2) participation in the EU project Terminet and 3) a specific literature study focusing on the state of the art of hub-and-spoke networks, hub exchange facilities and hub exchange operations in road-rail intermodal transport. The Terminet project ran from 1997 to 2000. I participated in two inventory studies: one on bundling networks and one on innovative intermodal terminals. I also carried out an evaluation study in which I analysed and compared the functioning and performances of different terminals.

Phase II can be seen as the preparatory phase of the simulation analyses, in which the following activities were carried out:
- Description of the empirical system.
- Conceptualisation of the empirical system.
- Specification of the conceptual model into a computer model.
- Verification and validation of the computer model.

Phase III consisted of the design of the experiments to be simulated with the model and the analyses of the simulation outputs.

```
Phase I: Comprehensive exploration
┌─────────────────────────────────────────────────────────────┐
│  ┌──────────────────┐    ┌──────────────────────┐           │
│  │ Inventory study  │───▶│ Specific literature  │◀──┐       │
│  │ within Terminet  │    │ review               │   │       │
│  │ project          │    │ Problem definition   │   │       │
│  └──────────────────┘    │ Research design      │   │       │
│                          │ (Chapter 1)          │   │       │
│                          └──────────────────────┘   │       │
│                                                     │       │
│                          ┌──────────────────────┐   │       │
│                          │ General literature   │───┘       │
│                          │ review (Chapter 2)   │           │
│                          └──────────────────────┘           │
```

Phase II: Modelling

```
            ┌──────────────────────────┐
            │ Descriptive empirical    │
            │ model (Chapter 3)        │
            └──────────────────────────┘
                        │                    Abstraction
                        ▼
            ┌──────────────────────────┐
            │ Conceptual model         │
            │ (Chapter 4)              │
            └──────────────────────────┘      Programming and determination of
                        │                     parameters and variables
                        ▼
            ┌──────────────────────────┐
            │ Computer simulation model│
            │ and costs model          │
            │ (Chapter 5)              │
            └──────────────────────────┘
```

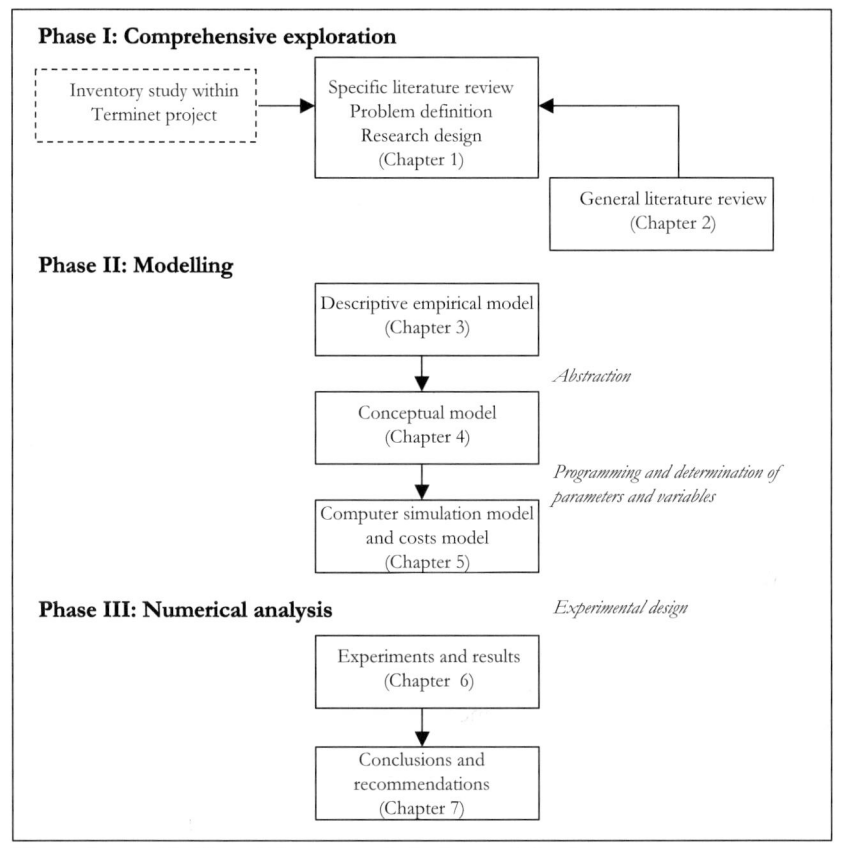

Phase III: Numerical analysis   *Experimental design*

```
            ┌──────────────────────────┐
            │ Experiments and results  │
            │ (Chapter 6)              │
            └──────────────────────────┘
                        │
                        ▼
            ┌──────────────────────────┐
            │ Conclusions and          │
            │ recommendations          │
            │ (Chapter 7)              │
            └──────────────────────────┘
```

Figure 1: Outline of the research design and thesis

For the description of the empirical system, system analysis was used as a general structural framework for the description of the empirical and proposed hub-and-spoke systems. Research techniques applied included the following:
- Desk research on publications in scientific journals, informal reports, professional magazines and commercial documentation.
- (Telephone) interviews with facility manufacturers, and facility and network operators.
- Site visits to shunting yards, rail-road terminals, pilot plants for new hub terminals.
- Observation of scale models and animations for new hub terminals.
- Case studies of specific hub facilities such as the Metz shunting yard, the Herne shunting yard and the application of new hub terminals for the Metz, Valburg and Venlo nodes.

Next, a conceptual model was constructed. The modelling objective was to:
- Develop a model in which different parameter and variable settings can represent different types of hub-and-spoke networks, hub exchange facilities and hub exchange operations.
- Keep the model as transparent and as aggregated as possible without losing typical features.

It turned out that one conceptual model could not sufficiently represent all variations of exchange operations due to fundamental differences between types of resources and routing of flows along these resources and train access and departure control routines to and from exchange operations. As a result one general and five derived conceptual models were constructed, which are all based on the same general framework and modelling principle. The general conceptual model for hub exchange operations is discussed below.

The conceptual models were then programmed into computer models, values for parameters and variables estimated, and the computer models verified and validated. ARENA was chosen as the modelling software.

Conceptualisation of the empirical system

Logistics and queuing theory were used as the theoretical modelling framework. The logistics theory regards thinking in flows, stationary points and flow control (De Vaan, 1998 in: Goor et al., 2000). In queuing theory servers process jobs according to a certain service time. Queues may occur in front of the server when the number of jobs exceeds server capacity. A group of similar servers is defined as a workstation. Jobs arriving as a group in the system are defined as batch arrival, jobs leaving as a group as batch departure (Hall, 1991). The general conceptual model is shown in Figure 2.

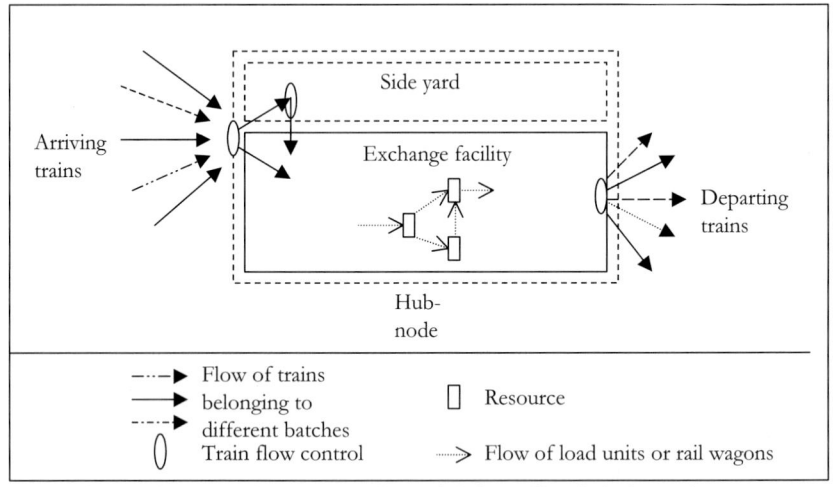

Figure 2: A general conceptual model for rail-rail hub exchange operations

The transparency of the model is obtained, because dimensions of infrastructure, exact origin and destination trains and exact unload and load positions on trains, in the storage area, on the transport system, or exact wagon positions, are not specified. Instead, the spatial characteristics of exchange operations are expressed in the service time distribution functions of the servers. This requires accurate data on locomotive and crane cycles, which could be obtained and validated. Furthermore, problems with modelling allocation related to trains and tracks or to equipment and jobs are minimised. Hence, the precise relocation of load units or rail wagons is not modelled. The model output I am particularly interested in is the time taken to complete processing of a train or a batch, in other words, the accumulation of side yard waiting time, operational service time and queuing time of load units or rail wagons into train and batch service and sojourn times. Train service time is defined as the time from which a train enters the exchange facility until the moment the train leaves it (= facility time). Waiting time at the side yard after arrival is not included. Train service time plus side yard waiting time is defined as train sojourn time. Batch service time is defined as the period of time from which the first train of a batch enters the exchange facility until the moment the last train of a batch leaves it. Adding side yard waiting time to the batch service time results in the batch sojourn time. In this modelling approach load units or rail wagons "flow" through the hub exchange node and are faced with time resistances that accumulate into train and batch service and sojourn times.

Simulation models

Eight computer models were constructed: one synchronised and one non-synchronised model per exchange facility. Crucial variables of the models are the service times of servers. Therefore special attention was paid to the data collection on service times and the estimation of theoretical service time distributions. Distributions were estimated for each type of server and each type of handling. To estimate distributions for cranes a crane cycle time micro simulation tool was developed. Using this tool, crane cycle times could be simulated for each type of transhipment.

Cost model

Since a simulation model does not include a cost evaluation module, a separate cost model was constructed in a spreadsheet. The cost model is a tool that can be used to easily calculate average costs expressed as costs per load unit. The "costs per load unit" for greenfield sites was chosen as indicator for comparison, because the study involves a general comparison of four hub exchange facilities. Since the comparison is not related to any specific hub-node with specific characteristics, facilities with different capacity levels were compared for various demand volumes. Costs calculations imply a total costs approach, implying that both capital (depreciation and interest) and operational costs are included.

Experiments

Many variables could be varied in the experiments. To focus the search for the most favourable operational conditions for new hub terminals, experiments were carried out in a controlled and structured manner. Controlled experiments imply that the effect of a single variable on certain performance indicators was studied. Structured experiments imply that the experiments in which single variables were studied were carried out in a specific order.

We started our series of experiments by studying three volume variables: number of load units/rail wagons per train, number of trains per batch and number of batches per day. The purpose of these experiments was to identify favourable demand, the required minimum demand volume for facilities to be economically feasible and to obtain general insight into costs structure and train sojourn times. See Table 1 for a specification of the initial experiments. Variables were studied in combination with differentiating the variable number of equipment for the new hub terminal and the three alternative hub exchange facilities hump shunting, flat shunting and road-rail terminals.

Table 1: Initial experimental design to determine favourable volume conditions for new hub terminals

Set of experiments	Number of load units (LU)/train; rail wagons/train	Number of batches	Number of trains in a batch
I – increase length of train	32 LU; 20 wagons 48 LU; 30 wagons	1	3
II – increase number of trains	48 LU; 30 wagons	1	4, 6, 8
III – increase number of batches	48 LU; 30 wagons	3	3, 4, 6

Once favourable options for variable demand were determined, the sensitivity of the results for changes in the variables load order and load factor as well as for different costs levels was studied. See Table 2 for a specification. Based on the findings of the initial experiments, only favourable demand conditions and capacity levels were further explored. To determine favourable conditions and facilities for time-sensitive flows, benchmark criteria of 120 minutes for train sojourn time and 50 euros for costs per load unit were applied.

Table 2: Experimental design sensitivity analysis for load order, load factor and costs

Set of experiments	Alternative value(s) sensitivity variable	Number of load units (LU)/train; rail wagons/train	Number of batches	Number of trains in a batch
V – sensitivity load order	planned	48 LU; 30 wagons	Depending on demand selected cases	Depending on demand selected cases
IV – sensitivity load factor	1.4 1.8	42 LU; 30 wagons 54 LU; 30 wagons	Depending on demand selected cases	Depending on demand selected cases
VI – sensitivity costs	- +25% investment equipment - + 25% investment infrastructure - 3% and 6% interest rate - cheaper, but slower cranes	48 LU; 30 wagons	Depending on demand selected cases	Depending on demand selected cases

In the final set of experiments, variations in arrival times and delays as well as strategic operations control principle were studied. See Table 3 for a specification of the experiments. With respect to variable arrival time first, the ideal *just-in-time* interarrival time was determined. With a *just-in-time* arrival schedule, trains do not have to wait for service, and equipment does not have to wait for trains. Ideal circumstances were studied for the purpose of comparison with realistic arrival schedules such as those of the Metz and Herne hubs.

In the previous experiments it was assumed that trains arrive according to schedule. However, in international hub-and-spoke intermodal traffic around 30% of trains are delayed each day. In national hub-and-spoke intermodal traffic 10% of trains are delayed each day. The delayed arrival time of trains varies from several minutes to 24 hours. The impact of delays was therefore studied.

All the abovementioned experiments focus on synchronised operations. However, at some level of non-synchronisation of arrivals or delays, train sojourn times may be better off with non-synchronised operations. In this last set of experiments the impact of non-synchronised operations on Herne and Metz, and a few selected delayed arrival schedules from the previous experiments were studied. For these experiments different models were applied to a few selected cases from the previous experiments with arrival times and delays.

Table 3: Experiments with arrival time, delay and strategic operations control principle

Set of experiments	Alternative value(s) sensitivity variable	Load order	Number of batches	Number of trains in a batch
VII – Arrival time	Ideal schedule	Unplanned/	3	3, 4, 6
	Herne/Metz schedule	Planned*	3	3, 6
	Herne/Metz improved schedule		3	3, 6
VIII – Delay	Ideal schedule	Unplanned/	3	3, 6
	- Random national	Planned*		
	- Random international			
IX – Strategic operations control principle	Non-synchronised operations	Unplanned/ Planned*	3	3, 6
	- Metz / Herne schedule			
	- Delayed ideal schedule			

* Planned load order applies to new hub terminals, unplanned load order to alternative facilities.

Main findings and conclusions

The objective to develop several simple and aggregated models without losing specific features was achieved thanks to the flow-oriented modelling approach. As a consequence of differences in the operations control between synchronised and non-synchronised operations two types of models for each type of facility had to be constructed. Furthermore, different models had to be constructed due to different features of the exchange facilities. However, differences between hump shunting and flat shunting could be overcome by different parameter settings in the same model.

The underlying principle of the models is that trains, load units or rail wagons "flow" through the hub exchange node and are faced with time resistances that accumulate into a train sojourn time. The transparency of the models is obtained, because dimensions of infrastructure, exact origin and destination trains and exact unload and load position on trains, in storage areas and in transport systems, and exact wagon position are not specified. The spatial characteristics of exchange operations are expressed in the service time distribution functions of the servers. Accurate estimated and validated service time distribution functions are crucial for the accuracy of the models and could be obtained.

A typical consequence of aggregation is the loss of real details, which, despite model validation, may influence results. Model assumptions with respect to:
- job assignment to cranes,
- volume per exchange relations,
- train entrance time,

- shunting time between side yard and facility,
- no equipment breakdowns,

lead to underestimation of the train service and sojourn times.

The first two assumptions only affect the results of the terminal simulations. Due to the first two assumptions I expect that train service and sojourn times in the terminal simulations are underestimated with a maximum of about 19 minutes, but more likely averaging to 10 minutes. The affect of the second assumption is difficult to quantify.

The first two assumptions only affect the results of the terminal simulations, which means that the mutual ranking of time performances may change. The latter three assumptions affect all results in the same way. The mutual ranking of performances of facilities does not change. All performances are underestimated with a similar period of time. With respect to the third assumption I expect an underestimation of the train service time and sojourn time of between 3 to 6 minutes. Results apply for all simulation for the projected operation in which the network locomotive remains attached to the train during operations, because the exchange facilities are assume to be electrified. If facilities are not electrified, a diesel locomotive must be attached to the train outside the facility, which implies an underestimation of the service time of about 12 minutes.

When applying the models and interpreting the model outputs the specific simplifications of reality applied should be considered. The models may be improved by integrating a number of further details.

The new hub terminal concept seems most suitable for larger hub-and-spoke networks with a minimum daily demand of at least nine trains of about 600 metres in length. The daily demand should preferably be structured into small batches of two or three trains instead of large batches of (for instance) four or six trains. Smaller batches lead to shorter train service times. Most favourable new hub terminals and their performances are presented in Table 4. These facilities remain below the benchmark criterion of 120 minutes for train sojourn time and 50 euro per load unit for costs for less favourable conditions for load factor, total annual costs and model assumptions.

The shortest train service times are achieved for ideally synchronised arrivals and synchronised operations. Ideal means a *just-in-time* arrival schedule in which trains do not have to wait for service, and equipment does not have to wait for trains. For new hub terminals ideal train interarrival times lie between about 3 and 25 minutes. For these ideal conditions trains and batch service time are equal to train and batch sojourn time. When train interarrival times deviate from the ideal schedule, which is entirely feasible due to planning problems and/or delays, train service and sojourn times in most cases will increase. This in itself is not problematic so long as interarrival times and delays do not amount to a train sojourn time higher than the train sojourn time benchmark criterion. The extent to which deviations from the ideal interarrival times and delays may accumulate depends on the one hand on the time window between the train service time and the benchmark criterion for train sojourn time and on the other hand on the type and size of deviation and delay. In general we can say that faster facilities (shorter service times) allow larger deviations and delays.

Table 4: Quantification of performances for favourable operational conditions of new hub terminals under the condition of ideal synchronised train arrivals

Demand*	Facility and capacity level	Train service time (minutes)	Batch service time (minutes)	Duration total operation (minutes)	Costs per load unit (euro)
3*3	C4_rr	68	77	244	29
3*3	C4	44	49	147	38
3*4	C6	37	55	166	37
3*4	C4	73	87	260	29
3*6	C10	31	49	163	37
3*6	C6	58	79	250	26

* 3*3 stands for three batches of three trains

Comparison of the ideal interarrival times with realistic arrival schedules and delays suggests that there is a large gap between intermodal practice and the preferred arrival schedules for new hub terminals. This discrepancy should be addressed before we consider implementing new hub terminals. The train sojourn times not only of new hub terminals but also of alternative hub exchange facilities are seriously affected by non-synchronised train arrivals and regular (and often lengthy) delays as is currently the case.

Under the condition of a planned load order there are alternative facilities for new hub terminals (see Table 5). The alternatives are competitive with new hub terminals for a demand of nine trains. The new hub terminals C4, C2 and C4_rr are (much) faster (and would be even faster for a planned load order), but the alternatives perform better in terms of costs per load unit. For a higher demand than nine trains there are no alternatives for new hub terminals.

The relatively high minimum demand volume (due to high investment costs) required to achieve a reasonable costs per load unit is not the main obstacle to implementation. Poor network conditions are the main obstacle, as was pointed out above. But if network-related problems are resolved, lower investments may make the new hub terminal more attractive. The greatest effect can be obtained by reducing equipment costs.

However, investors may prefer a more gradual path towards innovation. Existing road-rail terminals may be upgraded with a transport system. The results suggest that a transport system contributes significantly to a fast handling performance compared to a terminal without a transport system.

Table 5: Alternative hub exchange facilities that meet the benchmark criteria under the condition of planned load order

Demand*	Facility and capacity level	Train service time (minutes)	Batch service time (minutes)	Duration total operation (minutes)	Costs per load unit (euro)
3*3	RR4	94	157	300	21
3*3	H22	101	133	222	31
3*3	H12	108	131	248	35

* Three batches of three trains.

With respect to hump shunting and flat shunting, solutions for reducing the performance backlog of between 20 and 40 minutes due to the need to couple a network locomotive, fill air tubes and carry out a lengthy brake test, are required. Available techniques seem to be automated (un)coupling and self-propelled wagons. These innovations require modification of or investment in rolling stock. Further investigations into the feasibility of such solutions appear to be required.

Main conclusion

Average favourable operational conditions for new hub terminals are a minimum daily demand of at least nine trains organised into several small batches of two or three trains, train interarrival times within a batch of between about 5 and 25 minutes, arrival schedules with buffer time in between batches of about 60 minutes, and arrival delays of a maximum of about 60 minutes.

However, these conditions do not equate with current intermodal practice in any sense. Significant improvement of service network planning and control is required, not only for new hub terminals. For alternative hub exchange facilities it is even more crucial that train arrivals are synchronised and reliable.

Even if network-related problems are resolved, investing in a new hub terminal, even when modified to reduce costs, is still a risky business. Investors may prefer a more gradual path towards innovation. Existing road-rail terminals upgraded with a transport system seem to be an interesting solution for a demand of up to nine trains per day.

Findings and conclusions with respect to secondary objectives

The general literature review on road-rail intermodal transport presented as prologue to this thesis resulted in the first comprehensive review on road-rail intermodal transport. This first comprehensive review on road-rail intermodal transport, based on 92 publications from 1977 to 2000, was published in 2004 in Transportation Research A (Bontekoning et al., 2004).

The second secondary objective was "*Provide a thorough assessment of the functioning of (former) existing and proposed hub-and-spoke systems*".

The system description in Chapter 3 highlighted a lack of uniform terminology in intermodal hub-and-spoke practice, literature on proposed new hub terminals and literature on intermodal hub-and-spoke networks. Chapter 3 contributes to new or modified terminology in intermodal transport research with respect to terms such as hub exchange operations, batch, synchronisation of arrivals, synchronised operations, hub exchange facility and hub-node.

The assessment of hub-and-spoke systems in Chapters 3, 4 and 6 leads to the conclusion that different hub exchange facilities require the same demand characteristics to achieve efficient hub exchange operations. Typical features of train arrivals for efficient hub exchange operations are its batchwise structure and the synchronisation of train arrivals. For efficient exchange operations the presence of other trains in a batch is required. (Previous) existing hub-shunting seems slow, because a large part of the processing time at shunting yards is down to waiting time due to non-synchronised arrival schedules.

Finally, with respect to the last secondary objective, this thesis may contribute to other studies with more precise node time and costs data for hub-and-spoke networks. Chapter 6 and the appendices provide train sojourn times and related costs for various demand volumes, load order, load factor, batch sizes, arrival schedules, capacity levels and costs. This new data shows that time and costs performance may vary significantly under different conditions.

Recommendations for further research
Eight recommendations for further research were formulated. First, investigate the causes of and solutions for poor rail network service planning and control. Current railway practice hampers not only the development of hub-and-spoke networks, but any advancement of the competitiveness of intermodal transport.

Second, investigate among shippers, forwarders and intermodal and railway operators handling time-sensitive goods, the train sojourn times they consider to be acceptable for intermediate exchange and at what price.

Third, investigate the potential and possibilities for modifying existing road-rail terminals into hub exchange facilities with a transport system that supports the cranes.

Fourth, try to improve the models through the incorporation of a few more details in order to make the models more flexible and to apply different operations control principles.

Fifth, further investigate the impact of delays on operations and costs related to the rail haul.

Sixth, set up a central public database for costs, accounting rules, investments in equipment and infrastructure, etcetera for the rail network and nodes.

Seventh, investigate on which transport relations automated (un)coupling or self-propelled rail wagons could be implemented and to what extent time and costs performances at hump shunting and flat shunting yards will be improved.

Last, investigate how new hub terminals can be modified in order to realise a significant reduction in the amount of investment and at which greenfield locations new hub terminals may be implemented.

Samenvatting Yvonne Bontekoning

Probleemstelling
De implementatie van hub-and-spoke-netwerken in het intermodale transport wordt aangedragen als een mogelijke manier om het marktaandeel van intermodaal transport te vergroten (European Commission, 1997; Kreutzberger, 1999a; 1999b; Cardebring et al., 2002). De voordelen van hub-and-spoke-netwerken ten opzichte van point-to-point-netwerken zijn een hogere frequentie van transportdiensten per transportrelatie, een toename van het aantal transportrelaties (ten dienste van kleine stromen) en schaalvoordelen. In de loop van de afgelopen tien jaar zijn in Europa diverse intermodale rail hub-and-spoke netwerken in gebruik genomen. Twee daarvan worden sinds eind 2004 niet meer gebruikt, vanwege de onbetrouwbaarheid van de aankomsttijden van treinen op de hub (Arndt & Rozendaal, 2004). Traditioneel gezien worden de treinen op de hubs gerangeerd, wat een tijdrovend proces is. Begin jaren 90 is er in Europa een nieuw type intermodale terminal voorgesteld, dat is ontworpen voor snelle overslag op de knooppunten van hub-and-spoke-netwerken. Deze hub-terminals kunnen een einde maken aan het tijdrovende rangeren.

Ondanks diverse onderzoeken naar intermodale hub-and-spoke-netwerken (European Commission, 1997; Jourquin, 1999; Janic, 1998), rangeerprocessen (Ferguson, 1993; Timian, 1994; Wang, 1997; Kraft, 2000; 2002) en de werking van de nieuwe hub-terminals (Alicke, 1999, 2002; Meyer, 1998; Bostel, 1996; Bostel & Dejax, 1998), is er nog geen diepgaand onderzoek gedaan waarin hub-and-spoke netwerken met rangeerhubs worden vergeleken met terminal hubs. Van 1997 tot 2000 heb ik deelgenomen aan een EU-project genaamd Terminet. De conclusies van het Terminet-project waren eveneens aanleiding tot verder onderzoek naar hub-and-spoke-netwerken en nieuwe overslagfaciliteiten in vergelijking met alternatieve overslagfaciliteiten voor hubs. Een simulatiestudie kan meer inzicht verschaffen in de overslagprocessen met verschillende soorten hub-faciliteiten. Met behulp van een simulatie kunnen we verschillende batch samenstellingen en aankomsttijden en vertragingen van treinen bestuderen. Daarnaast kunnen we middels simulatie het overslagproces evalueren.
De voorgestelde hub operations in hub-and-spoke concepten voor intermodaal goederenvervoer wijken af van het huidige rangeren, van hub operations in andere goederenvervoer branches en van maritieme en road-rail terminal processen. Als gevolg kunnen bestaande modellen die gebruikt worden om deze processen te analyseren maar beperkt gebruikt worden.

Doelstellingen van het onderzoek
De hoofddoelstelling is als volgt geformuleerd: "*ontwikkel een model waarmee gunstige operationele omstandigheden voor nog te implementeren nieuwe hub-terminals kunnen worden geïdentificeerd en waarmee hun prestaties in verhouding tot alternatieve faciliteiten voor overslag op hubs kunnen worden gekwantificeerd*".

Van de modelontwikkeling wordt verwacht dat er een (of meerdere) simulatiemodel(len) worden ontwikkeld waarin verschillende instellingen van parameters en variabelen verschillende hub-and-spoke-systemen kunnen vertegenwoordigen, waarbij het model zo eenvoudig en geaggregeerd mogelijk is, zonder dat daardoor specifieke eigenschappen verloren gaan.

Gunstige operationele omstandigheden zijn gedefinieerd als kansrijke combinaties van volumegrootte, aankomsttijden van treinen en capaciteit van faciliteiten, die tot een bepaald prestatieniveau leiden.

Als aanvulling op het hoofddoel van het onderzoek zijn er drie secundaire doelen geformuleerd. Als eerste is, bij wijze van proloog op de formulering van het hoofddoel, de volgende doelstelling geformuleerd: *Een algemene evaluatie verschaffen van de huidige staat van het onderzoek naar intermodaal transport via spoor en weg.*

Als tweede subdoel is geformuleerd: *een diepgaande evaluatie leveren van het functioneren van (voormalige) bestaande en toekomstige hub-and-spoke-systemen.*

Ten slotte werd parallel aan het hoofddoel de volgende doelstelling geformuleerd, teneinde cijfers te verschaffen voor de parameters tijd en kosten voor modellen in hub-and-spoke-netwerkstudies: *Nieuwe en aanvullende prestatiegegevens leveren voor verschillende faciliteiten voor overslag op een hub onder verschillende operationele omstandigheden.* Tot nu toe zijn de parameters voor tijd en kosten in deze modellen altijd op aannames gebaseerd en lijken ze derhalve niet of nauwelijks op empirische gegevens te zijn gestoeld.

Aanpak van het onderzoek

Het onderzoek bestond uit drie fasen, die zijn weergegeven in figuur 1. Fase I kan worden gekarakteriseerd als een verkenning van het onderzoeksonderwerp en de probleemstelling. Deze fase bestond uit drie onderzoeksactiviteiten: 1) een algemene literatuurstudie naar de huidige staat van het onderzoek naar intermodaal transport via spoor en weg, 2) deelname aan het EU-project Terminet en 3) een specifiek literatuuronderzoek naar de huidige staat van onderzoek met betrekking tot hub-and-spoke-netwerken, faciliteiten voor overslag op hubs en overslagprocessen op hubs. Het Terminet-project liep van 1997 tot 2000. Ik heb meegewerkt aan twee verkennende onderzoeken: een naar het bundelen van netwerken en een naar innovatieve intermodale terminals. Daarnaast heb ik een evaluerend onderzoek uitgevoerd waarin ik het functioneren en de prestaties van verschillende terminals heb geanalyseerd en vergeleken.

Fase II kan worden beschouwd als de voorbereidende fase van de simulatieanalyse, waarbij de volgende taken zijn uitgevoerd:
- Beschrijving van het empirische systeem.
- Conceptualisering van het empirische systeem.
- Specificatie van het conceptuele model en het bouwen van een computermodel.
- Verificatie en validatie van het computermodel.

Fase III bestond uit het ontwerpen van de experimenten die met het model moesten worden gesimuleerd en de analyse van de output van de simulatie.

```
Fase I: Verkenning
┌─────────────────────────────────────────────────────────────┐
│  ┌ ─ ─ ─ ─ ─ ─ ─ ─ ─ ─ ─ ┐      ┌─────────────────────┐    │
│  │ Inventarisatie studie in │ ──→ │ Specifieke literatuur studie │    │
│  │   Terminet project    │      │    Probleem definitie    │ ←──┐ │
│  └ ─ ─ ─ ─ ─ ─ ─ ─ ─ ─ ─ ┘      │    Onderzoeksopzet       │    │ │
│                                  │      (Hoofdstuk 1)       │    │ │
│                                  └─────────────────────┘    │ │
│                                                              │ │
│                                       ┌─────────────────────┐│ │
│                                       │ Algemene literatuur studie ├┘
│                                       │      (Hoofdstuk 2)       ││
│                                       └─────────────────────┘│
Fase II: Modelleren
```

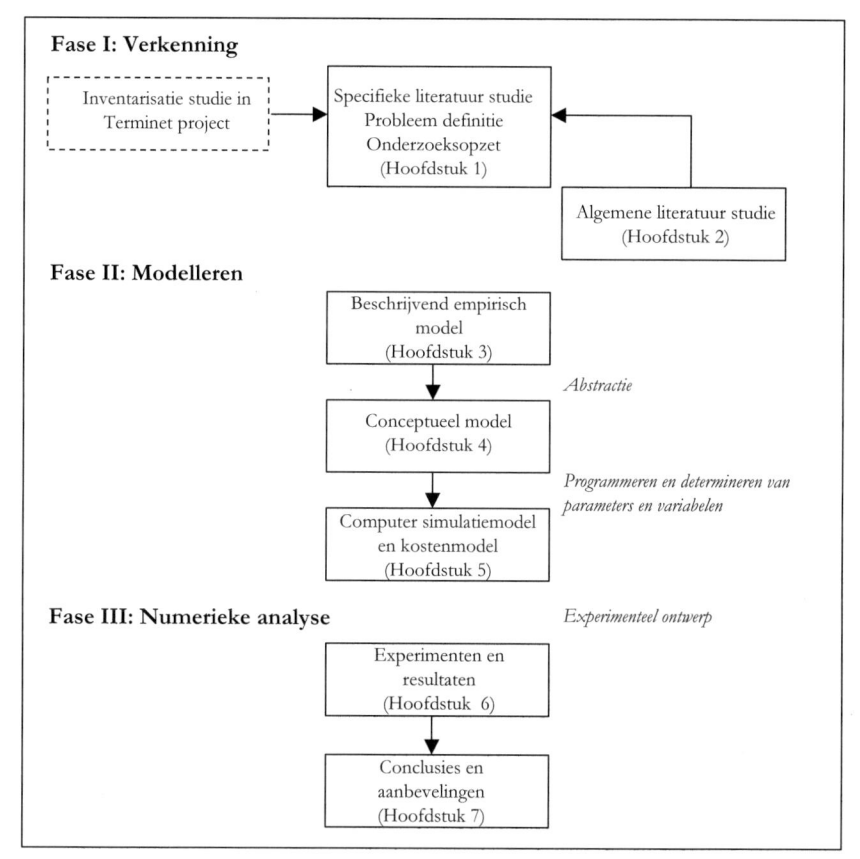

Figuur 1: Overzicht van de onderzoeksopzet en inhoud van het proefschrift

Voor de beschrijving van het empirische systeem is als algemeen structureel raamwerk systeemanalyse gebruikt voor de beschrijving van empirische en geplande hub-and-spoke-systemen. De gebruikte onderzoeksmethoden zijn onder meer:
- Literatuuronderzoek naar publicaties in wetenschappelijke tijdschriften, informele rapporten, vakbladen en commerciële documentatie.
- (Telefonische) interviews met de ontwerpers en bouwers van de faciliteiten en de exploitanten van de faciliteiten en netwerken.
- Locatiebezoek aan rangeerterreinen, railterminals en proefopstellingen van faciliteiten voor nieuwe hub-terminals.
- Observatie van schaalmodellen en animaties voor nieuwe hub-terminals.
- Casestudy's naar specifieke hub-faciliteiten, zoals het rangeerterrein te Metz en het rangeerterrein te Herne, alsmede naar de toepassingsmogelijkheden van nieuwe hub-terminals voor de knooppunten Metz, Valburg en Venlo.

Vervolgens is er een conceptueel model gemaakt. De doelstellingen voor de modellering waren:
- De ontwikkeling van een model waarin verschillende instellingen van parameters en variabelen verschillende soorten hub-and-spoke-netwerken, overslagfaciliteiten op hubs en overslagprocessen op hubs kunnen vertegenwoordigen.
- Het zo transparant en geaggregeerd mogelijk maken van het model, zonder dat er karakteristieke eigenschappen verloren gaan.

Uiteindelijk bleek dat één enkel conceptueel model de verschillende soorten overslagprocessen niet allemaal kon vertegenwoordigen, vanwege de fundamentele verschillen tussen de diverse soorten equipement, routes langs het equipement en aankomst- en vertrekprocedures van de treinen. Daarom zijn er zes conceptuele modellen geconstrueerd, alle gebaseerd op hetzelfde algemene raamwerk en modelleerprincipe. Het algemene conceptuele model voor overslagprocessen op hubs wordt hieronder beschreven.

Vervolgens werden de conceptuele modellen tot computermodellen omgevormd, werden er parameters en variabelen vastgesteld en werden de computermodellen geverifieerd en gevalideerd. Als modelleersoftware werd gekozen voor ARENA.

Conceptualisering van het empirische systeem

Als theoretisch modelleerraamwerk zijn logistieke theorie en wachtrijtheorie gebruikt. De logistieke theorie gaat uit van stromen, stationaire punten en stroombesturing (De Vaan, 1998 in: Goor et al., 2000). Bij wachtrijtheorie verwerken servers taken met een bepaalde servicetijd. Wachtrijen kunnen vóór de server ontstaan als het aantal taken de capaciteit van de server overschrijdt. Een groep gelijksoortige servers wordt gedefinieerd als een werkstation. Taken die als groep het systeem binnenkomen worden gedefinieerd als "batch arrival," taken die als groep vertrekken als "batch departure." Het algemene conceptuele model wordt getoond in figuur 2.

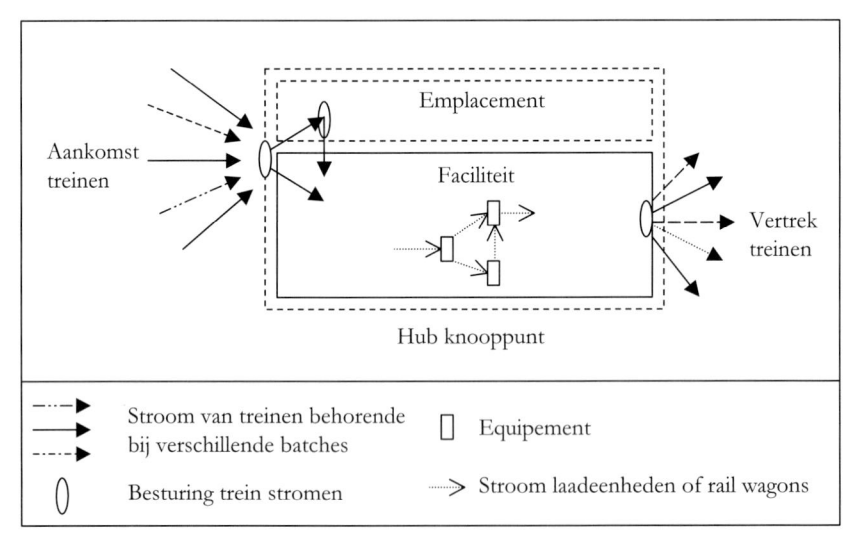

Figuur 2: **Algemeen conceptueel model voor overslagprocessen op rail-rail hub**

De modellen zijn transparant omdat de afmetingen van de infrastructuur, de exacte herkomst en bestemming van de treinen, de precieze los- en laadposities (op de treinen, in het opslaggebied, binnen het transportsysteem) en de exacte posities van de wagons niet zijn gespecificeerd. In plaats daarvan worden de ruimtelijke kenmerken van de overslagprocessen uitgedrukt in de verwerkingstijd-distributiefuncties van de servers. Daarvoor zijn juiste gegevens over de cycli van locomotieven en kranen nodig. Deze gegevens stond de onderzoekster tot haar beschikking en konden ook worden gevalideerd. Daarnaast zijn de problemen bij het modelleren van toewijzingen van treinen aan sporen en van equipement aan taken geminimaliseerd. Als gevolg zijn de precieze herlaadposities van laadeenheden of spoorwegwagons niet in het model opgenomen. De output van het model waar ik met name in ben geïnteresseerd is de tijd die nodig is om de verwerking van een trein of batch te voltooien. In andere woorden, de accumulatie van wachttijd en servicetijd. De servicetijd van een trein wordt gedefinieerd als de tijd tussen het binnenkomen van de trein op de overslagfaciliteit en het moment waarop deze trein weer vertrekt. Daarin is de wachttijd op een zijspoor na aankomst niet opgenomen. De verwerkingstijd van een trein plus de wachttijd op een zijspoor wordt gedefinieerd als de verblijftijd van een trein. De verwerkingstijd van een batch wordt gedefinieerd als de tijd tussen het binnenkomen van de eerste trein van een batch op de overslagfaciliteit en het moment waarop de laatste trein van deze batch weer vertrekt. Als we de zijspoorwachttijd optellen bij de verwerkingstijd van een batch, levert dat de servicetijd van de batch op. Binnen dit model "stromen" de laadeenheden of wagons door de hub overslagfaciliteit, waarbij ze te maken krijgen met tijdweerstanden die samen de service- en verblijftijd van treinen en batches vormen.

Simulatiemodellen

Er zijn acht computermodellen gemaakt: voor iedere overslagfaciliteit één gesynchroniseerd model en één niet-gesynchroniseerd. Cruciale variabelen voor deze modellen zijn de servicetijden van de servers. Daarom is er speciale aandacht besteed aan het verzamelen van gegevens over servicetijden en het schatten van de theoretische kansverdeling van de servicetijden. Voor ieder type server en ieder type overslag zijn verdelingen geschat. Om de verdeling voor kranen te schatten is er een micro simulatiemodel ontwikkeld waarmee de cyclustijd van een kraan kan worden nagebootst. Met behulp daarvan konden voor elk type overslag de kraancyclustijden worden gesimuleerd.

Kostenmodel

Aangezien in simulatiemodellen geen module voor de evaluatie van de kosten is opgenomen, is er een afzonderlijk kostenmodel opgezet in de vorm van een spreadsheet. Het kostenmodel is een hulpmiddel om gemakkelijk de gemiddelde kosten te kunnen berekenen in de vorm van kosten per laadeenheid. Er wordt uitgegaan van de "kosten per laadeenheid" voor nieuwbouw faciliteiten, omdat het onderzoek draait om een algemene vergelijking van vier hub overslagfaciliteiten. Aangezien de vergelijking niet gebonden is aan een specifiek hub-knooppunt met specifieke kenmerken, zijn faciliteiten met verschillende capaciteiten vergeleken voor verschillende hoeveelheden laadeenheden en wagons. De berekening van de kosten impliceert een benadering op basis van alle kosten, zodat zowel kapitaal (afschrijving en rente) als de operationele kosten worden meegeteld.

Experimenten

In de experimenten konden talrijke variabelen worden ingesteld. Om gericht te zoeken naar de meest gunstige operationele omstandigheden voor nieuwe hub-terminals, zijn er gestructureerde vergelijkende experimenten uitgevoerd. Vergelijkende experimenten wil zeggen dat de effecten van één enkele variabele op bepaalde prestatie-indicatoren zijn getest. Gestructureerd wil zeggen dat de experimenten waarin individuele variabelen werden bestudeerd in een specifieke volgorde werden uitgevoerd.

We zijn onze reeks experimenten begonnen door drie variabelen te bestuderen die te maken hebben met volume: het aantal laadeenheden of wagons per trein, het aantal treinen per batch en het aantal batches per dag. Het doel van deze experimenten was om naast een gunstige vraag tevens de minimumomvang van de vraag om de faciliteiten economisch levensvatbaar te maken vast te stellen en daarnaast algemeen inzicht te vergaren in de opbouw van de kosten en de servicetijden van treinen. Zie tabel 1 voor een specificatie van de eerste experimenten. Bij de bestudering van de variabelen is rekening gehouden met de verschillende hoeveelheden equipement van de nieuwe hub-terminals en de drie alternatieve overslagfaciliteiten op hubs: heuvelen, rangeren op vlak terrein en weg-spoorterminals.

Tabel 1: Experimenten voor het vaststellen van een gunstige overslagvolume voor nieuwe hub-terminals

Experimenten	Aantal laadeenheden (LE)/trein ; wagons/trein	Aantal batches	Aantal treinen per batch
I – trein verlengen	32 LE; 20 wagons 48 LE; 30 wagons	1	3
II – aantal treinen vergroten	48 LE; 30 wagons	1	4, 6, 8
III – aantal batches vergroten	48 LE; 30 wagons	3	3, 4, 6

Zodra er gunstige opties voor de variabele vraag waren gevonden, werd bestudeerd hoe gevoelig de resultaten waren voor wijzigingen van de variabelen laadvolgorde en laadfactor, alsmede voor verschillende kostenniveaus. Zie tabel 2 voor een specificatie.

Tabel 2: Experimenten naar de gevoeligheid van de variabelen: laadvolgorde, laadfactor en kosten

Experimenten	Alternatieve waarde(s) gevoeligheidsvariabele	Aantal laadeenheden (LE)/trein ; wagons/trein	Aantal batches	Aantal treinen per batch
V – gevoeligheid laadvolgorde	gepland	48 LE; 30 wagons	Afhankelijk van vraag geselecteerde case	Afhankelijk van vraag geselecteerde case
IV – gevoeligheid laadfactor	1,4 1,8	42 LE; 30 wagons 54 LE; 30 wagons	Afhankelijk van vraag geselecteerde case	Afhankelijk van vraag geselecteerde case
VI – gevoeligheid kosten	- +25% investering uitrusting - +25% investering infrastructuur - 3% en 6% rente - goedkopere, maar langzamere kranen	48 LE; 30 wagons	Afhankelijk van vraag geselecteerde case	Afhankelijk van vraag geselecteerde case

Op basis van de resultaten van de eerste experimenten zijn uitsluitend gunstige vraagvoorwaarden en capaciteitsniveaus verder bestudeerd. Om de gunstige omstandigheden en faciliteiten voor tijdgevoelige stromen te bepalen, zijn we uitgegaan van twee benchmark criteria, te weten maximaal 120 minuten servicetijd voor de trein en 50 euro aan kosten per laadeenheid.

In de laatste reeks experimenten werden variaties in aankomsttijden en vertragingen bestudeerd, alsmede verschillende strategieën voor de aansturing van de processen. Zie tabel 3 voor een specificatie van deze experimenten. Wat de variabele aankomsttijd betreft werd de ideale "just-in-time"-tussentijd bepaald. Met een aankomstschema met just-in-time als uitgangspunt hoeven treinen niet op afhandeling te wachten en hoeft equipement niet op beschikbare lading op treinen te wachten. De ideale omstandigheden zijn bestudeerd om deze te kunnen vergelijken met reële aankomstschema's, zoals die van de hubs in Metz en Herne.

Bij de voorgaande experimenten werd steeds aangenomen dat de treinen op tijd aankwamen. Binnen het internationale intermodale hub-and-spoke-verkeer loopt iedere dag echter zo'n 30% van de treinen vertraging op. Binnen het nationale intermodale hub-and-spoke-verkeer heeft iedere dag ongeveer 10% van de treinen vertraging. De vertraging van deze treinen varieert van enkele minuten tot 24 uur. Derhalve zijn ook de gevolgen van vertragingen bestudeerd.

Bij alle bovengenoemde experimenten lag de nadruk op synchrone processen. Maar bij een bepaald niveau van niet-synchronisatie van aankomsten als gevolg van vertragingen kunnen de servicetijden misschien beter worden geoptimaliseerd op basis van niet-synchrone processen. Bij deze laatste groep experimenten zijn de gevolgen bestudeerd van niet-synchrone processen op de hubs in Herne en Metz alsmede een selecte groep vertragingen uit eerdere experimenten. Voor deze experimenten zijn verschillende modellen toegepast op een klein aantal geselecteerde cases uit eerdere experimenten met aankomsttijden en vertragingen.

Tabel 3: Experimenten voor het bestuderen van aankomsttijden, vertragingen en strategieën voor de aansturing van processen

Experimenten	Alternatieve waarde(s) gevoeligheidsvariabele	Laadvolgorde	Aantal batches	Aantal treinen per batch
VII – Aankomsttijd	Ideaal schema	Niet gepland/ gepland*	3	3,4,6
	Schema Herne/Metz		3	3, 6
	Verbeterd schema Herne/Metz		3	3, 6
VIII – Vertraging	Ideaal schema - nationaal - internationaal	Niet gepland/ gepland*	3	3, 6
IX – Strategie procesaansturing	Niet-gesynchroniseerde processen: - Schema Metz/Herne - Ideaal schema met vertraging	Niet gepland/ gepland*	3	3, 6

* Geplande laadvolgorde heeft betrekking op nieuwe hub-terminals, niet-geplande laadvolgorde op alternatieve faciliteiten.

Belangrijkste bevindingen en conclusies
De doelstelling om verscheidene eenvoudige, geaggregeerde modellen te ontwikkelen zonder specifieke kenmerken te verliezen is behaald door de modellering vanuit een "stroom"-concept te benaderen. Gezien de verschillen in de aansturing van gesynchroniseerde en niet-gesynchroniseerde processen moesten er voor ieder type faciliteit twee soorten model worden geconstrueerd. Daarnaast moesten er meerdere modellen worden geconstrueerd als gevolg van de verschillende eigenschappen van de overslagfaciliteiten. De verschillen tussen heuvelen en rangeren op vlak terrein konden echter worden gemodelleerd door in hetzelfde model verschillende parameterinstellingen te gebruiken.

Het onderliggende principe van de modellen is dat de laadeenheden of wagons door het overslagpunt van de hub "stromen," waarbij ze te maken krijgen met tijdweerstanden die samen de servicetijd van de treinen vormen. De modellen zijn met succes transparant vormgegeven: de afmetingen van de infrastructuur, de exacte herkomst en bestemming van de treinen, de precieze los- en laadposities (op de treinen, in het opslaggebied en binnen het transportsysteem) alsmede de exacte posities van de wagons zijn niet gespecificeerd. De ruimtelijke kenmerken van de overslagprocessen worden uitgedrukt in de service-distributiefuncties van de servers. Juiste geschatte en gevalideerde distributiefuncties voor de servicetijd zijn van cruciaal belang voor de accuratesse van de modellen en bleken haalbaar.

Een typisch gevolg van aggregatie is het verlies van reële details die, ondanks de validatie van het model, van invloed kunnen zijn op de resultaten. Model aannames met betrekking tot:
- taaktoewijzing aan kranen,
- volume per uitwisselingsrelatie,
- trein inrijtijd,
- rangeertijd tussen emplacement en hub faciliteit,
- procesverstoringen,

leiden tot een onderschatting van de trein service- en verblijftijd. De eerste twee aannames beïnvloeden alleen de resultaten van de terminal simulaties. Als gevolg van de eerste twee aannames verwacht ik dat de trein service- en verblijftijden worden onderschat met een maximum van ongeveer 19 minuten, meer de kans is aanwezig dat het maar 10 minuten is. Het effect van de tweede aanname is moeilijk te kwantificeren.

De eerste twee aannames treffen alleen de uitkomsten van de terminalsimulaties. Dit kan leiden tot een wisseling in de rangschikking van de tijdsprestaties van de verschillende faciliteiten. De laatste drie aannames treffen alle resultaten op dezelfde manier en beïnvloeden niet de onderlinge rangschikking van de resultaten. Alle resultaten worden in gelijke mate onderschat. Met betrekking tot de derde aanname verwacht ik een onderschatting van de trein service- en verblijftijd tussen de 3 en 6 minuten. De resultaten hebben betrekking op de situatie waarin alle faciliteiten geëlektrificeerd zijn en waardoor de netwerklocomotief aan de trein gekoppeld kan blijven. Zouden faciliteiten niet geëlektrificeerd zijn dan betekent dat een onderschatting van de uitkomsten met 12 minuten.

Bij het toepassen van de modellen en het interpreteren van de output ervan moeten de specifieke vereenvoudigingen van de werkelijkheid dus in overweging worden genomen. De modellen kunnen worden verbeterd door een aantal verdere details te integreren.

Het nieuwe hub-terminalconcept lijkt met name geschikt voor grotere hub-and-spoke-netwerken met een minimale dagelijkse vraag van ten minste negen treinen van ongeveer 600 meter. De dagelijkse vraag zou idealiter moeten worden opgedeeld in kleine batches van twee of drie treinen in plaats van grote batches van bijvoorbeeld vijf of zes treinen. Kleinere batches leiden tot kortere verwerkingstijden voor de treinen. De gunstigste nieuwe hub-terminals en hun prestaties zijn opgenomen in tabel 4. Deze faciliteiten blijven met hun prestaties onder het criterium voor treinservicetijd van maximaal 120 minuten en het criterium voor kosten van maximaal 50 euro per laadeenheid; ook onder minder gunstige omstandigheden qua laadfactor, totale kosten op jaarbasis en model aannames.

De kortste verwerkingstijden worden bereikt met optimaal gesynchroniseerde aankomsten en gesynchroniseerde processen. Met optimaal wordt een aankomstschema met just-in-time als uitgangspunt bedoeld, waarmee treinen niet op afhandeling hoeven te wachten en equipement niet op treinen. Voor de nieuwe hub-terminals ligt de ideale tussentijd tussen 3 en 25 minuten. Bij deze ideale omstandigheden komt de servicetijd van treinen en batches overeen met de verblijftijd van treinen en batches. Als de tussentijd van een trein afwijkt van het optimale schema – wat zeker kan voorkomen als gevolg van problemen met de planning en/of vertragingen – nemen in de meeste gevallen de service- en verblijftijd van de trein toe. Dat is op zich geen probleem, zo lang de tussentijden en vertragingen maar niet leiden tot een langere treinservicetijd dan wij als maximum hebben gehanteerd (120 minuten). De mate waarin afwijkingen van de ideale trein aankomsttijden en vertragingen kunnen cumuleren, is aan de ene kant afhankelijk van het tijdsvenster tussen de servicetijd en de benchmark criterium voor treinverblijftijd, en aan de andere kant van het type en de omvang de afwijking van de treinaankomsttijd en de vertraging. In het algemeen kunnen we stellen dat snellere faciliteiten (met kortere servicetijden) grotere afwijkingen en vertragingen toelaten.

Tabel 4: Kwantificering prestaties nieuwe hub-terminals bij gunstige omstandigheden onder voorwaarde van optimaal gesynchroniseerde trein aankomsttijden

Vraag*	Faciliteit en capaciteitsniveau	Verwerkingstijd trein (minuten)	Verwerkingstijd batch (minuten)	Duur totale proces (minuten)	Kosten per laadeenheid (euro)
3*3	C4_rr	68	77	244	29
3*3	C4	44	49	147	38
3*4	C6	37	55	166	37
3*4	C4	73	87	260	29
3*6	C10	31	49	163	37
3*6	C6	58	79	250	26

* Drie batches van drie treinen.

Uit een vergelijking tussen de ideale trein tussentijden en reële aankomsttijden en vertragingen lijkt naar voren te komen dat er een grote discrepantie bestaat tussen de intermodale praktijk en de gunstigste aankomstschema's voor nieuwe hub-terminals. Deze discrepantie moet eerst worden aangepakt voordat we de implementatie van nieuwe hub-terminals overwegen. De treinservicetijden van niet alleen de nieuwe hub-terminals maar ook van de alternatieve overslagfaciliteiten op een hub hebben ernstig te lijden onder niet-gesynchroniseerde aankomsten van treinen en de regelmatig optredende (en vaak lange) vertragingen waarvan momenteel sprake is.

Onder voorbehoud van een geplande laadvolgorde zijn er alternatieven voor nieuwe hub-faciliteiten (zie Tabel 5). Deze alternatieven concurreren met nieuwe hub-terminals bij een vraag van negen treinen. De nieuwe hub-terminals C4, C2 en C4_rr zijn (veel) sneller (en zouden nog sneller zijn bij een geplande laadvolgorde), maar de alternatieven presteren beter wat betreft kosten per laadeenheid. Voor een grotere vraag dan negen treinen zijn er geen alternatieven voor nieuwe hub-terminals binnen het gestelde afwegingskader.

Tabel 5: Alternatieve faciliteiten voor overslag op hubs die onder voorwaarde van een geplande laadvolgorde voldoen aan de vergelijkingscriteria

Vraag*	Faciliteit en capaciteitsniveau	Verwerkingstijd trein (minuten)	Verwerkingstijd batch (minuten)	Duur totale proces (minuten)	Kosten per laadeenheid (euro)
3*3	RR4	94	157	300	21
3*3	H22	101	133	222	31
3*3	H12	108	131	248	35

* Drie batches van drie treinen.

De relatief hoge minimumvraag (die het gevolg is van hoge investeringskosten) die nodig is om billijke kosten per laadeenheid te realiseren vormt niet de voornaamste hindernis voor de implementatie. De grootste belemmering wordt, zoals hierboven al aangegeven, gevormd door slechte netwerkcondities. Maar als de netwerkgerelateerde problemen zijn opgelost, zou het te investeren bedrag voor een nieuwe hub-terminal aantrekkelijker gemaakt moeten worden. Het grootste verschil kan worden bereikt door de kosten voor equipement te verlagen.

Investeerders zullen echter mogelijk de voorkeur geven aan een gelijkmatiger innovatietraject. Bestaande weg-spoorterminals kunnen worden voorzien van een transportsysteem. De resultaten lijken erop te wijzen dat een transportsysteem een significante bijdrage levert aan een snelle verwerking in vergelijking met een terminal zonder transportsysteem.

Voor heuvelen en rangeren op vlak terrein zijn oplossingen nodig om de achterstand van 20 à 40 minuten weg te werken die het gevolg is van de noodzaak om een netwerklocomotief aan te koppelen, de luchtleidingen te vullen en de lange remtest uit te voeren. Mogelijk geschikte technieken zijn automatische (ont-)koppeling en zelfaandrijvende wagons. Voor deze innovaties zijn wijzigingen aan of investeringen in rollend materieel nodig. Er lijkt behoefte te zijn aan verder onderzoek naar de haalbaarheid van dergelijke oplossingen.

Voornaamste conclusie
De gemiddelde gunstige operationele omstandigheden voor nieuwe hub-terminals zijn: een minimale dagelijkse vraag van ten minste negen treinen, opgedeeld in meerdere kleine batches van twee of drie treinen; tussentijden voor treinen binnen een batch van 5 tot 25 minuten; een aankomstschema met een buffertijd van rond de 60 minuten tussen twee batches, en aankomstvertragingen van maximaal 60 minuten.

Deze omstandigheden komen echter in het geheel niet overeen met de huidige intermodale praktijk. Er is behoefte aan een significante verbetering van de planning en aansturing van het netwerk, niet alleen ten behoeve van nieuwe hub-terminals. Voor

alternatieve overslagfaciliteiten op hubs is het van nog groter belang dat de treinen gesynchroniseerd en met grote betrouwbaarheid op tijd aankomen.
Ook als de netwerkproblemen worden opgelost, blijft het een riskante onderneming om te investeren in een nieuwe hub-terminal, zelfs wanneer deze is aangepast om de kosten te verlagen. Investeerders zullen mogelijk de voorkeur geven aan een gelijkmatiger innovatietraject. Het van een transportsysteem voorzien van bestaande weg-spoorterminals lijkt een interessante oplossing te zijn voor een vraag kleiner dan negen treinen per dag.

Bevindingen en conclusies aangaande de secundaire doelstellingen
Het algemene literatuuronderzoek naar intermodaal weg-spoorverkeer dat de proloog voor dit onderzoek vormde, heeft de eerste integrale evaluatie van intermodaal weg-spoorverkeer opgeleverd. Deze eerste integrale evaluatie van intermodaal weg-spoorverkeer, gebaseerd op 92 publicaties uit de periode 1977 tot 2000, is in 2004 gepubliceerd in Transportation Research A (Bontekoning et al., 2004).

De tweede secundaire doelstelling was *"Een diepgaande evaluatie leveren van het functioneren van (voormalige) bestaande en toekomstige hub-and-spoke-systemen."*
Het in hoofdstuk 3 beschreven systeem wierp licht op het gebrek aan uniforme terminologie binnen de intermodale hub-and-spoke-praktijk, de literatuur over geplande nieuwe hub-terminals en de literatuur over intermodale hub-and-spoke-netwerken. Hoofdstuk 3 vormt een bijdrage aan nieuwe en gewijzigde terminologie voor onderzoek naar intermodaal transport wat betreft begrippen als overslagproces op de hub, batch, synchronisatie van aankomsten, gesynchroniseerde processen, overslagfaciliteit op de hub en hub-knooppunt.
De evaluatie van hub-and-spoke-systemen in hoofdstukken 3, 4 en 6 leidde tot de conclusie dat verschillende overslagfaciliteiten op hubs dezelfde vraagkenmerken moeten hebben om een efficiënt overslagproces op de hub te realiseren. Karakteristieke kenmerken van de aankomst van treinen voor efficiënte overslag op de hub zijn een batch-gewijze organisatie en de synchronisatie van de aankomsten. Voor een efficiënt overslagproces moeten treinen in dezelfde batch gelijktijdig op de hub aanwezig zijn. (Eerdere) bestaande rangeerprocessen op hubs lijken traag, omdat een groot deel van de verblijftijd van treinen op rangeerterreinen de vorm heeft van wachttijd die het gevolg is van niet-gesynchroniseerde aankomstroosters. Maar ook het overslagproces is te langzaam.

Tot slot moet met betrekking tot de laatste secundaire doelstelling worden opgemerkt dat dit onderzoek een bijdrage kan leveren aan ander onderzoek, namelijk met gegevens over preciezere knooppunttijden en kostengegevens voor hub-and-spoke-netwerken. In hoofdstuk 6 en de appendices staan de servicetijden van de treinen vermeld, alsmede de daarmee gepaard gaande kosten voor verschillende vraagniveaus, laadvolgordes, laadfactoren, batchgroottes, aankomstschema's, capaciteiten en kosten. Uit deze nieuwe gegevens blijkt dat de tijden en kosten van het overslagproces voor verschillende omstandigheden aanzienlijk kunnen verschillen.

Aanbevelingen voor verder onderzoek
Er zijn acht aanbevelingen voor verder onderzoek geformuleerd.
Ten eerste, onderzoek naar de oorzaken van, en oplossingen voor, slechte planning en aansturing van het railnetwerk. De huidige praktijk op het spoor staat niet alleen de ontwikkeling van hub-and-spoke-netwerken in de weg, maar iedere vooruitgang op het gebied van de concurrentiekracht van intermodaal transport.

Ten tweede, onderzoek onder expediteurs, verzenders en operators van intermodale transportmiddelen en spoorwegvoorzieningen die omgaan met tijdgevoelige goederen, naar de servicetijden die voor hen acceptabel zijn voor overslag op hubs, en tegen welke prijs.

Ten derde, onderzoek naar het potentieel en de mogelijkheden voor de verandering van bestaande weg-spoorterminals in hub-overslagfaciliteiten met een transportsysteem dat de kranen ondersteunt.

Ten vierde, verbetering van de modellen door het opnemen van een aanvullende details om de modellen flexibeler te maken en verschillende strategieën toe te passen op de procesaansturing.

Ten vijfde, nader onderzoek naar de gevolgen van vertragingen op processen en kosten die verband houden met vervoer per spoor.

Ten zesde, opzetten van een database voor kosten, calculatieregels en investeringen in equipement en infrastructuur voor rail netwerken en knooppunten.

Ten zevende, onderzoek naar de haalbaarheid van de implementatie van automatische (ont-)koppeling en spoorwegwagons met eigen aandrijving binnen diverse transportrelaties, alsmede de mate waarin de tijden en kosten die een rol spelen bij heuvelen of rangeren op vlak terrein kunnen worden verbeterd.

Ten slotte, onderzoek naar de manier waarop nieuwe hub-terminals zodanig kunnen worden aangepast dat er een significant lagere investering voor nodig is alsmede onderzoek naar locaties waar nieuwe hub-terminals kunnen worden gerealiseerd.

References

Alicke, K, (1999), *Modellierung und Optimierung von mehrstufigen Umschlagsystemen.* PhD Thesis, Karlsruhe: Wissenschaftliche Berichte des Institutes für Fördertechnik und Logistiksysteme der Universität Karlsruhe.

Alicke, K. (2002), Modeling and optimization of the intermodal terminal Mega Hub. *OR Spektrum,* 24, pp. 1-17.

Anderson, K.M. & Walton, C.M. (1998), *Evaluating intermodal freight terminals: a framework for government participation.* Austin: Southwest region University Transportation Center, Center for Transportation Research, The University of Texas at Austin, TX.

Anonymous (2004), Nürnberg Rbf.

Arndt, E.& Rozendaal, G. (2004), ICF voert grootscheepse reorganisatie door. *Transport Policy,* 36, pp. 24-25.

Arnold, P. & Thomas, I. (1999), Localisation des centres de transbordement dans un système multi-reseaux: essai de formalisation. *L'espace géographique,* 3, pp. 193-204.

Asariotis, R. (1998), Intermodal Transportation and Carrier Liability, in: Report of an ENO transportation foundation policy forum. *Towards improved intermodal freight transport in Europe and the United States: next steps.* Munich, Germany, pp. 33-40.

Assad, A.A. (1980), Models for rail transportation. *Transportation Research A,* 14, pp. 205-220.

Balci, O. (1998), Verification, validation, and testing. In: J. Banks (ed.), *Handbook of simulation: principles, methodology, advances, applications, and practice.* New York: Wiley & Sons.

Ballis, A. & Golias, J. (2002), Comparative evaluation of existing and innovative railroad freight transport terminals. *Transportation Research A,* 36, pp. 593-611.

Banks, J. (1998), *Handbook of simulation: principles, methodology, advances, applications, and practice.* New York: Wiley & Sons.

Barnhart, C. & Ratliff, H. (1993), Modeling intermodal routing. *Journal of Business Logistics,* 14, pp. 205-223.

Barton, J.E., Selnes, C.L., Anderson, R.J., Lindberg, D.L. & Foster, N.S.J. (1999), Developing a proposal for a multi-user intermodal freight terminal as a public-private partnership. *Transportation Research Record,* 1659, pp. 145-151.

Bartholdi, J.J. and Gue, K.R. (2001), The best shape of a crossdock. *Transportation Science,* 33 (4), pp. 419-428.

Beier, F.J. & Frick, S.W. (1978), The limits of piggyback: light at the end of the tunnel. *Transportation Journal,* 18 (2), pp. 12-18.

Beisler, L. (1995), Effiziente Produktionsstrukturen für den Kombinierten Verkehr (Efficient production structures for combined transport). *ETR Eisenbahntechnische Rundschau,* 44, 4, pp. 241-246.

Betak, J., Black, I. & Morlok, E. (1998), Interoperability in intermodal freight transport, in: *Report of an ENO transportation foundation policy forum. Towards improved intermodal freight transport in Europe and the United States: next steps.* Munich, Germany, pp. 17-31.

Biggler, M.P. (2003), *Questionnaire and interview,* 14 August. Employee ICF and representative for X-net and hub shunting yard Herne.

Black, I., Seaton, R., Ricci, A. & Enei, R. (2003), *Final Report: Actions to promote intermodal transport Cranfield*, Cranfield University and ISIS.

Boardman, B.S., Malstrom, E.M., Butler, D.P. & Cole, M.H. (1997), Computer assisted routing of intermodal shipments. In: *Proceedings of 21st International Conference on Computers and Industry Engineering*, pp. 311-314.

Boese, P., Hansmann, A., Nöthlich, M. (1989), Neue Betriebsverfahren im kombinierten Verkehr. *ETR Eisenbahntechnische Rundschau*, 38, 11, pp. 699-706.

Bontekoning, Y.M. (2000a), The importance of new-generation freight terminals for intermodal transport. *Journal of Advanced Transportation*, 34 (3), pp. 391-413.

Bontekoning, Y.M. (2000b), A jump forward in intermodal freight transport: are hub-terminals an alternative for shunting? In: *Conference Proceedings Part 1*, Trail 6th Annual Congress, The Hague/Scheveningen. Delft: TRAIL Research School, pp. 13-37.

Bontekoning, Y.M. & Kreutzberger, E. (1999), *Concepts of new-generation terminals and terminal nodes*. Delft: Delft University Press.

Bontekoning, Y.M. & Kreutzberger, E. (2001), *New-generation terminals: a performance evaluation study*. Delft: Delft University Press.

Bontekoning, Y.M. & Trip, J.J. (2004), Rail-rail hub-terminals as an alternative for shunting: an explorative comparative case study. In: (Eds) Beuthe, M., Himanen, V., Reggiani, A., and Zampari, L. *Transport Developments and Innovations in an Evolving World*. Berlin: Springer, pp. 235-251.

Bontekoning, Y.M., Macharis, C. & Trip, J.J. (2004), Is a new applied transportation research field emerging? - A review of intermodal rail-truck freight transport literature. *Transportation Research Part A - Policy and practice*, 38 (1), pp. 1-34.

Bookbinder, J.H. & Fox, N.S. (1998), Intermodal routing of Canada-Mexico shipments under NAFTA. *Transportation Research*, 34 (4), pp. 289-303.

Bosschaart, A, (2003), *Is de nieuwe generatie hubterminal echt beter dan de rangeerterminal?* Bachelor Thesis, Rotterdam: Erasmus Universiteit Rotterdam.

Bostel, N, (1996), *Méthodes de simulation et d'optimisation appliquées à la gestion opérationelle des chantiers de transbordement rapide*, PhD Thesis, École Centrale Paris, Châteney Malabry, Paris.

Bostel, N. & Dejax, P. (1998), Models and Algorithms for Container Allocation Problems on Trains in a Rapid Transshipment Shunting Yard. *Transportation Science*, 32 (4), pp. 370-379.

Bruins, H. (2003), *Questionnaire and interview* (27 November). Employee ProRail and representative for shunting yard Kijfhoek.

Brunner, J. (1994), Simulationprogramm „KLV Simu" zur Bemessung von Containerbahnhöfen, *ETR Eisenbahntechnische Rundschau*, 43 (10).

Bukold, S. (1996), *Kombinierter Verkehr, Schiene/Straße in Europa: Eine vergleichende Studie zur Transformation von Gütertransportsystemen*. Frankfurt am Main: Peter Lang.

Button, K.J. (1994), *Transport Economics*. Cambridge, UK, Cambridge University Press.

Campbell, J.F. (1994), *A Survey of Network Hub Location*. Studies in Locational Analysis, 6, pp. 31-49.

Cardebring, P.W., Fiedler, R., Reynaud, C. & Weaver, P. (2002), *Summary report of the IQ project, Hamburg*. Germany: TFK Transportforschung GmbH.

Charlier, J.J. & Ridolfi, G. (1994), Intermodal transportation in Europe: of modes, corridors and nodes. *Maritime Policy and Management*, 21 (3), pp. 237-250.

Chih, K.C.K., Bodden, M.P., Hornung, M.A. & Kornhauser, A.L. (1990), Routing and inventory logistics systems (Rails): a heuristic model for optimally managing intermodal double-stack trains. *Journal of Transportation Research Forum*, 31 (1), pp. 50-62.

Chih, C.K. & Van Dyke, C.D. (1987), The intermodal equipment distribution model. *Journal of Transportation Research Forum*, 27 (1), pp. 97-103.

Clarke, D.B., Chatterjee, A., Rutner, S.M. & Sink, H.L. (1996), Intermodal freight transportation and highway safety. *Transportation Quarterly*, 50 (2), pp. 97-110.

Clementson, T. (1988), *Strategy and uncertainty a guide to practical systems thinking*. Amsterdam: OPA B.V.

Cooper, H.M. (1989), *Integrating research: a guide for literature reviews*. Newbury Park/London/New Delhi: SAGE Publications.

Coyle, J.J., Bardi, E.J. & Novack, R.A. (2000), *Transportation*. Cincinnati: South-Western College Publishing.

Crainic, T.D. (1999), Long-haul freight transportation, in: R.W. Hall (ed.), *Handbook of transportation science*. Norwell: Kluwer Academic Publishers.

Crainic, T.D., Florian, M., Guélat, J. & Spiess, H. (1990), Strategic planning of freight transportation: STAN, an interactive-graphic system. *Transportation Research Record*, 1283, pp. 97-124.

Daganzo, C.F., Dowling, R.G. & Hall, R.W. (1983), Railroad classification yard throughput: the case of multistage triangular sorting. *Transportation Research A*, 17 (2), pp. 95-106.

DeBoer, D.J. (1992), *Piggyback and containers: A history of rail intermodal on America's steel highway*. San Marino, CA: Goden West Books.

Declercq, E. & Verbeke, A. (1997), Locatieanalyse en beleidsrelevantie met een toepassing voor de binnenvaartsector in Vlaanderen. *Tijdschrift Vervoerswetenschap*, pp. 195-211.

Declercq, E. & Verbeke, A. (1999), The EMOLITE Project: Evaluation Model for the Optimal Location of Intermodal Terminals in Europe. *Studies in Locational Analysis*, 13, pp. 77-90.

D'Este, G. (1995), An event-based approach to modelling intermodal freight systems, In: *Proceedings of 7th WCTR Volume 4*, Sydney, Australia: pp. 3-13

Dürr, E.H. (1994), Experience with a distributed information architecture for real-time intermodal tracking and tracing. In: *Proceedings of the first world congress on applications of transport telematics and intelligent vehicle-highway systems, Towards an intelligent transport system*, 30 nov. - 3 dec., Paris, France, pp. 1524-1531.

Eatough, C.J., Brich, S.C. & Demetsky, M.J. (2000), A statewide intermodal freight transportation planning methodology. *Journal of the Transportation Research Forum*, 39 (1), pp. 145-155.

Engel, M. (1996), *Modal-Split-Veränderungen im Güterfernverkehr: Analyse und Bewertung der Kosten - und Qualitätseffkete einer Verkehrsverlagerung Straße/Schiene*. Hamburg: Deutscher Verkehrs-Verlag.

European Commission (1997), *Smart intermodal European transport*. Luxembourg: Office for official publications of the European Communities.

European Commission (1997), *Smart intermodal European transport*. Luxembourg: Office for official publications of the European Communities.

European Commission (1998), *Osiris. Optimised system for an innovative rail integrated seaport connection*. EU project 4th FP. Luxembourg: Office for publications of the European Communities.

European Commission (1999), *Intermodal transportation and carrier liability*, Luxemburg:

European Conference of Ministers of Transport, United Nations Economic Commission for Europe & Statistical Division and European Union Eurostat. (1997), *Glossary for transport statistics*. http://www1.oecd.org/cem/online/glossaries/

Evers, P.T. & Emerson, C.J. (1998), An exploratory analysis of factors driving intermodal transport usage. *Journal of Transportation Management*, 10 (1), pp. 34-44.

Evers, P.T. & Johnson, C.J. (2000), Performance perceptions, satisfaction and intention: the intermodal shipper's perspective. *Transportation Journal*, 40 (2), pp. 27-39.

Evers, P.T. (1994), The occurance of statistical economies of scale in intermodal transportation. *Transportation Journal*, 33 (4), pp. 51-64.

Evers, P.T., Harper, D.V. & Needham, P.M. (1996), The determinants of shipper perceptions of modes. *Transportation Journal*, 36 (2), pp. 13-25.

Feo, T.A. & González-Velarde, J.L. (1995), The intermodal trailer assignment problem. *Transportation Science*, 29 (4), pp. 330-341.

Ferguson, R.T., (1993), *Mathematical modeling of the railroad switching process*. PhD Thesis. Charlottesville, Faculty of the School of Engineering and Applied Science, University of Virginia.

Ferreira, L. & Kozan, E. (1992), Intermodal terminals. In: *Papers of the Australian Transport Research Forum*, October 1992, Canberra, pp. 605-617.

Ferreira, L. & Sigut, J. (1993), Measuring the performance of intermodal freight terminals. *Transportation Planning and Technology*, 17, pp. 269-280.

Ferreira, L. & Sigut, J. (1995), Modelling intermodal freight terminal operations. *Road and Transport Research*, 4 (4), pp. 4-16.

Flood, R.L. & Carson, E.R. (1990), *Dealing with complextity: An introduction to the theory and application of systems science*. New York: Plenum Press.

Fonger, M. (1993), *Gesamtwirtschaftlicher Effizienzvergleich alternatiever Transportketten: eine Analyse unter besonderer Berücksichtigung des multimodalen Verkehrs Schiene/Strasse*. Göttingen: Vandenhoeck & Ruprecht.

Fowkes, A.S., Nash, C.A. & Tweddle, G. (1991), Investigating the market for intermodal freight technologies. *Transportation Research A*, 25 (4), pp. 161-172.

Fritsch, B. (2003), *Questionnaire* (31 July). Employee ICF: representative for ICF Quality Net and hub shunting yard Metz.

Hansen, I.A., (2004), Automated shunting of rail container wagons in ports and terminal areas. *Transportation Planning and Technology*, 27 (5), pp. 385-401.

Goor, van A.R., Ploos van Amstel, M.J. & Ploos van Amstel, W. (1992), *Fysieke distributie: denken in toegevoegde waarde*. Leiden/Antwerpen: Stenfert Kroese Uitgevers.

Goor, van A.R., Kruijtzer, A.H.L.M. & Esmeijer, G.W. (2000), *Goederenstroombesturing, voorraadbeheer en materials handling*. Leiden: Stenfert Kroese.

Groothedde, B. & Tavasszy, L.A. (1999), Optimalisatie van terminallocaties in een multimodaal netwerk met simulated annealing, In: *Proceedings van de Vervoerslogistieke Werkdagen 1999*, Connekt, Delft, pp. 43-57.

Gruppo Clas (2002), *Resource cost calculation for selected corridors*, Deliverable 3 EU project RECORDIT, http://www.recordit.org.

Gue, K.R. (1999), The effects of trailer scheduling on the layout of freight terminals. *Transportation Science*, 33 (4), pp. 419-428

Hall, R.W. (1991), *Queueing methods for services and manufacturing*. Englewood Cliffs, NJ: Prentice Hall.

Hall, R.W. (2001), Truck scheduling for ground to air connectivity. *Journal of Air Transport Management*, 7, pp. 331-338.

Harper, D.V. & Evers, P.T. (1993), Competitive issues in intermodal railroad-truck service. *Transportation Journal*, 32 (3), pp. 31-45.

Hayuth, Y. (1987), *Intermodality: concept and practice: structural changes in the ocean freight transport industry*. London: Lloyds of London Press.

Hee, K.M. van, Wijbrands, .R.J. (1988), Decision support system for container terminal planning. *European Journal of Operational Research*, 34, pp. 262-272.

Héjj, E. (1983), Analysis and comparison of rail and road intermodal freight terminals that employ different handling techniques. *Transportation Research Record*, 907, pp. 8-13.

Hengst-Bruggeling, M. den, (1999), *Interorganizational Co-ordination in Container Transport: a chain management design*. PhD Thesis. Delft: Delft University of Technology.

Hirsch, J.M.L. (1994), *Advanced Management Accounting*. Cincinnati, Ohio: South Western Publishing Co.

Höltgen, D. (1996), *Terminal, Intermodal Logistics Centres and European Infrastructure Policy*. Cambridge, UK: University of Cambridge.

Horn, K. (1981), Pricing of rail intermodal service: a case study of institutional myopia. *Transportation Journal*, 21 (Summer), pp. 63-78.

Howard, S.G. (1983), Large or small terminals in intermodal transport: what is the optimum size? *Transportation Research*, Record 907, pp. 14-21.

ICF (1999), Time table and train exchange relations.

Impulse (1997), *Operating forms for network modes*. Zürich: ETH-IVT.

Impulse (1999), *Cost effectiveness of intermodal transport*. Deliverable D13-D14.

Janic, M, Reggiani, A & Spicciarelli, T. (1998), The European freight transport system: theoretical background of the new generation of bundling networks. In: *Proceedings 8th World Congress of Transportation Research (WCTR)*, pp. 421-433.

Janic, M., Reggiani, A. & Nijkamp, P. (1999), Sustainability of the European freight transport system: evaluation of innovative bundling networks. *Transportation Planning and Technology*, 23, pp. 129-156.

Jennings, B.E. & Holcomb, M.C. (1996), Beyond containerization: the broader concept of intermodalism. *Transportation Journal*, 35 (3), pp. 5-13.

Jensen, A. (1990), *Combined transport: Systems, economics and strategies*. Stockholm: Swedish Transport Research Board.

Johnston, M.L. & Marshall, S. (1993), Shipper perceptions of intermodal equipment. *Transportation Journal*, 33 (1), pp. 21-29.

Jones, W.B., Cassady, C.R. & Bowden, R.O. (2000), *Developing a standard definition of intermodal transportation*. Department of Industrial Engineering, Mississippi State University.

Jourquin, B., Beuthe, M. & Demilie, C.L. (1999), Freight bundling network models: methodology and application. *Transportation Planning and Technology*, 23, pp. 157-177.

Kelton, W.D., Sadowski, R.P. & Sadowski, D.A. (1998), *Simulation with Arena*. Boston: WCB/McGraw-Hill.

Kindred, H.M. & Brooks, M.R. (1997), *Multimodal Transport Rules*. The Hague/London/Boston, Kluwer Law International.

Klincewicz, J.G. (1998), Hub location in backbone/tributary network design: a review. *Location Science*, 6, pp. 307-335.

Konings, J.W. (1996), Integrated centres for the transshipment, storage, collection and distribution of goods. *Transport Policy*, 3 (1-2), pp. 3-11.

Koningsveld, H. (1987), *Het verschijnsel wetenschap: Een inleiding tot de wetenschapsfilosofie*. Meppel: Boom.

Kraft, E.R. (2000), Implementation strategies for railroad dynamic freight car scheduling. *Journal of the Transportation Research Forum*, 39 (3), pp. 119-137.

Kraft, E.R. (2002a), Priority-based classification for improving connection reliability in railroad yards: part I: Integration with car scheduling. *Journal of the Transportation Research Forum*, 56 (1), pp. 93-105.

Kraft, E.R. (2002b), Priority-based classification for improving connection reliability in railroad yards: Part II: Dynamic block to track assignment. *Journal of the Transportation Research Forum*, 56 (1), pp. 107-119.

Kreutzberger, E. (1998), The performance of new-generation terminal concepts for hub terminals and collection and distribution terminals: balancing between effectivity and feasibility. In: *Proceedings 4th TRAIL Annual Congress 1998, Transport, Infrastructure and Logistics -Part 2*, December 15th, Scheveningen, The Netherlands.

Kreutzberger, E. (1999a), Innovative networks and new-generation terminals for intermodal transport. Improving the cost-quality ratio by bundling flows. In: *Proceedings 5th TRAIL Annual Congress 1999, Five Years "Crossroads of Theory and Practice" - Part 3*, December 1st, Scheveningen, The Netherlands.

Kreutzberger, E. (1999b), *Promising innovative intermodal networks with new-generation terminals*. Deliverable D7 of the Terminet project of the EU. Delft: OTB/TU Delft.

Kreutzberger, E. (2000), New-generation terminal concepts and innovative networks for combined transport. In: *Proceedings 6th TRAIL Annual Congress 2000, Transport, Infrastructure and Logistics -Part 2*, December 12th, Scheveningen, The Netherlands.

Kreutzberger, E. (2002), The impacts of innovative technical concepts for load unit exchange on the design of intermodal freight networks. In: *International Congress on Freight Transport Automation and Multimodality*, 23 and 24 May, Delft.

Law, A.M. & Kelton, W.D. (1991), *Simulation modeling and analysis*. Boston: McGraw-Hill.

Lennartz, K. (1991), Das elektronische Stellwerk für den Rangierbhanhof München Nord. *Rangiertechnik und Gleisanschlusstechnik*, 51, pp. 51-56.

Loureiro, C.F.G. (1994), *Modeling investment options for multimodal transportation networks*, PhD-thesis, University of Tennessee. UMI Dissertation Service, Ann Arbor, MI.

Ludvigsen, J. (1999), Freight transport supply and demand conditions in the Nordic Countries: recent evidence. *Transportation Journal*, 39 (2), pp. 31-54.

Macharis, C. & Verbeke, A. (1999), Een multicriteria-analyse methode voor de evaluatie van intermodale terminals. *Tijdschrift Vervoerswetenschap*, 4, pp. 323-352.

Mahoney, J.H. (1985), *Intermodal freight transportation*. Westport, Connecticut: ENO Foundation for transportation, Inc.

McKenzie, D.R., North, M.C. & Smith, D.S. (1989), *Intermodal transportation: the whole story*. Omaha, NE: Simmons-Boardman Books, Inc.

McWilliams, D.L., Stanfield, P.M. and Geiger, C.D. (2005), The parcel hub scheduling problem: a simulation-based solution approach. *Computers & Industrial Engineering*, 49, pp. 393-412.

Meinert, T.S., Youngblood, A.D., Taylor, G.D. & Taha, H.A. (1998), *Simulation of the railway component of intermodal transportation*. Fayetteville, AK: Arkansas University.

Meyer, P, (1998), *Entwicklung eines Simulationsprogramms für Umschlagterminals des Kombinierten Verkehrs*. PhD Thesis. Hannover, Department of Mechanical Engineering (Maschinenbau), University of Hannover.

Min, H. (1991), International intermodal choices via chance-constrainted goal programming. *Transportation Research A*, 25 (6), pp. 351-362.

Morash, E.A., Hille, S.J. & Bruning, E.R. (1977), Marketing rail piggyback services. *Transportation Journal*, 17 (Winter), pp. 40-50.

Morlok, E.K., Sammon, J.P., Spasovic, L.N. & Nozick, L.K. (1995), Improving productivity in intermodal rail-truck transportation. In: Harker, P. (ed.). *The service productivity and quality challenge*, pp. 407-434.

Morlok, E.K. & Spasovic, L.N. (1994), Redesigning rail-truck intermodal drayage operations for enhanced service and cost performance. *Journal of Transportation Research Forum*, 34 (1), pp. 16-31.

Morlok, E.K., Spasovic, L.N. & Vanek, F.M. (1997), *Regional options and policies for enhancing intermodal transport*. University of Pennsylvania and New Jersey Institute of Technology.

Muller, G. (1995), *Intermodal freight transportation*. Lansdowne, Virginia: Eno Transportation Foundation and IANA.

Murphy, P.R. & Daley, J.M. (1998), Some propositions regarding rail-truck intermodal: an empirical analysis. *Journal of Transportation Management*, 10 (1), pp. 10-19.

Nagy, G. & Salhi, S. (1998), The Many-to-Many Location-Routing Problem. *Sociedad Española de Estadística e Investigación Operativa*, 6 (2), pp. 261-275.

Newman, A.M. & Yano, C.A. (2000a), Centralized and decentralized train scheduling for intermodal operations. *IIE Transactions*, 32, pp. 743-754.

Newman, A.M. & Yano, C.A. (2000b), Scheduling direct and indirect trains and containers in an intermodal setting. *Transportation Science*, 34 (3), pp. 256-270.

Niérat, P. (1987), Organisation of road transport from terminals and combined transport accessibility. In: *OECD, Just-in-Time Transport: New Road Freight Transport Strategies and Management: Adapting to the New Requirements of Transport Services, Part I*, Gothenburg.

Niérat, P. (1997), Market area of rail-truck terminal: pertinence of the spatial theory. *Transportation Research*, 31 (2), pp. 109-127.

Nikoukaran, J., Hlupic, V. & Paul, R.J. (1999), A hierarchial framework for evaluating simulation software. *Simulation Practice and Theory*, 7, pp. 219-231.

Norris, F.B. (1995), *Spatial diffusion of intermodal rail technologies*. PhD Thesis. Seattle: University of Washington.

Nozick, L.K. & Morlok, E.K. (1997), A model for medium-term operations plans in an intermodal rail-truck service. *Transportation Research A*, 31 (2), pp. 91-107.

OECD (1997), Road Transport Research. Paris: OECD.

Petersen, E.R. (1977a), Railyard modeling: Part I. Prediction of put-through time. *Transportation Science*, 11 (1), pp. 37-49.

Petersen, E.R. (1977b), Railyard modeling: Part II. The effect of yard facilities on congestion. *Transportation Science*, 11 (1), pp. 50-59.

Plunkett, W.M. & Taylor, G.D. (1998), *Intermodal profitability analysis in the truckload and less than truck load industries*. Fayetville: Arkansas University.

Powell, W.B. & Carvalho, T.A. (1998), Real-time optimization of containers and flatcars for intermodal operations. *Transportation Science*, 32 (2), pp. 110-126.

Rizzoli, A.E., Fornara N. and Gambardella, L.M. (2002), A simulation tool for combined rail/road transport in intermodal terminals. *Mathematics and Computers in Simulation*, 59, pp. 57-71

Rotter, H. (2003), *Questionnaire* (August) . Employee KombiVerkehr, Frankfurt.

Rotter, H. (2002), *Telephone interview* (28 June). Employee KombiVerkehr, Frankfurt.

Rutten, B.J.C.M. (1995), *On medium distance intermodal rail transport*. PhD Thesis, Delft: Delft University of Technology.

Savy, M & Aubriot, C. (2005), *Intermodal transport in Europe*. Paris: Conseil National des Transports

Schijndel, W.J.V.D.J. (2000), Congestion and multimodal transport: a survey of cargo transport operators in the Netherlands. *Transport Policy*, 7, pp. 231-241.

Shannon, R.E. (1975), *Systems simulation: the art and science*. Englewood Cliff, NJ: Prentice Hall.

SIMET (1994), *Economic and technical research of the transfer of goods: design and evaluation of rapid transfer: future fast transfer technologies*. EU Project SIMET. Doc. EURET/410/94.

Slack, B. (1990), Intermodal transportation in North America and the development of inland load centers. *Professional Geographer*, 42 (1), pp. 72-83.

Slack, B. (1995), Along different paths: intermodal rail terminals in North America and Europe. In: *Proceedings 7th World Congres on Transportation Research Volume 4*, Sydney, Australia, pp. 123-131.

Slack, B. (1996), Services linked to intermodal transportation. *Papers in Regional Science*, 75 (3), pp. 252-263.

Slack, B. (1999), Satellite terminals: a local solution to hub congestion? *Journal of Transport Geography*, 7, pp. 241-246.

Southworth, F. & Peterson, B.E. (2000), Intermodal and international freight network modeling. *Transportation Research*, C 8, pp. 147-166.

Spasovic, L.N. (1990), *Planning intermodal drayage network operations*. PhD Thesis. Philadelphia, University of Pennsylvania: UMI Dissertation Service, Michigan.

Spasovic, L.N. & Morlok, E.K. (1993), Using Marginal Costs to evaluate drayage rates in rail-truck intermodal service. *Transportation Research Record*, 1383, pp. 8-16.

Stank, T.P. & Roath, A.S. (1998), Some propositions on intermodal transportation and logistics facility development: shippers' perspectives. *Transportation Journal*, 37 (3), pp. 13-24.

Sussman, J. (2000), *Introduction to Transportation systems*. Boston: Artech House.

Swain, J.J. (1999), Imagine new worlds. Informs, *OR/MS today simulation survey*, pp. 38-51.

Taha, T.T. and Taylor, G.D. (1994), An integrated modeling framework for evaluating hub-and-spoke networks in truckload trucking. *Logistics and Transportation Review*, 30 (2), pp. 141-166.

Taylor, J.C. & Jackson, G.C. (2000), Conflict, Power, and Evolution in the Intermodal Transportation Industry's Channel of Distribution. *Transportation Journal*, Spring, pp. 15-17.

Terminet (2000), *Performance analyses 5 new-generation terminal case studies*. Deliverable D10. Delft: TU Delft, OTB Research Institute for Housing, Urban and Mobility Studies.

Thuong, L.T. (1989), From piggyback to double-stack intermodalism. *Maritime Policy and Management*, 16 (1), pp. 69-81.

Timian, D.H. (1994), *Current methods for optimizing rail marshalling yard operations*. Manhattan, Kansas: Department of Industrial Engineering, College of Engineering, Kansas State University.

TRB (1998), *Policy options for intermodal freight transportation*. Washington D.C.: Transportation Research Board, National Research Council.

Tsai, J.F., Morlok, E.K. & Smith, T.E. (1994), *Optimal pricing of rail intermodal freight: models and tests*. Philadelphia, Department of Systems Engineering, School of Engineering and Applied Science, University of Pennsylvania.

Tsamboulas, D.A. & Kapros, S. (2000), Decision-making process in intermodal transportation. *Transportation Research Record*, 1707, pp. 86-93.

van Duin, R. & van Ham, H. (1998), Three-stage modeling approach for the design and organization of intermodal transportation services. In: *Proceedings of the IEEE International Conference on Systems, Man and Cybernetics. Part 4*, Oct. 11-14, San Diego, CA, pp. 4051-4056.

Vis, I.F.A. and de Koster, R. (2003), Transshipment of containers at a container terminal: an overview. *European Journal of Operational Research*, 147, pp. 1-16.

Vis, I.F.A. (2005), http://www.ikj.nl/container/

Vleugel, J., Kreutzberger, E. & Bontekoning, Y.M. (2001), *Concepts of innovative bundling networks*. Delft: Delft University Press.

Vogtmann, M. & Franke, K.-P. (2000), Case Metz. In: Terminet, Performance analyses 5 new-generation terminal case studies. Deliverable D10. Delft: TU Delft, OTB Research Institute for Housing, *Urban and Mobility Studies*, pp. 13-28.

Walker, W.T. (1992), Network economics of scale in short haul truckload operations. *Journal of Transportation Economics and Policy*, 26 (1), pp. 3-17.

Wang, X. (1997), *Improving planning for railroad yard, forestry and distribution*, PhD Thesis, Philadelphia, Graduate Group in Managerial Science and Applied Economics, University of Pennsylvania.

Wesseling, G. (2003), *Questionnaire and interview* (1 October). Railway expert.Employee Logitech B.V.

Wiegmans, B.W., Masurel, E. & Nijkamp, P. (1999), Intermodal freight terminals: an analysis of the terminal market. *Journal of Transportation Planning and Technology*, 23, pp. 105-128.

Winston, C. (1983), The demand for freight transportation: models and applications. *Transportation Research*, A 17 (6), pp. 419-427.

Winston, W.L. (1994), *Operations research: applications and algorithms*. Belmont, California: Duxbury Press.

Woxenius, J. (1994), *Modelling European combined transport as an industrial system*. Göteborg, Sweden: Department of Transportation and Logistics, Chalmers University of Technology.

Woxenius, J. (1998), *Development of small-scale intermodal freight transportation in a systems context*. Göteborg, Sweden: Department of Transportation and Logistics, Chalmers University of Technology.

Yan, S., Bernstein, D. & Sheffi, Y. (1995), Intermodal pricing using network flow techniques. *Transportation Research*, B 29 (3), pp. 171-180.

Zavattero, D.A., Rawling F.G. & Rice, D.F. (1998), Mainstreaming intermodal freight into the metropolitan transportation planning process. *Transportation Research Record*, 1613, pp. 1-17.

ZEW, IER, ISIS, Gruppo Clas & Tetraplan (2000), *Accounting Framework*. Deliverable 1 EU project RECORDIT. ZEW: http://www.recordit.org.

Zijderveld, E.J.A. van (1995), *A structured terminal design method: with a focus on rail container terminals*, PhD-Thesis, TU Delft, Faculty of Mechanical Engineering.

Zlatoper, T.J. & Austrian, A. (1989), Freight transportation demand: A survey of recent econometric studies. *Transportation*, 16, pp. 27-46.

Zografos, K.G. & Giannouli, I.M. (1998), A methodological framework for introducing ITS applications for improving the performance of intermodal freight terminals. In: *Proceedings of the 5th world congress on intelligent transport systems*, 12-16 October, Seoul, Korea, Paper No. 2080.

Websites
http://home.arcor.de/klausrost/Wagenmeister/rbf.htm
www.stinnes-freight-logistics.de (2003).

Appendix A Specification of parameters and variables of the crane service time simulation tool

In this Appendix parameters and variables applied in the crane service time simulation tool are specified for various types of transhipment at respectively the new hub-terminal and the road-rail terminal. The kinematics parameters applied and the terminal layouts used are provided in Chapter 5 section 5.4.1.

Crane service times at new hub-terminal
Transhipment from train to train
Specific parameters and assumptions for this job incorporated in the simulation tool are:
- Range drop-off position: 60 meter, which implies 30 meters to the left or 30 meters to the right of the crane pick-up position. The range is based on the assumption that within a range of five 40 feet containers a drop off position can be found.
- $d_{z(E)}$: 1.75 meter.
- $d_{z(F)}$: 3.5 meter.
- From initial to pick-up position the trolley moves from any of the tracks, storage per transport outer transport system lanes to any of the six tracks.
- From pick-up to drop-off position the trolley moves from a certain track to any of the six tracks.

Transhipment from train to storage or from storage to e train
Specific parameters and assumptions for this job incorporated in the simulation tool are:
- Range drop-off position: 60 meter, which implies 30 meters to the left or 30 meters to the right of the crane pick-up position. The range is based on the assumption that within a range of five 40 feet containers a drop off position can be found.
- $d_{z(E)}$: 1.75 meter.
- $d_{z(F)}$: 4.25 meter.
- From initial to pick-up position the trolley moves from any of the tracks, storage or outer transport system lanes to any of the six tracks.
- From pick-up to drop-off position the trolley moves from the two tracks on the left side to the storage lane on the left side, from the two tracks in the middle to the centre storage lane and form the two tracks on the right to the storage lane on the right.

Transhipment from train to transport system or from transport system to train
Specific parameters and assumptions for this job incorporated in the simulation tool are:
- Range drop-off position: 15.5 meters. There are 45 parking positions for the roller pallets at each side of the travelling lanes of the transport system. That implies for a track length of 700 meters one parking lot at every 15.5 meters.

- $d_{z(E)}$: 1.75 meter.
- $d_{z(F)}$: 4.25 meter.
- From initial to pick-up position the trolley moves from any of the tracks, storage lanes or left and right outer transport lane to any of the six tracks.
- From pick-up to drop-off position the trolley moves from a certain track at the left side of the transport system to the left sided parking lane of the transport system and from a certain track at the right side of the transport system to the right sided parking lane of the transport system.

Transhipment from storage to transport system
Specific parameters and assumptions for this job incorporated in the simulation tool are:
- Range drop-off position: 15.5 meters. There are 45 parking positions for the roller pallets at each side of the travelling lanes of the transport system. That implies for a track length of 700 meters one parking lot at every 15.5 meters.
- $d_{z(E)}$: 1.75 meter.
- $d_{z(F)}$: 4.25 meter.
- From initial to pick-up position the trolley moves from any of the tracks, storage lanes or left and right outer transport lane to any of the six tracks.
- From pick-up to drop-off position the trolley moves from the storage lane on the left side of the transport system to the left sided parking lane of transport system, and from the storage lanes on the right side of the transport system to the right sided parking lane of the transport system.

Crane service times at road-rail terminal
Transhipment from train to train
Specific parameters and assumptions for this job incorporated in the simulation tool are:
- Range drop-off position: 60 meter, which implies 30 meters to the left or 30 meters to the right of the crane pick-up position. The range is based on the assumption that within a range of five 40 feet containers a drop off position can be found.
- $d_{z(E)}$: 1.75 meter.
- $d_{z(F)}$: 3.5 meter.
- From initial to pick-up position the trolley moves from any of the tracks or storage lanes to any of the four tracks.
- From pick-up to drop-off position the trolley moves from a certain track to any of the four tracks.

Transhipment from train to storage or from storage to train
Specific parameters and assumptions for this job incorporated in the simulation tool are:
- Range drop-off position: 60 meter, which implies 30 meters to the left or 30 meters to the right of the crane pick-up position. The range is based on the assumption that within a range of five 40 feet containers a drop off position can be found.
- $d_{z(E)}$: 1.75 meter.
- $d_{z(F)}$: 4.25 meter.
- From initial to pick-up position the trolley moves from any of the tracks or storage lanes to any of the four tracks.

- From pick-up to drop-off position the trolley moves from a certain track to any of the three storage lanes.

Transhipment from train to edge of crane section in storage or from edge of crane section in storage to train
Specific parameters and assumptions for this job incorporated in the simulation tool are:
- $d_{z(E)}$; 1.75 meter.
- $d_{z(F)}$; 4.25 meter.
- From initial to pick-up position the crane moves from any longitudinal position in a crane section to any other longitudinal position.
- From pick-up to drop-off position the crane moves from a certain longitudinal position in a crane section to the edge of the crane section. Edge is determined as length of train divided by number of cranes.
- From initial to pick-up position the trolley moves from any of the tracks or storage lanes to any of the four tracks.
- From pick-up to drop-off position the trolley moves from a certain track to any of the three storage lanes.

Transhipment from storage to edge of crane section in storage
Specific parameters and assumptions for this job incorporated in the simulation tool are:
- $d_{z(E)}$; 1.75 meter.
- $d_{z(F)}$; 4.25 meter.
- From initial to pick-up position the crane moves from any longitudinal position in a crane section to any other longitudinal position.
- From pick-up to drop-off position the crane moves from a certain longitudinal position in a crane section to the edge of the crane section. Edge is determined as length of train divided by number of cranes.
- From initial to pick-up position the trolley moves from any of the tracks or storage lanes to any of the three storage lanes.
- From pick-up to drop-off position the trolley moves from a certain storage lanes to any of the three storage lanes.

Transhipment from storage at edge of crane section to storage at other end of crane section (transport)
For operations with 2 cranes these job does not exist. However, it is modelled in the computer model, but setting the service time for this job at zero can solve this. For operations with more than 2 cranes the following parameters apply.
Specific parameters and assumptions for this job incorporated in the simulation tool are:
- $d_{z(E)}$; 1.75 meter.
- $d_{z(F)}$; 4.25 meter.
- From initial to pick-up position the crane moves from any longitudinal position in a crane section to lower edge of crane section. Lower edge is determined as x-coordinate is zero.
- From pick-up to drop-off position the crane moves from edge at lower crane section to edge at opposite side of crane section. Edge at opposite side is determined as length of train divided by number of cranes.
- From initial to pick-up position the trolley moves from any of the tracks or storage lanes to any of the three storage lanes.

- From pick-up to drop-off position the trolley moves from a certain storage lanes to any of the three storage lanes.

Appendix B Justification of the number of crane service times to be generated by the crane service time simulation tool

How many crane service times are sufficient to fit a distribution function on? This has been determined as follows. For the transhipment type "from train to train" in road-rail hub operations data sets with respectively N=5, N=10, N=25, N=50, N=100, N=200, N=500 and N=1000 crane service times were generated. The data sets with a higher number of generated service times contain the generated crane service time of the data set with a lower number of generated services times. So, the data set N=10 consists of N=5 plus an additional 5 generated crane service times, and the set N=200 consists of N=100 plus an additional 100 generated crane service times. Next, the mean and standard deviation were compared in order to see at which number of observations they stabilise when the number of crane service time increases. If there is a lot of variance between single observations, variance will average out when the number of observations becomes larger. At a certain number of observations additional observations will not lead to further significant changes of the mean and standard deviation.

As Table B–1 indicates the mean and standard deviation slightly vary for the different numbers of observations. But the differences are a bit larger for N=5 to N=50. From N=100 onwards it seems that the standard deviation stabilises at between 36 and 39 seconds and the mean at about 122 to 125 seconds. Therefore the number of crane service times that must be generated to fit a distribution function is determined at 100. It is assumed that 100 crane service times is also sufficient for other types of transhipment and transhipments at the new hub-terminal.

Table B–1: Mean and standard deviation for different number of generated service times for crane cycle relate to direct train to train transhipment at a road-rail terminal

Number of replications	Standard deviation (seconds)	Mean (seconds)
5	35	122
10	33	130
25	44	124
50	54	127
100	37	123
200	36	122
500	38	125
1000	39	123

Appendix C Validation of the crane service time simulation tool

The crane service times generated by the tool have been validated for a road rail terminal with 2 cranes and a new hub-terminal with 10 cranes. The validation included:
1) A comparison of the average of 100 generated $d_{x(L1)}$, $d_{x(L1)}$, $d_{y(W1)}$ and $d_{y(W2)}$ with the by hand account estimated expected average value calculated. This was done for each type of job and for both type of terminals
2) A comparison of the average of 100 generated crane service times with service times obtained in the data collection.

The generated service times and those used for validation are presented in Table C–1.

Table C–1: Validation of average crane service times generated by the simulation tool

Terminal	Type of transhipment	Tool values (seconds)	Validation values (seconds)
Road-rail	1. direct transhipment from train to train	122	90-300 (SIMET, 1994);
	2. transhipment from train to storage and from storage to train	134	95-180 (Rotter, 2003) 129-164 (Ballis & Golias, 2002)
	3. transhipment from train to edge of storage and from edge of storage to train	207	
	4. transhipment from storage to edge of the storage	201	
New hub	1. direct transhipment from train to train	61	
	2. transhipment from train to storage and from storage to train	61	
	3. transhipment from train to transport system and from transport system to train	59	
	4. transhipment from storage to transport system	64	
	Average 4 types	61	61 (Meyer, 1998, p. 131)

Comparison of service times is not that straight forward. The tool generates service times for each type of transhipment while the data obtained from practise and the literature does not make that distinction. Therefore for the validation an average crane cycle time was calculated for the validation of the cycle times of the new hub-terminal. For the new hub-terminal the generated average cycle time and that of Meyer match.

In addition, service times for road-rail terminals are most likely based on road-rail transhipment and not on hub-exchange operations. Transhipment types 1 and 2 are most related to the crane movement in road-rail transhipment. Transhipment type 3 and 4 are specific for hub operations. Therefore only the cycle times of transhipment type 1 and 2 of the road-rail terminal are used for validation. The validating values for the road-rail terminal represent a range, because they include time for disturbances and waiting and depend on the mix of load units. For instance, in the case with only containers and hardly any disturbances the average crane cycle at a road-rail transhipment may be only 95 seconds (Rotter, 2003). Swap body and trailers may take more time due to (un)folding grip arms and more difficult positioning. The cycle time generated by the tool is based on the assumption only containers and no disturbances or waiting time. So, the cycle times of transhipment type 1 and 2 should be close to the lower part of the validating ranges from the different sources. Which is more or less the case.

Appendix D Overview of collected time data on hump shunting activities

Based on the data presented in the table below the service times of various hump shunting activities were determined.

Activity	Time	Source
Activities related to sorting		
Uncoupling network locomotive	2-3 min.	Bruins (2003)
Changing from network locomotive to shunting engine	15-20 min./train	Rotter (2003)
Uncoupling rail wagons	*10-15–30 min./30 wagons	Fritsch (2003)
	2- 3 min. per "cut" plus 1-1.5 min. per wagon emptying air reservoirs	Bruins (2003)
	30 min./30 wagons	Terminet (2000)
Coupling switch locomotive to train and pushing train to shunting hill	*4-6-10 min./train	Fritsch (2003)
	2-3 min. (coupling loc.)/15 km/h and various 100 meters (1-3 minutes)	Bruins (2003)
	10 min./train	Terminet (2000)
Previous two activities combined	20 min./train	Ferguson (1994)
Pushing one wagon over the hump	*10-20-30 sec./wagon	Fritsch (2003)
	11 sec./wagon	Bruins (2003)
	14-24 sec./wagon***	Wesseling (2003)
	30 sec. /wagon	Terminet (2000)
	40 sec. /wagon	Ferguson (1994)
	5 –7.5 sec./wagon	Huet/Vallet (1977/78)
Return trip of switch locomotive to next train to be shunted	*5-8-15 min./train	Fritsch (2003)
	5-6 min./train	Bruins (2003)
Coupling wagons	5-8-19 min./30 wagons	Fritsch (2003)
	2-3 min. per coupling	Bruins (2003)
All activities together	1 min./wagon	Turnquist and Daskin (1982)

Activities related to assembly		
Correcting false runners by the yard engine	*5-10-20 min./false runner **40 min./ batch of 6 trains 60 min./false runner	Fritsch (2003) Terminet (2000) Bruins (2003)
Pushing wagons together (by locomotive, not automated)	20 min./batch of 6 trains	Terminet (2000)
Assembly	40 min./train 120 min./train	Terminet (2000) Ferguson (1994)
Coupling the network locomotive to the departing train	5-8-10 min./train 10 min.	Fritsch (2003) Bruins (2003)
Brake test	15-20-30 45 min. (incl. inspection) – 2*600m walking is about 18 min.	Fritsch (2003) Bruins

*   Minimum time – most likely time – maximum time.
**   Happens once for every 10 trains.
***   Hill speed is 3 to 5 km per hour.

- Ferguson (1994) in Timian: location: unnamed rail hump yard USA;
- Turnquist and Daskin (1982): location unknown; 1 minute per wagon total classification time (all in) mean train length 60 wagons;
- Huet/ Vallet (1977/78): location Sotteville and Hourcade, France;
- Fritsch (2003): location Metz, France;
- Bruins (2003): location Kijfhoek, The Netherlands.

Appendix E   Simulating sorting locomotive behaviour and service times at a flat shunting yard

With the data collected for sorting related activities the behaviour of a shunting locomotive could be simulated. The data consists of the speed of a shunting locomotive, yard lay-out and distances and duration of sorting related activities such as (un)coupling wagons. This data was provided in Chapter 5. With this data an imaginary sorting case was simulated, and for each wagon group the duration of sorting calculated. For each wagon group the duration of the following are activities determined and summed up to a service time:
- coupling shunting locomotive to train at arrival track (only when a new train is being sorted);
- pulling train out of track (first time out of arrival track, succeeding times out of sorting tracks);
- pushing train to sorting track;
- pushing train into sorting track till end of track in case of empty track or till previously shunted wagon group if not empty;
- coupling wagon group to wagon group already standing in sorting track, except if there is no other wagon group yet;
- uncoupling sorted wagon group from rest of train or in case of last wagon group of train from shunting locomotive;
- driving shunting locomotive to arrival track to pick up next train to be sorted (only when previous train is completely sorted).

The case that was simulated consisted of 6 trains and 39 wagon groups. These six trains can be a batch of trains or a set of six individual trains. The data in Table E–1 show the number of wagon groups per train and the length of each wagon group. The distances related to the lay-out provided in Chapter 5 section 5.4.3 are used for the simulation. Joint arrival/departure tracks are 700 meters long, sorting tracks 350 meters. The distance between tracks is 40 meters. Due to the shorter sorting tracks than train length, each departing train is assembled at the departure track and is composed of two blocks. However, this is assembling time is not included in the sorting time but in the assembly time (workstation 2). The speed of the shunting locomotive is between 5km (long train) and 10 (short train) km/hour. For the calculations a speed of 7.5 km per hour is used. For each pushing and pulling activity the distance travelled by the locomotive has been determined and the travelling time been calculated. The order in which the wagon groups are dropped off at the various sorting tracks has arbitrarily been determined.

Table E–1: Features of the 39 wagon groups to be sorted

Number of wagon group	1	2	3	4	5	6	7	8	9	10
Train	Length of each wagon group in meters									
1	60	40	120	80	20	100	60	20		
2	120	120	80	40	180					
3	200	200	60							
4	20	20	60	100	40	120	80	40	20	100
5	140	40	180	20	60	80				
6	20	40	100	160	60	180	20			

The simulation provided 39 service times, which are shown in the left graph in Figure E–1. The outliers in Figure E–1 are the service times of each first wagon group of a train. These service times include the coupling of the locomotive to the new train, which takes 12 minutes. Those outliers cause difficulty to fit a distribution. Since the coupling of the locomotive may be viewed as a general activity for all wagon groups of a train, it is argued that the sum of coupling times can be distributed over all 39 service times. The data set with adjusted service times is shown in the right graph of Figure E–1. This data set is used to fit a distribution.

Figure E–1: 39 simulated observations of a cycle of a sorting locomotive at a flat shunting yard

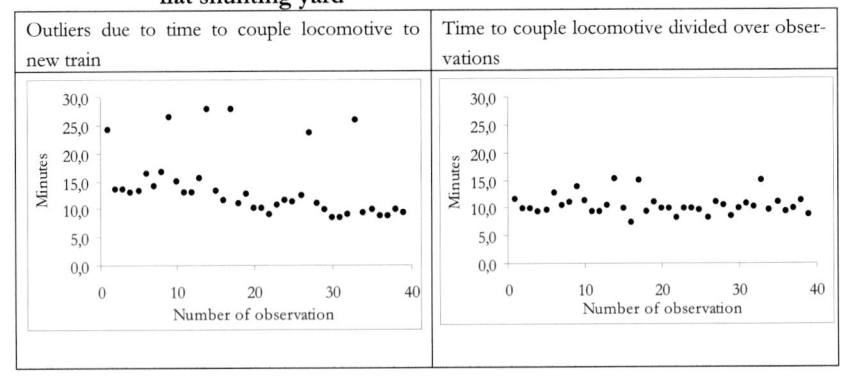

Appendix F Specification of variables in the cost model

In Chapter 5 section 5.5 the contents of the cost model was described. In this Appendix values applied in the costs model in Chapter 6 are specified in four tables.

Table F–1: Specification of investments

Equipment	Unit price (euro)	Source
New hub-terminal crane (including foundation)	5.000.000	Terminet (2000)
Road-rail terminal crane	1.500.000	Terminet (2000); Rotter (2003); Gruppo Clas (2002)
Foundation road-rail terminal crane	2.000.000	Terminet (2000); Rotter (2003); Gruppo Clas (2002), SIMET (1994)
Electricity supply	120.000	Terminet (2000)
Shunting locomotive	1.000.000	Impulse (1999, p. 9) Wesseling (2003); Gruppo Clas (2002); Bruins (2003)
Operations control system		
- new hub terminal/hump shunting yard	1.200.000	Terminet (2002)/estimated
- road-rail terminal/flat shunting yard	62.500	Terminet (2000)/estimated
Infrastructure		
Land		Terminet (2000)
- Purchase (m²)	22	
- Preparation (m²)	44	
Building	1.000.000	Terminet (2000)
Foundation building	406.250	Terminet (2000)
Rail tracks – concrete (m)	375	Estimated based on Terminet (2000); Rotter (2003); Bruins (2003)
Rail tracks – gravel (m)	625	Estimated based on Terminet (2000); Rotter (20003); Bruins (2003)
Switches	50.000	Terminet (2000)
Braking system	250.000	Estimated based on Lennartz (1991); Anonymous (2004)
"Beidruck" system	450.000	Estimated based on Bruins (2003); Lennartz (1991); Anonymous (2004)
Pavement storage area (m²)	45	Terminet (2000)

Table F–2: **Specification of depreciation periods**

Equipment	Lifetime (years)	Source
Cranes	15	Estimated based on Terminet (2000); Rotter (2003); Gruppo Clas (2002)
Electricity supply	15	Terminet (2000)
Transport system	20	Terminet (2000)
Shunting locomotive	15	Estimated based on Impulse (1999, p. 9); Bruins (2003);Wesseling (2003); Gruppo Clas (2002)
Operations control systems	6	Terminet (2000)
Infrastructure		
Land	none	Terminet (2000)
Building	20	Terminet (2000)
Foundation building	20	Terminet (2000)
Foundation crane	20	Terminet (2000); Rotter (2003)
Rail tracks	50	Terminet (2000)
Switches	20	Terminet (2000)
Braking system	15	Estimated
Pavement storage area	20	Terminet (2000)

Table F–3: Specification of parameters for the estimation of operational costs

Consumption costs	Unit	Source
Fuel	14.6 euro/hour	Estimated based on Impulse (1999, p.9); (Gruppo Clas (2002)
Electricity	0.8 euro/LU	Estimated based on Terminet (2000); Gruppo Clas (2002)
Operating costs		
Equipment	0.8% of total investment in equipment	Estimated based on Terminet (2000); Gruppo Clas (2002)
Infrastructure	2% of total investment in infrastructure	Gruppo Clas (2002)
Maintenance costs		
Equipment terminal	1.25% of total investment in equipment	Estimated based on Terminet (2000); Gruppo Clas (2002)
Equipment shunting yard	6 cost/hour	Estimated based on Impulse (1999, p.9); Bruins (2003); Wesseling (2003); Gruppo Clas (2002)
Infrastructure	1.5% of total investment in infrastructure	Estimated based on Terminet (2000); Rotter (2003); Gruppo Clas (2002)
Operations control system	10.0% of total investment in operations control system	Terminet (2000)
Labour costs		
Crane driver	38,500 euro/year	All labour costs estimated based on:
Pinsetter/ radioman	37,500 euro/year	Terminet (2000); Bruins (2003); Fritsch (2003)
Locomotive driver	29,000 euro/year	Biggler (2003); Rotter (2003); Gruppo Clas (2002)
Shunting assistant	27,000 euro/year	
Pinpullers/cableman	27,000 euro/year	
Operation control	37,500 euro/year	
Maintenance and repair	36,500 euro/year	
Administration and management	39,000 euro/year	

Appendix G Specification of additional costs per load unit due to changes in rail haul costs

Table G–1: Costs data network locomotive and locomotive driver

Investment network locomotive	4,4 million euro (Gruppo Clas, 2002, p. 87)
Depreciation period	20 years (Gruppo Clas, 2002, p. 48)
Average mileage	150,000 km/year (Gruppo Clas, 2002, p. 48)
Salary costs	40 euro/hour (Gruppo Clas, 2002, p. 88)

Costs calculation additional costs per load unit due to waiting time network locomotive
Depreciation costs/year are 4,4 million divided by 20 = 220,000 euro.
Depreciation costs/km are 220,000/150,000 = 1.47 euro per km.
If we translate waiting time at the new hub-terminal into the distance that the locomotive could have driven with a speed at 80 km/h, we can estimate the waiting costs per hour: 80 km/h multiplied by 1.47 euro/km = 117,60 euro/hour.
Each train carries 48 load units (LU) in the experiments. 117,60 euro/hour divided over 48 load units results in additional costs/LU of 2,45 euro if the train sojourn time is 60 minutes.

Costs calculation additional costs per load unit due to waiting time network locomotive driver
The salary costs for a network locomotive driver is about 40 euro per hour (Gruppo Clas, 2002, p. 88).
Each train carries 48 load units (LU) in the experiments.
40 euro/hour divided by 48 results in an additional costs of 0.83 euro/LU if the train sojourn time is 60 minutes.

Appendix H Specification of half-width confidence intervals average train sojourn times

Facility	Demand	Capacity level	Average train sojourn time (minutes)	+/- Absolute (minutes) from average	+/- Relative (%) from average
New hub-terminal	1*3	C2	115	0.5	0.4%
		C4	43	0.02	0.0%
		C6	26	0.02	0.1%
		C10	16	0.02	0.1%
	1*6	C2	288	1.6	0.6%
		C4	89	1.4	1.6%
		C6	53	0.1	0.2%
		C10	33	0.02	0.1%
	1*8	C2	398	2.1	0.5%
		C4	124	2.3	1.9%
		C6	71	0.1	0.1%
		C10	44	0.01	0.0%
	3*3	C2	113	0.2	0.2%
		C4	44	0.05	0.1%
		C6	26	0.0	0.0%
		C10	15	0.0	0.0%
	3*4	C2	201	0.3	0.1%
		C4	74	0.3	0.4%
		C6	42	0.0	0.0%
		C10	20	0.0	0.0%
	3*6	C2	301	0.5	0.2%
		C4	101	0.5	0.5%
		C6	58	0.1	0.2%
		C10	31	0.0	0.0%
Hump shunting yard	1*3	H11	229	9.7	4%
		H12	194	4.0	2%
		H21	162	8.6	5%
		H22	127	3.0	2%
	1*6	H11	427	13.6	3%
		H12	357	5.6	2%
		H21	291	12.4	4%
		H22	217	4.4	2%
	1*8	H11	559	29.5	5%
		H12	458	8.7	2%
		H21	379	29.0	8%
		H22	278	7.9	3%
	3*3	H11	247	46	19%
		H12	196	2.8	1%
		H21	254	26	10%
		H22	141	6.7	5%
	3*4	H11	324	40	12%
		H12	248	1.8	1%
		H21	323	30	9%
		H22	173	9	5%

	3*6	H11	467	42	9%
		H12	359	2.3	1%
		H21	472	44	9%
		H22	242	11	5%
Flat shunting	1*3	F11	492	17	3%
		F12	454	16	4%
		F21	301	8	3%
		F22	263	7	3%
	1*6	F22	480	7.1	1%
Road-rail terminal	1*3	RR2	206	4.7	2.3%
		RR3	222	1.7	0.8%
		RR4	149	0.4	0.3%
	1*6	RR3	592	2.2	0.4%
		RR4	545	1.3	0.2%

Appendix I Specification of number of load units and rail wagons to be exchanged per train

Table I–1 provides some background information for various experiments. Table I–1 shows the number load units, rail wagons or wagon groups to be exchanged in relation to the variables length of train, assumed length of rail wagons, load factor, planned or not planned load order and number of trains per batch.

Table I–1: Exchange volume per train related to various demand variables

Length of train	Number of wagons*	Load factor	Number of LU's	Number of trains in batch	Exchange factor**	LU's for exchange per train	Wagons for exchange	Wagon groups for exchange***
600	30	1.6	48	3	0.67	32	30	12
600	30	1.6	48	4	0.75	36	30	12
600	30	1.6	48	6	0.83	40	30	12
600	30	1.4	42	3	0.67	28	30	12
600	30	1.4	42	4	0.75	32	30	12
600	30	1.4	42	6	0.83	35	30	12
600	30	1.8	54	3	0.67	36	30	12
600	30	1.8	54	4	0.75	41	30	12
600	30	1.8	54	6	0.83	45	30	12

*   Each rail wagon has a length of 20 meters.

**   The exchange factor (the number of load units on train that have to be exchanged) equals (n-1)/n, n being the number of trains in a batch. Thus, 1/(n-1) of the load units remains on the train.

*** Related to planned load order for shunting; for terminals planned load order does not effect the number of l load unit but the distribution of load units over the routes.

Appendix J Specification of results of cases in quadrants II, III and IV

Table J–1: Specification of cases in quadrant II: options for time sensitive flows

Demand condition*	Facility and capacity level	Train service time(minutes)	Costs per load unit(euro)
1*3 (short trains)	C10	13	311
1*3 (short trains)	C6	17	209
1*3 (short trains)	C4	27	159
1*3 (short trains)	C2	72	108
1*3 (short trains)	RR4	97	68
1*3 (short trains)	H22	103	108
1*3 (short trains)	RR3	114	59
1*3	C10	16	207
1*3	C6	26	140
1*3	C4	43	106
1*3	C2	115	72
1*4	C10	21	156
1*4	C6	35	105
1*4	C4	62	80
1*6	C10	33	104
1*6	C6	53	70
1*6	C4	89	53
1*8	C10	44	104
1*8	C6	71	71
3*3	C10	15	72
3*4	C10	20	54

* Number batches x number of trains per batch.

Table J–2: Specification of cases in quadrant III: options for costs sensitive flows

Demand condition*	Facility and capacity level	Train service time (minutes)	Costs per load unit (euro)
1*3 (short trains)	RR2	171	50
1*3	RR4	149	46
1*3	RR3	176	40
1*3	RR2	266	34
1*4	RR4	233	34
1*4	RR3	279	30
1*4	RR2	424	25
1*6	H22	217	41
1*6	C2	288	37
1*6	H21	291	38
1*6	H12	352	38
1*6	RR4	394	29
1*6	H11	427	42
1*6	RR3	470	21
1*8	H22	278	34
1*8	H21	379	40
1*8	C2	398	37
1*8	H12	458	38
1*8	H11	559	35
3*3	H22	141	31
3*3	RR4	153	21
3*3	RR3	181	19
3*3	H12	196	35
3*3	H11	247	32
3*3	H21	254	36
3*3	RR2	271	15
3*4	H22	173	25
3*4	C2	201	22
3*4	H12	248	28
3*4	H21	323	29
3*4	H11	324	25
3*6	H22	242	22
3*6	C2	300	16
3*6	H12	359	23
3*6	H11	467	21
3*6	H21	472	24

* Number batches x number of trains per batch.

Table J–3: Specification of cases in quadrant IV: no options

Demand condition*	Facility and capacity level	Train service time (minutes)	Costs per load unit euro)
1*3 (short trains)	H21	138	110
1*3 (short trains)	H12	147	108
1*3 (short trains)	H11	182	99
1*3	H22	127	80
1*3	H21	162	75
1*3	H12	194	73
1*3	H11	229	67
1*4	H22	154	61
1*4	C2	172	54
1*4	H21	204	57
1*4	H12	244	55
1*4	H11	294	51
1*6	RR2	-	-
1*8	RR4	-	-
1*8	RR3	-	-
1*8	RR2	-	-
1*8	C4	124	54
3*4	RR4	-	-
3*4	RR3	-	-
3*4	RR2	-	-
3*6	RR4	-	-
3*6	RR3	-	-
3*6	RR2	-	-

* Number batches x number of trains per batch.
- No performances calculated, because previous demand level exceeded the 8 hours.

Appendix K Specification of infrastructure dimensions, number of equipment and labour in cost model

For the costs calculations in Chapter 6 an initial costs level is used which is based on the so-called basic capacity. The basic capacity consists of a fixed basic infrastructure for the exchange facility, no side yards, and the required equipment and personnel related to the capacity level. The basic capacity is applied in costs calculations related to single batch demand, except for the demand of one batch of 8 trains. This demand requires additional infrastructure. In addition, for the road-rail terminal additional infrastructure had to be included for a demand of one batch of 6 trains. For costs calculations related to multiple batch demand, costs for side yard infrastructure are added to the costs for the basic capacity. Table K–1 to Table K–4 provide an overview for each exchange facility of their layout dimensions, number of equipment and labour applied in the costs calculations.

Table K–1: Specification of layout dimensions, number of equipment and labour new hub-terminal

Demand	Basic capacity 1*3, 1*4, 1*6	Additional side yard capacity 1*8	3*3	3*4	3*6
Infrastructure					
Number of tracks	6	8	6	6	6
Number of storage lanes	3	1	3	3	3
Number of road lanes	2	2	2	2	2
Number of switches	10	14	14	16	18
Average width per track/lane	5	5	5	5	5
Facility length (m)	700	700	700	700	700
Number of arrival tracks	-	-	3	4	6
Number of departure tracks	-	-	3	4	6
Total surface (m^2)	45500	45500	66500	73500	87500

	Facility and capacity level C2	C4	C6	C10
Equipment				
Cranes	2	4	6	10
Number of roller pallets in transport system	13	18	23	33
Labour per shift				
Crane driver*	3	5	7	11
Pinsetter/radioman	2	4	6	10
Operation control	2	2	2	2
Maintenance and repair	2	2	2	2
Administration and management	3	3	3	3
Total	12	16	20	28

* Assumed is one additional person who can replace any of the other function due to holiday, Illness, etc.

Source: Based on (Terminet, 2000).

Table K–2: Specification of layout dimensions, number of equipment and labour hump shunting yard

Demand	Basic capacity 1*3, 1*4, 1*6	Additional sideyard capacity 1*8	3*3	3*4	3*6
Infrastructure					
Number of tracks arrival yard	6	8	6	6	6
Number of tracks departure yard	6	8	6	6	6
Number of switches	24	32	36	40	48
Brake units*	9	12	13	15	18
Assembly units**	6	8	9	10	12
Round tracks + lead track to and from hump	3400	3400	3400	3400	3400
Average width per track/lane	5	5	5	5	5
Length arrival tracks (m)	700	700	700	700	700
Length departure tracks (m)	700	700	700	700	700
Additional number of arrival tracks (side yard)	-	-	3	4	6
Additional number of departure tracks (side yard)	-	-	3	4	6
Total surface (m^2)	59000	73000	80000	87000	101000

	Facility and capacity level H11	H21	H12	H22
Equipment				
Locomotives***	3	4	4	5
Labour per shift				
Locomotive driver ****	3	4	4	5
Shunting assistant	2	3	3	4
Pinpuller	1	1	1	1
Cableman arrival yard*****	6	12	6	12
Cableman departure yard*****	4	4	8	8
Operation control	2	2	2	2
Maintenance and repair	2	2	2	2
Administration and management	3	3	3	3
Total	23	31	29	37

*   Estimated as number of departure tracks plus additional number of departure tracks plus 0.5 times number of switches.
**   Equal to number of departure tracks plus additional number of departure tracks.
***   Assumed is one locomotive reserve capacity.
****   Assumed is one additional person who can replace any of the other function due to holiday, illness, etc.
*****   This is the assumed minimum required number of labour for (un)coupling wagons and air tubes to keep with the cycle of the locomotive.

Sources: based on (Fritsch, 2003), (Bruins, 2003).

Table K-3: Specification of layout dimensions, number of equipment and labour flat shunting yard

Demand	Basic capacity 1*3, 1*4, 1*6	Additional side yard capacity 3*3
Infrastructure		
Number of tracks arrival yard	3	6
Number of tracks departure yard	3	6
Number of sorting tracks	6	
Number of switches	24	36
Round tracks + lead track to and from hump	2400	2400
Average width per track/lane	5	5
Length arrival/departure tracks (m)	700	700
Length sorting tracks (m)	350	350
Additional number of arrival tracks (side yard)	-	3
Additional number of departure tracks (side yard)	-	3
Total surface (m²)	45600	66600

	\multicolumn{4}{c}{Facility and capacity level}
	F11	F21	F12	F22
Equipment				
Locomotives*	3	4	4	5
Labour per shift				
Locomotive driver **	3	4	4	5
Shunting assistant	2	3	3	4
Operation control	2	2	2	2
Maintenance and repair	2	2	2	2
Administration and management	3	3	3	3
Total	12	14	14	16

*   Assumed is one locomotive reserve capacity.

** Assumed is one additional person who can replace any of the other function due to holiday, illness, etc.

Source: based on (Biggler, 2003).

Table K–4: Specification of layout dimensions, number of equipment and labour road-rail terminal

Demand	Basic capacity 1*3, 1*4	Additional side yard capacity 1*6	3*3	3*4	3*6
Infrastructure					
Number of tracks	4	6	4	4	-
Number of storage lanes	3	1	3	3	-
Number of road lanes	2	2	2	2	-
Number of switches	6	10	10	12	-
Average width per track/lane	5	5	5	5	-
Facility length (m)	700	700	700	700	-
Total surface (m²)	31500	31500	31500	31500	-
Number of arrival tracks	-	-	3	4	-
Number of departure tracks	-	-	3	4	-
Additional surface (m²)	-	-	21000	28000	-

	Facility and capacity level		
	RR2	RR3	RR4
Equipment			
Cranes	2	3	4
Labour per shift			
Crane driver*	3	4	5
Pinsetter/ radioman	2	3	4
Operation control	2	2	2
Maintenance and repair	2	2	2
Administration and management	3	3	3
Total	12	14	16

* Assumed is one additional person who can replace any of the other function due to holiday, illness, etc.

Sources: based on (Rotter, 2003), (Terminet, 2000), (Gruppo Clas, 2002).

Labour costs depend on the number of shifts required to deal with a certain demand. The duration of operations, which is an output variable of the simulation, is used to determined whether 1, 2 or 3 shifts are required. Table K-5 provides an overview of number of shifts applied in the costs model for specific demand and facility. Labour for administration and management are assumed only to work 1 shift.

Table K–5: Number of shifts per facility, capacity level and demand level

Facility and capacity level	Number of batches* number of trains per batch					
	1 * 3	1 * 4	1 * 6	3 * 3	3 * 4	3 * 6
C10	1	1	1	1	1	1
C6	1	1	1	1	1	1
C4	1	1	1	1	1	1
C2	1	1	1	1	2	2
H22	1	1	1	1	1	2
H21	1	1	1	2	2	3
H12	1	1	1	2	2	2
H11	1	1	2	2	2	3
RR4	1	2	2	2	-	-
RR3	1	2	2	2	-	-
RR2	1	2	2	2	-	-
F22	1	1	2	2	-	-
F21	1	1	2	2	-	-
F12	2	2	-	3	-	-
F11	2	2	-	-	-	-

Appendix L Selected cases for sensitivity analyses

Demand*	Facility	Service time (minutes)	Costs per load unit
400m*1*3	RR3	114	59
400m*1*3	RR2	171	50
400m*1*3	F21	235	60
1*3	RR4	149	46
1*3	RR3	176	40
1*4	C2	172	54
1*4	H21	204	57
1*4	RR4	233	34
1*6	C4	89	53
1*6	H22	217	41
1*8	C6	71	53
1*8	C4	124	40
3*3	C6	26	49
3*3	C4	44	38
3*3	C2	113	27
3*3	H22	141	31
3*3	RR4	153	21
3*3	RR3	181	19
3*3	H12	196	35
3*4	C10	20	54
3*4	C6	42	37
3*4	C4	74	29
3*4	H22	173	25
3*4	C2	201	22
3*6	C10	31	37
3*6	C6	58	26
3*6	C4	101	20

* Number batches x number of trains per batch.

Appendix M Specification of results flat shunting alternatives

Flat shunting alternatives have only been simulated under the condition of planned load order. Therefore these alternatives were not included in Appendix J with the initial experiments to which the unplanned load order applies. The flat shunting alternatives shows up in two quadrants of the benchmark graph. In Table M–1 the alternatives in quadrant III -options for costs sensitive flows- are presented. In Table M–1 the alternatives that are no options (quadrant) are presented.

Table M–1:   Specification of cases in quadrant IV: no options

Demand*	Facility and capacity level	Train sojourn time (minutes)	Costs per load unit (euro)
1*3 (short trains)	F22	198	73
1*3 (short trains)	F21	235	60
1*3 (short trains)	F12	325	67
1*3 (short trains)	F11	362	55
1*3	F12	454	53
1*6	F12	-	-
1*6	F11	-	-
1*8	F22	-	-
1*8	F12	-	-
1*8	F21	-	-
1*8	F11	-	-
3*3	F11	-	-
3*4	F22	-	-
3*4	F12	-	-
3*4	F21	-	-
3*4	F11	-	-
3*6	F22	-	-
3*6	F12	-	-
3*6	F21	-	-
3*6	F11	-	-

*   Number of batches * number of trains per batch.
-   Alternatives were not included in the experiments.

Appendix N Specification of results for different load orders

Table N–1: Train service times for a demand of one batch of three trains for different load orders for a few selected facilities (in minutes)

Facility and capacity level	Unplanned	Planned-realistic	Planned-ideal	Planned-ideal with locomotive remaining attached to train
F11	-	492	197	162 (149 short brake test)
F12	-	454	131	-
H11	229	126	75	-
H12	194	108	54	-
H21	162	103	73	-
H22	127	101	52	-
RR3	176	113	78	-
RR4	149	91	60	-
C4	43	35	29	-
C6	26	20	19	-

Appendix O Specification of results for different load factors

Demand (number of batches * number of trains)	Facility and capacity level and load factor	Train service time (minutes)	Costs per load unit (euro)
400m*1*3	RR2	171	50
	LF1.4	157	56
	LF1.8	201	43
400m*1*3	RR3	114	58
	LF1.4	102	66
	LF1.8	133	51
400m*1*3	F21	235	60
	LF1.4	235	67
	LF1.8	235	52
1*3	RR3	176	40
	LF1.4	163	44
	LF1.8	211	35
1*3	RR4	149	46
	LF1.4	137	51
	LF1.8	176	40
1*4	C2	172	54
	LF1.4	151	62
	LF1.8	194	48
1*4	H21	204	57
	LF1.4	204	65
	LF1.8	204	51
1*4	RR4	233	34
	LF1.4	201	39
	LF1.8	265	30
1*6	C4	89	53
	LF1.4	81	61
	LF1.8	101	48
1*6	H22	217	41
	LF1.4	217	46
	LF1.8	217	36
1*8	C4	124	40
	LF1.4	107	46
	LF1.8	135	36
1*8	C6	71	53
	LF1.4	63	61
	LF1.8	77	48

Continuation

Demand (number of batches * number of trains)	Facility and capacity level and load factor	Train service time (minutes)	Costs per load unit (euro)
3*3	C2	113	27
	LF1.4	100	29
	LF1.8	131	23
3*3	C4	44	38
	LF1.4	38	43
	LF1.8	50	34
3*3	C6	26	49
	LF1.4	23	56
	LF1.8	29	44
3*3	H12	196	29
	LF1.4	196	33
	LF1.8	196	26
3*3	H22	141	31
	LF1.4	141	36
	LF1.8	141	28
3*3	RR3	181	17
	LF1.4	150	20
	LF1.8	304	16
3*3	RR4	153	20
	LF1.4	137	23
	LF1.8	281	18
3*4	C10	20	54
	LF1.4	19	62
	LF1.8	22	48
3*4	C2	201	22
	LF1.4	176	24
	LF1.8	227	19
3*4	C4	74	29
	LF1.4	56	33
	LF1.8	91	26
3*4	C6	42	37
	LF1.4	38	43
	LF1.8	46	33
3*4	H22	173	23
	LF1.4	173	25
	LF1.8	173	18

Continuation

Demand (number of batches * number of trains)	Facility and capacity level and load factor	Train service time (minutes)	Costs per load unit (euro)
3*6	C10	31	37
	LF1.4	29	42
	LF1.8	34	33
3*6	C4	101	20
	LF1.4	79	23
	LF1.8	122	18
3*6	C6	58	26
	LF1.4	50	29
	LF1.8	65	23

Appendix P Specification of results of costs per load unit for different increases in costs

Facility, capacity and demand level	Initial situation	+25% on amount of investment in equipment	+25% on amount of investment in infrastructure	3% interest rate instead of 2.3%	6% interest rate instead of 2.3%
RR4 (1*3)	46	51	47	46	51
RR3 (1*3)	40	44	41	40	44
RR4 (1*4)	42	47	44	43	47
H22 (1*6)	41	43	45	43	47
C4 (1*8)	40	48	42	42	47
C6 (3*3)	49	58	50	51	58
C4 (3*3)	38	45	39	39	44
H12 (3*3)	35	36	39	36	39
H22 (3*3)	31	33	35	33	36
H11 (3*3)	31	32	35	32	36
C2 (3*3)	27	31	28	27	31
RR4 (3*3)	21	23	22	22	24
RR3 (3*3)	19	20	20	19	21
F11 (3*3)	17	18	19	18	20
C6 (3*4)	37	44	39	39	44
H22 (3*4)	25	26	28	26	29
C2 (3*4)	22	26	24	23	26
C4 (3*4)	29	34	30	30	34
C10 (3*6)	37	44	38	38	44
C6 (3*6)	26	31	27	27	31
C4 (3*6)	20	24	21	21	24

Costs per load unit (euro)

Appendix Q Specification of results for initial versus ideal train interarrival times

Demand number of batches * number of trains per batch	Facility and capacity level	Train service time (minutes)		Costs per load unit (euro)
		Initial 8-minute interarrival times	Ideal interarrival times	
3*6	C10	31	28	37
3*3	C2	113	100	27
3*3	C4	44	38	38
3*4	C4	74	73	29
3*6	C4	101	85	20
3*3	C4_rr	77	68	29
3*4	C6	42	37	37
3*6	C6	58	51	26
3*3	H12_planned	108	91	35
3*3	H22_planned	101	74	31
3*3	RR3_planned	115	93	19
3*3	RR4_planned	94	76	21

-rr: facility with roadrail cranes.
_planned: under condition of planned load order.

Curriculum Vitae

Yvonne Bontekoning was born in Berkhout in the Netherlands on 26 January 1968. She completed her VWO (pre-university education) at RSG Westfriesland in Hoorn in 1987. From 1984-1985 she spent a year studying and graduating at Kennewick High School, Kennewick (WA) in the USA. After finishing her pre-university studies she studied French for one year at the Université de Savoie in Chambéry, France. From 1988 to 1993 she studied Agricultural Economy at Wageningen University. She wrote two Masters theses: one in the field of logistics management on optimal location choice for the distribution centres of a large organic fruit and vegetable distributor, the other in the field of agricultural business economics which involved comparing the performance of a mixed organic farm with that of a semi-organic farm.

Upon finishing her studies she worked for three and a half years as a management trainee at the Stevedory container company based at ECT Rotterdam. There she became involved in automated and robotised terminals. In 1996 she continued as a researcher at the OTB Research Institute for Housing, Urban and Mobility Studies where she undertook a 2-year post-doctoral study on policy analysis in the fields of Housing, Urban Studies and Mobility. Yvonne was involved in the EU project Terminet as researcher and technical coordinator and participated in the Dutch project FAMAS. From 1 April 2002 to 1 January 2005 she was co-ordinator of the department of Transport and Infrastructure.

In her spare time Yvonne enjoys training for and competing in short triathlons and going on cross-country ski vacations. She is a Nordic Walking instructor and trainer and is also a cross-country ski instructor during the winter season.

TRAIL Thesis Series

A series of The Netherlands TRAIL Research School for theses on transport, infrastructure and logistics.

Nat, C.G.J.M., van der, *A Knowledge-based Concept Exploration Model for Submarine Design*, T99/1, March 1999, TRAIL Thesis Series, Delft University Press, The Netherlands

Westrenen, F.C., van, *The Maritime Pilot at Work: Evaluation and Use of a Time-to-boundary Model of Mental Workload in Human-machine Systems*, T99/2, May 1999, TRAIL Thesis Series, Eburon, The Netherlands

Veenstra, A.W., *Quantitative Analysis of Shipping Markets*, T99/3, April 1999, TRAIL Thesis Series, Delft University Press, The Netherlands

Minderhoud, M.M., *Supported Driving: Impacts on Motorway Traffic Flow*, T99/4, July 1999, TRAIL Thesis Series, Delft University Press, The Netherlands

Hoogendoorn, S.P., *Multiclass Continuum Modelling of Multilane Traffic Flow*, T99/5, September 1999, TRAIL Thesis Series, Delft University Press, The Netherlands

Hoedemaeker, M., *Driving with Intelligent Vehicles: Driving Behaviour with Adaptive Cruise Control and the Acceptance by Individual Drivers*, T99/6, November 1999, TRAIL Thesis Series, Delft University Press, The Netherlands

Marchau, V.A.W.J., *Technology Assessment of Automated Vehicle Guidance - Prospects for Automated Driving Implementation*, T2000/1, January 2000, TRAIL Thesis Series, Delft University Press, The Netherlands

Subiono, *On Classes of Min-max-plus Systems and their Applications*, T2000/2, June 2000, TRAIL Thesis Series, Delft University Press, The Netherlands

Meer, J.R., van, *Operational Control of Internal Transport*, T2000/5, September 2000, TRAIL Thesis Series, Delft University Press, The Netherlands

Bliemer, M.C.J., *Analytical Dynamic Traffic Assignment with Interacting User-Classes: Theoretical Advances and Applications using a Variational Inequality Approach*, T2001/1, January 2001, TRAIL Thesis Series, Delft University Press, The Netherlands

Muilerman, G.J., *Time-based logistics: An analysis of the relevance, causes and impacts*, T2001/2, April 2001, TRAIL Thesis Series, Delft University Press, The Netherlands

Roodbergen, K.J., *Layout and Routing Methods for Warehouses*, T2001/3, May 2001, TRAIL Thesis Series, The Netherlands

Willems, J.K.C.A.S., *Bundeling van infrastructuur, theoretische en praktische waarde van een ruimtelijk inrichtingsconcept*, T2001/4, June 2001, TRAIL Thesis Series, Delft University Press, The Netherlands

Binsbergen, A.J., van, J.G.S.N. Visser, *Innovation Steps towards Efficient Goods Distribution Systems for Urban Areas*, T2001/5, May 2001, TRAIL Thesis Series, Delft University Press, The Netherlands

Rosmuller, N., *Safety analysis of Transport Corridors*, T2001/6, June 2001, TRAIL Thesis Series, Delft University Press, The Netherlands

Schaafsma, A., *Dynamisch Railverkeersmanagement, besturingsconcept voor railverkeer op basis van het Lagenmodel Verkeer en Vervoer*, T2001/7, October 2001, TRAIL Thesis Series, Delft University Press, The Netherlands

Bockstael-Blok, W., *Chains and Networks in Multimodal Passenger Transport. Exploring a design approach*, T2001/8, December 2001, TRAIL Thesis Series, Delft University Press, The Netherlands

Wolters, M.J.J., *The Business of Modularity and the Modularity of Business*, T2002/1, February 2002, TRAIL Thesis Series, The Netherlands

Vis, F.A., *Planning and Control Concepts for Material Handling Systems*, T2002/2, May 2002, TRAIL Thesis Series, The Netherlands

Koppius, O.R., *Information Architecture and Electronic Market Performance*, T2002/3, May 2002, TRAIL Thesis Series, The Netherlands

Veeneman, W.W., *Mind the Gap; Bridging Theories and Practice for the Organisation of Metropolitan Public Transport*, T2002/4, June 2002, TRAIL Thesis Series, Delft University Press, The Netherlands

Nes, R. van, *Design of multimodal transport networks, a hierarchical approach*, T2002/5, September 2002, TRAIL Thesis Series, Delft University Press, The Netherlands

Pol, P.M.J., *A Renaissance of Stations, Railways and Cities, Economic Effects, Development Strategies and Organisational Issues of European High-Speed-Train Stations*, T2002/6, October 2002, TRAIL Thesis Series, Delft University Press, The Netherlands

Runhaar, H., *Freight transport: at any price? Effects of transport costs on book and newspaper supply chains in the Netherlands*, T2002/7, December 2002, TRAIL Thesis Series, Delft University Press, The Netherlands

Spek, S.C., van der, *Connectors. The Way beyond Transferring*, T2003/1, February 2003, TRAIL Thesis Series, Delft University Press, The Netherlands

Lindeijer, D.G., *Controlling Automated Traffic Agents*, T2003/2, February 2003, TRAIL Thesis Series, Eburon, The Netherlands

Riet, O.A.W.T., van de, *Policy Analysis in Multi-Actor Policy Settings. Navigating Between Negotiated Nonsense and Useless Knowledge*, T2003/3, March 2003, TRAIL Thesis Series, Eburon, The Netherlands

Reeven, P.A., van, *Competition in Scheduled Transport*, T2003/4, April 2003, TRAIL Thesis Series, Eburon, The Netherlands

Peeters, L.W.P., *Cyclic Railway Timetable Optimization*, T2003/5, June 2003, TRAIL Thesis Series, The Netherlands

Soto Y Koelemeijer, G., *On the behaviour of classes of min-max-plus systems*, T2003/6, September 2003, TRAIL Thesis Series, The Netherlands

Lindveld, Ch..D.R., *Dynamic O-D matrix estimation: a behavioural approach*, T2003/7, September 2003, TRAIL Thesis Series, Eburon, The Netherlands

Weerdt, de M.M., *Plan Merging in Multi-Agent Systems*, T2003/8, December 2003, TRAIL Thesis Series, The Netherlands

Langen, de P.W, *The Performance of Seaport Clusters*, T2004/1, January 2004, TRAIL Thesis Series, The Netherlands

Hegyi, A., *Model Predictive Control for Integrating Traffic Control Measures*, T2004/2, February 2004, TRAIL Thesis Series, The Netherlands

Lint, van, J.W.C., *Reliable Travel Time Prediction for Freeways*, T2004/3, June 2004, TRAIL Thesis Series, The Netherlands

Tabibi, M., *Design and Control of Automated Truck Traffic at Motorway Ramps*, T2004/4, July 2004, TRAIL Thesis Series, The Netherlands

Verduijn, T. M., *Dynamism in Supply Networks: Actor switching in a turbulent business environment*, T2004/5, September 2004, TRAIL Thesis Series, The Netherlands

Daamen, W., *Modelling Passenger Flows in Public Transport Facilities*, T2004/6, September 2004, TRAIL Thesis Series, The Netherlands

Zoeteman, A., *Railway Design and Maintenance from a Life-Cycle Cost Perspective: A Decision-Support Approach*, T2004/7, November 2004, TRAIL Thesis Series, The Netherlands

Bos, D.M., *Changing Seats: A Behavioural Analysis of P&R Use*, T2004/8, November 2004, TRAIL Thesis Series, The Netherlands

Versteegt, C., *Holonic Control For Large Scale Automated Logistic Systems*, T2004/9, December 2004, TRAIL Thesis Series, The Netherlands

Wees, K.A.P.C. van, *Intelligente voertuigen, veiligheidsregulering en aansprakelijkheid. Een onderzoek naar juridische aspecten van Advanced Driver Assistance Systems in het wegverkeer*, T2004/10, December 2004, TRAIL Thesis Series, The Netherlands

Tampère, C.M.J., *Human-Kinetic Multiclass Traffic Flow Theory and Modelling: With Application to Advanced Driver Assistance Systems in Congestion,* T2004/11, December 2004, TRAIL Thesis Series, The Netherlands

Rooij, R.M., *The Mobile City. The planning and design of the Network City from a mobility point of view,* T2005/1, February 2005, TRAIL Thesis Series, The Netherlands
Le-Anh, T., *Intelligent Control of Vehicle-Based Internal Transport Systems,* T2005/2, April 2005, TRAIL Thesis Series, The Netherlands

Zuidgeest, M.H.P., *Sustainable Urban Transport Development: a Dynamic Optimization Approach,* T2005/3, April 2005, TRAIL Thesis Series, The Netherlands

Hoogendoorn-Lanser, S., *Modelling Travel Behaviour in Multimodal Networks,* T2005/4, May 2005, TRAIL Thesis Series, The Netherlands

Dekker, S., *Port Investment – Towards an integrated planning of port capacity,* T2005/5, June 2005, TRAIL Thesis Series, The Netherlands

Koolstra, K., *Transport Infrastructure Slot Allocation,* T2005/6, June 2005, TRAIL Thesis Series, The Netherlands

Vromans, M., *Reliability of Railway Systems,* T2005/7, July 2005, TRAIL Thesis Series, The Netherlands

Oosten, W., *Ruimte voor een democratische rechtsstaat. Geschakelde sturing bij ruimtelijke investeringen,* T2005/8, September 2005, TRAIL Thesis Series, Sociotext, The Netherlands

Le-Duc, T., *Design and control of efficient order picking,* T2005/9, September 2005, TRAIL Thesis Series, The Netherlands

Goverde, R., *Punctuality of Railway Operations and Timetable Stability Analysis,* T2005/10, October 2005, TRAIL Thesis Series, The Netherlands

Kager, R.M., *Design and implementation of a method for the synthesis of travel diary data,* T2005/11, October 2005, TRAIL Thesis Series, The Netherlands

Boer, C., *Distributed Simulation in Industry,* T2005/12, October 2005, TRAIL Thesis Series, The Netherlands

Pielage, B.A., *Conceptual Design of Automated Freight Transport Systems,* T2005/14, November 2005, TRAIL Thesis Series, The Netherlands

Groothedde, B., *Collaborative Logistics and Transportation Networks, a modeling approach to network design,* T2005/15, November 2005, TRAIL Thesis Series, The Netherlands

Valk, J.M., *Coordination among Autonomous Planners,* T2005/16, December 2005, TRAIL Thesis Series, The Netherlands

Krogt, R.P.J. van der, *Plan Repair in Single-Agent and Multi-Agent Systems,* T2005/17, December 2005, TRAIL Thesis Series, The Netherlands

Bontekoning, Y.M., *Hub exchange operations in intermodal hub-and-spoke networks. A performance comparison of four types of rail-rail exchange facilities,* T2006/1, February 2006, TRAIL Thesis Series, The Netherlands